THE ULTIMATE SUCCESS GUIDE

THE ULTIMATE
SUCCESS
GUIDE

CONTENTS

CHAPTER 1

START YOUR OWN BUSINESS

BY BRIAN TRACY

One of your goals, in achieving all the success that is possible for you, is to earn a lot of money, and then, to hold on to it. Your financial and material goals can only be accomplished when you create sufficient value for yourself and your company, and then keep some of that value for yourself. No matter what your goals, you will either have to achieve them through working for the business of someone else, or by starting and building your own business. In either case, the more you know about how a business begins and grows, the faster you will be successful in whatever you do.

More people are forming more businesses today than at any other time in American business history. Last year, more than 820,000 new businesses were incorporated, more than 1,500,000 sole proprietorships were formed, and more than a million partnerships were established. Tom Peters, the business author, says that the primary driving forces of innovation and job creation in America today is in the small and medium-sized business sector.

In a time of rapid economic expansion in all directions, it is easier and more possible for you to start your own business and to be successful than it has ever been before. The good news is that, every single different type of person, from every kind of background, with every limitation you can imagine, has started and built successful businesses. And so can you.

The most important quality you need in starting and building your own successful business is *courage*. Like the Starship Enterprise, you have to have the courage "to go where no one has ever gone before." You must have the courage to step out in faith, and take risks with no guarantees of success. When you embark on your first business venture, you will feel like you are the first person who has ever done it. And in a certain sense, you are.

SUCCESS IN AMERICA

Ivan Sergevitch emigrated from the Soviet Union to the United States about five years ago. He did not speak a word of English when he arrived. He had everything he owned in a cardboard box tied up with string. For his first year in America, he lived in the "Little Russia" district of New York. He made his living delivering pizzas out of a Russian pizza parlor to Russians in the neighborhood who spoke his language.

But he was determined to get a piece of the American dream. Throughout his first year, he studied English as well as American business and success ideas. After one year of delivering pizzas, his English was good enough for him to get a job selling printing services to businesses. In his third year, he started his own business as a printing broker and sold one million dollars worth of printing, earning a 20% commission on sales. The next year, he sold two million dollars worth of printing and earned $400,000 dollars. In his fifth year in America, he sold three million dollars worth of printing and earned more than $600,000 dollars for himself. He now lives in a beautiful house and drives a Mercedes-Benz, his long-term goal.

NO LIMIT THINKING

A Vietnamese couple, who had escaped from Vietnam by boat to Thailand, arrived in the United States a few years ago, penniless. The only person they knew was a cousin who had a small bakery in Houston. He took them in and gave them minimum wage jobs working in the bakery. But he was getting older, and he told them that if they could come up with $30,000, he would sell them the bakery. That became their goal.

They lived in the back of the bakery, sleeping on flour sacks. They sent their two children to the local schools. They got up at 3 o'clock in the morning and worked 14 and 15-hour days. Between them, they earned

$8,000 per year after taxes and they saved $6,000. They did this for five years until at last they had the $30,000 they needed to buy the bakery.

Today, they own a chain of bakeries. They live in a beautiful home. Their children are in top universities and they are financially independent.

SELF-MADE MILLIONAIRES

Fully 74% of all self-made millionaires in America today got there by starting and building their own successful businesses. And here is an important point. Not one of these people had ever owned a business before they started. They came up with an idea to produce a product or service better than someone else and then started right where they were. This is the story of virtually all business success in America.

You do not need to have experience in entrepreneurship. Most people who start businesses have none. You do not need a lot of money. Most people start on their kitchen tables, or working out of their garages. You simply need to learn everything that is necessary and then apply it to your work as you go along. And what hundreds of thousands, and even millions, of other people have done, you can do as well.

Perhaps the best motto for small business success is the Michael Jordan advertisement for Nike running shoes, "Just Do It!"

Confucius said, "A journey of a thousand leagues begins with a single step."

START WHERE YOU ARE

What does it take to start your own business in America? Absolutely nothing. You can start your own sole proprietorship, and name it after yourself, "John Jones Enterprises" right where you are, right now. If you use your own name, you don't even have to register it. You can decide, this very minute, reading these words, that you are going to start your own business. You do not need permission or approval from anyone.

Having selected the name for your business, you are ready to take action. You can now stop at your nearby bank, and open a bank account in the name of your company. As a sole proprietorship named after yourself, you can use your social security number for tax purposes. You can make a minimum deposit, order checks, and you are on your way.

If you pick a name other than your own personal name, you will have to register it at a cost of about $25. This will assure that no one else is doing business under the same name, and to protect the name for yourself. You don't even need a lawyer. You can call the appropriate government office in your city/state yourself.

Remember the great philosophical principle, "If you build it, they will come."

Nature abhors a vacuum, and strives to fill it. If you take the steps to start your own company, even if you are not sure what business you are going into, you will create a natural vacuum in your personal universe. By some strange principle, business opportunities will begin emerging to fill that vacuum. Your business life will begin to change.

If you have a clear idea of the kind of business that you want to start, that is even better. But the very act of starting your own company and opening a bank account for it will cause things to happen in your life that you cannot today imagine. You will create a force field of magnetism that will begin attracting people and opportunities to you to make your business a successful enterprise.

START SMALL

In starting your own business for the first time, it is better not to incorporate at the beginning. If you create a corporation, which can cost you several hundred dollars, there are definite disadvantages for the first-time entrepreneur. These have to do with revenues, losses and taxes.

With a sole proprietorship, you can deduct everything you invest in your business to get it going against your current income. But with a corporation, you can only deduct losses against profits in the company. Since you will not have profits at the beginning, you will have nothing to deduct your expenses from. You will be unable to deduct them from your taxes, thereby making them twice as expensive. It is best to use a sole proprietorship, or perhaps an S corporation when you begin, so that all income and losses can be deducted from your personal income.

SELECTING A BUSINESS

How do you select a business to start or go into? There are a hundred different ways. But the most important determinant of all is that you get into something that you really like, enjoy and care about. *Passion* is the critical factor in determining small business success.

Peter Drucker wrote, "Whenever you see something getting done, you find a *monomaniac* with a mission."

Every business, and every product line within a business, needs a dedicated *champion* who is passionately committed to the success of that business. He or she thinks day and night about sale and profitability for that business and product. Without a champion, without a person who is passionately committed to making that business successful, the business will definitely fail.

Even with a champion, there is no guarantee of success. But without someone who cares more about the business, the products and services and the customers than anything else, the business has very little chance of surviving and thriving in a competitive market.

This is why it is essential that you pick a product or service that you really believe in and care about. You choose an area where you feel you can really help customers by giving them a value or benefit that they cannot get from any other product or service. Many people start businesses selling products that they enjoy using themselves. Other people start businesses because they are passionate about the technology or the science involved. Some people start businesses that are outgrowths of their hobbies or their other interests in life.

Look for a product and service that you use personally and which you can enthusiastically recommend to others. Identify the products and services that you have the strongest feelings about. Look for something better that no one else is offering. There may be a need or demand that your current customers have that your company is not interested in satisfying. Many people start businesses because their current companies are not interested in their ideas and they are convinced that they can make them successful.

Often people start businesses because of what is called a "significant emotional experience." Something happens in their life that triggers a strong emotion, and propels them into entrepreneurship. Sometimes it is the unexpected loss of a job. Sometimes it is the story of another person who started his or her own business and become outrageously successful. Sometimes a person gets fed up with a low salary and limited prospects, and decides to 'bust loose.' Any one of these events can make you decide to set off on your own.

FREEDOM IS THE GOAL

Many people think that the major motivation behind entrepreneurship is to make a lot of money. However, interviews with thousands of entrepreneurs prove that this is not the case. The primary reason that people turn to entrepreneurship is for the sense of personal freedom that it offers. Many entrepreneurs don't earn as much after taxes as they would if they were working at an ordinary job. But as entrepreneurs, they are their own bosses. They are free. They answer to no one. This is worth more to them than the security and higher pay of a corporate environment.

There is an old saying, "When you start your own business, you only have to work half days. And you are free to decide whichever 12 hour period it will be."

Whatever your motivations, if you have ever thought of starting your own business, you should make a decision and just do it. Don't procrastinate and delay. Get on with it, right now. You can start small, with a network marketing business. You can work part-time, evenings and weekends, offering a service out of your own home. You can work temporarily in someone else's entrepreneurial business to learn the ropes. You have to get your feet wet in some way. If you are eventually going to be a big success, you have to get some entrepreneurial experience. There is no better way to learn what you need to learn except by plunging in and picking it up as you go along.

LEARN AS YOU GO

Of all creatures on earth, human beings are wonderful in that they are "learning organisms." They are constantly taking in new information from their environments, adding it to what they already know, and moving forward.

You can learn at an incredible rate, depending upon the number of new experiences you have. Entrepreneurs who become successful only achieve their goals after many months and even years of success and failure. They have been through every difficulty, setback and challenge that is possible for a small businessperson to experience. As a result of these learning experiences, they become more alert and aware. They develop wisdom and knowledge. They make fewer and fewer mistakes. They do more and more of the right things and fewer of the wrong things. They not only earn more from their efforts, but they hold onto a greater percentage of their profits. Over time, step-by-step, inevitably, they achieve their goals of financial success and independence.

MINIMIZE RISK

One of the myths of entrepreneurship is that entrepreneurs are *risk takers.* However, this is not true at all. Successful entrepreneurs are actually "risk-avoiders." Successful entrepreneurs are focused on earning a profit from their activities. They do everything possible to minimize the risks involved in earning that profit. To the degree to which they successfully control risk, they increase the likelihood of profit, and succeed at their ventures. As an entrepreneur, profit-seeking must be your central focus as well.

Once you have decided that you want to enjoy the rewards of entrepreneurial success in particular, the next step is for you to explore every detail of the business you are thinking of going into. You must investigate before you invest. You must accept nothing on trust and leave nothing to chance. You should talk to lots of people in that business and get lots of input. Your aim is to minimize, reduce, and even eliminate risk wherever possible in the pursuit of profit. Your goal is to assure potential profits are real and potential losses are minimal or controllable.

 Whenever a person reaches the point where they say that they can "afford to lose" a little bit of money, you can be sure of just one thing. They are going to lose their money, and probably lose a lot. The very attitude of being willing to "lose money" seems to assure that the money will be lost in some way.

The only thing that is easy about money is losing it. Making money is hard, harder and harder still. As the Japanese proverb says, "Making money is like digging in the sand with a pin. Losing money is like pouring water on the sand."

When you decide to start your own business, begin by reading several books on small business formation. Some of the best books ever written are on the bookstands today. Read about every single aspect of market planning, market research, financing, delivery and distribution systems, people, processes, promotion, advertising and especially *sales*.

SALES IS ALL IMPORTANT

The most critical element in an entrepreneurial business is your ability to sell the product or service in sufficient quantity to pay all your costs and make a profit. Every successful entrepreneurial business starts off with someone who is very good at sales. Without a top salesperson, no business can survive or succeed for long.

Dun & Bradstreet summarized 50 years of research into thousands of successful and unsuccessful businesses recently with the conclusion that, "The reason for business success is *high sales*; the reason for business failure is *low sales*. All else is commentary."

Your ability to sell the product or service is the primary driving engine of entrepreneurship. This is because cash flow is the lifeblood of the enterprise, and cash flow comes from sales. Every business start-up is a race against time. Can the entrepreneur generate enough cash to support the business before the existing cash runs out? There must be a total, one hundred percent commitment to selling until the business gets off the ground. Otherwise, it will surely fail.

All successful entrepreneurial businesses focus on sales single-mindedly at the beginning. However, there is a common mistake that many entrepreneurs make once the business gets going. Because selling is hard work, the entrepreneur starts thinking about backing off into management of the enterprise, and getting someone else to do the selling.

The entrepreneur hires a salesperson to sell, and becomes the manager, for which he or she is usually not suited either by temperament or ability. Now the company has an average salesperson on the outside and a mediocre manager on the inside. Invariably, the company's sales begin to decline and the business starts to lose money. It has the worst of all possible situations.

Usually, before the company hits bottom, the entrepreneur fires the salesperson and goes back to selling, where he should have been in the first place. Very quickly, the company recovers and begins to grow again.

BOOTSTRAP YOUR BUSINESS

Many people think that the key to starting a new business is to have lots of money. The primary reason that people don't start their own businesses is because they say, "I don't have any money."

They often feel that they have to arrange all the money in advance. I heard a business professor giving recommendations to a roomful of entrepreneurs recently and I almost fell off my chair. He said, "When you start your own business, don't put any of your own money into it. Borrow all the money from the bank. Save your own money for your personal expenses."

Nothing could be further from the truth. When you start your own business for the first time, 99% of the money you will raise will be "love money." This is money that you provide yourself or that people lend or give you because they love you. No bank or venture capitalist will touch a new business start-up. It is simply too risky.

Banks and bankers are not in the business of taking risks. They are in the business of *making good loans* on which they earn interest and which they are absolutely sure can be repaid. When I started my first business some years ago, I was amazed to find that no banker anywhere had any interest whatsoever in lending me a single penny for my business. Most of them treated me as though I were a combination of a failure and a pickpocket when I went into see them. I learned that this is quite common. There should be a sign in every bank lobby that says, "No Small Business Start-Ups Need Apply."

Most venture capitalists today will only lend money to a company that has been in business for at least two years and that has a solid track record of increasing sales, earnings and profits. Banks will only lend money to you if you can show them that you can cover the amount you want to borrow by about five times. This means that they want you to prove that you have $5.00 worth of tangible assets for every dollar that you want to borrow.

In addition, they want personal guarantees from you and your spouse that will outlive a bankruptcy and last all of your life. They will want an assignment of every single piece of property that you own, and many banks will even ask you, if you can believe this, to deposit the amount that you want to borrow in a certificate of deposit with them.

The best and usually the only way to start your own small business is for you to accumulate the money that you need personally. You will have to use your savings, loans against your home, and money from your friends and family. When I started my first business many years ago, I learned how to sell again. I sold my house, my car, my furniture and all my investments. This is quite common.

Plan to grow your business by bootstrapping, one of the most popular and powerful routes to entrepreneurial success. In bootstrapping, you pull yourself up with your own efforts. You start small and you grow on a solid foundation of sales and profits. This takes longer than if you were to start off with money in the bank, but it has one distinct advantage. Bootstrapping forces you to develop the knowledge and skills you need to be successful as you go along. Because you do not have money to throw at your problems, bootstrapping forces you to become more creative in generating sales and profits. You learn early on to rely on yourself and your own abilities to succeed. Your skills develop as your business grows. You learn strategies and techniques of business success that last you all your life.

Many of the biggest businesses in America started on a hope and prayer, and the strategy of bootstrapping, on the part of an under-funded entrepreneur. Some examples are Ford Motor Company, Hewlett-Packard, Microsoft, Apple and even McDonalds. What thousands of successful businesses have done, you can do as well.

BE REALISTIC WHEN YOU START

When you begin your business, you must practice the "two times, three times rule." This rule says that, no matter how conservative your financial projections, everything will end up costing you *twice* as much as you have budgeted and everything you need to do will take *three* times as long.

For example, if you think that it will cost you $1,000 to develop a product and bring it to the market, it will invariably cost $2,000 or more. Some start-ups actually end up paying ten times what they had planned to get the first product out the door. If you think that it will take you three months to break even once you have started, you should triple that number and calculate that it will take you at least nine months. I have worked with companies that have taken three years instead of three months to get their first product to the market.

CASH IS KING

The key to survival to any small business is *cash*. Cash is king. Cash is critical. Cash is everything. You must become an absolute fanatic about generating and conserving cash. You must postpone, delay, defer and abandon every conceivable expense that you possibly can to assure an adequate supply of cash. You must not spend a single penny on anything that you cannot turn quickly back into cash.

When I started my first new business many years ago, I made the most common mistakes of new entrepreneurs. I went out and bought furniture, office fixtures, and a large photocopier and invested thousands of dollars in printing. Within 90 days, I had burned through all my savings and still had no sales or revenues. I went so broke so fast I could hardly believe it. In no time, I was selling off my possessions, taking out a new loan on my car, and borrowing money from my friends and relatives. I almost went under because I did not realize how important it was to conserve cash at the outset.

Whenever a banker or anyone else looks at your business, the very first and most important number that they will turn to will be the amount of cash you have on hand. Cash is like blood or oxygen to the brain. If you have it, you can survive. If you run out of it for any period of time, you will die. Without cash, the enterprise will fail, no matter how good its prospects may be for the future.

To preserve cash, never buy when you can rent, borrow or lease. Never buy anything new if you can get it used. Postpone all major purchase decisions for at least 30 days before you make them. Then reevaluate them again. Most major purchase decisions postponed for 30 days are never made at all. Never buy large quantities of stationery or promotional materials unless you have immediate use for them. Buy only the amount of materials that you absolutely need at the moment to conduct the business in the present. Forget all the economies of mass production and saving where you can get better prices by ordering large quantities.

When you start your own small business, you will be offered a thousand different ways to waste money and a thousand different people encouraging you to spend your money on things that are not helpful to you. You must become as careful as a miser and as crafty as a fox.

INVEST YOUR HUMAN CAPITAL

When you start your new business, the most valuable assets you have are your energy, imagination, character and discipline. This is what you use to get in there and do the work and get the results. Your assets are your abilities to make the key decisions, to get out there face-to-face with customers and make the sales. Your most valuable assets are your abilities to follow through on your commitments and promises.

Ralph Waldo Emerson once wrote that, "A great institution is the length and shadow of a single man."

Even a small organization or company is the length and shadow of a single person. You are your business. The business is you. The business can never be more or less, better or worse than you are, on an hour-by-hour, minute-by-minute basis. The business is really a mirror image reflection of your character and ability. Your business tells you, and the world, who you really are.

More than 30,000 businesses were studied over a twenty-year period to determine their reasons for success and failure. The statistics that emerged from these studies seem to hold true for almost all businesses over the years.

In general, they found that it takes about two years for a new business to break even and start to make a profit. Most business that fail do so in the first two years. They run out of money and credit before they figure out how to earn more than they are spending.

During the first two-year period, the business will suffer mostly losses that will have to be made up from the energy and resources of the entrepreneur. In the second two years, the business will start to make a profit. These profits will go into paying back the debts and losses that were incurred in the first two years.

After four years, the business will start to generate net profits, having paid back all its start up cost. It will break into the clear and the entrepreneur will start to make good money. But it is only after the seventh year of entrepreneurship that the business starts to be really successful and the entrepreneur begins to make an excellent living.

Most of the highest paid people in America, and most self-made millionaires, are entrepreneurs who have passed the seven-year point in building and running their own businesses. They have stayed the course and paid the price of success - but it took more than seven years.

Of course, it is possible to beat the odds. Everyone who got caught up in the dotcom boom was convinced that business success was achievable almost overnight. It may be possible to build a successful business in less than seven years. But beating the odds in entrepreneurship is very similar to the occurrence of miracles. It is not that miracles don't happen; it is just that you cannot depend upon them.

CAREFULLY PLAN YOUR BUSINESS IN ADVANCE

When you decide to start your own business, you may launch impulsively because of a significant emotional experience or event in your life, like the loss of a job or the appearance of an opportunity. You may do it slowly and deliberately by spending several weeks or months in study and preparation.

Whichever you choose, investigate before you invest. It is much easier to get *into* a new business than it is to get *out* of it. It is therefore important that you spend sufficient time investigating, in advance, before you commit time and resources to a particular business venture. This careful assessment can be critical to your long-term success.

Remember the 80/20 Rule. This rule says that 20% of what you do will account for 80% of your results. One application of the 80/20 Rule says that the first 20% of time that you spend in planning and evaluating your business at the beginning will determine 80% of the results that you eventually get.

When you decide to start your own business, you should draw up a complete business plan. There are several books on the bookstands that you can get for a few dollars that will give you all the ingredients of a business plan. There are computer programs that will walk you through the process of building a business plan. They make the process simple and straightforward.

The assembling and putting together of a complete business plan is a key *test* of the entrepreneur. If you have the discipline to do it, you will find that it alerts you to many factors that you may not have considered. It will take a lot of work on your part to generate the various numbers that you will need to complete the different parts of the plan. But the contribution it can make to your success can be decisive.

Inc. magazine reported on study of 100 start-ups a few years ago. Fifty of these new businesses had created detailed business plans before they began. Fifty of them had started on the back of an envelope or with little more than an idea in the mind of the entrepreneur.

After five years, they returned to interview the business founders and evaluate the results. They found that most of the companies that had started *without* a business plan had gone bankrupt, ruining the founders and usually their families and friends in the process.

On the other hand, virtually all of the companies that had started with a written business plan were flourishing. Many of the company owners made up complete business plans again every year, sometimes spending several weeks per year putting them together.

PLANNING REVEALS THE PITFALLS

But here was the most important point. They asked the company founders how important the business plans had been in actually running their businesses on a day-to-day basis. The answer they received was surprising. Almost all the successful entrepreneurs said that once the business plan was complete, it was usually put in a drawer and hardly referred to again throughout the year. They said that it was the exercise of thinking through the ingredients of the business plan prior to starting work that was more important than anything else.

By creating a business plan, you are forced to think honestly and objectively about every part of the business before you begin. The business plan requires that you project sales and revenues, and then back up your projections with research and analysis. It forces you to think through all revenue and expense estimates for the year, and determine if they are realistic and achievable. The business plan will end up saving you an enormous amount of time and energy in executing it. It will do more to guarantee your success than any other investment of time you can make.

Time is money, but money is time as well. If you have to work for five years to assemble $20,000 to invest in your business, that $20,000 represents five years of your life. You must invest this piece of your life very carefully, and a business plan enables you to do it.

A business plan begins by your defining clearly the product or service you are going to offer. You must determine exactly how much you will be able to charge for the product or service. You must calculate how much you will have to pay to make your product or service available in the first place.

MARKETING MASTERY

Before you enter the market with a new product or service, you must ask, "Why would someone switch from what they are currently using to my product? Why would they buy from me rather than from someone else?"

For a new product or service to sell in a competitive market, it must have at least three factors about it that make it superior to whatever else is available. It must have three features or benefits that make it stand out from the competition. It must have a "unique selling proposition" and at least three competitive advantages. It must offer something more and better than whatever else customers are already using.

A new product or service must be faster, cheaper, easier to use or possess different features, factors or ingredients that competitive offerings don't have. It must cause customers to see it and say, "That's for me!"

A business plan is usually a month-by-month projection, going forward about 18 months, of how much you intend to sell of your product each month. You put these numbers along the top line. Below each of these numbers, you list every expense necessary to generate and fulfill those sales. You then deduct all your expenses from your sales figure to get your amount of profit or loss for the month.

When you assemble these numbers, imagine that you are going in front of a board of bank examiners and they are going to ask you to explain and to defend every number on your plan. Discipline yourself to carefully calculate every number and base it on the most verifiable facts and details possible.

WHERE WILL THE SALES COME FROM?

If you project a certain level of sales, you should be able to show exactly where those sales are going to come from. How much advertising will you need to do and how many leads will the advertising generate? You should be able to show exactly who will call on or speak to each of these customers and how many sales can be expected from this prospect base. You must be able to estimate the exact amount of sale per satisfied customer and the amount of growth and net profit per sale, per product, per customer, per call.

The measure of your ability as an entrepreneur is your ability to create a business plan and a budget, and then to achieve those results on schedule. Anyone can pull numbers out of a hat. But the best business people are the people who meet or exceed their numbers consistently and dependably. This is the true measure of how good you really are.

First, you determine how much you are going to sell, how you are going to sell it, and who you are going to sell it to. Second, you determine how you are going to deliver the product or service and collect payment for it. Third, you estimate all of the expenses involved in achieving the sales on the top line.

Take every single conceivable expense, in order, from the largest expenses to the smallest, from cost of goods sold, salaries, rent, utilities and transportation all the way down to the cost of shipping and postage stamps. It is useless to play games with yourself, or to ignore unavoidable expenses. There is nothing that makes a business plan less believable than the failure of the entrepreneur to include every expense that will be incurred.

Once you have added up all your expenses, you then create a "fudge factor" of 20% of that total number. For example, if your top line sales for the month are going to be $10,000 and your total expenses to achieve those sales will be $5,000, you create a fudge factor of 20% or $1,000 and you include that as a real expense. Believe me, it will become a real expense, no matter what you do.

Now you have an accurate projection of your net income for that month. You do this for every month, taking into consideration seasonal fluctuations, vacations, cycles and trends in demand over the year, and estimate your financial results for the next 12-18 months.

FOCUS ON THE NUMBERS

Every month, you review your actual figures against your projected figures to see how close you were. By using a spreadsheet program like "Excel," you can keep accurate and current books. By changing any one of the numbers in your financial plan, you can then push a button and change all the subsequent figures so they are more in conformance with your real experience rather than your projections.

Over time, you will become more and more accurate at projecting exactly how much you will sell, how much it will cost to make those sales and how much profit you will earn each month. The better you become at making and meeting your financial projections, the better an entrepreneur you become in every other area as well.

BUYING A BUSINESS

There are two more points with regard to starting a new business. The first has to do with buying an existing business. Here is the rule. No one sells a *profitable* business. If someone has a business for sale, it usually has a hidden flaw of some kind. Perhaps you can compensate for the flaw and make the business prosper. Perhaps you cannot. But in any case, you must find out what it is.

I have spoken with many entrepreneurs who have been offered businesses for sale. When they heard this rule from me they went back and investigated, seeking the hidden flaw. In every case, they found that there was something negative about the business that the seller had not told them.

In one situation, the major customer for the business was closing down and fully 50% of the revenues would disappear by the end of the year. In another case, a competitor was bringing out a better product at 25% lower cost than the best product of this company and their sales would be non-existent within 12 months. Find the hidden flaw and if you can't compensate for it, don't buy the business at all.

If someone wants to sell you a business and it has problems, offer to pay them for the business out of the profits of the business. If there are no profits, there is no payment. Anybody who is selling a profitable business will be open to receiving a substantial part of their return in the form of ongoing profits. If a person is reluctant to be paid out of profits, you can judge for yourself whether you want to pursue it.

NETWORK MARKETING

The second area of starting a business has to do with network marketing. There are many outstanding network marketing companies in America today. Unfortunately, there are a large number of poor companies as well. Here is the rule. Everything that applies to starting your own business, in terms of business planning, selling, budgeting, projecting, and investing many months and even years, applies to building a successful network marketing business. If you are not prepared to invest 3-5 years building your business, don't get into it in the first place.

The greatest trap for would-be entrepreneurs in America is the lure of get-rich-quick schemes, easy money, something-for-nothing ideas that are advertised and promoted everywhere. There is within the psyche of most young people a passionate desire to shortcut the process of success. They are looking for a quick, easy way to jump the line and get to the head of the class without paying the full price in terms of hard work and sacrifice.

Make the decision that this is not for you. Refuse to look for or listen to any get-rich-quick schemes. If it sounds too good to be true, it probably is. Walk away. The very idea of looking for something for nothing can be fatal to your future.

TIME AND KNOWLEDGE

Once you decide on a new business, remember that the primary sources of value in America today are time and knowledge. Time refers to the speed at which you can deliver your product or service to your customers. Knowledge refers to the intellectual content that you put into your product, service or business. This is what makes what you do more important and valuable to your customers than what your competitors are doing.

By starting your new business at home, you can enjoy special financial and tax benefits. Do your homework. Find out what they are. Be perfectly correct in all of your financial dealings, with everyone in your financial life. Be straight with your bankers, your suppliers, your customers and with the tax people. Remember, life is very long and everything you do financially trails behind you for years and years.

There has never been a better time for you to achieve financial independence by starting your own business than there is today. Anything that anyone else has done, and especially something that hundreds and thousands and millions of other people have done, you can do as well, and maybe even better.

START YOUR OWN BUSINESS

You can piggyback on the knowledge and experience of hundreds of thousands of entrepreneurs who have put their best ideas and insights into books, audio programs and seminars. You can become one of the most successful business people in America by simply doing what others have done before you. There are no limits except the limits you place on your own imagination.

About Brian

Brian Tracy is Chairman and CEO of Brian Tracy International, a company specializing in the training and development of individuals and organizations. Brian's goal is to help people achieve their personal and business goals faster and easier than they ever imagined.

Brian Tracy has consulted for more than 1,000 companies and addressed more than 5,000,000 people in 5,000 talks and seminars throughout the US, Canada and 58 other countries worldwide. As a Keynote speaker and seminar leader, he addresses more than 250,000 people each year.

For more information on Brian Tracy programs, go to www.briantracy.com

CHAPTER 2

DO YOU WISH YOU COULD MAKE A $MILLION$ SHARING YOUR MESSAGE?

BY ALFONSO CASTANEIRA

Believe it or not, THE biggest obstacle, THE one thing getting in your way to selling your first million is NOT your ability as a speaker, nor the content of your message, nor even your marketing expertise.

Are you ready for the truth?... Can you handle the TRUTH?

I ask because when I heard and understood what I am about to share with you, I could not handle the truth. I listened to THE reason I was not able to break past the $200,000 mark and it made me MAD, so angry that I could not see straight for days, so furious that I could not go back and listen to the recording again. I had found a priceless nugget of radioactive information; it felt like my insides were burning from the moment the spoken words had vibrated in my eardrums. It took me months to swallow the pill I was given, but once I processed and released my fear, the floodgates opened and prosperity beyond belief began to flow.

Pay attention, for one of two things will happen now; you will either miss what comes next, or it will hit you like a ton of bricks.

YOUR biggest challenge, THE biggest obstacle, is the SPEAKER in the mirror! It is YOU!!!... The most important lesson you will ever learn about reaching the coveted Million Dollar mark is this: The hardest sale of your life is the one to yourself! No customer objections will be as insurmountable as your own excuses as to why you can't reach your next target revenue goal, on your way to the coveted yet elusive Million Dollar mark.

I had great objections; my first language is NOT English, how could anyone pay me to speak if I can't speak and pronounce proper English? I have no formal speaker training! Of course, the economy was in shambles and unemployment was high. It was an election year and hearing Ronald Reagan deliver a brilliant speech really had me believing that it was NOT possible, I couldn't do it! Besides, the most I had ever earned for an hour as a 'top flight' consultant was $200. Why would anyone in their right mind pay me an unbelievable $10,000 to hear my crummy speech?

In that self-pity frame of mind, I heard Earl Nightingale speak the radioactive words, "You are where you are, because that is where you really want to be, whether you'll admit that or not!" Not easy words to hear, particularly if your life is falling apart.

I managed to overcome my objections with the help of my best friend and mentor, my Dad. I began to understand how to chip away at my excuses and how to turn my objections into powerful reasons why I am worth a million. My mental breakthrough happened after I called him and said, "Dad, I am an idiot..." To which he quickly responded, "You are probably right, but tell me, what's wrong?" It was the conversation of a lifetime; he brought me to understand the biggest lesson of my career: The hardest sale you will ever make is the one to yourself. If you can't convince yourself, you don't have the backbone to convince anyone else. People will pay exactly what you believe in your gut you are worth and not a penny more. Ask yourself this question: Am I worth a MILLION? Your honest true-to-your-heart answer to that question is precisely the reason your income is what it is.

You are probably asking, how do I take this sort of abstract knowledge and create clear actionable steps that will help me make the shift? I agree, the knowledge that your income is directly connected to your self-worth is true, but what do you do about it?

Here are five actionable tools that have helped many to make the mental shift necessary to double, triple or quadruple their income, or finish their book, or take the next big leap.

Tool 1. Learn to change your focus. Shifting your focus of your own volition at any time, under any circumstances, will change your life and your income forever! This deceivably simple skill will give you the super-human ability to see that which everyone else misses.

Years ago, I had the great fortune of having a conversation with one of my heroes, the great speaker and mentor Earl Nightingale (the first person who sold a million copies of a voice recording "The Strangest Secret"). He told me an unbelievable truth: the news is the exception, NOT the rule. For every plane crash, a million land successfully and safely, for every car crash reported millions of others bring their occupants safely home to hug their children; for every negative thing the news reports, there are a million good people around the world doing good things to help each other through this adventure we call life. Earl taught me a most important lesson of my early career: It is YOU who decides what to focus on!!! By the way, find and listen to Earl's original recording on YouTube. It sold a million copies in 1956 for a reason.

Action: Find people focused as a herd on something. Deliberately and with complete consciousness of your actions, look at everything else BUT what the crowd is looking at. Discover one, two, three, or a hundred things the group missed.

Tool 2. Discover your fans before you have any. Once you realize who is in charge of your focus, it will be a simple shift in your focus which will bring about your ability to see yourself as worth the time and attention of the people that are out there praying for you to appear in their lives. YES! You read that right; there are thousands if not millions of people out there simply wishing and hoping that you appear in their path to bring your message of transformation; they yearn everyday, and that feeling in the bottom of your gut, or the loud voice in the back of your head, telling you that you have a personal mission to bring your message to the world. THAT voice, and THAT feeling, is the manifestation of the people you have not met yet, who wish for you to appear and help them along in their journey.

I know some of you are saying right now, this guy is crazy! Well, try this: Go out and find a speaker – any speaker that is already earning a good living with their speaking ability – and ask them if this happens to them with any regularity: A man or a woman they've never met before approaches them and says something like: "It is as if you were sent specially to speak to me." Ask the successful speaker point blank if there is ANY truth in this tool and pay close attention to what they say.

Action: Go out and speak, ready or not, for free or a fee and find your fans as they will do more for your sense of value than anything else in the world. Once you discover that people you've never met are waiting for you to come speak to them; you will discover an interconnectedness that exists which no scientist can explain.

Tool 3. Rediscover Socrates and the power of the Socratic Method. The entire bedrock of modern western thinking and its civilization can be traced back to the work of Plato's teacher, Socrates, who lived in Greece about 2,500 years ago. Socrates was a professional speaker! He never wrote anything down, yet he deeply influenced Plato, who in turn influenced Aristotle, and the trio influenced the way every human being on this planet thinks and acts today! How's that for the power of the spoken word!

Socrates helps us understand the single most important tool of the human race: THE Question. Within these 3 words: 'Who Am I?' you will find the essence of the entirety of the human consciousness experience. Socrates teaches us that armed with nothing but our ability to ask questions, we can shape or reshape our world into anything we could possibly imagine and even beyond.

Action: Ask questions like the one that liberated me from my mental jail: What if I could turn my biggest obstacles into my assets and the reasons people will hire me at a high fee? Get weird! Really weird!!! Ask things like: How can I turn this horrible experience I am having into THE most empowering experience of my life? Powerful questions will change your life forever!

Tool 4. Action item: Find new friends and if possible befriend your family. It is imperative that you surround yourself with people who believe in you. If you are having a hard time believing you are worth more, one reason is because you have negative people in your life who remind you every day how little you are worth. Their petty message is penetrating your subconscious and is hurting your chances of breaking out of your box. Shift focus, get better friends!

Tool 5. Authenticity trumps polished! Authentic speakers will trump polished ones every time – especially on income. If you find yourself losing your authenticity because you are choosing polished over authentic, stop! Authenticity will not only bring you more income, it will make you a happier human being.

Action: Develop your skill and your craft. Your increased ability will impact your self-worth, but when choosing between polished and authentic, go for authentic!

About Alfonso

Alfonso Castaneira is a Professional Speaker Coach. Alfonso coaches professional speakers to develop and accomplish step-by-step their million-dollar profit plan. Alfonso is passionate about helping speakers and coaches to craft their million-dollar story.

Among Alfonso's biggest professional speaker fans is Pat Williams, co-founder and Senior Vice-President of the NBA's Orlando Magic. Pat, a high demand Professional Speaker and a 40-year veteran in the speaking industry, dedicated his latest book to Alfonso, calling him the best coach in the speaking industry and the coach that most influenced his professional speaking career.

Among Alfonso's greatest success stories is Pegine Echevarria; she was recently accepted into the National Speakers Association's Million Dollar club and became the cover girl for Speaker Magazine!

Contact Alfonso at:
www.ProSpeakCoach.com
Alfonso@ProSpeakCoach.com

CHAPTER 3

AERODYNAMICALLY SPEAKING, A BUMBLEBEE SHOULD NOT BE ABLE TO FLY– BUT IT DOESN'T KNOW THAT, SO IT GOES ON FLYING ANYWAY

BY ALONZO KELLY

Have you ever wondered why some people from the same neighborhoods, who went to the same schools, and survived similar circumstances are more successful than their peers? Perhaps the bumblebee provides all the answers we need to answer that question. If you have ever really noticed, the bee has a body too large for its wings, and flaps them entirely too slow to actually lift it off the ground. They also spend most of their time transporting things which would seem to make flight that much more impossible. Despite all the reasons it should stay grounded, the beauty of the bee is the ability to ignore 'laws of science' and go about its business with style and grace. The bee does not concern itself with the doubts of others and certainly does not let logic get in the way of achieving its goals.

Successful people behave in a way that seems utterly impossible to others, but perfectly natural to them. They exhibit strength and confidence in situations that fill others with fear and doubt. The lessons from the bee that can guarantee our success and ultimate victory are highlighted in the following reflections.

CONTROL WHAT YOU CAN CONTROL

I can remember the first time I mentioned out loud that I was going to become a successful businessman. Eyebrows were raised, giggles broke the silence, and doubt seemed to suck the air right out of the room. There were too many reasons to count why people thought I could not be successful. Maybe the reason was because it was rare for someone in my neighborhood to actually make it out with a smile on their face. Perhaps it was because I wasn't seen as being overly-gifted in the classroom. Or maybe it was because they thought I didn't have all the resources I needed in order to build a business. No matter the reason, like the bumblebee, I did not realize I wasn't supposed to be successful, so I went after my dreams without being concerned about what others said is impossible or beyond my means. The early lesson learned was that I needed to do the best I could with what I had at the time. I could not control everyone's thoughts and opinions, but I could control my response. As a result of ignoring someone else's logic, I have been able to serve thousands through my consulting practice across the country and host a radio show that is featured in 7 major cities.

IF A HAMMER IS THE ONLY TOOL YOU HAVE, THEN EVERY PROBLEM WILL LOOK LIKE A NAIL

After careful reflection and an honest review of my life journey thus far, it became apparent that all my failures can be attributed to one source; my ego. Having a certain level of self-confidence can serve a person well, but not at the expense of growth and maturity. I let the circumstances of environment convince me that unless I won the game, finished in first place, led the team in points, or had the last word in a spirited debate, it was pointless to even compete. The sacrifices I've made to put myself in a position to win have produced personal and professional gains, but the costs for this mindset have been painful life lessons. My reflection unveiled for me the truth behind all the experiences I should have had along my life journey but completely missed them. I missed my daughter's first word, I failed to visit my mom as often as I should have while she was alive, and I completely missed the boat on the importance of patience and balance. I had become accustomed to attacking every challenge, every issue, and every goal with my trusty hammer in hand. The problem I now realize is that it's hard to stop a hammer in the middle of a full swing. Even if I wanted to slow down it felt too late. Perhaps the problem wasn't with the hammer, but my lack of options to use another tool.

In order to evolve personally and professionally, I had to put the hammer down and pick up a tape measure, a pencil, and a flashlight. I used the tape measure to examine whether or not the things that I put the most effort into are producing real measurable results. I sharpened my pencil and committed to documenting a blueprint for the next phase of my life. I used the flashlight to explore the dark corners of fear that prevented me doing what I really wanted to do. Hammers have their purpose, but it's unnecessarily difficult to build a home or live an enjoyable life if it's the only tool you've got.

IF WE HAD NO WINTER, SPRING WOULD NOT BE SO PLEASANT; IF WE DID NOT TASTE ADVERSITY, PROSPERITY WOULD NOT BE SO WELCOME

I have heard when it rains it pours. I have also heard there is a light at the end of tunnel. Now that I think about it, I am constantly reminded that all things happen for a reason. Every time I heard such phrases, it was in the midst of a bad situation or a series of unfortunate events. Why hasn't someone coined a phrase that reminds me that when it rains it was necessary, the light at the end of the tunnel is the same light that guided me into it in the first place, or the reason for whatever is happening does not always have to make sense? The fact is that we will be presented with highs and lows, surprises and disappointments, good times and bad. Rather than wait until something unfortunate happens only to then invoke the power of the clever phrase to get us through, we should anticipate certain things happening and get our recovery tools in order. In other words, be prepared. Have an umbrella on hand for the rainy days, flashlight for the dark days, and a good laugh ready in waiting when something out of the ordinary decides to make a surprise appearance.

Ensure you have a few strong relationships intact to help you see through the dark days and cover your back when it decides to rain. Disappointment does not have to linger long or cause us to lose focus for a prolonged period of time. Chalk up the event as a 'life' happening – embrace it, learn from it, and move on. Find a way to start each day with a hearty laugh about something in recent history that didn't go as planned. Rejoice in the fact that you have learned from the experience and it hasn't repeated itself!

WE IMAGINE THAT WE WANT TO ESCAPE OUR SELFISH AND COMMONPLACE EXISTENCE, BUT WE CLING DESPERATELY TO OUR CHAINS

I once heard someone say that in the absence of fact, people use cliché. Clichés are over-used phrases that a person will lean on because they are lacking original thought. How many times this week have you heard someone at work use one of the following phrases?

• Think outside-the-box

• Win-win situation

• Give 110%

• Push the envelope

• Hit the ground running

• Today, more than ever...

• Perfect storm

• Cast a wider net

Why do we as leaders insist on evolving our technology and way of thinking but refuse to let go of outdated rhetoric and expression? Why are we smart enough to agree that there is a time and place for everything, but struggle to let go of that which may be getting in the way of our success? Something worth considering is that perhaps the reason we are unable to obtain the results we seek (personally or professionally) is due to our reliance on well-intentioned clichés. In other words, there was a time when the person who hit the ground running as an outside-the-box thinker that gave 110% resulted in the casting of a wider net which yielded a win-win situation for all. Today more than ever, I say enough with the clichés already! Today is as good a day as any to leave clichés to the amateurs. Successful people dare to be original and inspiring. You are not a cliché and your body of work should not be either.

TELL ME TO WHAT YOU PAY ATTENTION AND I WILL TELL YOU WHO YOU ARE

Health experts suggest that we should make a point to 'shop the perimeter' first in the grocery store. The perimeter of the grocery store is typically where you will find the freshest fruits, vegetables, meats, bread, dairy, and liquids. The closer to the center of the store you patronize, the more likely you are to find processed, prepackaged, and canned foods. From a leadership perspective, I am starting to realize that the same perimeter philosophy about food also holds true when talking about human beings.

We have never been apologists for convenience when it comes to people and relationships. Just like our food, we would prefer that we have to do as little as possible in terms of preparation but still expect the maximum return. We lose patience with those that are not as polished as we need them to be. We forget that we too were once 'perimeter professionals' and that although we were rough, unpolished, slightly less attractive to the eye, and not yet perfectly packaged, we were also the freshest, most unique, most innovative, most daring, and produced the best results.

Successful people continue to shop the perimeter. They take a second look at people and ideas that may require a more hands-on approach than desired. They are mindful of how an accumulation of degrees, awards, promotions, and bonuses may have pushed them away from the freshness of the perimeter to the dullness of the center. Let me be the first to remind you that for every 'perimeter professional' you ignore for sake of convenience, an observant shopper (client) can easily spot an unhealthy 'processed professional' and 'canned consultant.' Take a look in the mirror and ask yourself which you one you see.

GOOD COMMUNICATION IS AS STIMULATING AS BLACK COFFEE, AND JUST AS HARD TO SLEEP AFTER

Successful people create environments where communication is authentic, and are thankful when critical news about their performance is brought to their attention. We are not perfect and the opportunities to learn and grow will be endless on the leadership journey. I can remember receiving some feedback that I felt should have been delivered years ago. Feeling blindsided and unappreciated, I slipped into behavior reserved for high school kids in an after school 'spirited debate.' I lashed out in my best defense about why the feedback was wrong and how I should have received the message a long time ago. After getting over my two-minute ego trip, I allowed the feedback to sink in and realized of course they were right. I was still miffed about not having received the news that I needed years ago, but I was nonetheless thankful it was finally brought to my attention. I often wonder why it takes us so long to share insight or observations necessary for growth. I can only conclude one of two things is happening. Either we haven't learned how to give and receive feedback, or we do not create environments where feedback from our relationships is not only encouraged but also expected.

In order to be victorious we must always be mindful of our communication. It must be clear, authentic, relevant, and specific. This applies not only to providing such messages, but receiving them as well. Our ability to evolve as leaders demands that we are consistent with our communication and regard it as a core principle of who we are personally and professionally.

CONCLUSION

Knowing the tips for success does not automatically make you a success any more than owning a piano automatically makes you a pianist. Commit to taking action on the following tips:

1. Do not concern yourself with what others believe you are capable of achieving. Your job is not to prove anyone wrong but to prove yourself right. Nothing great was ever invented because we followed the rules of logic at the time. You are an amazing person capable of producing incredible results.

2. Control what you can control. Success requires that we master utilizing the resources available to us, no matter how limited. You will always be able to accomplish more with additional time, talent, and resources. What will separate you from the amateurs however, is your ability to refuse to let what you do not have access to, be reason for your failure. Our history is filled with stories of winners who were perceived to be not as talented, not as strong, and not as smart. Imagine a world where the bee is still sitting in the hive waiting to grow bigger wings because all the other flying creatures have them.

3. Use more than one tool to solve your problems. There are many different ways to solve a problem and twice as many tools to assist in the effort. If you find yourself confronting your challenges with the same aggressive approach, you will find that more problems have been inadvertently created. If you insist on being soft-spoken and always needing consensus, you may be perceived as being weak and indecisive. Develop a balance of comfort with being collaborative when you need to be and an authoritative decision-maker when the situation requires. Both will be necessary on your journey of success.

4. Embrace adversity as teachable moments worth remembering. The best way to prevent negative surprises is to plan and prepare relentlessly. Part of planning and preparing includes your response to phenomena that happen without your control. You take an extra jacket on a hike because you remembered that last time you left one behind. You arrive at the airport 90 minutes early, because you remember what happed the last time you only prepared for a minimum delay. Adversity turns to failure only when you ignore the wealth of information that the experience provided.

5. You are better than a cliché! Success demands that you release mediocrity and embrace excellence. In order to do that, you must avoid the temptation to blend in at all costs. Add value to your clients by delivering in unique and innovate ways.

6. Shop the perimeter. Welcoming the challenge of molding a raw idea into an incredible final product is what motivated you in the first place. Never forget your roots when partnering with businesses and individuals. The times demand that you invest in yourself and your business in a way that guarantees fresh ideas and more meaningful results.

7. Demand feedback that fosters growth. I absolutely agree that we should be proud of who we are and the service we provide. It is hearing about the opportunities to grow that separate the mediocre from the elite.

About Alonzo

Alonzo M. Kelly is President & CEO of Kelly Leadership Group, LLC. Born and raised in Detroit, MI, Alonzo migrated to Wisconsin to attend St. Lawrence Seminary High School. Molded in the home of a loving grandmother and groomed in an institution of faith, his passion for service and leadership is unparalleled. He is the architect behind the first Teen Court Juvenile Correction Program for the state of Wisconsin, and has extensive leadership experience in the non-profit, healthcare, and financial industries.

Today he is the founder of Kelly Leadership Group, LLC. Since forming the organization in 2009, KLG has served over 1,000 individuals through personal and professional development, delivered training to a plethora of Fortune 500 companies and non-profit organizations, and is consistently retained to be the keynote speaker at large and small events across the country. Kelly is the host of a dynamic live Internet radio show *'Leadership; The Way I See It'* that boasted over 10,000 weekly listeners within the first 8 weeks of launching in April of 2012. Tune in and evolve your leadership today at: www.blogtalkradio.com/alonzokelly.

Alonzo Kelly holds a Bachelor's degree in Accounting, a Master's degree in Public Administration, a Master's degree in Human Resources & Labor Relations, and a Master's degree in Business Administration. He is a member of Alpha Phi Alpha Fraternity Incorporated, and has received countless awards for his leadership and service – including the United Way Philanthropic Five Award, Central Region Young Professional of the Year from the National Urban League, and the TRIO Achievement Award.

Visit: www.kellyleadershipgroup.com to learn more about how KLG is building stronger leaders that produce unimaginable results.

CHAPTER 4

CREATE YOUR OWN SUCCESSFUL BUSINESS IN 5 SIMPLE STEPS — OUT OF NOWHERE

BY BETTINA J. VIERECK

*"Any goal can be accomplished if you break it down
into enough small steps. "*
~ Henry Ford

This is a great quote and absolutely true. It works in all areas of life, and if you always stick to it, you've already mastered an important step in connection with creating your own successful business – out of nowhere. But it is not enough, because all these small steps make only sense for your success if you take action:

*"The world seems to belong to those who reach out and grab
it with both hands. It belongs to those who do something rather
than just wish and hope and plan and pray, and intend to do
something someday, when everything is just right."*
~ Brian Tracy

That's another great quote. Combine it with the first one and you already have the complete basis for your business success. Read these two quotes again and again, keep them always in mind and apply them – regardless of what you do:

- Do you have to do something you really dislike? Divide it into lots of small steps and perform one by one.

- Do you have to solve a problem? Divide it into lots of small parts and solve one by one.

- Do you want to learn something new? Divide it into lots of small lessons and learn one by one.

- Do you ... ?

This always works and if you select small enough steps or parts or lessons or whatsoever, you can really do and achieve all – independent of your actual situation – at least as long as you take action, because *without appropriate action* the very best defined steps or parts or lessons or whatever are completely useless and just a waste of time.

And never think that you're not able to create a successful business of your own – that is definitely not true. It does not matter where you are today, because you have all you need for starting and building up a successful business: Your ability to think, to plan, to learn and to focus on the things that must be done. And even if you have some problems in one or several fields at the moment that is definitely no obstacle, because you can change all, if you really want to do it and take all necessary actions in this regard. All skills you need for having a successful business are learnable. And it is not necessary to be an expert in all fields, often it is completely sufficient to have a good overview, and to know whom you have to ask for help or where you can get the necessary information or resources. And now let's start.

STEP 1 – YOU NEED A GREAT IDEA FOR THE BUSINESS YOU WANT TO CREATE

This is very important for your successful business. You must offer a great product or service to your customers, because they are already surrounded by huge amounts of average products and services. Besides that, the product or service you intend to offer to them must be something you can do in an excellent way and there must be a market for it, because the best product or service will not help you to build up a successful business if there's no market. Try for example to sell pork ham in an area where only Muslims live and you'll have no success – no matter how good your pork ham tastes, how excellent your customer service is, and how low your prices are fixed.

Depending on your abilities, your knowledge and your personal values develop your idea and define your goal. It must be something that fills you with enthusiasm and the burning desire to do and to achieve it; you must be fascinated by it and really love it. You must feel great whenever you just think of it. But never make the mistake to walk around wearing rose-colored glasses. Think deep and very critically about your idea, examine the market, look at the products and services your future competitors already offer, evaluate their strengths and weaknesses and find out what you have to do to offer the most attractive, desirable and helpful product or service to your future customers. Be honest with yourself and think always in a simple way. And never forget that the first objective of your successful business has to be selling lots of products or services at profitable prices, all other things are of minor relevance and just means to the end.

STEP 2 – CREATE A COMPREHENSIVE AND WRITTEN BUSINESS PLAN

This comprehensive and written business plan is the basis for all your further activities in connection with creating your successful business. It must contain all relevant information. Look at it as a kind of blueprint for your business, because you will not only use it to present it for example to your bank, in case you intend to take a line of credit, but you will work with it each day as your personal guideline for your business success. Therefore, invest enough time in its creation and include all relevant information in connection with your business idea. While preparing it, think about your entire business, consider each single aspect and do not overlook anything. Go through all details that are vital for you to build up your successful business, and always keep in mind that good and detailed planning before starting your business will save you much frustration, failure, work, time and money during the following years. And besides that, you always know exactly what you're doing, you know all aspects of your business by heart and you are able to take the right decisions and actions just in time.

Writing a business plan is no cabala, even if you've never done that before. It is a job you can manage, because writing a business plan can be divided into lots of several sections with ease. Focus always on one of these sections and look at it from several points of view. The main sections you have to cover in any case are the following:

- Define a clear and comprehensive mission statement for your intended business. You need clarity about your own values as well as the values your business stands for, the purpose of your business and its long-term vision.

- Set the strategic goals for your business, the goals you must achieve for success. And be very clear in your formulations, because only unambiguous defined goals with measurable statements lead to success. In connection with your strategic goals, it is of utmost importance that you concentrate on the basic success factors each business must have: the reputation of your business on the market, the level of sales under short-, mid- and long-term considerations as well as their level of profitability.

- The next section of your business plan is the definition of the tactical goals which you derive from your strategic goals. Think carefully about this point, because it is a kind of daily instruction for your successful business. Define exactly which products or services you intend to offer, and develop an appropriate marketing and sales plan which allows you to gain profit in accordance with your strategic goals. Your marketing and sales plan is a mighty tool for your daily successful work, because it always gives you the guideline policy in connection with: your products and services, your pricing, your contribution, your customers and your competitors as well as your investments. Determine in a clear and precise way which resources you need for building up your successful business, do not focus on an "as-much-as- possible", but on an "as-much-as-necessary" solution.

I always recommend people to set high and demanding goals, and I also do that in connection with your successful business; but in connection with your business plan, I suggest that you look at all ingredients from several points of view. A pessimistic one, an average one and of course, an optimistic one. Include some reserves in your figures, because it's normal in business that even with the best planning, unforeseen things happen or costs change. And ask yourself always what could happen in the worst case if one or several things do not work in the planned way –

that will help you to set the right priorities, find solutions in a quick and easy way and to focus on the things that are really important for your business and your success.

STEP 3 – FIND THE NECESSARY RESOURCES FOR BUILDING UP YOUR BUSINESS

One of the main reasons why people do not start up their businesses is an assumed lack of money for providing the necessary resources. Even with the best business plan, it is sometimes not possible to find for example a financing bank or private lender, because securities and guarantees are not available or other conditions or requirements cannot be fulfilled. But there is no need to resign and give up at that point. Take this as a challenge, start immediately with finding a sufficient solution, and always keep in mind that for each problem, there exists at least one solution that works.

If you have your own successful business, you always are a problem solver at first, before all other things. And finding a solution in connection with financing your business is a really great experience and training for your whole business life – especially if you have to start with nothing. I hope you've done your job in connection with the preparation of your comprehensive business plan with accuracy, because now you'll need it. It should include a list with all resources you need to start, and give you all relevant details in connection with the money you need for financing your intended business. Take this list and analyze each individual item: What alternatives do you have for reducing your costs? Be creative in connection with each point and also take unconventional measures into consideration:

- Do you really need everything right from the start?

- Do you really have to buy everything or is it possible to rent them for some time, or maybe just for those projects for which you really need them?

- Which points can be simplified in a way that you can reduce your costs?

- Is it possible to do things with used equipment, because you can very often buy it for a fraction of what a new item would cost?

- Can you out-source some things for which you would need cost-intensive room and equipment?

- Do you really need for example the planned location, equipment, staff or whatever else right from the start, or is it also possible to start smaller with less expenditure?

The questions you have to ask yourself depends on your business idea, but it is in nearly all cases possible to reduce the money needed in a significant way. And as soon as you've started your business and created your first revenues, you can permanently reinvest your profits in the originally-intended way.

The next thing you have to do is to find one or several solutions in connection with organizing the above determined minimum amount of money you need for starting. Therefore you can do several things:

- You can look for an additional job and use the earnings from that job as start-up money for your business.

- You can go through all the things you own. It is very likely that there are lots of things you do not really need. Try to sell them either on the Internet or with the help of small advertisements, which you often can place for free in supermarkets.

- Due to the fact that you're a problem solver and a goal achiever, you can ask your family and friends to lend you the necessary money you need for starting. The worst thing that could happen is that they say no, but that is no catastrophe, and sometimes you'll be really astonished at who will support you.

- Look for your first customers and agree on a 30 or 50% deposit, or even ask for a 100% advance payment.

- Negotiate with your suppliers long payment targets and with your customers short ones. If you do that right on the basis of a clear and comprehensive calculation as well as a serious, accurate check of the creditworthiness of your customers, that can be a great possibility even to perform a big project with less or even no money.

There are many more possibilities we can think of. Be creative in this regard and try all things that could lead to success. Never give up if something does not work, try the next possibility – as long as necessary and until you have success or in other words: the necessary money for getting started.

STEP 4 – START AND TAKE ACTION

Now the great moment is here. If you've done your homework and performed the above steps with seriousness, discipline and accuracy, you can make the first real step in connection with creating and building up your successful business:

You can start!

And you should do that immediately. Do not wait for 100% perfect conditions and circumstances, because that never will happen. Just now is the right time for you to begin. You've defined a clear mission statement and you know exactly what you want to achieve. The very best moment to start and move in the right direction – step-by-step in accordance with your business plan – is NOW. I am quite sure that you'll have to make some corrections and adjustments from time to time, but that's the normal way of life. Due to the fact that you clearly know what you want to achieve and always follow that direction, you recognize the necessity of corrections and changes in time, and can immediately react and adjust your business plan as well as your actions.

STEP 5 – NEVER LEAVE THE ROAD OF SUCCESS

Become a great leader with successful habits. Focus always on the output you can achieve. Invest your time wisely and in a highly profitable way. Set clear priorities and do the most important things first. Do all necessary things when they have to be done. Avoid procrastination. Take decisions quickly, but always in accordance with your mission statement and after an accurate analysis of the situation. Trust in yourself and your abilities and never lose self-confidence. Develop your skills and increase your knowledge – invest in yourself and each day reserve some time for that. Lead a well-balanced and comprehensive life, because life does not only consist of business. Give enough room to family, fun, sport, health, friends and whatever else you appreciate. Always be clear about the persons and things you want to have in your life. Avoid too much clutter and keep your life simple - leave the boat behind you after crossing the river. Use the great tool of asking: Ask for help, ask for additional information, ask for opinions, ask about any topic you can think of.

…And last but not least, take responsibility for your life and for your decisions!

ABOUT BETTINA

Bettina Viereck was born and lives in Waldshut, a beautiful, small town in the South of Germany near the Swiss border. She studied Business Management with the main focus on International Marketing as well as Finance & Accounting. She graduated in summer 1988 and worked for many years in various management functions in Switzerland, Austria and Germany. Besides that, she pursued further education as a Quality Assurance Manager at the German Society for Quality (DGQ) and helped several companies to build up, implement and certify simple and working Quality Systems – based on the standard series DIN EN ISO 9000.

Bettina has deep knowledge in connection with the overall analysis of companies, the work out as well as the implementation of necessary corrective actions for ensuring the long-term success of businesses. Bettina believes in lifelong education, and permanently keeps her knowledge and expertise up-to-date. Her passion is helping other people improve their lives and to achieve what they want to have, always based on their individual personal values. She performs personal coaching on an overall basis – which considers all areas of life always with the aim to enable her clients to create free, well-balanced and happy lives, discover their best selves and live their dreams. In addition, she has developed several training programs on important business matters as well as personal growth such as time management, coping with stress, communication and presentation skills, organization of work, project management, setting and achievement of strategic and tactical goals and self-improvement. Besides that she is engaged in the field of human rights based on the Universal Declaration of Human Rights by the United Nations with special focus on the equality of all human beings and freedom of speech as well as religion.

Outside of work, Bettina loves to spend time with her family and close friends. She loves art, music and literature, is interested in international political developments as well as world religions. She is dedicated to environmental protection and engaged in well-selected charity events with direct influence. She likes to paint, make music and enjoy the beauty of nature. In her leisure time, she writes non-fiction books and creates photographic art.

For more information on Bettina's work you can visit:
www.mentalpower4u.com
www.selbstlernseminare.com
Or follow Bettina on twitter: twitter.com/BettinaViereck

WWW.GOLF.COM/subscribe

BUSINESS REPLY MAIL
FIRST-CLASS MAIL   PERMIT NO. 22   TAMPA FL

POSTAGE WILL BE PAID BY ADDRESSEE

GOLF®

PO BOX 62120
TAMPA FL 33663-1201

CHAPTER 5

EVOLVE OR DIE!

BY BOBBY BRYANT

It was a crisp cool day in October 2007. During this time, the real estate industry began to drastically deteriorate. Banks were imploding by the day, people throughout the United States were losing their jobs in record numbers, foreclosures around the country were aberrant, and everybody knew somebody that was being evicted from their home because they could no longer afford to pay their mortgage. The climate of my profession was something like a horror movie without a heroic ending. It was as though someone had turned off the lights to my lucrative business and walked away with no intentions of returning things back to normal. Little did I know, in 2007, we were in the infancy of a recession.

Months earlier, I owned a thriving Mortgage Brokerage Company. At that time, most banks had very competitive loan products that allowed Mortgage Brokers like myself to shop the best deal and place most potential homebuyers in a program that required little or no money down. Dozens of lenders competed for our business. Once the lenders began to implode, shopping for the best deals and programs started to become a daunting task. Lenders began losing more money due to foreclosures than they were loaning out for new mortgages. This fact alone resulted in a credit crunch. In other words, it increasingly became more and more difficult to obtain a mortgage.

Due to the mortgage debacle, I regrettably decided to close my Mortgage Brokerage Business. Countrywide Home Loans had been courting me for a while to join their team. They saw how small Mortgage

Brokerages like mine were struggling and was heavily pursuing me to manage one of their branches. My options limited, I accepted their offer. I accepted an offer that would drastically change the lifestyle I had grown accustomed to. A single father at the time, I knew I was going to have to sell my beautiful home and cars, and unfortunately, the stability my kids were used to was about to be drastically interrupted (School, Friends, etc.).

Optimistically, I began working at Countrywide Home Loans with the task of turning around a struggling branch. It was in a great location, newly-built office, and they currently had 17 Loan Officers. I came in the door, introduced myself, and began immediately re-interviewing everyone to see if I thought they had the ability and burning desire to succeed or let them go. After this uncomfortable, but necessary beginning, I had a team of only four (4) Loan Officers that I kept from the original team. I also had four (4) Loan Officers that I brought with me from my previous Mortgage Brokerage Company to join me on this new journey. Now, the recruiting began as I had a Countrywide Branch to rebuild.

Being that my Mortgage Brokerage Firm was not the only one going through a transition, I had the opportunity to recruit and build a solid team of high producing Loan Officers that were in limbo. I quickly built a sound team of producers. My struggling Countrywide Branch went from the weakest in the region to one of the top three (3) producing Branches. Then, a few months later, we began getting word that Bank of America was interested in buying Countrywide. At this time, Countrywide and Bank of America took turns in the #1 and #2 spot in the country as the BEST mortgage originator of home loans.

The rumors became a reality. Bank of America was actually buying Countrywide. My new team feared how these changes would impact their production. Weeks went by as everyone was anticipating the merger of the two companies and whose programs we would use. Are we going to use Bank of America's FHA Guidelines or Countrywide's FHA Guidelines? The concern was the same for all of our other loan programs. Due to the turbulent uncertainties, I began one at a time losing my new All-Star TEAM. Most of the guys/gals I recruited at this time were exhausted with the mortgage industry and had enough with change and how drastically our lives were spinning out of control with all the adjustments. The size of my team immediately became anorexic, and I now only had seven (7)

Loan Officers. All of the "used-to-be" Countrywide Branches around the country were going through the same experience that I was going through at my new Bank of America Branch. My area Sales Manager had encouraged me and the other "now" Bank of America Branch Managers to just hold on and that things would get easier soon. However, it seems like I was losing a Loan Officer everyday as they were aggressively seeking stable shelter within Corporate America.

Then, the defining moment that changed my life. It was a normal morning as I made my hike into the office. I pulled up, parked, walked in, and sat my things down on my desk. The floor where my Loan Officers sit in their cubicles was empty. The office was very quiet. I'm early, just like any other day. The only thing is, more than half of them weren't going to show up because they had already quit. For some reason, it was like everything was happening in slow motion as I was reflecting on the last few months. Sitting at my desk looking out the office window onto the floor, my elbows up, my fingers crossed, as I'm in a thinker pose, I eventually **decided** to begin considering my options. I remember saying to myself "Bobby, you have to reinvent yourself." Abruptly, the office phone rang!!

"Thanks for calling Bank of America Home Loans, my name is Bobby Bryant, how may I help you?" is what I said as I answered the phone. The voice on the other end said, "Bobby, this is Mr. Johnson! I'm coming to your office before lunch, are you going to be there?" Shaking off my self-meditative moment, I told Mr. Johnson to come to the office and that I would be here waiting for his arrival. He confirmed and stated that he would see me soon.

During my 11 years in the mortgage industry, I have worked with hundreds of Buyers. Some buyers needed their hand held, and others showed up with a folder full of documentation to complete their files because they understood the loan process. As an Owner and Branch Manager in the Mortgage Industry for several years, my experience has afforded me the opportunity to have dialog with some of the best Real Estate Brokers, Managers, Owners, and Realtors in this business with different perspectives on the real estate industry. In a reflective state of mind, it was the accumulation of phenomenal dialog, and experiencing a shift in our industry that all aligned on this opportunistic day that unknowingly started me on a journey to create a real estate company that had the potential to revitalize homeownership in America.

Mr. Johnson arrived at my office to bring me some paperwork to begin processing his loan. He handed me a folder of all the documents I had requested in order to put his file in underwriting. Obviously a little frustrated, as he sat in the chair across from me, he began talking about the process of finding his new home. Mr. Johnson just like so many other buyers I've worked with uttered this exact comment "I found my own home by searching on the Internet and my Realtor didn't do anything other than write up the contract!" He went on to say "And just think, my Realtor is going to make a full commission and I did most of the work!!" To say the least, Mr. Johnson was a little perturbed. The more he talked through his subtle frustrations about how the Realtor was going to make a full commission, he ended up talking himself into asking the Realtor for a portion of their commission due to him finding his own home.

Mr. Johnson was buying a $310,000 property in which the Realtor was due to make $9,300. Although I have heard Mr. Johnson's story a few hundred times over the years from different buyers, his talking out loud to make sense of his situation allowed me to observe his thought process and how it made him feel. I was blown away! I thought to myself, "I have heard too many people complain about the same issue." I went on to think, "What is going on? What are Realtors doing or not doing that has so many people feeling like Mr. Johnson?" Well, that afternoon I shared this story with a friend (a Real Estate Broker) as I tried to quantify how many people that my Loan Officers and I have worked with over the years that have made this same statement over and over again. I thought to myself, "This is a new problem that needs a solution! But why is this happening?"

Being a Realtor and Broker for several years, I asked a close friend a plethora of questions like: How many clients have you worked with that have found their own home? How many times have you worked with buyers and they already had a list of properties they wanted to see? How many times have you worked with a buyer and you have to hold their hand through the entire process? How many times are you asked for a portion of your commission? How has the Internet helped your business? How has the Internet hurt your business? Are buyers changing, and if so how? Are sellers changing, and if so how? How many times do you list a house for sale and you charged less than the traditional 6%? How many times have sellers asked you to lower your fee? How often do sellers sell their house and in-turn buy a home using you for both transactions? And, to what extent do innovative websites like Zillow, Trulia, Sawbuck, and other consumer-centric sites empower buyers and sellers in a way that changes how you as a Realtor conduct business?

As I shot out questions and we discussed the current state of the real estate industry, a problem was obviously and vividly identified. A problematic opportunity that resulted in my seeking a solution. My questions, his answers, along with statistical data from NAR (National Association of Realtors) conceived a business model that would revolutionize the real estate industry.

The answer to my earlier question about what Realtors are doing or not doing? Nothing! Realtors simply haven't changed!! The Internet was changing and reshaping our industry right under our (Realtors) noses!! As the Internet evolves, it empowers consumers and begins to change their buying and selling habits due to their having access to excess information. Access to view homes at their own leisure, view tax values, home values, days on the market, view foreclosures, view Open Houses, and conduct aerial views all from the comfort of their own home or office. Access. Access. Access. Mr. Johnson found his own home because he had access to just about all information at his fingertips!

THE FACTS: Buyers and Sellers are evolving every day! Why? Because the Internet is giving consumers information today that they didn't have access to just a few years ago. How does a Realtor preserve their way of doing business? They can't! The cat has been let out of the bag years ago. It's only going to evolve more rapidly. Consumers to some degree can access just about anything about a property that a Realtor used to hold sacred. Do consumers need Realtors like they use to? Of course not! However, consumers need Realtors to facilitate and navigate them through the potential pitfalls and to a successful closing. When people have access to information, it changes everything. The founders of Redbox, Netflix, and Amazon conceived a more efficient and effective way of delivering a service by leveraging technology. These ideas successfully lowered the PRICE in their respected industries! Why do we think the real estate industry is exempt from this equation?

THE PROBLEM: The housing market changed the moment the financial industry changed. You affect the money, you affect purchasing power. Unless you have cash, financing a home is like buying back in the 1980's. You must have: Credit, Money, and the Ability to demonstrate that you can continue to make payments over time.

Over 260 banks closed their doors in 2008. Today, more banks are consolidating to survive their demise. Lenders evaluated what types of loans should be eliminated in order to keep the market from repeating the same mess that caused all these banks to implode. Millions of homeowners lost their homes due to risky loans. Public Down Payment Assistance programs like Nehemiah were voted out of existence by the New Housing Bill, and became illegal as of October 1, 2008.

The market got tighter, job loss throughout the United States topped 10%, banks increased credit card interest rates, decreased credit limits, there were record foreclosures in several areas of the country, and a full-blown credit crunch slowed down consumer spending. Consumers started holding their money because they didn't know what to expect. Buyers couldn't buy, and sellers couldn't sell. Credit Crunch!!

THE SOLUTION: Given this information, I began researching to find a cure for the real estate industry. My goal was to find a new way to execute the basics. To find a solution that provides an answer to everything mentioned in this chapter. A company that meets buyers at their individual point of need by providing an opportunity to receive a rebate that lowers their closing cost. A concept that helps sellers preserve their hard-earned equity by reducing the cost to list their house on the MLS. A concept that gives Realtors a vehicle that will allow them to prospect less, facilitate more, and increase their income. I wanted a business method that embraces where the industry is going. However, to accomplish this, I had to understand what consumers want, how their buying and selling habits have evolved at the hands of technology, and how to deliver a comprehensive service that created a win-win situation.

I took the time to research and understand the evolving dynamics of the real estate industry and the new direction that was being driven by the consumer. Given technology today, can you imagine what the real estate industry will be like in five years? Can you imagine what Zillow and Trulia will be like in 5 years? Can you imagine how many more new real estate search sites will be up and running in 5 years? It's inevitable!!! This new understanding commands that Realtors let go of the old traditional way of practicing real estate and embrace the change that is happening right now. TODAY! Nothing stays the same forever. I hope we learned that by what Redbox and Netflix did to Blockbuster. I hope we learned that by what the Internet did to the Travel Industry and the Stock Brokerage Industry. I hope we learned that by what Amazon did to Barnes and Noble.

On this day, I decided to be open to new opportunities, to reinvent myself, to listen to my clients frustrations, to research the changes that inflicted itself upon the real estate industry, and to methodically understand what consumers want. To be "Ultimately Successful" you have to be open to new opportunities and have a burning desire to unequivocally be your personal best. One has to be passionately in the pursuit of perfecting their craft. If not, you are going to quit. It's your passion that becomes the everlasting fuel that drives you thru' the peaks and valleys of your journey. Altering my mindset, my opportunity immediately presented itself because I was willing to see past my comfort zone. This fact alone allowed me to conceive an idea that is progressively gaining momentum and national attention with the potential of changing the game of real estate. iBuy Realty: Revitalizing Homeownership in America by making the purchase of a home more rewarding and the selling of a house more economical. I had to EVOLVE, or DIE!

About Bobby

Bobby Bryant is the Founder/President of iBuy Realty and iBuy University. Originally from Mobile, AL, Bobby is a triple-degreed Educator. With two Masters Degrees in Education, he taught five years in the public school system(s) of Alabama and Texas.

Bobby's experience in real estate dates back to 1995. Three years after moving to Houston, TX he became a Mortgage Broker and opened his own brokerage firm called Texas Guaranteed Mortgage. After several successful years and a struggling economy, Bobby accepted a Branch Manager position with Countrywide Home Loans. His task was to turn around a struggling branch on the Northeast side of Houston, Texas. Bobby fulfilled that task and shortly afterwards, Countrywide was bought by Bank of America.

It was while Bobby Bryant was at Bank of America that the idea and vision for iBuy Realty was conceived. Seeking a new challenge, Bobby paid close attention to the transition of the real estate industry and how consumers were adapting and changing their buying and selling habits due to the economy. His mission was to create a solution for an industry that desperately needed to provide some type of relief for cash-strapped buyers and equity-deprived sellers. With higher down payment requirements and declining home values, Bobby Bryant found the antidote for an ailing real estate industry: iBuy Realty! His mission: To revitalize homeownership in America by making the purchase of a home more rewarding and the selling of a house more economical. With a Mission Statement like that, how can you go wrong?

Leveraging his educational background, Bobby is an Author, Instructor, Mentor, Professional Speaker, and Trainer for hundreds of professionals (Realtors) that seek to learn how to thrive and survive in today's real estate industry. Bobby is a TREC (Texas Real Estate Commission) Certified Real Estate Instructor. He teaches and trains new and experienced Realtors/Brokers and Mortgage Professionals at iBuy University (Real Estate School) in Mid-Town Houston, Texas.

As the Owner of iBuy University, Mr. Bryant believes that the real estate industry needs fresh and new ideas. His vision is to encourage and assist the next generation of real estate professionals by offering relevant education and tools that will drastically increase their success. iBuy University: Education. Evolved.

Bobby Bryant is sincerely one of the industries newest pioneers of real estate. His desire and ability to understand the changes that have inflicted itself upon the real estate industry is what makes him unique and successful. He understands real estate, the unforeseen changes, and the challenges before us. Furthermore, this is someone on a national scale to keep your eyes and ears open for. I introduce to you, Bobby Bryant! The next BIG name in real estate…

CHAPTER 6

BRAND AND GROW RICH - STRATEGIES TO POSITION, PACKAGE AND PROMOTE YOU AS AN EXPERT AND CASH IN ON YOUR BUSINESS OR LIFE KNOWLEDGE

BY DANIEL CALIGUIRE

Are you an aspiring online entrepreneur? I believe that right now is the single greatest time in the history of mankind for aspiring entrepreneurs to rise up and take the stage. 85% of the entire human race is connected through the Internet performing 7 billion searches a day for some type of information. People have a burning desire for guidance, mentoring, coaching and information that solve their problems. People all over this world are extremely passionate about so many different topics and you can position yourself as the expert who delivers the in-demand information making a massive online fortune.

Based on this belief I created the website www.AspiringEntrepreneurs Academy.com to give you the processes, systems, platforms and strategies to become a published author on Amazon, the world's biggest stage for authors and create informational products that answer the questions that solve the problems people are searching for – all the while building your personal brand that positions you as the expert.

What's my story? I entered the world of online marketing for one reason; I wanted to be a Dad and husband who could spend as much time as I wanted with my family. You see, just 5 years ago I was doing very well in life, I had a corporate job where I spent ten years as a technology Consultant and Recruiter. My salary was increasing each year as I became more of an expert in my field, my benefit package was decent and my overall lifestyle was what most people would classify as upper middle class. I want you to know that this is not a "rags to riches story, I wasn't homeless or bankrupt or on my last dollar, I thought I had all the things you need in life. I drove a nice car, had a big beautiful house.

In the early months of 2007, something profound happened to me and it happens to millions of people every day, my new wife Leah and I found out we were expecting our first child and it was a girl!. Those of you who are parents know the journey my wife and I were about to embark on. This included things like regular doctor's visits and all the planning to get ready to welcome our little girl to the world. I used up all my vacation time spending time with my wife as her support, it was super exciting and extremely emotional for both of us, I just could not wait to be a daddy! My daughter Giada Isabella Caliguire was borne on September 28th 2007; she was an angel from God, the most precious little girl I have ever laid eyes on. After Giada was born, I asked my boss at the time to take a couple weeks off so that I could be a dad and supporting husband. Unfortunately, I did not get the response I was hoping for. At that very moment I decided to stop giving all I have to my corporation where I was merely trading my time for a paycheck. Instead I was going to be an Entrepreneur so that I could get the one thing that mattered most, time to spend with Giada. This is how it all started; I just wanted to be a daddy!

In five short years I built two online companies. My First Company generated 4.5 million dollars in five years in Internet marketing consulting fees coaching small business owners on their Internet Marketing strategy. (I was really just selling my information as a service.) My second company was an online niche product, outdoor wood-fired pizza ovens. I built a drop ship company where I held no inventory and generated over 2 million dollars in sales in the first two years. Below are some of the strategies I used and hope that you do the same, but surpassing me. This is my way to give back, this is all about YOU.

Becoming an online entrepreneur starts with overcoming the common fears or myths. These are the typical myths that keep people stuck in the 9-5 rat race and the exact fears I had when I launched my online career. I knew if I succeeded I could live a fulfilled entrepreneurial lifestyle and spend as much time as I wanted with my family and friends.

Myth No. 1: I'm not an expert so why would anybody buy from me? Not true, you are most likely more of an expert than you think. You have experience in life, business, and you might have a hobby you are passionate about. The first thing we teach at: www.aspiringentrepreneurs academy.com is how to **position** yourself as an expert in whatever field you choose. I knew nothing about Internet Marketing when I started five years ago. I spent my entire career in corporate America as a Technology Consultant and Recruiter. I quickly branded myself as an Expert in the field of Internet Marketing and generated 4.5 million in consulting fees in a field I just learned.

Myth No. 2: I don't have a website and no one knows who I am. The Aspiring Entrepreneur's Academy will position and brand you as an expert, and build your marketing funnel. I will go into greater detail on why you need a funnel (not a website) and how it works. My Marketing funnel works for me 24/7. It's a process where your customers come in to a series of websites that offer valuable content and training. They are also receiving automatically from you a series of emails that further position you as an expert, build trust and get the customer to know, like and trust you.

Technology has made it extremely easy and affordable to launch an international online business but you need the right positioning, packaging and marketing funnel. The Aspiring Entrepreneur's Academy can quickly launch your online career.

Myth No. 3: I don't know how to make an informational product and I have no experience selling online. Don't worry, we have this system set up that will build your informational product for you and even better, broadcast it all over the Internet for people to buy. Once we set up your branded marketing funnel, it works 24 hours a day 7 days a week, it never sleeps or calls off and works for you while you're out doing what your calling is, spending time with your family, friends or helping make the world a better place. Before I started online marketing I had absolutely no experience selling or marketing online, in four short years I raked in almost 6 million dollars in sales and fees!

In all seriousness, those three myths derail a lot of people from living a fulfilled life. The reality is that becoming an online entrepreneur has never been easier and faster if you have the right platform, message and system. Below are the strategies that will get you started, these are the same steps I took that ultimately lead me to build several multi-million dollar businesses and live the ultimate Entrepreneur's lifestyle where I spend a majority of my time being a daddy.

FOUR PROVEN STEPS TO BECOME A SOUGHT-AFTER EXPERT

1. **Position and Brand.** This is the heavy lifting and the foundation when it comes to building your online expert empire. **This is where you claim your topic and own it.** The first step and key is to know what's already been said so you can formulate your own opinion and even more important, differentiate yourself. In general, you can start by studying the work of the ten most influential people in your desired subject. You should be on every email list of the current experts in your industry; you should also buy their books and products, and attend as many seminars as you can. Pay close attention to how others are positioning themselves and the sales process they take you through.

   Every online Entrepreneur must master positioning and self-branding. You should be thinking about questions like; *why is my content more valuable than others in my space? How Am I different that everyone else?* Educate, don't sell! I want you to be obsessed with value based content. The more value people perceive in you the more you can charge. When I started as an Internet Marketing coach to small business owners, I studied the most creative thought leaders in my field, I studied what they were doing, how they spoke and their positioning strategies. I generated millions in consulting and coaching fees because I was able to articulate at a high level internet marketing strategies, thus business owners put me in the "expert" class.

2. **Find a problem And Answer It.** The best strategy to further your position and brand yourself as an expert in your space is to identify the ten most pressing questions your audience has and then answer them. If you can publish content or even better, videos that answer the questions people are asking, you are immediately the expert. When I was consulting for business owners, the two biggest questions they had for me was how could they generate more targeted website traffic to their website and convert those visitors to sales. I made videos and published content answering those two questions. The videos and content all had a call-to-action that pointed back to a consultation with me. So in short, you are solving the most pressing questions and in return generating business for yourself and positioning YOU as the expert.

3. **Create a series of digital products** - Positioning, packaging and profiting from your online content is fast and profitable, here are two reasons you should create, package and promote your knowledge.

   • *You pay to create it, but after that, there is no production or manufacturing costs to cut into your profit. Nor are there shipping costs to deliver the product to your clients. Plus, your product doesn't need to be stored in a warehouse—and you won't ever have to worry about running out of stock. Online products also infinitely scalable.*

   • *Digital products are delivered immediately, providing your customers with instant gratification, so they can consume your product while they're still in a state of excitement. Most importantly, your product can be accessed anywhere in the world, instantly.*

4. **Build Your Marketing Funnel.** Do this correctly and you win! Notice how I say funnel and not website. A Marketing Funnel is a system that you set up once but works while you sleep 24 hours a day 7 days a week and it never calls off. It delivers your message systematically the exact same way to every one of your prospects. Its a way to get prospects to know, like and trust you so that they become your fan and paying client. My funnel starts with a lead capture page with a bold claim (this is

your Mac Machine) that is structured in a way to position you as an expert. Your claim goes something like this; The Aspiring Entrepreneurs Academy will give you to the tools necessary to make a fortune online as an expert, and allow you to get paid based on the value you offer – not the hours you work even if you have little or no experience as an online entrepreneur. I like to use a video to deliver my claim front and center – filled with valuable content and an email opt in form to the right of the video with a compelling headline and sub headline at the top. The call to action is in the video and on top of the opt-in form. Once a prospect sees your video that starts to answer questions they have they will begin to know, like and trust you in return for their email address. They will give you their information to receive more training or content from you.

The second stage to my funnel is a series of automatically generated emails that are sent to the prospect answering the 10 most pressing questions you have identified above; I like to again use video content as they are seeing a real person professionally present valuable content. Each email builds upon the last. The emails are alongside access to your video's that are stored on your website, each week they get access to a new video and an email that is further positioning your message and brand. The #1 objective of your entire funnel is to teach, not sell. I was able to outsell my competitors who had more experience than me when I was an Internet Marketing Coach to small business owners because my entire presentation was education based, not a sales pitch. Once a prospect went through my education based webinar, I had them hooked; I was a true teacher and very transparent. We spend a lot of time teaching and setting up marketing funnels at:
www.aspiringentrepreneursacademy.com

The fact that you are reading this book tells me you are a passionate person who most likely has extremely valuable experience in life or business. If you want to learn how to take what you already know and love, and position yourself as the voice, www.aspiringentrepreneursacademy.com will give you everything you need to package, promote and profit from your passion. Remember, this all started because I was passionate about being a dad!

About Daniel

Daniel Caliguire is a serial Internet entrepreneur who is ranked #1 in the world on Linked In for the search term "Internet Marketing Strategist." Daniel is the founder of The Online SEO Agency who is partnered with the #1 SEO Ranked firm in the world, National Positions. Daniel helped grow National Positions to the Inc. 500 award winner for 2009, 2010 and 2011. Mr. Caliguire is a personal branding advocate who is releasing his first book titled "Brand Spanking You" in early 2013.

Daniel has helped hundreds of business owners generate millions of dollars in new business revenue via modern search engine marketing strategies. Mr. Caliguire is also the founder of The Aspiring Entrepreneur's Academy, where anyone with any background can brand themselves as an expert authority and cash in on their passion.

Daniel is a devoted husband married to the love of his life, Leah and they have 2 children, Giada and Lydia. Daniel is extremely passionate about working with and being an entrepreneur so he can spend time with his family. If you want to work with Daniel directly and receive free entrepreneur training you can visit one of his sites:
www.www.danielcaliguire.com or
www.aspiringentrepreneursacademy.com

CHAPTER 7

HOW TO NEVER RUN OUT OF MONEY WITH YOUR IRAs AND RETIREMENT ACCOUNTS

BY TROY M. BENDER

I will never forget being 16, driving my first car, and picking up one of my first dates. I was on top of the world, but the feeling didn't last long.

…In fact, we did not even make it two miles. The car ended up puttering to a stop on the side of the road, where my ego deflated as the last drops of gas evaporated from my tank.

The change is incredible, if you think about it. Seconds before, we were laughing and thinking about the future, even if we could not see past cheeseburgers and a movie. Then, in the blink of an eye, we were stuck on the side of the road, watching others drive past. She jumped in the drivers seat and I pushed the car to the nearest gas station. Talk about embarrassing!

If I have learned anything over the years, it is the importance of preparation.

I suppose I ran out of gas on the way to eat because I just was not thinking. I risked the wrong thing. There was just too much to lose when I picked up Stacy on less than a quarter tank. The date ended there, by the way. It is a lesson that life will keep teaching you if you do not learn. You never want to run out of gas, and that only becomes truer and truer as life goes on.

Knowing what is worth risking and what is not, is important. It is something I help people decide everyday as a safe money planner. I make sure my clients never run out of money after retirement.

I like to help people.

Everyone has had plans backfire because they either have not prepared well enough or did not know enough about what they were doing. I like to help my clients plan for their financial future, and teach them a thing or two that others in my field do not usually mention.

With the stock market crashes over the last decade, my clients are increasingly worried that their money will not last through retirement. I work with them to make sure their hard-earned money does not evaporate by avoiding crucial mistakes.

KEEPING THE RIGHT THINGS SAFE

First of all, know what you should keep safe. Here is a hint: it is your retirement account!

I meet with both pre-retirees and others who are decades into their retirement on a daily basis. I work with both age groups to make sure each and every one of them does the same thing; keep their principal retirement funds steady through market ups and downs.

It is not enough to simply save money and grow an IRA and 401K. If those accounts are not protected, you may wake up one morning to see your retirement fund shrink drastically. Unfortunately, it happened to millions after the financial crashes of 2000 and 2008.

According to the ISI Group, Inc., the Standard & Poor's 500 fell from March 24, 2000 through October 9, 2002 a total of 49.10%. It fell even more from October 9, 2007 through November 20, 2008. This time period it fell 51.93%.

One couple I currently help saw their $180,000 savings in retirement accounts fall to $32,000 in just three years. Their broker promised them the money would come back. It did not.

By the time they came to me, they had no idea what to do.

What their broker should have done is ensure that their retirement principal was safe from risk, despite what happened in the global market. Instead, he put their life savings in risky accounts. Those accounts backfired in 2008.

That couple wanted to make money in stocks and bonds, which certainly is not a bad thing. But they did not want to lose everything, which is nearly what happened. The broker should have known what to risk and what to keep safe.

Their savings were up for grabs everyday. On dozens of different trading days, they lost a lot of money. And it continued until they left that broker and came to me.

WHAT DO I DO DIFFERENTLY?

Ask my happy clients in Orange County, California. Many of them have taken my financial classes, which I teach three times a month. I do nearly the same thing for each and every one of my clients. I put their retirement principal where it can receive a certain amount of market growth while losing none of the principal when the market crashes.

We look to win a safe amount each year. We never lose anything, no matter how bad things are everywhere else. We do this by putting their retirement principal in a Fixed Indexed Annuity (FIA), also called hybrid annuities. Our goal is not to hit a home run out of the park, hear the crowd cheer, and make a victory lap. We just want to make it to base, I like to tell clients, and stay in the game.

By putting their money in a FIA, my clients' goals are to receive enough interest to offset inflation. This past decade, most clients were very happy to average 5 to 6%. How do my clients average 6% when everyone else is losing money? One aspect of the FIA is Annual Reset - when the Standard & Poor's 500 is falling, you lose nothing, in exchange for a cap on the upside. This eliminates the greatest fear of investing for someone heading into retirement, which is loss of principal.

The worst any client of mine has ever earned in any one-year period over the past 14 years is a 0% return. There has never been a loss! The best any client of mine has done in any one year is 22%, but most are

5 to 6%. If they were to put their money in a CD, for example, they can expect to make around 0.05% a year, up to nearly 1%. Other options? They can find a money market account, or settle with a savings account. In all likelihood, neither option will offer even as much as 1% interest. They would be making less than inflation, meaning they will lose money every year.

After all, 2011's inflation was 3.2% and 2012's inflation was 2.1%. It is a safe bet that you will lose money picking any of the three options above.

During some years, clients have made more than 10%, but they don't expect it every year. They reap enough benefits to stay even, and never lose a dime. Again, it is like going in for a layup in basketball. Our goal is to be safe, and we want to score an easy point, not a difficult one.

PLAN WELL, PLAN EARLY

The second thing I do differently is I tell my clients to start preparing for retirement early. My mother taught me the multiplication tables before I could read. She is a math wiz herself, and I like to think of myself as numerically inclined. One of my most treasured childhood memories is going out to eat with my parents. At the end of the meal, my dad always gave me the bill. I'd say I was about five when he started doing it. I'd take it to the counter, count the change, and figure out the tip.

Going back even farther, my mother said at 4 years old, I was checking to make sure the numbers were correct at the grocery store! I like to think of those exercises as preparation for my career today.

Planning is key to staying afloat during retirement, and planning early is another thing I suggest my clients do. General advice, in my experience, says that people should start planning for retirement five years before their working life ends.

I disagree. I tell them to keep one number in their heads – 70 ½. At the age of 70 ½, no matter how well preserved your IRAs and other retirement accounts are, you will be forced to begin taking a certain amount from them each year. These withdrawals are called required minimum distributions (RMDs), and they are required. What is worse, the percentage amount you have to withdraw grows each year.

At the time of this writing, if you have, say $100,000 in retirement accounts, you must withdraw nearly $3,650 or 3.65% of that account at 70 ½. The percentage that you must withdraw continues to increase through age 100. At age 85, you will take out nearly 7%.

I tell each of my clients they need to begin preparing for retirement anywhere between 1 and 15 years before they turn 70 ½. I warn my clients of what I call the "Perfect Storm". This happens more often than you would imagine, and it's financially devastating.

WHAT'S THE PERFECT STORM?

It is a little like running out of gas, then having to push your date to the station in the pouring rain. Say you have lost a good portion of your IRA or 401K, like the clients I mentioned earlier. They lost nearly $150,000 of their retirement principal by putting it in risky stocks and investments. Then, the government came knocking. They had to withdraw their RMD. At their ages, their RMD was already nearly 5% per year and was continuing to increase.

I beg you - be careful. There is just too much at risk. The fixed indexed annuity (FIA) provides a guaranteed stream of income for life with a contractual guarantee that is issued by a life insurance company.

They may be the best chance of covering the money, without risk, that is lost due to mandatory required minimum distributions.

A few benefits of the (FIA) hybrid annuity include:

1. Preservation of principal and earnings

2. Automatically locks in gains

3. Never lose money due to a market downturn

4. Guaranteed lifetime income and guaranteed death benefit

5. Provide a high probability of an inflation hedge

6. Effective in all market cycles

7. Can be set up as a stretch IRA or multi-generational IRA

Protect your principal as soon as you can in case another financial crash hits us. You will reach that golden age of 70 ½ in much better spirits, and with much more money.

PLAN FOR FUTURE GENERATIONS

I am up bright and early every morning. I just love my career, and it is usually still dark when I head to the office. I use the time to answer emails, plan to check in on some clients I haven't heard from in a while, and organize my day. I don't expect any visitors. Who is as crazy as I am about retirement finances?

As it turns out, there are more than a few.

I have one client, Ruth, who spends her early mornings in a slightly different way than I do. She goes to the gym, where she uses the elliptical and watches the morning news. One morning she did not like what the news told her. She ran out of the gym and drove to my office at about 6:45am, knowing I would be there.

The Dow Jones Index fell more than 500 points that morning, and she was done with the volatility. She wanted to move her money to something safer to eliminate losses. We sat at my desk and got to work with the front door still locked and the closed sign still swinging in the window from her loud knocking.

I take care of my clients, and many of them want to take care of their children by planning some form of inheritance. It is not as easy as one might think. And it is especially hard with 10,000 baby boomers turning 65 everyday, according to Bloomberg.

With our aging population, Social Security is dwindling, and it is falling fast. By some estimates, it will be depleted by 2033. A young 23-year-old professional straight out of college, for example, is unlikely to receive social security. And my one year old or nearly three year old? Not a chance.

Clients like Ruth want to prepare a portion of their savings to pass on to their children. Like the majority of my clients, Ruth wanted to make sure she provided a legacy her children would inherit and benefit from.

We make sure that happens properly by setting up a Stretch IRA, or Multi-Generational IRA.

KNOW WHAT YOU WANT

In my experience, my clients want two things. They want preservation and income. That is it! I work with them to obtain both. They want preservation because they have worked hard all their lives. They do not want to see the savings they take with them when they enter retirement fall for the wrong reasons. They want their principal to stay intact, and they want to know they will not lose what they worked for all their lives.

And finally, they want income because people want to enjoy life. Clients understand they need to shift their thinking from growth, while they were working, to income, when they are nearly retired or are in retirement.

My clients do not just want to survive – they want to go on vacations, they want to move closer to their grandkids, and they do not want to have to check the markets every morning. I work with them to promise they will have both. For 14 years we have not seen a single client lose any of their retirement with vehicles they have purchased from our company.

To learn more about fixed indexed annuities (hybrid annuities) go to: http://indexedannuitiesinsights.com.

To learn more how we can help you, visit our website at:
www.Asset-Retention.com
or call our office locally at: 949-595-4409 or toll free at: 877-707-4409.

We are happy to help you with your retirement concerns.

About Troy

Troy Bender is President and CEO of Asset Retention, founded in 1999 in Orange County, CA.

"Protecting and Growing Your Retirement" is the company's motto. Their main focus is retirement planning, income planning, estate planning, and wealth management. Basically, unlike other risky advisors on Wall Street, Troy's goal is to create income streams that last through retirement.

Asset Retention is an accredited business with the Better Business Bureau and member of the National Ethics Association (www.ethics.net). He is also ranked among the elite in the industry as a 5-Star Best, which is awarded to less than 7% of all wealth managers.

Mr. Bender was recently featured on ABC, CBS, NBC & Fox affiliates around the country. He was seen on the Consumer's Advocate Show with Nick Nanton, 2011 Emmy Award winner. Troy was recently quoted and featured nationwide in *Newsweek* as one of America's Premier Experts® and known as a Financial Trendsetter.

Locally, Troy has been seen many times on Channel 6 TV, featured exclusively for 10 years in the Orange County Resource Guide for seniors, and heard on Orange County and Los Angeles radio stations, KLAA Sports and KABC Talk Radio.

A Southern California native, Troy understands that his clients look beyond themselves, and he helps prepare their financial well-being to transfer to their loved ones. Through Troy, there is no more letting Uncle Sam take all of the hard-earned money that your elders worked for decades to accumulate.

Troy attended the University of California at Los Angeles and has grown to love his community, contributing to it well after his office closes for the day. He chose this career to see people sleep soundly at night, knowing their money will last.

His father, also a longtime California resident, went to USC, and his mother was a real estate agent, who graduated #1 in her class in college at the sister school of Notre Dame. There is a long tradition of not just hard work, but also community service in the Bender family.

As a self-described 'Safe Money Planner,' Troy Bender looks out for those he helps.

To learn more about Troy Bender, the 'Safe Money Planner' and how you can receive the Special Report "10 Things to know about Planning Your Retirement Income," visit our website at: www.Asset-Retention.com
Or call locally at: 949-595-4409
Or toll free at: 877-707-4409

CHAPTER 8

IT'S NOT ABOUT THE MONEY

BY CHRISTY SMITH

I have been very blessed over my lifetime. I have a great family, an exceptional business and I'm surrounded by outstanding people that have become a very important part of my life. Unlike many people, I don't believe money should be the determining factor of success. In fact, I'm sure we all have heard of people that have accumulated a tremendous amount of wealth, but have been extremely unhappy. Some have even taken their own lives because they found no satisfaction in money. Personally, I have never allowed money to be a measure my success. Money may be a by-product of success, but it doesn't define success.

Success can be defined in many different ways, but for me success is about reaching your established goals. I believe I have been successful in life, not just in business. I am achieving my business goals as well as my personal goals. I don't think there's any one thing that can make any of us successful, but it is a combination of many things, and finding the right combination is what is important. Overall success is basically the accumulation of smaller successes throughout our lifetime. Each success you achieve is leading you to overall success. It takes a great deal of determination to make that happen, but it's very achievable. Very honestly, I can't remember one time when my husband and I said we were going to do something, that we didn't accomplish it. That is because we have learned to set realistic and achievable goals, we set our minds to it, put in the necessary effort, and watch it happen. I have found that my goals have changed over the years as I have grown as a person, but the process whereby I achieve my goals and experience success seems to remain the same.

I would have to say, from a personal and business perspective, the main element of my success is related to my faith. I let God guide me in every decision I make. While not everyone will subscribe to my opinion, I have found this component of my life to be the most influential and it has allowed me to make decisions that have proven extremely beneficial for me personally and professionally, as well as financially. In addition to this solid foundation, I have also experienced other components that have allowed me to experience success – which I would like to share with you.

BE A DREAMER

I dream big! I always dream big dreams and I keep those dreams in the forefront of my mind. I maintain a three-ring binder filled with sheet protectors in which I put pictures of things that I want to accomplish. I look at that binder on a regular basis because it represents the dreams and ambitions in my life. I think many people fail to accomplish their dreams because they keep their dreams in the back of their mind and just think about them on occasion. They don't write them down and they don't actively remind themselves of their big dreams. Most people think, "It will never happen for me." They sabotage themselves before they even make an attempt to fulfill their dreams. I encourage you to write down your dreams and even go as far as cutting out pictures and placing them in a binder so you can be reminded often of where you are headed.

I think it's very important to point out that my dreams are not always about what I can do for me. It's also about what I can do for others. It was a pivotal point in my life when I realized everything was not about me. I regularly think about and dream about making a difference in the lives of other people. I strongly believe God has me here for a reason and I believe it's my responsibility to fulfill that purpose. One of my dreams is to buy a house and donate it to a mother with children who may be struggling. In fact, I would like to be able to do that annually and make a difference in the lives of others in a tangible way. What are your big dreams? Do you desire to make an impact on the lives of others? I challenge you to expand your dreams to include blessing others in some way.

When you do something to benefit another, keep in mind that giving shouldn't be about wanting the recognition for giving. It has to be because you just want to make a difference. For example, I don't want to be acknowledged when I give away a house to someone that has that need. In fact, I may try to do it in such a way that the recipient doesn't even know where it came from. My husband and I do that now. A few weeks ago we sent cash in the mail to a couple of families that we knew needed money. We didn't put a return address on the envelope and we didn't put our name on a note inside the envelope. We wanted it to be completely anonymous. It's not about giving to receive recognition or to receive something in return. I believe God gives us the means to bless others because he knows we have a heart to give to people in need.

So many times people think of success and achievement as accumulating "things," but I don't think of achievement in that way. For me, achievement is what I can do to make a difference in the lives of others. The more I can do to make a difference, the more successful I am. Certainly we don't give away all our money, but helping others gives me a greater sense of fulfillment than any possession I may ever obtain.

ESTABLISH WRITTEN GOALS

Another very important component that has led me to success is proper planning and specific goal setting. I believe a lot of people don't reach their full potential because they don't set specific goals. I find it helpful for me to write down my goals so that I can look at them on a regular basis. For example, I currently have a nice boat that my family and I enjoy, but I have my eyes set on a significantly larger boat. So, I have a picture of the boat I want sitting on my desk. Every day when I see that picture it reminds me of one of my long-term goals. I am very visual when it comes to my dreams and goals. I write them down and I keep pictures in front of me to remind me of where I'm going and what I want to accomplish.

Setting long-term goals is essential, however, setting short-term goals is also imperative because short-term goals are the stepping-stones to get us to our long-term goals. I recommend first establishing your long-term goals and then working backwards to establish your short-term goals. Placing these goals in writing allows you to refer back to them, measure your progress and hold yourself accountable for your accomplishments.

In my office we sit down every December and outline our goals for the upcoming year. After establishing the specifics related to these long-term goals, we then plan what needs to be done the week before the goal, the month before, and the other months preceding the event date. Then, every week at our staff meeting we discuss where we are in our progress toward accomplishing those monthly goals. It's easy to lose track of the big picture when you're working every day and day-to-day life comes into play. So, every week we evaluate our monthly goals and determine what needs to be done in that particular week to get us closer to the fulfillment of that monthly goal and ultimately the overall long-term goal.

I encourage you to develop your own system to track your goals and your progress. You will be surprised at how much more productive you will become.

SURROUND YOURSELF WITH THE RIGHT PEOPLE

It is very important to have someone that you can talk to and who will support you in your dreams and goals. For me, that person is my husband. We discuss how we can accomplish things and we do it as a team. If you don't have a spouse that can help you get there, you can find a mentor. If you can't afford to pay for a mentor, find a friend or someone that you can connect with, who you can talk with about your dreams and what you want to do to make a difference in your life as well as in the lives of others. That person can help keep you on track as well.

My husband is probably the biggest reason why I am where I am to-day. I'm not a risk taker, that's why I'm so good at what I do. I invest people's money safely in environments where they cannot lose money. I can guarantee that because I use investment products that are not at risk in the market. My personality is couched in safety and my nature is the very opposite of a risk taker. However, my husband believes sometimes we have to take chances in life to get what we want. When I want to go into my protective and safe mode, he is standing back there saying, "We're not going to be able to make enough money to give that house away unless you do this or unless you do that." He's always the one that's guiding me to make good decisions. I'm very fortunate to have a husband and mentor who shares in my vision for the future. If he were not a giving and caring person and a visionary, then I would never be able to reach my goals.

Mentors may actually change throughout your career. My mentor when I first got into the financial services business was the person that hired me, trained me and taught me how to be a successful financial planner. However, as I grew as a person and as my goals began to change, I had to find a different mentor that could help me through that period of time. It's always important that we have mentors in our lives, someone we can look up to and who can help guide us and give us inspiration. You always need someone to be there, to be an inspiration and to help keep you going when everyday life gets tough. That mentor can also hold you accountable for your goals and offer guidance when you get off track.

You can find a mentor in many different ways. The easiest way may be to hire one if finances are not an issue. However, mentors can be quite expensive and many people are not able to afford to hire one. In the past, when I wasn't in the same financial position that I am in now, I would always look for that person who is more successful than me. I've never been the type of person that needed an ego boost or felt like I was always the best. So, I would find the people that were better than me and I would develop a relationship with them. My friend and mentor, Brian Van Winkle, is a great example of an individual who has been extremely inspirational and beneficial in my life. Brian and I met on a business trip about seven years ago and we have been able to develop and maintain a great business relationship. He lives in another state and does the same thing that I do, only in a bigger way. He has always given me great advice. Anytime I was considering making a change, or had an idea, or faced some kind of an obstacle, I could call him and tell him what was going on and ask for his advice.

There is one basic rule when shopping for a mentor: Your mentor must be someone who has already achieved what you want to achieve. I always made it a point to make friends and develop relationships with people who were already what I wanted to become. Most successful people like to help others become successful. You would think that in the financial services business they might refuse your request for help – because they would view you as their competition. But, highly successful people are not that way. They don't worry about the competition. They're smart enough to realize that there are enough people out there that we all can help. So they are open to developing relationships rather than considering other advisors as competition.

Another very important consideration when choosing a mentor is that of values. Make sure the values of your mentor are consistent with your values. That will be key to a successful mentoring relationship. I have a person that came to my firm as a new financial advisor about five years ago. He had a very successful career in radio, but was new to the financial services industry. I have had the good fortune of developing a mentoring relationship with him. I talk with him on a daily basis, encourage him and help him reach his goals. He has very specific goals that he has outlined for himself and because of the success that I have had, I can help him achieve those goals. However, the overall reason that mentoring relationship has been so successful is because we share very similar values.

ALWAYS MAINTAIN THE PROPER PERSPECTIVE

My greatest successes in life have nothing to do with money. If I had to tell you what my biggest success was, I would say it's my children. From the time they were born it was my responsibility to raise them to be Christians and to be productive adults. That has been the most challenging and the most rewarding part of my life. My priorities have always been and will always be God, my family, and then my job. I sincerely believe I am successful today in all areas of my life because I established and practiced a healthy balance in life and I have been very careful to maintain those priorities.

My challenge to you is to find the right balance in your life. Don't work so many hours chasing an income at the expense and neglect of your spouse and children. Establish your priorities and stick to them. It's not about money, it's about creating the life you desire by achieving multiple successes – which lead to overall success.

About Christy

Christy Smith is the Founder and President of The Presley Group, LLC, a retirement planning firm in Denham Springs, Louisiana. Christy is a fully licensed insurance agent and has earned recognition as a Certified Estate Planner and Certified Long Term Care Specialist and is a long standing member of the National Ethics Bureau. As a long time member of the Million Dollar Roundtable, Christy has worked tirelessly to make a difference by devoting her life to helping retirees and those approaching retirement understand their retirement needs and goals. Christy specializes in providing "safe money" retirement strategies that allow her clients to create financial security in any economy, providing not only a sound financial future but peace of mind during retirement.

As one of the nation's leading retirement, estate planning and insurance specialists, Christy hosts a weekly radio show, "Your Money Matters," featuring industry experts like former U.S. Comptroller David Walker and Erwin Kellner, Chief Economist for Market Watch. Christy has been hosting "Your Money Matters" for the past five years, providing sound financial planning and retirement advice to the Baton Rouge community. In addition to her popular radio program, Christy has also authored two books, Plan, Protect, and Preserve and The Ultimate Retirement Guide.

Christy lives in Denham Springs, LA with her husband Richard and her three children-Alexis, Coleman and Presley. Christy is a devoted mother and proud Christian, and attempts to maintain her strong family and Christian values in both her personal and professional life. Faith is the foundation of both Christy's personal life and The Presley Group's mission to serve and, inline with the Bible verse "everything in heaven and earth is yours" (1 Chronicles 29:11), she believes that people should be good stewards with their money – and that includes making responsible decisions about putting it in environments where it can best serve people's needs during their later years.

You may contact The Presley Group at: 225-791-5773
or by visiting their website: safemoneyplan.net

CHAPTER 9

COLLEGE WITHOUT STUDENT LOANS

BY DAVID SMITH

One of the keys to being successful is having the right education. A crucial part of that education is a college degree that centers on your interests, goals, and passion. How can you make that happen in a time when:

- Average Cost of Attendance (COA) $40,000+
- Average Time to Graduate (Undergrad) 5.8 years
- Average Cost—Undergrad Degree $232,000
- Average Student Loan Debt—approx. $ 30,000+

THE S-A-F-E WAY

We have developed a process that helps parents and their children, working in concert to obtain the best, most relevant education possible with the minimum out-of-pocket expense as possible. By following our guide to Selection, Acceptance, Funding, and Execution, you will be well on your way to obtaining the relevant education necessary to be successful in today's world.

SELECTION

The first critical step is to align your student's unique talents and abilities with an elite, selective, or competitive school that will offer attractive admissions and financial aid packages. There are approximately 2,000 non-profit institutions in the U.S. College and university system.

There is a specific breakdown of how schools are ranked. Schools such as Stanford, Harvard, MIT, Duke, Vanderbilt, Yale, and Pomona are some of the 50 "Elite" schools. Next are "Selective" schools made up of roughly 150 institutions including USC, Cal, UCLA, Santa Clara, Cal Tech, and Pitzer. The third category is made up of approximately 250 "Competitive" colleges such as Pepperdine, USD, Occidental, LMU and UC Davis. The remaining 1,750 are basic, standard colleges such as state schools and universities.

The sheer number of students following the herd mentality of attending state and local colleges reduces the amount of merit based and academic awards available there. Elite, selective, and competitive colleges typically perceived as too expensive or exclusive have ample means of discounting their tuition for those students deemed as desirable. Merit-based aid has no income requirement or limitations; it's the school's subjective decision. The more valuable your student is to them, the more they will discount their services in order to secure their attendance.

Selecting the right college requires a thorough analysis of multiple factors that are unique to your student's career objectives and lifestyle. Using their time in high school to develop interests and to make connections to a possible career path is one of the most effective ways for your student to fine-tune their decision-making process. Rather than arbitrarily deciding to be a doctor or a lawyer, this process helps them gain a better perspective of what they are truly interested in. It allows them to gain an understanding of what their career path entails and the options that are available within it.

No other decision has such lasting academic and financial impact as the choice of the college your student attends. Most families use emotional criteria such as a school's proximity to home, school reputation or even the best football team in order pick a school and just assume that the student will fit in. They are not aware that there are schools out there that will be a good fit based on class size, major offerings, environment, and overall attitude.

Here is a quick review of what needs to happen before your student begins to fill out an application form:

- Set the expectation – In families where college is an expectation from an early age, students rise to the challenge and select colleges, majors, and careers and usually finish college in four years.

- Fit, Fit, Fit – An education that fits your student's goals, aspirations, talents, and personality is priceless. This leads to happiness, contentment, higher productivity, and eventually to just the right career. Keep your eyes open for the clues.

- "Why" is more important than "How" – Your student needs to answer; Why am I going to college; why should I put out the effort; why is it important? This helps provide the motivation necessary for a successful college experience.

- Utilize all of the available tools – Science-based selection programs, Internet searches, volunteer activities, and job shadowing. Thorough preparation helps guarantee success.

ACCEPTANCE

Although the institution makes the final decision regarding acceptance or rejection of the admission applications, knowing and then utilizing some of the selection criteria can put your student at the top of the list.

Let's change the paradigm. It's vital to replace the common mindset of "How can my student compete?" with "Which colleges are willing to compete for my student?"

While a central part of the admission process is to know which colleges your student prefers, you can take it a step further and apply to colleges of equal quality that compete for the same students. Research can uncover these "unknown" colleges that will provide award letters that your student can use as leverage. Test scores and GPAs are just starting points or the common denominator among applicants. Tagging, legacies, and demonstrable interest play an important role in the acceptance process.

Tagging

A "Tag" is a positive mark added to a student's admissions application that indicates that he or she is of special interest to the college. Children of alumni get tags known as "legacies," the size of the tag or size of their advantage is usually measured by the depth of the parent's generosity to the school. Students with special talents also get tagged. Students with outstanding academic qualities, athletic qualities, or musically/artistically- inclined students are of special interest to the colleges.

Your student's intended school may need three tuba players for the marching band and have a glut of saxophone players. This may not help

95

your saxophone-playing student, but be aware that sometimes it's enough of an advantage to help them get in at competing, equally attractive institutions. Having more than one school choice gives your student an edge because the other school just may need another saxophone player.

Underrepresented minorities, sexes, and students from underrepresented states receive tags. Based on federal funding requirements your student may receive a tag if they are from a certain state, female, male, etc.

Once an application is tagged, the individual is removed from the common pool of applicants and moved to an entirely new level for special consideration. An applicant that normally may not have been looked at twice may find that being tagged opens many doors. It's vitally important to know in advance which colleges give extra attention to specific tags.

Packaging

Imagine looking out over a cornfield. There are thousands of stalks of corn all planted in neat, evenly-spaced rows. Now imagine that several of these stalks are three feet taller than the rest. Help your student stand out like those taller stalks amid all of the remaining freshman applicants and you make it easier for the admissions officer to find them.

College is big business loaded with rules and procedures geared to help fill their classrooms with students that have a high probability of success. The key to making your student one of the desirable ones is by promoting their value to each school. Make it obvious to the school that your child is the one that they have been looking for.

You must "Package & Position" your student based on the College Acceptance Profile (CAP) that is unique to each school. The students with the highest CAP scores are most attractive to colleges and are eligible for the best financial aid packages. These students receive more grants and free money versus them having to obtain student loans and participate in work-study programs.

The CAP criteria used by selective and elite institutions includes:
- Awards – National, Regional, State, County, and School
- Academics – Standard Test Scores
- Activities – School and Outside (Leadership is important)
- Community Service – Volunteerism, Helping Others

- Character Traits – Teacher/Counselor Ratings

Admissions committees rely on CAP to objectively review each applicant and then compare them to the established selection criteria for the school. In a survey by the National Association of College Admission Counselors, 54% of the colleges that responded said that they use preferential packaging.

FUNDING

Financial aid can be made up of these sources:

- Need-Based
- Merit-Based
- Scholarships
- Endowments

College costs money…whether it's your money, the government's money, or the school's money depends on smart strategy and a winning formula. Since the goal is for your student to attend a great school without student loans the first step is to understand Need-based Financial Aid. Applying for need-based aid is essential even if you don't think that you're eligible because many schools won't even consider your student for "non-need" based aid if you don't apply. This is done through the Free Application for Federal Student Aid (FAFSA) which is available online at www.fafsa.ed.gov.

The Higher Education Act of 1965 states that it is the parents' responsibility to educate their children beyond the 12th grade. The law states that if a family can demonstrate "Need," the government will assist in paying for the education. The good news is "Need" is not subjective but is based on a formula and you can estimate your contribution much easier by understanding the calculation.

The financial aid administrator at each school develops the average Cost of Attendance (COA) for all categories of students. The COA = Tuition & Fees + Room & Books + Transportation + Miscellaneous Expenses. The law also provides limited allowances for computer expenses, dependent care, and expenses for handicapped students. The COA can vary for each student at the same school but students in the same situation must have the same COA.

The next part of the formula is the Expected Family Contribution (EFC), which is the amount you as a family are expected to contribute toward your student's education expenses, and is recalculated each academic year during the FAFSA process.

After subtracting your EFC from the college's COA the remainder is need. Your EFC is the same at every college but your need at each college will vary according to the college's COA. If your EFC is $10,000 and the COA at college A is $13,000 and college B, which happens to be an elite school is $43,000 it may make perfect sense to choose college B. FAFSA is just the first step of the funding process however.

Once your student has filed the FAFSA you are able to explore various financial aid opportunities that can make the difference between affording your student's first choice school and having to settle for less. It has been estimated that an excess of $60 billion is available every year that goes untouched by students.

In many cases parents assume that Scholarships, monies distributed by entities such as civic organizations or corporations, are the key to making up the difference for them financially. These funds are paid directly to the student to offset the cost of college but they represent less than three percent of the total money available for education. A college plan that counts on scholarships to pay the majority of costs is an ill-fated strategy that will have disastrous results for most families.

Merit-based aid is an incentive to attract students considered valuable to the institution in the "subjective" areas of academics, arts, athletics, or outside activities. Merit awards are distributed by the Admissions Office of each school in the form of distributional discounts and loans subsidized by endowment funds. Colleges control over $150 billion in endowment funds, the 2nd largest pool of money behind Federal Aid, meaning they are choosing who gets this money. Properly positioning and demonstrating the value of your student is not just a good idea but imperative if you want to make college affordable today.

Generally private schools exhibit the highest COA and many families eliminate them believing that they cannot afford the high expense. While this thinking seems reasonable it is faulty thinking. Private institutions have the largest endowment funds available and therefore offer the largest awards to students that meet or exceed the school's criteria.

Accessing this additional money at selective and elite schools may require more effort but is certainly worth it. The keys to properly position your student includes them having achieved strong scores on the SAT or ACT, maintaining contact with the Department Chairman at their selected schools, and demonstrating their direction and focus along with the other qualities potential schools are searching for.

EXECUTION

Now that you have an inside look at how desirable schools will compete for your student, it's time to use that information to your student's best advantage. It's time to implement the plan that hopefully has been in place since your student's sophomore year in high school.

Applying early is a form of demonstrable interest and typically results in a favorable review from admissions. It is a great strategy and can be used as leverage against other schools with attractive offers. In essence the longer your student waits to apply, the fiercer the competition becomes for the remaining seats. With an admissions process that is both objective and subjective in a highly competitive environment, the odds of success increase dramatically as your student ferrets out the ideal fit from the good fits that we discussed in the Selection section.

Working ahead of schedule allows your student time to fine tune the applications and get valuable unhurried input from counselors or professionals. Requesting high school transcripts, letters of recommendation, and SAT/ACT scores all take time to coordinate. Exceeding deadlines can work wonders in getting a school's attention and it also takes the last minute pressure off you and your student.

Timeline:

- **Freshman & Sophomore Year** – Focus on SAT/ACT preparation and fine tune career interests.

- **Junior Year** – Continue preparation for SAT/ACT. Participate in volunteer and extracurricular activities that will strengthen their overall profile.

   o January through May – Refine list of schools to apply to and ensure a good fit.

   o Summer – Obtain requirements plus all admission applications and begin to complete them and work on the required essays.

- **Senior Year** – Continue participation in volunteer and extracurricular activities.
  - o September – Fine tune applications and request letters of recommendation from teachers, counselors, coaches, and mentors.
  - o October – Submit applications and begin applications for financial aid.
  - o November and December – Contact potential schools and arrange for personal visits and interviews.
  - o January – Submit the FAFSA and CSS profile.
  - o February and March – Follow up with potential schools and schedule personal visits with additional schools if desired.
  - o March – Acceptance/Waiting List/Denial letters will start arriving.
  - o April – Student Aid Report (SAR) awards and offers of acceptance from individual schools will begin to arrive. Review each SAR for accuracy and notify the school's department of admission prior to end of month.
  - o May – Commit to the school of choice.

Through the S-A-F-E process you and your student will exercise due diligence, carefully consider what constitutes a good fit, apply with confidence, and then have the opportunity to choose between attractive offers made by your collection of ideal schools.

Getting the right education is not a four-year decision, but a decision that will help guarantee a lifetime of success!

For more information and to let us know how helpful this information has been please visit us and give us your feedback at: www.CollegeFundingConnection.org.

ABOUT DAVID

D.A. "Dave" Smith has been tagged by his clients as "The College Strategist" – a moniker he is very proud of earning by helping students attend the best colleges in the USA. Additionally, his proprietary process saves an average of $21,783 annually for the parents of undergraduates. Proving this fact by working with over 500 families, he has saved his clients over $53 million in the last four years. All the students graduated without any student debt in five years or less.

A resident of San Diego, California, he has established himself as a subject matter expert for college-related topics, and can be regularly seen on the most watched television show in the county, "Good Morning San Diego" – KUSI TV channel 51. He provides 5-6 educational workshops per month to educate the community on the always-changing landscape for higher education.

Dave's expertise comes from his research and then application of the insights college administrators gave him as he sought the answers that would allow a student to attend college, receive a Bachelor's degree, and move on to a career without the burden of being in debt. He is neither an educator nor a parent, just a son striving to fulfill his commitment to his mother who passed away from the complications of breast cancer. His motivation is from the great saying by Zig Ziglar, "You will get everything you want out of life, IF you help enough people get what they want."

Today he is documenting his successes and expanding the scope of his message to families across the United States. Dave does not believe that the $1 trillion student loan bubble should exist, and he is standing up and educating families about the educational opportunities available today and seldom used by college bound students.

He is proud of each family that works with him, because he is changing lives one family at a time. Please review the video testimonials by families touched by Dave and his team at: www.collegewithoutstudentloans.com

CHAPTER 10

YOUR MOST IMPORTANT FINANCIAL DECISION

BY DAVID BOIKE
WITH DJ BOIKE

By now, we all know that a "Perfect Storm" has arrived for many Americans. This convergence of several key factors is threatening the financial security of many folks, but especially citizens age 55 and over. For this group of people who are about to retire or have already retired, the threat is very real. According to well-documented sources, most pension funds are underfunded and future benefits may be in jeopardy. The cost of the Social Security, Medicaid, and Medicare programs are exploding as more folks move into retirement and fewer tax payers remain in the workforce. Inflation continues to raise the costs of key goods and services such as health care, alternative housing, utilities, and food. In the meantime, most investors have earned very poor returns on their retirement accounts over the past ten years. On top of all this, taxes are likely to increase again and guess who will be paying the bulk of these tax increases. You're correct. People with money. People who earn over $58,000 per year. People whom our government considers "rich." Hard working people who have saved and invested for their retirement years. If that describes you, then get ready. You have a great big bulls eye on your back.

SO WHAT CAN YOU DO TO PROTECT AND PROFIT FROM THE COMING FINANCIAL STORM? IT ALL BEGINS WITH CHOOSING THE RIGHT ADVISOR

The most important financial decision that you will ever make is the selection of your financial advisor. This one choice will influence almost every other financial decision you will make.

WILL YOU BE YOUR OWN ADVISOR?

That is kind of like a doctor trying to do his own brain surgery. Not impossible, I guess, but extremely dangerous!

Will you rely on what you can learn from reading books by people like Dave Ramsey or Suze Orman?

> *Before becoming a broker with Merrill Lynch, Suze Orman, the best-selling financial author and TV personality, was a waitress for the Buttercup Bakery in Berkeley, California. Why would Merrill Lynch hire a waitress? According to Ms. Orman: "They weren't hiring a waitress. What they saw in me was that I would be an excellent saleswoman."*
> ~ Arthur Levitt – *Taking on the Street*

Maybe you could get your advice from *Money Magazine*, or one of the other money financial publications that now cover the walls of area bookstores. "The rich are taking their advice from professional financial advisors. The poor are getting their advice from *Money Magazine*," Robert Veres, financial author, explained. Again, it is not impossible to find good solid advice and help this way, but it can be very time-consuming and eye-straining.

You could watch hours and hours of financial news programs on TV every day: *CNBC, The Wall Street Report, Mad Money,* etc. Good info? Usually. Good entertainment? Often. Good for your marriage? Hardly ever!

The most logical choice for most people is to find a highly qualified, well-seasoned, honest, ethical, and trusted financial advisor. You may think that this sounds like an impossible task. Though I agree it can be quite difficult to find a trusted advisor, our firm's 30-year track record of being chosen by people just like you tells me it can be done.

WHAT ARE THE DIFFERENT KINDS OF FINANCIAL PROFESSIONALS?

Did you know that though there over 90 different titles for financial professionals, yet the federal government only recognizes three types? The three types of federally-recognized financial professionals are Registered Representatives, Insurance Agents, and Investment Advisor Representatives. The following describes each group's capabilities and services.

"BESIDES BEING 'SMARTER THAN THE AVERAGE BEAR', WHAT OTHER QUALIFICATIONS DO YOU HAVE?"

Registered Representatives

The first and most common type of financial professional is called a Registered Representative, or stockbroker. Registered Representatives are regulated by Financial Industry Regulatory Authority (FINRA), which operates under the oversight of the Securities and Exchange Commission (SEC). All Registered Representatives must be employed by a FINRA Member Broker Dealer to sell financial products such as stocks, bonds, and mutual funds. In addition, Registered Representatives must hold a series G3 State license and either a Series 6 or Series 7 securities license.

FINRA calls a person who holds these licenses a *Registered Representative* because he or she is *registered* with FINRA and is a *representative* of the brokerage firm with which he or she is affiliated. Brokers are considered by FINRA and the SEC to be product salespeople whose job is to represent the best interests of their firms. According to the regulators, brokers sell investment products in order to earn commissions; they are not paid to give advice, and any advice they do give is considered "incidental" to the sale of their products. In fact, the SEC requires that monthly statements issued by brokerage firms include the following disclosures: "Your account is a brokerage account and not an advisory account. Our interests may not always be the same as yours…Make sure your understand…. The extent of our obligations to disclose conflicts of interest and to act in your best interest….Our salespersons' compensation may vary by product and over time."

Registered Representatives make money by selling financial products that their broker dealer represents. The most common products sold are investments called retail mutual funds. With mutual funds, your money is "pooled" with other investors' money and managed by a fund manager. You are a shareholder, granting you a proportionate share of the funds' gains, losses, and fees. Mutual funds charge shareholders fees in order to pay commissions and ongoing rewards to Registered Representatives.

The key point here is that Registered Representatives by license and employment contract are commissioned-based salespeople.

> *"Commissions distort brokers' recommendations in many other ways. Some firms, for example, have special arrangements to sell mutual funds in exchange for above-average commissions. If a Merrill Lynch broker knows he'll get 25 percent more money for selling a Putnam mutual funds over an American Century fund, guess which fund the broker will try to sell you? Most large brokerage firms today sponsor their own funds, and my try to steer you to one of those. That way, the fee you pay to the manager of the mutual fund remains in-house and adds to the firm's profits. The problem is that brokerage firm funds don't necessarily perform better than, or even as well as, independent funds."* ~ Arthur Levitt – *Taking on the Street*

Insurance Agents

Another type of professional whom many people rely on for financial advice is an Insurance Agent. Every Insurance Agent must hold a state insurance license. An agent must hold a license based not on his state of residency, but based on the residency of his clients. For example, if a New Jersey agent has clients who live in Delaware, he must hold a Delaware license. There are four main types of insurance licenses:

1. **Property/Casualty license** This allows the agent to sell homeowners, automobile, and liability insurance.

2. **Life/Health license** This allows the agent to sell life, health, accident, and disability income insurance, as well as fixed annuity products.

3. **Long-Term Care Insurance license** This allows the agent to sell long-term care insurance.

4. Variable Annuity license This allows the agent to sell variable annuity products, provided that the agent also holds the FINRA Series 6 or Series 7 licenses described earlier.

Like stockbrokers, Insurance Agents' licenses are held with one or more insurance companies. <u>And, like stockbrokers, agents legally represent the insurers, not their customers.</u> Also like stockbrokers, agents earn commissions from the sale of products; they do not give or earn fees for rendering advice.

"Captive" agents are employees of a particular insurance company. These agents sell that company's products only, similar to how salespeople at Ford dealers only sell Ford automobiles.

"Independent" agents operate their own businesses or work for a general agent. Independent agents hold their licenses with many insurance companies, giving them access to a wider product line.

To make it even more complicated, some insurance companies employ their own agents while also allowing independent agents to sell their products.

INVESTMENT ADVISOR REPRESENTATIVES

Unlike Registered Representatives and Insurance Agents, an Investment Advisor Representative represents and works for you instead of a *Wall Street* firm or insurance company. In fact, Investment Advisor Representatives have a "fiduciary duty" to serve your best interests. They have a legal responsibility to do what is best for you. This is in sharp contrast to a Registered Representatives or Insurance Agents whose duty is to a home office. An Investment Advisor Representative must hold one of the following FINRA licenses:

- **Series 65: Uniform Investment Adviser Law license:** Before practicing, the Investment Advisor Representative must also obtain the Series 63 state license.

- **Series 66: Uniform Combined State Law license:** This license combines the Series 65 and Series 63 into one examination.

The SEC regulates Registered Investment Advisory firms and their Investment Advisor Representatives. Each state also regulates Investment

Advisor Representatives. In addition to passing the necessary requirements to become an Investment Advisor Representative, many of these advisors are also "dually licensed" so they can help their clients with the investment and insurance services they wish to obtain. This allows Investment Advisor Representatives to provide holistic financial planning services to their clients.

So when you are in need of a trusted advisor, remember there are only three types of federally and state-recognized advisors. Two of the three types, Registered Representatives and Insurance Agents, by license legally represent their company. They are paid by commissions to sell you their company's products. Investment Advisor Representatives legally represent *you* and *your best interests*. They are paid to *advise* and not to *sell*. Because of this, most people pay fewer fees when working with an Investment Advisor Representative than when working with a Registered Representative.

The 3 Types of Federal & State Recognized Advisors			
Advisor	Contractually Represents	Compensated By	Products Offered
Registered Representatives	A Broker Dealer	Selling Investment Products	Limited to Broker Dealer offerings
Insurance Agents	An Insurance Company	Selling Insurance Products	Limited to Insurance Company offerings
Registered Investment Advisors	The Client	Advising and Monitoring	Unlimited access to most financial products and services

SOME FINAL THOUGHTS ABOUT THE VALUE OF A TRUSTED ADVISOR

Sound financial advice is not expensive. An effective advisor can add value equal to many times his fee simply by preventing you from making some very poor investment decisions (like chasing yesterday's hot sector).

It is my experience that many investors view fee structures from an incorrect perspective. They concern themselves with either the amount of time an advisor spends with them personally (effort) or the size of the fee (looking for lowest cost). Instead, investors should be concerned with how much *value* the advisor adds *relative* to the *cost.* If the value exceeds the fee charged, even if the fee seems high in absolute terms, you will have received value. On the other hand, if the value does not exceed the fee, no matter how low the fee, it is still too high.

> **A Startling Fact: Total fees paid by a client utilizing a Registered Investment Advisor are often substantially less than what would be paid using a Registered Representative (Broker).**

Remember that while good advice may not be cheap, it is far less expensive than bad advice.

CONCLUSION

The Perfect Financial Storm is fast approaching. Those who don't prepare will most assuredly suffer grave financial consequences. Those who do prepare properly will reap the rewards. The more a person has, the more they are at risk of losing. The old saying, "you can't get blood out a rock" is so true. People with little assets and low income will not be affected as much as affluent savers and investors. If you are "rich" by the government standards, meaning you have $58,000 or more in annual income and you have investable assets of $500,000 or more, seek out a trusted financial advisory firm that utilizes a proven, systematic process like our ARK program to help you protect what you currently have, and to profit in the years ahead.

WHAT IS THE ARK PROGRAM AND HOW CAN IT BENEFIT ME?

The ARK program is our unique financial planning strategy that was designed to protect our clients from the growing risks associated with the upcoming financial storm as well as to profit over the years ahead. The ARK program utilizes a systematic approach to help our clients:

1. Clarify their financial goals and concerns.

2. Identify their financial risks.

3. Establish a plan to reach goals and address financial risks.

4. Assistance with implementing all aspects of the plan including coordinating, tax planning, legal documents, investments, and insurance.

5. Ongoing monitoring and updating of your program to make sure all aspects of the plan continue to achieve your financial objectives and properly address your financial concerns.

WHAT MAKES THE ARK PROGRAM DIFFERENT FROM PROGRAMS OFFERED BY OTHER FINANCIAL ADVISORS?

The key difference between our ARK program and the other programs offered by most financial advisors around the country is that we designed our program specifically for our clients. The ARK program is not a sales pitch designed by some investment or insurance company to promote their financial products and services. Our ARK program is the result of what we have learned from helping hundreds of affluent clients over the past 30 plus years. It is not created by, owned by, or funded by any investment or insurance company. It allows us as Registered Investment Advisors to create an unbiased plan of action specifically for each of our clients. Most other "financial plans" simply lump all people into the same basic categories and end with recommending their company's products as the "solution." As Registered Investment Advisors, we get paid to advise not to sell. We have no company products to push. This is the big difference between the ARK program and other programs offered by most other financial advisors.

WHAT IS THE NEXT LOGICAL STEP TO CONSIDER?

Hope for the best, but plan for the worst. The problem with the *Titanic* wasn't that the owners thought the ship was safe. It was that they didn't order enough lifeboats for everyone on board. There's nothing wrong with hoping the stock market will go up 10 percent a year. Maybe it will. The mistake for the past 20 years has been planning on it.

You have to take charge of your own finances. No one else can.

Over the past 30 years our firm has helped hundreds of people plan for a worry- free retirement. Through our systematic financial planning process, we have helped our clients reduce their investment fees, avoid unnecessary taxes, protect their retirement accounts, maximize their returns, and establish a predictable source of supplemental income. I am sincerely happy for these fine folds.

But I can't help think about the thousands of other folks who have heard us speak in person, on TV, or on the radio, and decided not to take action. Some of these folks eventually do decide to come in for a Second Opinion. Unfortunately, their situation is usually worse off than they were when they first met with us. Like most areas of life, procrastination is a costly mistake when it comes to your financial planning.

So now that you have finished this chapter, let me strongly encourage you to find yourself a personal Trusted Financial Advisor, and get your financial house in order. For more information, you can request our free report on "How to Choose a Trusted Advisor" by going to our website: www.TheRetirementResource.org.

Timeless Wisdom

"The plans of the diligent lead surely to advantage."
Proverbs 21:5

We wish you a happy, healthy, and financially worry-free retirement!

David and DJ Boike

About David

- Host of NBC 25's *"Money Matters"*
- Founder of Retirement Resources, LLC
- Chartered Financial Consultant

Dave Boike, ChFC is a locally well-known financial educator, host of NBC 25's *"Money Matters"* and author of *High Tide: A Practical Guide for Affluent Retirees to Protect, Profit and Prosper from the Coming Financial Storm.* Dave's goal on *"Money Matters"* is to discuss pertinent, current, and helpful financial information. For 32 years, Dave has been teaching investors how to preserve their assets, increase their income, and reduce income taxes.

Dave also serves as a Chartered Financial Consultant, a designation awarded only to experienced advisors who have completed a 10-course study program, through the American College in Pennsylvania, focusing on Tax, Investment, Risk Management, Retirement and Estate Planning. In addition, he is an approved member of the International Association of Registered Financial Planners, and the Society of Financial Service Professionals.

Dave is also a contributing author of *21st Century Wealth*, an easy-to-read book for those already retired or those planning for a financially rewarding retirement. His insight and opinions are sought after by various media sources including *The Wall Street Journal, Smart Money* Magazine, Detroit Business Hour, TV 25, TV 12, and various radio stations. Dave was also recently featured in Senior Market Advisor magazine for his outstanding service to the community.

For three years in a row, Dave has been named a 5 Star Wealth Manager, an award only given to the top 7% of advisors in each state. The 5 Star Wealth Manager status is only for advisors who have a 95% or higher client satisfaction rating. His Firm, Retirement Resources, LLC, has been recognized annually as one of the top Advisory firms in the country and has an A+ rating from the Better Business Bureau.

Recently Dave was featured on a new T.V. series created to educate Retirees on key issues named *The Consumer Advocate* which is to air on many of the major networks in 2013.

Dave and his wife, Cherie, are the proud parents of 2 sons and 6 grandchildren. They are active members of a church, where he has served on the Deacon's board for over 15 years. In his free time, Dave enjoys playing basketball, going up north, reading, meeting new people, spending time with family and friends, and traveling.

About DJ

DJ Boike, RFC is host of NBC 25's *"Money Matters."* He is Vice President of Retirement Resources, LLC and an Investment Advisory Representative.

DJ is a locally well-known financial educator and co-author of *High Tide: A Practical Guide for Affluent Retirees to Protect, Profit and Prosper from the Coming Financial Storm.* DJ's goal in *High Tide* is to discuss pertinent, current, and helpful financial information Retirees need to know. For over 10 years, DJ has been teaching investors how to preserve their assets, increase their income, and reduce income taxes.

DJ also serves as an Investment Advisory Representative a license awarded only to experienced advisors who have completed a series of tests administered by the State of Michigan, focusing on Tax, Investment, Risk Management, Retirement and Estate Planning. In addition, he is an approved member of the International Association of Registered Financial Planners.

High Tide is an easy to read book for those already retired or those planning for a financially rewarding retirement. His insight and opinions are sought after by various media sources including The Clarkston News, Tri-County Times, TV 25, TV 12, and various radio stations. DJ was also featured in *INC. Magazine* for his outstanding service to the community.

Recently DJ was featured on a new T.V. series created to educate Retirees on key issues named *The Consumer Advocate,* which is out to air on many of the major networks in 2013.

DJ has been married to his lovely wife, Jennifer, for 10 years. He is the proud father of 4 children, Gwyn, Ava, Boston, and Cooper. He is also a faithful member of Bethany Baptist Church.

CHAPTER 11

NATURAL ACTIVITY, SUPERNATURAL RESULTS

BY DAVID PICKARD

At some point in your life or career comes the moment when you compare yourself with someone and wonder, "How did so and so become so successful? What has he done to create such abundance in his life?" Comparing yourself with others is natural. Ask yourself what else you can do to achieve greater results. Let's face it; we have goals we wish to achieve and challenges that we must overcome to achieve them. Often, the obstacles we face are what prepare us for what lies ahead.

Like most people, I've had successes in my career and faced temporary failures. I've been fortunate to learn from my mistakes and have been asked to share advice on how to succeed. That is why I am writing this chapter. There is a simple formula that I use, and I believe it translates into a true advantage. The formula is a simple Biblical principle, and, I'd like to share with you my ideas in parallel to a story so that maybe it, too, can help you along your special success journey. The story of David and Goliath exemplifies what happens when the natural occurrences in a person's life lead to supernatural outcomes.

Long before David became the great King of Israel he began his career as a lowly shepherd boy. He was the youngest and smallest in his family. His brothers ridiculed him because of his small frame, and he was denied the opportunity to participate in the military and enjoy its benefits. So, he was given the dead-end job of tending to the family's sheep. As you can imagine, this path did not look very promising for David. He spent many days and nights in the wilderness looking after his flock and playing the harp, as he had plenty of free time on his hands.

He became so skilled at playing the harp that he was called by the prophet Samuel to play for the king of Israel, Saul, to help bring peace to Saul in a time of war. The war was between the Philistines and Israelites, and Goliath, a Philistine, stepped out of the Philistine camp and announced that whoever took him down would join the two warring factions and become their leader. David, who had earned King Saul's favor after bringing him peace with music from his harp, asked if he could be the one to fight Goliath. David drew from his past experiences in the fields, where he had used his slingshot to kill predators such as lions and bears in order to protect his sheep. Little did he know God would use those skills and experiences to bless him down the road. Saul finally agreed and let David face the great giant Goliath with no more than the tools he used everyday—a stone and a slingshot. David killed Goliath with one shot, and, as a result, David saved his country from the Philistines and would eventually become king of Israel.

The story of David and Goliath has long been a favorite of mine because of the message it conveys: every step of a journey has value and prepares you for the next step. No experience is without value; therefore, it benefits you to do the very best at the job you have at the present. Exceed expectations, because you have no way of knowing what you will be asked to do next. David did things in his everyday, natural, life that brought to him blessings of supernatural proportions.

Success, like David's, requires commitment. The success that I have achieved in my career certainly did not come to me by luck or overnight. At various stages of my career, I've remembered this story and asked myself, "What can I do in the natural that will help bring about supernatural blessings in my life like David had?" The number of things that we experience—those things we do in the natural world—correlate directly to the way in which we manage the gifts we have been given.

One of my favorite verses in the Bible is "The horse is made ready for the day of battle, but the victory rests with the Lord." Proverbs 21:31. This illustrates the great law of the universe--cause and effect. I believe that just like David in the Bible, God entrusts each of us with certain gifts: time, talent, and treasure—which will hereafter be called the three T's—of which you are the steward. Managing and measuring the three T's is the key to abundant success and is how I measure my business and progress.

"T" #1 - TIME:

Our time is our most valuable resource. How we use it determines our level of success in life. God (supernatural) used David's time in the wilderness to prepare him for something larger. Without David's willingness (natural) to prepare himself by learning to use his weapons, and to play the harp, God could not have used him for his needs.

We all experience the same number of hours in a day, a week, or a year. Have you ever noticed that the busiest people are the ones who always have time to help someone else? This is no accident. Top producers are better stewards of their time. When we make the best use of our time, spending our days in productive pursuits and managing our time well, we can always find time for something more.

I have found that the more time I give to help others; the more others take the time to help me. This past summer, my wife and I volunteered at our church to teach a life skills class to those in need of education but lacked the funds to pay for it. We developed the curriculum, set aside 10 hours a week to prepare, and spent eight weeks teaching 10 students computer skills. At the end of the summer, we were overjoyed with the progress, and our community leaders noticed, as well. We were recognized, and our program is being modeled for future training courses. And, very surprisingly, unseen opportunities have literally come out of nowhere for both my wife and I in our work and personal lives, as a result of our giving.

I try to remember the more I give the more I receive. I have to do my part in the natural to receive the supernatural blessing I can't see. It does not matter where you offer the extra time: you can attend a church, volunteer, or help homeless families, all that matters is you put forth the extra effort.

"T" #2 - TALENT:

The second gift that each person receives is a unique talent. Now, some talents we are born with and some we have to learn or develop to the fullest potential. When you develop your talents, you are becoming an even better version of the person you want to be. When you teach other people what you know, you reinforce your own talents while also making the world around you better. You are being a good steward of your talents.

Samuel was a mentor to David and recognized David's heart and willingness to prepare himself. Although, David did not know Samuel had a direct line with the King, his preparation in becoming a skilled musician made it possible for a poor shepherd boy with no future to stand before the king. Proverbs 22:29 says, "Do you see a man skilled in his work; he will serve before kings, he will not serve before obscure men."

I have been fortunate enough to have a mentor assist me from the very beginning of my career, and subsequently have been promoted 13 times in 13 years. Finding someone that is successful in your field, and modeling that person, is the fastest way to achieve superior results. I've been mentoring someone for many years, and he has since attended a top business school and is now on the fast track at a major corporation.

Spending time with someone who has already done something you strive to do shortens your learning curve. You can take years to learn it all by yourself, or you can listen to your mentor, apply his or her advice, and achieve success in a shorter time. One caveat: make sure the people who mentor you are qualified to teach what you desire to learn. Look for the number one person in the field of your interest.

When you are growing your talents, growth will follow in other areas as well, most notably in the treasure you receive. Treasure is the fruit of our labors and is the third "T gift" that we receive, of which we must become good stewards.

"T" #3 - TREASURE:

As the story goes, David did the things in the natural that he needed to become the wealthiest person in his day and ultimately, King.

Making it to the top 1% in income and wealth is undoubtedly hard and can take many years to accomplish. For me, it took over 15 years of going to school, laboring days, nights, and weekends, moving around the country, and being open to projects and traveling to places I couldn't pronounce, much less find on a map. Whatever your financial goals may be, I've found that the more you give in the natural the more you receive in the supernatural.

Of the three T's, treasure is the easiest to measure. We measure it every time we deposit money into the bank account. The treasure we receive, in my experience, correlates directly to the manner in which we are stewards of this gift. My personal approach to managing my treasure involves the Christian approach of tithing or giving 10% of whatever money I earn back to my church. But, I believe that giving to a church is not the only way in which to become a successful steward of one's treasure. If you attend a church that promotes tithing, ask yourself "Am I tithing?" If you do not attend a church or other religious organization to which one can give, then ask, "Am I making donations to charity?"

The point is to believe that you will always have enough, so you can afford to share or to give some of it away. God does bless this faith in His provision. The more you give, the more opportunities for amassing treasure you'll have for yourself and the more you'll have to give away. Give what your heart tells you to give, which is what 2 Corinthians 9:7 tells us to do, and to do it "not reluctantly or under compulsion." Try this: track what you receive and what you in turn give away. Challenge yourself to give more and see if, in fact, you receive even more in return. God has a way of blessing those who do good deeds and assist the world around them.

BEGIN NOW:

The best part about the natural experiences of our lives yielding supernatural results is that it does not matter where you are in your life or your career to begin. You are ALREADY living the natural everyday. Begin today to utilize the natural time, talent and treasure you have, coupled with your experiences to achieve supernatural results. Keep in mind the story of David, and how he used his time to prepare and develop his talent, and how God blessed him in the supernatural to gain favor with the King, kill the enemy, and eventually become King.

Whether you are starting a new business venture, planning a career or life change, or simply want to energize your current career or life path, your first action each morning must be planning time. Spend an hour or so getting focused and balanced every day. Whether it is prayer, meditation, journaling…whatever will focus you personally, use it. Write down your goals. Create goals for your personal growth and for the ways in which you can help someone else to grow.

Acknowledge that there will be set backs in the new way of living the natural to achieve the supernatural. What we view as problems or set-backs just might be those natural, day-to-day activities--like David's in the Bible--that provide us with the experiences and the skills for a calling somewhere down the road. Appreciate each of the natural occurrences in your life for the simple experience of them, become a better steward of the gifts of Time, Talent, and Treasure, and you will reap supernatural rewards in your life and your career.

About David

David Pickard is a creative executive who has advanced consistently in his 13 year sales and marketing career. David, who is currently a Senior Vice President with a large consumer goods manufacturer, began his career as a sales intern dusting off shelves at home centers, and through hard work, relentless preparation and persistence, eventually gained responsibility of managing multi-million dollar portfolios at the world's largest retailers. He attributes his continued success to the formula he has created that grew out of his faith-based upbringing.

David received his Bachelor of Science in Management from Southwestern Assemblies of God University in Waxahachie, TX and his MBA from the University of South Florida in Tampa, FL. A proponent of continuing education, he has also taken Financial Skills Training, Advanced Presentation Skills and Product & Sales Development I & II, to name a few.

David is a member of Toastmasters International, the National Association of Sales Professionals, and the Bentonville/Bella Vista Chamber of Commerce. He also spends his free time mentoring others or volunteering at his church and other local charities. He believes that everyone can and should mentor someone toward greater success, which has served him well during his career building and managing sales teams. David has consistently earned awards and honors for exceptional sales performance and for top growth in product placement and revenue increase.

Among his varied areas of expertise is sourcing, which has taken him to Asia over 15 times since 2009. Although he has lived and traveled all over the world, David is happy to be living with his family in Arkansas.

To learn more about David, feel free to visit his website at: www.david-pickard.com.

CHAPTER 12

RISK VS. SAFE RETIREMENT INCOME

BY JAMMIE AVILA

"Is there anything you can do to help me?" was the question Ms. Browne asked me – as we sat across from each other at her kitchen table. It was February of 2009, and I had met Ms. Browne at a Financial Workshop I hosted earlier in the month. At the close of every workshop I have an evaluation form that I have each attendee fill out. Not only does it let me know how I did as a presenter, but also it gives each person in attendance an opportunity to request a free one-hour consultation either at my office or in the comfort of their home. Ms. Browne had enjoyed the financial workshop and wanted an appointment with me as soon as possible in her home. Since she wanted to meet right away, I adjusted my schedule so we could meet the next day. I could tell by the look on Ms. Browne's face when she answered the door the next day that she was anxious and worried. Though that was not uncommon with many of the people I met with during this horrible financial time. We had just come off 2008 – which was by far the worst Stock Market correction since the Great Depression. There was a lot of financial uncertainty at that time and anyone that had their personal nest egg invested in The Stock Market was dealing with some serious losses.

When I start any consultation I like to find out a little about whom I am meeting with. Where they are from? What they did for a living? How old they are? Are they married, etc.? I could tell going through this fact-finding process that it was starting to annoy her. So I put my pen down and stopped asking questions and just began to listen. Ms. Browne then began to tell me her story and why she wanted an appointment with me. She told me she was 71 years old and divorced a long time ago. She had worked for a major corporation for over 30 years and had regularly contributed to her company 401k and enjoyed the match from her employer all those years. By the time she was about to retire she had amassed close to 1 million dollars in her 401k account. With confidence, she decided to retire in 2007 after slowing seeing her 401k come back to life after the tech bubble nearly wiped her out in 2001. During that time her advisor had told her not to panic and that The Stock Market would come back and he was right.

After 5 years of market recovery from 2003-2007, she had gotten all of her losses back and more, thanks to her continued contribution as well as the company 401k match. Needless to say, she felt confident after talking to her broker in 2007 that she could take 7% withdrawals from her $1,000,000 401k every year and her principal would remain the same. She would never have to worry about running out of money. I could tell from the home she lived in and the car she drove that this was the retirement she had always hoped for. She was taking close to $70,000 a year from her 401k and had an additional $20,000 a year coming from Uncle Sam through social security. With over $90,000 a year in income, she could meet all of her obligations with the house she lived in and the car she drove. She even had enough money to take trips a couple times a year with family and friends. Life was great.

Then something happened that was even worse then what she experienced in 2001 and 2002 from The Stock Market – the Real Estate Bubble of 2008. In Las Vegas, Nevada where we live, we experienced record depreciation in the housing market. Home values had dropped by 50% when it was all said and done. Nobody could escape the Real Estate correction. Timing is everything and if you bought a home between 2004-2007 chances are you were completely upside down on your mortgage by the end of 2008. If that was where the bad news ended, she could probably live with it. Although she was upside down in her mortgage she could still afford the payment with the income she had coming in.

Unfortunately during that same year she experienced a huge Double Whammy. Not only did her home value take a big hit, but as she continued to receive her monthly statements from her brokerage account, she watched in horror month after month as her account value kept plummeting. She would call her broker worried, looking for some guidance and counsel, and it seemed he kept saying the same thing every time she would call, "Don't worry, the market will come back." She had faith in that statement as she had learned first hand from the tech bubble in 2001-2002. It did come back. So the rest of the year she tried not to worry and ignored the brokerage statements that came every month. By the end of 2008 her 401K account was down to $550,000. She could not believe it.

How would she ever get the money back that she lost. She did not work anymore nor was she contributing to her 401K and she definitely was not getting a match from her employer any longer.

Then the dreaded phone call from her broker came. He was now advising her that if she did not want to possibly run out of money before she ran out of life, she had to drop her withdrawal amount to 3-4% of her total account value per year. What was once a healthy $70,000 a year income turned to a very measly $20,000 a year withdrawal. Together with her social security check, she had gone from $90,000 a year to $40,000. That was not enough income for her to meet her financial obligations and the standard of living she had grown accustomed to in the last two years.

The broker had made some major mistakes in the retirement planning for Ms. Browne. Lets tackle the Broker's first downfall – asset allocation during the retirement years. Brokers generally do a great job during the working years of their clients – which we commonly refer to as The Accumulation Phase. The problem is that when their clients start their Distribution Phase they usually continue with the same mix of asset allocation they used in the capital Accumulation Phase – meaning a high percentage of the portfolio in stocks and mutual funds. In the case of Ms. Browne, her Broker had her 100% invested in stocks and mutual funds. That is absolute craziness to have a 69-year-old woman, who has just retired, allocated with that much risk. Unfortunately, that became one of her downfalls. You see, in 2008 when the stock market dropped by over 40%, Ms. Browne was allocated 100% to risk by her Broker. So when the market had a major correction, so did ALL of her holdings. There is a system that I always adhere to with my clients. If most financial advisors used this system in their planning, it would save the client a lot of heartache. It's called the Rule of 100.

The Rule of 100 is a tool used by financial professionals to provide you with general guidelines for the proper allocation of your retirement and investment assets. The Rule of 100 takes into consideration your age and investment time horizon to better define your risk tolerance. The results of this can be used to determine how much of your retirement and investment assets should be exposed to risk and loss.

The Rule of 100 uses your age as a baseline in the calculation to appropriately allocate your portfolio. The calculation begins with the number 100. Subtracting your age from 100 provides an immediate snapshot of what percentage of your retirement assets should be in the market (at risk) and what percentage of your retirement assets should be in safe money (no-risk) alternatives. This strategy will reduce your exposure to market risk and the volatile market swings that most people experienced in 2008 resulting in major losses.

EXAMPLE: A 69-year-old client has $100,000 saved for retirement. To apply the Rule of 100, start with 100 and subtract 69 to leave a remaining value of 31. In this illustration, the client should have no more than 31%, or $31,000, of his or her assets at risk in stocks or equities. This leaves 69%, or $69,000, of his or her assets to be allocated to safe money alternatives.

Let's assume that a client had 100% of their assets invested in The Stock Market. If the market declined 40%, a significant portion of their nest egg would have experienced a loss. When I ask clients the question, "If The Stock Market falls by 40% what percentage will it take for you to get your money back?" They almost always answer that it will take a 40% gain to get the money they lost back. However, that is wrong. It will take a 66.6% return on their investments to regain their original principal because they are now working off of a smaller principal. As you can see applying the Rule of 100 to asset allocation could be the saving grace you need when the market decides to correct again like in 2008.

The Brokers second downfall was income planning. He had assumed that since The Stock Market had rebounded after the tech bubble from years 2003-2007, that it was appropriate to tell his client she could take a 7% withdrawal during her lifetime and not run the risk of running out of money in her lifetime. Anytime you are in an account that has risk you cannot guarantee that your money will last as long as you do.

In 1994, William Bengen published a paper in the Journal of Financial Planning. This article has had the biggest impact on retirement income planning. It was titled "Determining Withdrawal Rates Using Historical Data." Bengen looked at actual Stock Market returns and retirement scenarios over the past 75 years.

He concluded that retirees who draw down no more than 4 percent of their portfolios every year stand a chance their money will outlive them. Retirees who draw down 5 percent a year run a 30 percent chance of jeopardizing their nest egg and those who take 6-7 percent are taking a much greater risk.

A 2006 study by Ibbotson Associates, an affiliate of Morningstar Inc., found that systematic withdrawals from retirement savings plans can be problematic if individuals withdraw more than 3% to 4% annually. The study found that, based on historical rates of return of a balanced stock and bond mix, a 7% annual withdrawal rate lasts just nine years. At a 5% withdrawal rate, the money lasts about 22 years and individuals would have to reduce their withdrawal rates to 4% or less to make portfolios sustainable for at least 30 years. It's easy to see where the broker went wrong with this information. He was having Ms. Browne take out way too much money from her portfolio. He set her up with the expectation that she could take a $70,000 a year income from her $1,000,000 401K account and never run out of money. Now to the defense of the Broker. He did not know that a 2008 was looming in the future. However, if you want predictable income during retirement, you should never have that income tied to an account that has risk.

Unfortunately, there was nothing I could do to help Ms. Browne. The damage had been done. If we could go back in time and I had met Ms. Browne back when she retired, we would have done things a lot differently. We would have used a Hybrid Annuity for a few different reasons. First, it provides a safe guaranteed lifetime income that she could never outlive. Using the rule of 100, when Ms. Browne retired at age 69 we could have put 69% or $690,000 in a Hybrid Annuity for guaranteed lifetime income. She could have taken a guaranteed withdrawal of 5.9% a year for the rest of her life at that age, which would be right around $40,000 a year. Then she could have kept the other 31% or $310,000 in a brokerage account with the potential for future growth. Taking 4% (less the 7% she was taking) withdrawals from that account she would have received an additional $12,000 a year bringing her income up to $52,000 a year income from her retirement accounts. Although Ms. Browne's investment is far from the $70,000 a year she was taking, it is much more safe, predictable and realistic.

Secondly, some of these Hybrid Annuities have a Long Term Care feature that is built into the contract. If my client's health changes in the future and they are unable to perform at least 2 of 6 daily living requirements, which are Bathing, Dressing, Eating, Transferring, Continence, and Toileting, then they qualify for the Home Healthcare Doubler, which doubles your income for up to 5 years. In Ms. Browne's case it would have hypothetically taken her income on the Hybrid Annuity from $40,000 a year to $80,000 a year. What a great guarantee built into the contract that protects my clients in the event they need long-term care. More importantly it allows the client to stay at home while getting the care they need and does not require them to be checked into a long-term care facility.

In the case where you do not need income right away like Ms. Browne, the Hybrid Annuity allows you to grow your income account value every year you defer taking withdrawals. It grows the income account value by 6-7% a year followed by guaranteed lifetime income at a future date that you decide. For example, if you are age 60, you do not need to start taking extra supplemental income from the annuity until age 70. If you started with $100,000, your benefit base would be worth a guaranteed $207,000 (including an initial 5.5% upfront bonus from the company). You could take a guaranteed 6% withdrawal rate from that at age 70. That is over $12,452 a year in additional lifetime income. Also if you have health issues in the future, they double the income for up to 5 years to $24,900. This is not only a great way to provide a safe guaranteed lifetime income, but also to protect yourself in the event you need some type of home healthcare in the future.

In the consultations I do with my clients, I always ask when it comes to their future income they are looking for if they want MAYBE income or GUARANTEED lifetime income? I believe now, after hearing Ms. Browne's story… you know why.

About Jammie

Jammie Avila is the CEO of Cornerstone Retirement and Insurance Services in Las Vegas, Nevada. He has been the "go to" expert in the area of Income Planning for the last 15 years. The number one fear retirees have heading into retirement is the fear of outliving their money. Jammie's income planning strategies remove that fear his clients have and ensure that their income will last as long as they do.

Jammie has also been interviewed on ABC, NBC, FOX, and CBS as well as spotlighted in *USA Today, Newsweek*, and *Forbes Magazine*. To find out more about Jammie, visit his website at: http://www.cornerstonevegas.com.

CHAPTER 13

HOW TO ACHIEVE YOUR DREAMS — AND CREATE YOUR IDEAL LIFESTYLE TOO

BY JEFF SALZENSTEIN

*"Twenty years from now you will be more disappointed by
the things that you didn't do than by the ones you did do.
So throw off the bowlines. Catch the trade winds in your sails.
Explore. Dream. Discover."*

~ Mark Twain

When I was a 12-year-old youngster and asked what I wanted to do when I grew up, my answer was clear: "I'm going to play tennis for the Stanford University tennis team."

Without knowing it, I had thrown a pebble in the pond of my life....and the ripples began.

To be honest, as a junior tennis player from Denver, Colorado, I had no idea how I was going to realize my dream of playing for mighty Stanford. Colorado wasn't exactly a tennis hotbed like California or Florida, but I was determined to find a way.

After years of working extremely hard, in both school and tennis, my dream was fulfilled when I accepted a tennis scholarship to matriculate at Stanford. Even more amazing was that I went on to succeed as an All-American and National championship tennis player on "the Farm." Fortunately, I was able to use my Stanford education on and off the tennis court to become one of the top 100 players in the world on the men's professional tennis tour.

When I think back on how I envisioned my future when I was 12, I recognize that I was artfully creating my desired future by crafting my unique version of the perfect "lifestyle"...for me.

You may have heard of the term "lifestyle design" popularized by best-selling author Tim Ferriss:

It's the idea that you can consciously create the life of your dreams filled with abundance, passion, and fun while fulfilling your true purpose in life. Many visionary leaders show us that you don't have to follow the 9 to 5 corporate "American Dream" model. I've chosen to become one of those visionaries by creating a lifestyle filled with freedom and fun that revolves around following my passion and mission to contribute to the world.

As Tim Ferriss explained in the **4 Hour Work Week: Escape 9-5, Live Anywhere, And Join the New Rich,** "The New Rich (NR) are those who abandon the deferred-life plan and create luxury lifestyles in the present using the currency of the New Rich: time and mobility. This is an art and a science we will refer to as Lifestyle Design (LD)."

It has been a life-changing experience for me to question the concept of working tirelessly for 45 plus years before retiring into the sunset at age 65.

Unless it's actually your idea of the ideal lifestyle, you really don't need to follow this more predictable way of living anymore. Ultimate freedom is very possible for you. What's really cool about the information age today is that multi-media platforms are readily available for you to share your message. You now have ample opportunities that were never possible before. All you have to do is expand your awareness and change your definition of "work."

The truth is that a VERY small minority of individuals has been lucky enough to have someone in their lives that went against the grain to become a successful entrepreneur and create abundance in more ways than just dollar signs. I've personally committed myself to this kind of abundance and now leverage each opportunity that comes my way to create more time and flexibility with creativity and purpose.

It can be downright scary and frustrating at times to step outside the box and search for solutions that don't follow typical cultural norms. But once you start getting creative, taking action, and getting results with your lifestyle plan, you'll begin to feel the powerful forces that will allow you to experience the most rewarding life possible.

Following a systematic road map to design your ideal lifestyle won't be perfect. You'll likely stumble and fall along the way, but if you stay the course, and redirect your personal road map when necessary, you'll be happy to find the pot o' gold at the end of your rainbow.

My lifestyle, passions, goals, and work may be completely different from yours, but I know enough about creating success to give you steps you can take to create your own lifestyle masterpiece. Apply this formula, take action, and enjoy the unfolding of your new life.

1. VISUALIZE YOUR IDEAL LIFESTYLE

*"Anyone who lives within their means suffers
from a lack of imagination."*

~ Oscar Wilde, Irish dramatist and novelist

Get your creative juices flowing and imagine everything you want your life to look like.

Dream big and let your imagination run wild.

What is your purpose or calling in life?

What type of profession would you like to pursue?

Who do you want to help?

Do you want to be married with kids?

Do you want to work from home?

How much time do you want to travel, play, and have fun?

How much money do you want to make to adopt your own "perfect" lifestyle?

Ask yourself these types of questions as you let your imagination create possibilities in your mind.

You're never too old, too young, too rich, or too poor to start this exercise. Heck, just look at what I did when I was 12 years old...I knew I wanted play tennis for Stanford and found a way to get there.

To help you make your dreams a reality, let's look at my favorite sport, tennis, as a comparison.

As a high performance tennis coach (with a professional tennis pro career behind me), I now teach an integrated tennis system through online training courses. I've had the unique opportunity to help thousands of players all over the world transform their tennis. The total tennis system I created came from many years of testing, developing, tweaking, and perfecting techniques that provides the best tennis training possible. The amazing feedback I've received from my offline and online students is proof that my teachings are founded on rock solid principles that deliver big time results.

Just like any sport, the foundation of playing great tennis is based on developing clear visualization techniques combined with great technical strokes and skills. So when evaluating the strokes of players, I strategically show them how they can improve their ability to visualize what they want to achieve on the court while improving stroke mechanics at the same time.

The power of visualization can't be underestimated when learning how to play successful tennis. In fact, even if you have the absolute worst technique in the world, you can ALWAYS visualize where you want to hit each ball. The ball might not go where you want it to each time (even the great champion, Roger Federer, doesn't hit his spots every time), but having the visual image in mind of your exact target puts you in the right state to execute each shot to the best of your ability. Your mind and body become laser-focused on finding the intended target.

Visualizing your targets on the court for ALL of your shots is just like seeing how you want your own life to look like. If you can't clearly see the picture of your dream job, dream house, dream family, and dream lifestyle, how can you consciously create it for yourself?

My advice to you is: Don't rely on blind luck to create your ideal life.

Start visualizing your ideal lifestyle and believe in it enough to make it happen... because it will!

2. FOCUS ON THE FINISH: CREATE YOUR BHAG

"A true BHAG is clear and compelling, and acts as a catalyst to work towards a clear finish line so the organization can know when it has achieved the goal; people like to shoot for finish lines."

~ Collins and Porras - *Built to Last: Successful Habits of Visionary Companies*

Now that you've been using your imagination more to see the end point of how you see your lifestyle coming together, it's time to create a Big Hairy Audacious Goal (BHAG) for your life.

I created my BHAG a while back when I realized what could be done for tennis players around the world with the use of my skills, experience, and the internet. I became clear, I dared to dream big, and I decided that I would help 1 million tennis players around the world improve their tennis games and their lives.

Can you begin to see how this kind of BHAG would inspire and motivate you? It sure works to motivate me! Each day I get closer to my BHAG, AND I get to reap the rewards of more resources that flow into my life, which enables me to create my ideal lifestyle as well.

This is why I want to motivate you to find a BHAG that will serve as a catalyst to your success in lifestyle design.

- Fast-forward into the future - 10 years - what is possible for you?
- Who are you helping?
- How are you making a difference in the world?
- How many people have you reached?
- How does this make you feel and what kind of rewards come with it?

Dare to make your BHAG so far-fetched that even you can't believe it's possible to attain. It doesn't have to feel "possible" right now. Be ready to stretch your mind, shake up your confidence level, and you'll love the self-inspired action that comes of it.

Don't worry about too many details yet. Over time, your BHAG will direct your body, mind, and spirit to come up with all the steps required for you to succeed. Stay focused on the end result of your BHAG, just like the finish positions on a tennis player's strokes.

Speaking of tennis, one of the most powerful concepts in the tennis system I teach involves having players focus on the "finish" of their strokes. This may seem a bit counterintuitive, especially if you know all the details that go into hitting the little yellow fuzzy ball.

Traditional coaches give tips like watching the ball, bending your knees, taking the racquet back, and hitting the ball more in front of you. Any player who's tried to apply all these tips at the same time knows "paralysis-by-analysis" well, which is far from the best way to have success in tennis. On the flip side, most players benefit tremendously from focusing on the **"finish"**. Being "finish focused" keeps things *simple* and helps you avoid thinking too much while successfully completing a solid stroke.

When a player focuses on creating a beautiful finish, their minds slow down because they're "dialed in" to the ending rather than trying to perform all the moving parts in the middle of the stroke. Having one directed focus on the finish gives players a better chance to make the right calculations every time they hit the ball. The feedback a player gets at the finish is very powerful in learning what worked and what didn't. The bottom line is that things move way too fast in tennis to analyze every part of the stroke as the ball approaches, and that's one reason why it's truly best to stick with the finish.

Executing the correct finish with tennis strokes is just like having your BHAG in mind. Visualizing your BHAG allows you to get to the final destination with passion and efficiency. Start by visualizing, get yourself a BHAG, and focus on that finish.

3. WRITE DOWN SHORT TERM GOALS AND TAKE ACTION

Every day is the perfect day to ask yourself questions about your life goals, and how you plan to address those goals.

~Jonathan Lockwood Huie

No matter how good of a dreamer you are, and no matter how inspiring you make your BHAG, that alone won't complete the entire picture. To achieve your BHAG and start living the life you desire, it's absolutely vital that you set clear and attainable short-term goals too.

Let's bring it back to tennis again where, in my system, I not only stress the importance of the finish and having a clear target on each shot, but I also make sure players get the beginning of their strokes down pat too, so that they can perform admirably on the court.

Several details can limit a tennis player's success when performing a proper stroke: the way they hold the racquet, having a bad grip, their ready position, and/or how they make their first move with their body as the ball comes their way. Without enough skill and precision at the beginning of the stroke, their chances for hitting solid shots dwindle.

Just like a tennis players' grip and first move to the ball can make all the difference with their strokes, being skillful and clear about the first steps for creating the ultimate lifestyle is equally important.

Here's how this can work for you. Start by setting daily action lifestyle goals that you'll successfully achieve everyday:

- How much sleep do you want to get?
- What time do you want to wake up?
- How much will you exercise?
- What kind of food will you eat?
- What habits will you change?
- What hobbies will you do that make you smile?
- Who will you spend time with?
- What line of work are you passionate about pursuing each day?

Answer the questions that make defining your ideal lifestyle more complete for you. Write them down. What will you do each day that will get you closer to living your life with true fulfillment and purpose?

If doing the things you love on a consistent basis isn't a habit, make a "to-do" list the night before and write them down.

Your "to-do's" can be anything you want them to be as a part of your new lifestyle. It could be tasks or activities like writing a book, making three phone calls to potential clients, planning a vacation, going for a walk, learning to cook, etc.

Take the concept of just writing out these "to-do" items one step further by writing your tasks out as "appointments" in a calendar. It works best for me to put these appointments on my iPhone calendar as soon as I make them. Having an organized schedule each day, hour by hour, makes it easier to stay on track and gives you more power to follow through on your action steps.

The secrets to success are quite simple. Performing daily actions that align with your BHAG will get you closer to achieving your dreams. Start with the end goal in mind, set a daily plan for yourself, take massive action every day, and watch the momentum propel you forward to the lifestyle of your dreams.

To recap, follow these 3 steps and you'll be golden:

1. VISUALIZE YOUR IDEAL LIFESTYLE
2. FOCUS ON THE FINISH (YOUR CLEAR BHAG)
3. WRITE DOWN SHORT TERM GOALS AND TAKE MASSIVE ACTION DAILY

Oh yeah...and don't forget to have fun along the way. I wish you all the best and much success in creating your inspiring and fulfilling life.

About Jeff

Jeff Salzenstein is the founder and president of JRS Sports, LLC, an organization focused on helping tennis players all over the world improve their tennis with world-class tennis instruction in the areas of technique, footwork, nutrition, injury prevention, motivation, and athletic development training.

Jeff has blended his immense skills as a sought-after high performance coach and online direct response marketing expert to develop a highly successful website: www.JeffSalzensteinTennis.com where he shares cutting edge tennis tips and lessons to help players transform their games. He has created several successful online instruction courses including the Tennis Forehand Solution and the Tennis Serve Secrets. Jeff also has a vibrant online tennis instruction membership site called the Total Tennis Training Inner Circle that has hundreds of members with over 25 countries represented. These online tennis courses and programs are setting a new standard in tennis learning online.

A member of the Colorado Tennis Hall of Fame, Jeff set the standard for tennis in Colorado with an unsurpassed record as a player at the amateur and professional levels.

Early in his career as a player, Jeff committed to learning and mastering the techniques and practice regimens that distinguish great players from good players. Today, this devotion and passion for the game are being borne out in the athletic and personal accomplishments of the players he coaches.

Jeff turned professional and joined the ATP Tour immediately after his 1996 graduation from Stanford University, where he earned a B.A. in Economics. He quickly rose through the ATP rankings while playing in all the Grand Slam events (Wimbledon, French Open, Australian Open and US Open).

In 1997, Jeff was named Rookie of the Year by *Tennis Week* magazine. At the 1997 US Open, Jeff played a nationally televised 2nd round feature match against Michael Chang (then ranked No. 2 in the world), losing in four sets. In 2004, despite having two major surgeries in the first three years of his professional career, Jeff broke into the top 100 in the ATP rankings for the first time which included eight years on tour. Jeff was the first American to accomplish this feat after his 30th birthday. At that time, Jeff was the 10th ranked American in the ATP world rankings, which included such notables as Andy Roddick, Andre Agassi, James Blake, Todd Martin, and Taylor Dent.

Jeff's academic and tennis excellence earned him an athletic scholarship to Stanford.

At Stanford, Jeff was named team captain his junior and senior years, and played No.1 singles. He led the Cardinals to back-to-back NCAA national team champion-ships, meriting all-American recognition in his junior and senior years in singles. Jeff received Stanford's Senior Athlete of the Year award in 1996, and was a semifinalist in the NCAA singles championship in 1995.

In addition to being a United States Professional Tennis Association Level 1 teaching professional and USTA High Performance Coach, Jeff is a Certified Nutritional Therapy Practitioner.

CHAPTER 14

THE FIVE KEY STRATEGIES IN TEAM BUILDING

BY JEREMY LARSON

There is something magical that takes place when a group of like-minded people come together. I was in the back of the room about to jump out of my seat the first time I was able to sit in on a sales team meeting. I was completely transformed. The idea of taking a current reality and going to work on what it takes to achieve a desired reality shocked my system. At a time when I was searching for a direction, I was given something to believe in.

I quickly learned that the myth that all you need to do is describe your vision and belief and people will line up to support you is the exact opposite of the truth. The goal of achieving something worth talking about is what every team strives for, and this quest will always be accompanied with resistance. Every step of progress is face-to-face with mediocrity trying to stop it in its tracks. I discovered that people pushing against your mission to do something extraordinary is what makes the journey worth doing.

I have been building sales/marketing teams ever since. I have seen: (1) incredibly talented individuals leave their team and take a pay cut to be a part of a winning team, (2) dream teams crumble in record time, (3) teams never get past step 1, and (4) teams overcome incredible adversity to achieve their goal and have a blast in the process.

The bigger your dream, the more important your team is. Not the bigger your dream, the bigger the team. Size does matter, but most important is the level of belief.

The main constraint on high performing companies is the ability to effectively and efficiently recruit and grow key people to match the growth of the company. When executed properly, building a team has the power to leverage the talent of the people around you to dramatically multiply results. How important is team building? 65-80% of operating costs is consumed in salaries and wages. The typical person works 50% of capacity (chitchat, Internet, email, personal business, distraction). I feel this is the leadership's fault. Everything sinks or flies on leadership. Businesses are not balance sheets, businesses are people serving people. Get the people right and the people will take care of the rest.

The best companies have the best teams. If you want a high-performing business, you need to recruit, hire, and retain high-performing people. Studies show that only 25% of hires end up becoming top performers, 50% are disappointing, and 25% are chronic under-performers. With the following Five Keys to Infinite Team Building we expect to double the percentage of new team members becoming top performers. When people ask me about the secret ingredients for building a team, I let them know there is nothing extravagant about team building, nothing that demands a special power, rather it requires discipline to adhere to the following Five Key Strategies To Infinite Team Building.

1. TRUST

Trust has the ability to speed up the development of, or destroy a team. You have to start by trusting the ideas and actions of the team. It is important to point out that you do not have to approve, but you do have to trust their intentions. Be honest with yourself and your team with the task at hand. Having goals and expectations that are not honest in the situation can create a thick layer of fog amongst your team's ability to focus. When Trust is high, the level of belief is high, when the level of belief is high the action taken is high. No one will continue to be on a team if trust has been breeched. Columbia Business School did a study that showed that mistrust doubled the cost of business – making lack of trust the largest expense. Assuming the team trusts the leader, a new team member will automatically begin to tap into what is called a transfer of trust and start trusting the leader fast, therefore resulting in quick action orientation, versus a new team member who is on the fence with their level of trust. Trust = level of belief = level of action taken.

Trust is also the greatest competitive advantage. The most trusted organization will always get the extra treatment and capture the largest market share. At all costs do not work with anybody on your team that you do not trust. I have never regretted going separate ways with somebody that I felt I could not trust. To do what's right over what's easy is always recognizable, and has a huge impact. To be confidently believed in with trust is the key to your team taking massive actions to achieve the collective goals.

2. GRATITUDE

Expressing gratitude through appreciation and celebration. The #1 most attractive trait is gratitude. We love to be around grateful people who are genuine and authentic. Studies found gratitude as the most common trait of those that are most happy. With a clear presence of appreciation for your team, you will attract top achievers. A Gallup study showed the number one reason you could lose top achievers or not attract top achievers is not compensation, but rather its not feeling appreciated. Top achievers that go above and beyond will have a tendency to grow resentful if they are not getting the appreciation that their efforts deserve. Top achievers are also talent magnets. A great way to leverage this and express gratitude is to have a reward program for recruiting. Reward all team members who recruit additional team members. Birds of a feather flock together. This is a valuable exercise on which to reward handsomely; plus, a majority of potential new team members will relate to someone working in the position considered versus a recruiter or top level supervisor. Reward the hero of the week, have pizza parties, and sit the team down to stop and appreciate efforts taken. Appreciation also needs to be given when communicating. If you want to hire top achievers and have them work on your team, you have to listen to them. Be open to all ideas, regardless of position or title. Celebrating helps create energy and momentum. People psychologically get hooked on momentum, it is a feeling we love. You don't ever want to be so busy to not stop and make time to celebrate, avoid waiting to the end of the quarter or the end of the year. Celebrate not only productivity achievements, but also quality control, efficiency, and team players. The most impactful form of celebrating is celebrating a collective win that involves the whole team. A team that celebrates together, stays together.

3. CLARITY

High performance requires clarity. There is no room for uncertainty. It is vital that the following questions can be answered by the leadership and the entire team any day of the week:

- Why was the team created? When the vision is clear people want to follow. When the vision is uncertain, the dedication of the team is uncertain.

- What is the expectation for each team member's performance and the team as a whole? Its Important for team members in various different roles to know their expectations are different. A lot of confusion and questioning is eliminated when individual team members roles are clearly defined and furthermore explained how those roles contribute to the over all performance goal. You can't hit unidentified targets.

- What is the benefit for each team member and the team as a whole if the desired performance is achieved? Risk is eliminated when the benefits are clear.

- What is the expected outcome for each team member and the team as a whole if the desired performance is not achieved? Everyone needs to know they are held accountable individually and collectively.

- How does the organization consistently demonstrate support for the team with resources, support, time, and money? Top achievers want to be certain that they are playing for the winning team with the industry's best support, resources, and innovation.

- Is leadership crystal clear on the attributes to look for in individuals to gel with the team culture? Top achievers do not like to work with less focused people that are lazy with action orientation. Critically important, Identify DNA and personality of the team's culture. Right person can be wrong in wrong culture. Be clear on the qualities we are looking for. I have always focused on: 1) Character, 2) Intelligence, and 3) Energy. I recruit character over experience any day of the week.

- Is the compensation model clear? This sounds obvious, but needs to be certain.

- Is the leadership dedication to the mission clear and evident in the interactions with the team? People trust those that stand through adversity.

- Is leadership clear on the signs and behaviors that are detrimental to the success of the team and the effective way to correct? I have seen very driven leaders hesitate to call their peers on actions and behaviors that seem counter-productive to the good of the team. Usually the tough decision is what's required to move on. I have never regretted firing someone.

- Is leadership clear that the highest focal point is on the collective achievement of the team not individuals? Too often do amateurs make the mistake of letting team members focus on their individual goals, ego, or career path and it suffocates the collective results.

- What is the team's psychological approach towards the mission? It is always best to think and act like the underdog.

4. MENTOR

Your job as the leader is to challenge the self-limiting beliefs that may exist with in your teams' minds. The leader has to paint an accurate picture of the future for the team to see. A big part of developing top achievers is giving feedback both candidly and inspirationally. Top achievers strive to work in an environment where they can grow their talents and become more of who they are meant to be. To take people from where they are now to where they never dreamed of being is the essence of leadership. If you accomplish this, you will get their loyalty. Top achievers want to work around people who are fresh and capable that are continuously learning, that have mentors, implement book, article, and audio program studies focused on achievement. Input leads to Output.

One of the biggest mistakes that I see organizations make with a new team member is breaking them in slowly or softly. It is very important to show the speed of production from the start. The pace that a new team member begins with will greatly determine the pace of their career with you. You want them to be stimulated, challenged, and feel speed from the start. Help people with their personal goals. Find out what their personal goals are and what their 'why' is. Find out what their passions in life are. If you don't care about people getting better and achieving what's important in their lives, leadership is not for you. You have to want to see your people grow.

5. PASSION.

One of the few things the web cannot do is produce leadership, which still has to come from individuals who have passion for something. Every single person needs to feel they are a part of something special. People need to feel they are part of an environment where they work and make human connections. Always be bold in expressing your passion. At the end of the day, everyone wants to feel they are making a difference. Passion is contagious not only amongst the team, but to customers as well. Passion drives purpose. People put faith in those that believe beyond themselves with a purpose. If the team recognizes that you care more about the purpose than your personal gain and want to do work that goes beyond yourself they will enthusiastically want to take part.

A clear purpose will provide the ability to collaborate and connect beyond personal desires. This gives everyone something to fight for. Your job is to constantly communicate the difference you want your organization to make through your products and service. Trying to please everyone is a recipe for disaster; focus on building a passion-filled, like-minded, laser-focused team compared to a bigger team that may have a few less interested people. When its time to hit the field, a focused and connected team will always be more powerful than a larger less-focused group could ever be. Great leaders are constantly sharing a clear bold vision of the future that their team can fall in love with, and rally their daily talents around. If you consistently pour out your passion and higher purpose so that your team feels they are making a difference, they will give you their energy, talent, and loyalty.

Like a car with a flat tire, if the team building fails to execute one single key strategy, they wont get far and the speed of growth will be slow and bumpy. This sounds simple because it is; the challenge is in sticking with the discipline to implement all five key strategies to infinite growth.

About Jeremy

Jeremy A. Larson is the founder and CEO of Deluxe Marketing Inc. (DMI) which has been featured by *Inc. Magazine* on three different occasions as one of Americas fastest-growing private companies as part of the Inc. 500. In 2010, DMI was ranked the 85th fastest-growing company in the nation with a 2,822% growth rate. The Business Journal has recognized DMI as the 3rd fastest-growing private company in its area.

Jeremy's passion is leadership. The opportunity to take someone from the back of the line and give them the tools and resources to work to the front of the line is what excites him.

Jeremy is known as "The Real Deal" amongst his clients and peers. He has built over a hundred sales teams in multiple locations across the globe from the ground up. He has become the trusted authority among top name Fortune 500 companies for designing and building direct face-to-face marketing programs that lower the cost of customer/subscriber acquisition – while exceeding desired goals.

Jeremy is a bestselling author and entrepreneur that is sought out for his opinion on direct marketing. Jeremy has been seen on NBC, CBS, ABC and FOX affiliates.

To learn more about Jeremy A Larson, Deluxe Marketing Inc., and how you can receive the free Special Report "The 3 Qualities To Look For When Hiring Top Talent" visit: www.JeremyALarson.com,
www.DeluxeMarketingInc.com
Or call Toll-Free 1-866-DMI-9419.

CHAPTER 15

ACHIEVING ULTIMATE SUCCESS IN PERSUASION: STORYSELLING IS BELIEVING

BY NICK NANTON & JW DICKS

So, in January of 1967, Paul McCartney, then-member of the Beatles (we assume you've heard of them), was in a car accident in London. A brief rumor gripped England that Sir Paul was actually killed in the crash. The next month, the official Beatles "fanzine" verified that Mc-Cartney was, in fact, alive and well, and life went on as normal - for a while, anyway.

A little over two years later, however, in the autumn of 1969, the stress of superstardom had pulled apart the world's most popular rock group. The Beatles were splitting up, and Paul was spending more and more time in Scotland with his new wife Linda, out of the public eye.

And that's when the weirdness really kicked in. With Paul in hiding for the first time since he and his mates became superstars, the student newspaper at Drake University in Iowa printed a story that seriously asked the question, "Is Beatle Paul McCartney Dead?" The rumor had grown in strength on the campus – and suddenly the students were hunting down clues that had supposedly been placed on the group's most recent albums. For instance, when part of the "Revolution #9" track on *The White Album* was played backwards, a voice said, "Turn me on, dead man." Others swore that, as the end of "Strawberry Fields Forever" faded away, another voice clearly said, "I buried Paul."[1]

Suddenly, Derek Taylor, the Beatles' press rep back in London, was inundated by calls – was Paul in fact deceased? He denied that he was. Because…well, he wasn't.

But then, the rumor made its way to Detroit – where another college newspaper made fun of the gossip by writing a satirical article detailing the "clues" that proved that McCartney was no longer living. Unfortunately, the story was picked up as *fact* by newspapers across the U.S. – and soon the subject was burning up the radio airwaves in New York City, among other major cities.

The "real story" was revealed as this: McCartney had died in that London car crash a few years ago. The Beatles, desperate to continue their success, had replaced him with a guy named William Campbell, the winner of a Paul McCartney look-alike contest, who coincidentally enough, evidently *sounded just like him and had the same incredible musical talent.* Huh?

Three songs were written and released by other rockers about the "death" of Paul. A television special was produced and syndicated nationally, in which a courtroom "trial" was held to decide if Paul was, in fact, dead; F. Lee Bailey, a leading celebrity lawyer at the time, cross-examined "witnesses." The verdict? Well, that was left in the hands of the viewers.

And finally, Paul McCartney decided to rise from the dead - and give an interview to *Life* magazine declaring he was alive and well – and just enjoying being "not famous" for the first time in many years.

Now, we will grant you, there have been plenty of movies about look-alikes taking over for famous people (starting with about eighty versions of *Prisoner of Zenda* over the years). But, as far as we know, there's never been an example of this actually happening in real life – let alone it happening with a worldwide superstar subject to intense media scrutiny who continued to publicly perform and create new music.

So…*how could anyone swallow this story???*

How could anyone believe that someone could quickly and easily take

---

1 John Lennon later revealed, the voice was saying "Cranberry sauce."

the place of someone as talented and singular as Paul McCartney was at the time? Even while new records featuring his instantly recognizable voice were still being made and released? How could anyone for a minute not only buy this whopper – but continue to spread it all across the globe?

Well, there is a very good reason many people actually believed it (or, at the very least, took it seriously) – and that's because it was *a great story.* And, as we'll see in this chapter, a great story causes people to believe fiction over fact – *because the human brain can't tell the difference.*

Scary? A little bit.

In this excerpt from our upcoming book, *StorySelling to Success,* we'll explain exactly why this happens – and what it means in terms of what we call "StorySelling" – the process in which you tell a powerful story to create a powerful Celebrity Brand.

FACT VERSUS FICTION: WHEN THE TRUTH DOESN'T MATTER

There are two important points we want to make about stories, points that have been backed up by tons of scientific research (which we'll discuss in detail in our book). Point one: Stories aren't necessarily a *creative* process – your brain generates and uses them as a *tool* to explain your life and what's happening around you. Point two: Good stories hit your brain in its "reward centers" – they actually cause chemical reactions that make you feel good in fundamental ways.

Now, let's apply those two points to the Paul is dead story and why it developed such a massive following, even though it was patently absurd.

To the first point, the "Paul is dead" story *explained* why Beatles fans were suddenly not seeing one of their idols anymore, after nonstop public exposure since the group became famous. After all, everyone knew where his creative partner John Lennon was – (this was the period when John was running around with new wife Yoko making headlines with outrageous stunts) – and Paul's absence from the spotlight stood out in comparison.

To the second point, the Paul-Is-Dead rumor made those believing the story feel good in the way that "Truthers" (people who believed 9/11 was an "inside government job") and "Birthers" (people who believed that Barack Obama wasn't born in the U.S.) felt good about their conspiracies – even though both those ideas are very distasteful concepts to many people. A fantastic story that seems to have a basis in actual ascertainable "facts" (shaky as those facts might be in reality) gets the listener excited; not only does it make sense of something strange, it also makes believers feel that *they're* in on a secret that has everyone else fooled, and, thus, they feel *smarter* than everyone else. They also feel part of an "inside group" - and that sense of belonging to an exclusive community makes them feel more important.

Primarily for those two reasons, a great story has the ability to "carry your brain away" – literally – through a concept that researchers call "transportation." Now, this isn't the kind of transportation that gets you to work or to the supermarket; *this* mode of transportation was discovered by researchers Melanie C. Green and Timothy C. Brock of Ohio State University[2] and it involves just how stories can impact your belief systems – even if those stories aren't necessarily factually accurate.

To quote the researchers, "...the reader loses access to some real-world facts in favor of accepting the narrative world that the author has created. This loss of access may occur on a physical level - a transported reader may not notice others entering the room, for example - or, more importantly, on a psychological level, a subjective distancing from reality. While the person is immersed in the story, he or she *may be less aware of real-world facts that contradict assertions made in the narrative."*

To put that in plain English, a *compelling story can be more important to someone than the facts.*

Want proof? Okay, check out this album cover from the last album the Beatles made together, *Abbey Road.*

Now, you and I might look at that picture and say, "Hey, sure looks like Paul's alive to me – there he is, walking across the street with the other three Beatles. Hey, shouldn't he be able to afford a nice pair of loafers?"

---

2 Melanie C. Green and Timothy C. Brock, "The Role of Transportation in the Persuasiveness of Public Narratives," Journal of Personality and Social Psychology, Vol. 79, No. 5.

But, when it came to those who had bought into the Paul-Is Dead conspiracy, here's what *they* saw: The four Beatles dressed to symbolize nothing less than a funeral procession, with John, dressed in white, as the minister, Ringo, dressed in black, as the undertaker, George, in denim jeans and shirt, as the gravedigger and Paul (or, more accurately, Mr. William Campbell, the guy who *looked* like Paul), barefoot and out of step with the others, as the corpse.

Oh, and that Volkswagen parked in the background? If you look closely, you'll see it has "28IF" as part of its license plate number – which, naturally to true Paul-Is-Dead conspiracy buffs, signified that Paul would have been 28 years old at that point - *if* he had lived.

In other words, all these obscure hidden meanings were more important to believers than the fact that *Paul was actually shown alive and well on the album cover.* And, since this was in an era that was well before Photoshop, it was pretty obvious that the photo was the real deal.

Again, this is just more evidence that the brain can't really distinguish between fact and fiction when a person has decided to buy into a story. As a matter of fact, it actively fights the impulse – because it's more important that *the brain defends the integrity of the story.*

This doesn't just apply to scurrilous dead Beatle stories. We all buy into narratives in our everyday lives – and when those narratives are challenged, we push back against the contradictions. How hard we push back depends on how invested we are in the particular story.

Think of someone who's a rabid Republican or Democrat who's confronted with information that contradicts his or her position. How many times have you said to yourself, when having a discussion with that kind of person, "This person is completely irrational – I have to stop arguing, there's no point!"

Odds are you're right. The person *is* being irrational – because the overall story he or she wants to believe in is more important than individual facts that conflict with it.

Getting back to the research of Green and Brock, the doctors discovered that it didn't matter if a story was presented as fact or fiction; if the story was compelling enough, if it had enough ability to "transport" people, it would directly impact their beliefs about the subject matter of the story.

And *that's* how someone could see Paul McCartney walking in a contemporary photograph – and still assume it was a big put-up job to send a hidden message about his death. In the words of Green and Brock, "Individuals may believe realistic fictional programs while discounting news reports that seem implausible."

As a matter of fact, that sounds a lot like our world today, doesn't it?

WHY STORIES WIN ARGUMENTS

Transportation is the ultimate goal for any good storyteller. And obviously, it should be the goal of a StorySelling effort as well.

Just as obviously, however, not just *any* story is going to prompt transportation (in later chapters, we're going to dig deeper into what ingredients are needed to create the kinds of story that enable this transformative process to happen).

What we want you to understand in *this* chapter, however, is that StorySelling is the most powerful tool you can use to communicate your personal brand and your company brand. All the research is very consistent on this fact (including the studies we've shared with you so far): *stories are the best way to make your "argument."*

Why?

For the simple reason that the people hearing (or watching) the story... *don't perceive it as an argument.*

Instead, they identify with the leading character (providing he or she is likeable and interesting enough), put themselves in their shoes, feel what they feel and respond to what the story says about that person and the situation. They shut off the questioning part of their brain, as we've discussed, and give themselves over to the story's events and the consequences of those events.

And remember, since we do use stories to explain things, if we accept the narrative, then we will accept the conclusion. If the story is about how a murderer got away because of a court foul-up, we will feel more inclined to favor tougher laws. If the story is about how an innocent man is put on death row, we will feel more inclined to protect the rights of the accused. The story leads us to those ways of thinking not through direct persuasion, but by dramatic license.

We will only change or modify those beliefs so easily, however, if *we don't know an argument is being made.* To us, it's just a story; it's not supposed to mean anything beyond the beginning, middle and end of a tale. And that's how a story's so-called "moral" can sneak up on us and have an impact.

We use stories to process reality. Think about how powerful a statement that is. Think about how, whatever situation we find ourselves in, we must immediately concoct some kind of story to explain it, even though, ultimately, the story may be false. We still need to have something to hang onto until the "real story" is finally revealed.

StorySelling becomes invaluable when you want other people to process *your* reality in a memorable, effective way – the way you want them to see you.

Think about a trial lawyer doing his closing argument. How does he persuade the jury? Ninety-nine times out of a hundred, he'll frame what he wants the jury to believe in the form of a story – retelling the events crucial to the case in the way he wants them to be perceived.

In a sense, that's exactly what you do for yourself with StorySelling. You're telling a story about you and/or your business in the way you want them to perceive you. And because it's not seen as straight sales pitch, your audience's guard is significantly lowered and they're more willing to accept what you have to say.

THE VALUE OF AUTHENTICITY

We feel the need to end this chapter with a word about the truth.

This chapter may read as if stories are a license to lie – but there is great peril in that approach. Obviously, the Paul-Is-Dead conspiracy was pretty much dead and buried itself when Paul came out of hiding and began to give interviews. Whoever William Campbell might have been, he couldn't have been good enough to look exactly like Paul *and* sound exactly like Paul, unless someone was doing *Mission: Impossible* for real.

When a big lie is aggressively sold, it's only a matter of time before it does catch up with you. And with social media ready to blow the whistle at the drop of a hat and virally bust you, your window for successful deception is very short – as short as a few minutes, in some cases.

The fact is, even when your StorySelling is effective, your audience won't be as heavily invested in your narrative as they are in, say, their religion, their politics or their relationships. That means that, while you *can* achieve "transportation," it's still a tenuous ride that could be quickly derailed - *if* the story you're telling is ultimately a false one.

StorySelling offers you your best chance at reaching people on a deep, meaningful level that can genuinely motivate them to buy from you. Long term, however, you can't misuse that power – or it will come back to haunt you in ways you won't want to happen.

About Nick

An Emmy-winning director and producer, Nick Nanton, Esq., is known as the top agent to celebrity experts around the world for his role in developing and marketing business and professional experts through personal branding, media, marketing and PR to help them gain credibility and recognition for their accomplishments. Nick is recognized as the nation's leading expert on personal branding as *Fast Company* magazine's expert blogger on the subject and lectures regularly on the topic at major universities around the world. His book *Celebrity Branding You*® has also been used as the textbook on personal branding for university students.

The CEO of The Dicks + Nanton Celebrity Branding Agency, an international agency with more than 1000 clients in 26 countries, Nick is an award-winning director, producer and songwriter who has worked on everything from large-scale events to television shows with Bill Cosby, President George H.W. Bush, Brian Tracy, Michael Gerber and many more.

Nick is recognized as one of the top thought leaders in the business world and has co-authored 16 best-selling books alongside Brian Tracy, Jack Canfield (creator of the "Chicken Soup for the Soul" series), Dan Kennedy, Robert Allen, Dr. Ivan Misner (founder of BNI), Jay Conrad Levinson (author of the "Guerilla Marketing" series), Leigh Steinberg and many others, including the breakthrough hit *Celebrity Branding You!*

Nick has led the marketing and PR campaigns that have driven more than 600 authors to best-seller status. Nick has been seen in *USA Today, The Wall Street Journal, Newsweek, Inc., The New York Times, Entrepreneur Magazine* and FastCompany.com and has appeared on ABC, NBC, CBS, and FOX television affiliates around the country, as well as on FOX News, CNN, CNBC and MSNBC, speaking on subjects ranging from branding, marketing and law to "American Idol."

Nick is a member of the Florida Bar and holds a J.D. from the University of Florida Levin College of Law, as well as a B.S./B.A. in Finance from the University of Florida's Warrington College of Business Administration. Nick is a voting member of The National Academy of Recording Arts & Sciences (NARAS, home to the Grammys), a member of The National Academy of Television Arts & Sciences (home to the Emmy Awards), co-founder of the National Academy of Best-Selling Authors®, and an 11-time Telly Award winner. He spends his spare time working with Young Life and Downtown Credo Orlando and rooting for the Florida Gators with his wife Kristina and their three children, Brock, Bowen and Addison.

About JW

JW Dicks, Esq. is America's foremost authority on using personal branding for business development. He has created some of the most successful brand and marketing campaigns for business and professional clients to make them the credible celebrity experts in their field and build multi-million dollar businesses using their recognized status.

JW Dicks has started, bought, built, and sold a large number of businesses over his 39-year career and developed a loyal international following as a business attorney, author, speaker, consultant, and business experts' coach. He not only practices what he preaches by using his strategies to build his own businesses, he also applies those same concepts to help clients grow their business or professional practice the ways he does.

JW has been extensively quoted in such national media as *USA Today, The Wall Street Journal, Newsweek, Inc.*, Forbes.com, CNBC.com, and *Fortune Small Business*. His television appearances include ABC, NBC, CBS and FOX affiliate stations around the country. He is the resident branding expert for *Fast Company's* internationally syndicated blog and is the publisher of *Celebrity Expert Insider*, a monthly newsletter targeting business and brand building strategies.

JW has written over 22 books, including numerous best-sellers, and has been inducted into the National Academy of Best-Selling Authors. JW is married to Linda, his wife of 39 years, and they have two daughters, two granddaughters and two Yorkies. JW is a 6th generation Floridian and splits his time between his home in Orlando and beach house on the Florida west coast.

CHAPTER 16

THE ABC'S OF BUYING CASH FLOW REAL ESTATE LIKE BILLION-DOLLAR PRIVATE EQUITY FUNDS:
A STEP-BY-STEP GUIDE TO IDENTIFYING HIGH-GROWTH, HIGH-CASH FLOW MARKETS

BY JOHN CHIN

Too many of us are unprepared to create comfortable futures for our-selves and those we care about. Inflation continues to erode our quality of life and our savings. Mortality rates climb, compounding our fears of running out of money before we die. Constant reminders of the financial state of our government and unfunded "entitlements" continue pushing us to become more self-reliant. Quality, safe investment options are few, and so-called "experts" can't be trusted as far as we can throw them.

I don't know about you, but I don't want to be a financial burden to my family during my golden years. I also don't want to be forced to greet Wal-martians during the final chapter of my life. That's not why I make the sacrifices I do today. We work our tails off and suffer through too much to go out like that.

As much as we try to be present - to enjoy life with the people we care about - there is always that nagging voice of the diligent ant that keeps us discontent, that keeps us stock-piling for the inevitable cold season of our future. It's a healthy voice.

The only problem is the voice gets louder as we get older. Are we ready? What if I get sick? What if something happens to the kids? What if hyper-inflation visits? What if China's economy collapses? What if Medicare takes a hit? What about Social Security? What if we were wrong about the Mayan calendar and the End is actually 2020? What if? What if? Fact: the future is uncertain. We need to prepare.

So, we hunt.

We hunt for ways to make and save more money. And we hunt for ways to make the money we save work harder for us. Since the beginning of our credit crisis, we have been pounded by waves of real estate media headlines. The average spectator watched in frightened paralysis. No action. No opportunity. No progress.

Others of us who abide by Warren Buffet's "buy when there's blood in the streets" investment philosophy licked our chops and got hungry. The biggest opportunists of us all were institutions that stepped up to drop billions of dollars in chips on the table, to bet on the recovery of residential housing.

And it was an easy bet. Unlike the speculative nature of investing that skyrocketed prices to artificial heights from 2004 to 2007, these yield-driven buyers focused on properties with tangible, immediate cash flow, ranging from 8% to 15% net return. Rich, huh? If you currently aren't in the markets these institutions are playing – and most of us aren't – you might think returns like this are unrealistic and/or high-risk. Well, they're not.

There is a way to find these markets with just a little common sense and some public information. That's what I'm here to teach you: how to identify real estate markets that billion-dollar funds discovered to find investments that out-perform more traditional "paper" alternatives.

I'll walk you through the macro-steps to find the right region or local market, then, I've made available additional free resources to help you tactically follow-up on your up-front homework. Everything you need is here to help you make consistent income regardless of your background as a real estate investor. You can access all the tools and complimentary education here: www.SafeCashFlow.com

I'm excited for you! Let's start this journey with a quick 3-question self-assessment...

Landlord Quiz:

<u>**Question 1:**</u> Which of these homes is the better investment?

Home "A"	Home "B"

Price: $58,900	Price: $101,500
Rent: $850 per month	Rent: $1,100 per month
Cap Rate: 15.3%	Cap Rate: 9.8%

<u>**Question 2:**</u> Which of these properties is better for wealth building?

Home "A"	Home "B"
Today's Price: $104,000	*Today's Price: $104,000*
(2006: $170,000)	*(2006: $420,000)*

| *Atlanta, GA* | *Orlando, FL* |
| *Single Family Home* | *Condominium* |

Question 3: How many hotdogs can Takeru Kobayashi eat in 12 minutes?

Answer to question 1: Trick question. If you picked home "A," you would be correct based on the snippet of info provided, but this "high cash flow home" sits in a high-risk neighborhood, in one of the worst school districts in U.S. history. Home "B" will generate a higher return on cash, long term, with a lot less hassle.

Answer to question 2: Home "A" will build wealth faster. 2006 prices offer zero indication of future values. We'll cover why "peak pricing" is not relevant as an indicator of growth in the pages ahead. There are much better ways to determine if a property is truly discounted when you buy it.

Answer to question 3: It doesn't matter! It's not an important question...just like many of the questions real estate investors use in their hunt for profitable cash flow properties. Arm yourself with *quality questions* and you will be better prepared to make money in real estate safely.

That's what you'll learn in these next few pages: *better questions*. I'll share with you the basics of buying like a billion-dollar private equity fund: a road map to identify markets with high growth potential and healthy cash flows: yields that dwarf traditional paper investments.

"It is better to know some of the questions than all of the answers."

~James Thurber

Below are the seven steps to make money in remote (not local) real estate markets. In the pages ahead, we'll dive into details of step 1. I call this the Macro Research. Then, you can follow up on the subsequent steps at: www.SafeCashFlow.com.

1. Macro Research - Identify a safe, high-growth market

2. Micro Research - Locate pockets within that market for safe, long-term cash flow

3. Your local help - Select an investment-minded real estate agent to be your on-the-ground assistant

4. Leverage - Set-up financing (if available)

5. Buy - Secure a property

6. Prepare the home – Renovations

7. Make money – Property management

STEP 1: MACRO MARKET - IDENTIFY A SAFE, HIGH-GROWTH MARKET OFFERING HEALTHY CASH FLOW

SAFETY and GROWTH POTENTIAL are found in vibrant, strong economies. No need to over-think this. You don't need to be an economist to know where real estate prices and rents are likely to rise, or at a minimum, hold strong. All we need to know are some very basic economic fundamentals:

• GDP per capita

• Population growth trends

• Affordability

Let's break it down very simply.

GDP per capita – Gross Domestic Product (GDP) is simply an all-encompassing measure of economic output in a given area. GDP equals jobs. Jobs equal the capacity for tenants to pay rent and families to buy houses. All economic data should be researched by MSA as this information is most relevant to real estate investing. We need local data, not information based on State or region. You can see GDP rankings by MSA at the link provided here: www.SafeCashFlow.com

Population growth – Early in my career, one of my mentors shared his simple success formula for virtually guaranteed appreciation: "Buy houses where people want to go." Simple, right?

Common sense tip: Ask yourself if the area you are researching is at-tractive to retirees. The 55+ age group in the U.S. controls over three quarters of America's wealth, according to the International Council of Shopping Centers. This is why I like the Sunbelt (Southern Hemisphere of the U.S.): warmer climates in front of Boomer migration from cold, Northern states.

A link is provided to view population growth trends by MSA here: www.SafeCashFlow.com

Affordability – This is my favorite area of research. This lesson con-tradicts popular thinking that peak market values, from 2004 to 2007, reflect future prices. Let me illustrate why this isn't the case.

Picture two entrepreneurial-minded grade school children selling candy bars. One kid sells them for 50-cents, the other for $1. The student sell-ing his chocolate bars for $1 only asks for 5 cents now, with the 95-cent balance due at the end of the semester. Which kid is likely to sell more candy bars? Right! The kid that appeals to our short-sighted nature, of-fering a deferred payment plan. Now, think about this for a second… if she sells a box of her goods at $1 per candy bar, with these terms, does it mean the market value of candy bars rises to $1? Heck no! At the end of the semester, most of her customers will default on their promise. She'll stop offering such lenient purchase terms, and candy bars will be sold for 50 cents again.

And there we have our credit crisis in a nutshell. During the height of our market, in '06 and '07, buyers were borrowing up to NINE TIMES their annual income to purchase properties, many of them as specula-tors: absentee owners with no physical or emotional tie to their proper-ties. It's not a coincidence this happened most in the high foreclosure states: Florida, California, Nevada, and Arizona.

When you have buyers purchasing homes via stupidly-attractive finance terms, prices with those purchase arrangements are NOT relevant. So, why do so many investors ask "What did the property sell for during the height of the market?" The answer is they don't have smarter questions that point to TRUE value:

1. What is the cost per square foot of this property vs. replacement cost?

2. How much income does the property produce relative to price (capitalization rate)?

3. How does the purchase price compare to local incomes?

I'll expound on the relevance of each question.

Cost per square foot vs. Replacement cost: If it costs $15,000 to build a car, including material costs and labor, and you are able to buy that vehicle for $10,000, it's obvious to see you achieved a legitimate discount. Likewise, if you can buy a house for less money than it costs to build it brand new, you may have a legitimate deal.

Considering the cost of land, entitlement, horizontal infrastructure (power, water, sewer, roads, street lights, sidewalks, etc.), material costs to go vertical, labor, marketing and selling costs, and the builder's profit, it's hard to deliver a brand new single family home for less than $80 to $100 per square foot.

Due to an over-saturation of inventory, resale homes are available all over the country for $40 to $70 per square foot (or less). If you buy a home, at say $50 per square foot, and the replacement cost is $90 per square foot, it's just a matter of time before you see the gap close between your price and the price of new construction. For the most part, this is inevitable as resale inventory is absorbed and financing becomes more readily available, thereby bolstering home buyer demand.

Income approach to value: When you're dealing in the entry-level housing space, where many homes are purchased as investments, the income approach to value helps us establish a price ceiling for property values. If the income is high on a property, the price ceiling is softer than if incomes are low.

Let's look at an example (refer to Question #2 at the beginning of the chapter):

Home A and B are both priced at $104k. Coincidentally, both rent for $1,100 per month, but due to lower expenses (property taxes and HOA dues), the net annual income on Home A is more than double that of Home B. If both properties are in comparable risk neighborhoods, Home A has more room for appreciation (a softer price ceiling) than Home B due to the higher returns. All other variables the same, Home B will have less buyers when it is sold again.

It is very realistic to find properties with net returns north of 8% on capital invested. Don't settle for less. Don't make the common mistake of justifying lower returns by speculating on appreciation. Tangible cash flow – a check deposited into your account each month – trumps speculation and provides an added buffer of safety.

$104,000

$104,000

$45 per square foot

Net yearly cash flow: $9,305 (9.9%)

$98 per square foot

Net yearly cash flow: $3,480 (3.7%)

PURCHASE PRICE COMPARED TO MEDIAN INCOMES

Historically, in the U.S., home buyers pay about 3.5 times their annual income for a home. This means a household income of $100k, would, on average, purchase a home priced around $350k. Obviously, some markets like Los Angeles and New York are higher, with home values 5 to 6 times income, but the norm is 3 to 3.5. When home prices run too far from local incomes, housing affordability is stretched and prices have a hard time sustaining. Conversely, if home prices are low relative to local incomes, values have more room to climb.

During the real estate collapse, post-2007, we saw the effect of housing prices that soared way beyond affordability. In my hometown of Orlando, for example, properties were purchased by buyers who borrowed 100% (or more) of purchase prices that were 9 to 10 times their annual income. Like a stretched rubber band, we witnessed prices snap back as hundreds of thousands of borrowers defaulted on their over-extended purchases.

Today, though, this can work FOR us, going the other direction. If affordability is stretched, home prices hit a ceiling. If home prices are low relative to local incomes, the opposite occurs: home prices will rise to match traditional debt to income ratios, with prices between 3 to 3.5 times median annual incomes.

Common sense tip: stay away from liberal, tenant-friendly states. A good starting point to identify easy eviction states is to check out at an Electoral College map that illustrates traditionally red and blue states. Start with red, capitalist states. Then, interview local property managers for average eviction costs and timeframes. If it generally takes more than 2 months to evict a tenant, RUN!.

Quite simply, a safe real estate market has a healthy economy with strong population growth trends. And if it's an affordable market, you'll see higher net returns on your cash and sound appreciation potential. Additionally, if you stay in front of retiree movement within the U.S. and are in a landlord-friendly state, you have further protection from falling prices and rents.

If you follow the steps to identify a bullet-proof macro market, your checklist should look like this:

- High GDP per capita
- High population growth trends
- Affordable market
- Southern hemisphere of the U.S.
- Landlord-friendly state

Now that we've narrowed our high-level search to one or two ideal markets, let's zoom in with a microscope to areas within this market where prices are trending the right direction, absent high crime and bad schools. From there, we'll start putting our local team in place to ensure a seamless, hands-off ownership experience.

If you've been diligent enough to follow the steps above, you are well on your way to establishing long-term financial peace of mind. I'm anxious to continue this journey with you. Go to: www.SafeCashFlow.com for resources to help you start building a high-performing portfolio of homes.

I can't wait to see you on the other side!

P.S. If you were really curious to know how many hotdogs Takeru can inhale in 12 minutes, the answer is 64.5. Got Tums?

About John

John Chin is an investor, real estate coach, and educator. He is the founder of US Investor Network, which provides a full-service solution for investors seeking to capitalize on emerging U.S. markets. His firm provides consultation services, including project feasibility analysis, income evaluation, renovation oversight, and local property management. This "turn key" model enables remote buyers the ability to safely and passively invest in residential income properties.

A U.S. Air Force veteran, John is a licensed real estate broker with over 17 years of experience serving commercial and residential investors, both foreign and domestic. Professional designations include:

CDPE – Certified Distressed Property Expert

GRI – Graduate, Realtors Institute

CIAS – Certified Investor Agent Specialist

CRS – Certified Residential Specialist

TRC – Trans-Referral Certified

ABR – Accredited Buyer Representative

John is passionate about teaching children lessons in self-reliance, love, and sustainability. He believes our social and economic problems can't be solved by adults who currently control the system that created these problems. Driven by a fire to smash the paralyzed status quo, he and a growing community of proactive parents are arming our next generation of INFLUENCE - our youth - with mindsets and skills to make the planet a more prosperous place for all of us. Lemonade businesses, backyard organic farms, and communication games are just a few of the fun ways they are helping children grow into independent-thinking adults. Parents and grandparents can join the movement at: www.ProsperitySeeds.com.

John resides in Orlando, FL with his wife, Amanda, and son, Ethan.

CHAPTER 17

SEVEN I.T. "MUST HAVES" TO RUN A SUCCESSFUL BUSINESS

BY KATHY DAVID, THE "IT" GIRL OF I.T.™

Today, we're much more informed about what's going on around the world than ever before, and we receive information at a much faster pace than we've ever experienced. This is due to the rapidly changing world of Information Technology (I.T.). Professionals are expected to perform at increased levels because of what technology tools can help them achieve.

To grow a successful business, you need to have the right technology tools to market, operate, expand, and optimize it to be competitive in a global economy. Yes, you're part of the global economy; everyone is. Your reach with the help of the Internet currently has no boundaries. You have access to all sorts of information, and you can do business with people from all over the globe…so having the right tech tools in place is essential to the success of your business. Without them, you'll find it difficult to expand your organization in a demanding market-place. In this chapter, I'll be sharing with you seven I.T. "must haves" to run a successful business right now.

1 - WHAT'S YOUR WMP? *WHAT IS WMP?*

WMP is Web Marketing Presence. If you're in business, you must have a WMP! If you don't, and if you think you don't need one, think again. As of June 30, 2012, there were 2,405,510,036 Internet users worldwide according to Internet World Stats. In the U.S., there are 245,203,319 Internet users, representing 78.3% of the U.S. population (as of December 31, 2011). Imagine if you have goods or services you want to promote; the opportunity is vast over the Internet. Having a website and social media presence on Facebook, Twitter, LinkedIn, Instagram, and others is key to the success of your web marketing campaign. Not having a website means you're missing out on new revenue for your business. It's easy to create a website using Wordpress and other online website services.

If you need help, hire someone to create a website for you. Your website, if done correctly, is the hardest-working sales tool you'll ever have to generate more business. Your potential clients access the web 24 hours a day, 7 days a week. WMP really means Winning Marketing Position. When you get new clients through your website, you have a winning marketing position.

2 - IF I GOOGLE YOU, WHAT WILL I FIND? *CAN YOU BE STALKED?*

If I stalk you over the Internet right now using your name, or type in keywords related to your products or services, will I find you? Will you show up in the first page? If not, you need to optimize your website. The first step to successfully marketing your company is building a website, but a website is useless if your customers can't find it. The next step is for you to optimize your online web presence. Here's a short list of optimization actions you can easily take:

SEO – Search Engine Optimization (SEO) is creating content that's relevant to your products or services. Include keywords commonly used in your industry throughout your website. Think about the words people use to search for your products and services online. Over time, Google will index the keywords on your site and help you organically increase your web ranking.

Site Linking – If other sites are linking to your site, your site is popular; therefore, it's useful and gives your website a ranking boost. Once your site page ranking increases, people can find your site faster and easier. The best way to increase your site linking is to comment on blogs, articles, and other online forums and reference your website address. If you have social media accounts, make sure to include your company website in all your profiles. Another way to increase site links to your website is by placing news, press releases, and article syndications over the Internet. The more inbound links you have to your site, the more success you'll have in increasing your World Wide Web ranking.

Google Webmaster Guidelines – Make sure your website is compliant with Google. If your website is full of errors, your website ranking will suffer. To find out how you can optimize your site with Google, sign up for Google Analytics. Then, follow the steps to validate and scan your website. For more information, go to http://support.google.com/webmasters/. Another tool you can use to help improve your website ranking is http://alexa.com.

Once your site is optimized and ready to go, make sure to submit it to the main search engines like Google, Amazon, Yahoo, and Bing, just to name a few. There are other ways you can optimize your site like PPC, Google Ads, Facebook Ads, etc. This is just a short list to get you started. The takeaway here is that you have to become search friendly, or "stalk-able" over the web! The easier it is for your potential clients to find you, the better chance you have to get new opportunities and customers.

3 – WHAT'S YOUR PSA? WHAT ABOUT BAS? *HUH?!*

PSA or BAS aren't the latest teenage communications texting acronyms; they're acronyms for important systems every business should use. PSA is short for Professional Services Automation. BAS is short for Business Automation Solutions. In essence, these two are synonymous, but PSA is used in service-based companies and BAS is used in manufacturing and industrial-type industries.

PSA integrates most or all business productivity functions, like sales, marketing, project tracking, products, inventory, client agreements, client financials, invoicing, trouble tickets, and many more. Typically, a robust PSA has the capability to run your business using one system. Having standalone Customer Relationship Manager (CRM), marketing, financial, project, inventory, procurement, and time and expense tracking software makes it difficult to track and manage "the big picture" because they're separate systems. When you use PSA, all these components are integrated. Using PSA helps you manage all the important aspects of your business in a streamlined and efficient way.

For manufacturing or industrial-type companies, the best BAS to use is Enterprise Resource Planning (ERP) software. All your operations and different departmental functions are all rolled into a system that cross-communicates. This makes it easy to manage your production, and monitor costs, sales, customers, inventory, and much more.

Regardless of what industry you're in, PSA or BAS solutions will help streamline you company's operations. There's nothing more frustrating than using systems that don't talk to each other, plus it makes your work more challenging because additional time is spent with redundant data entry. This can be avoided with PSA or BAS.

4 - SHOW ME THE MONEY!
IN BUSINESS, HAPPINESS IS A POSITIVE CASH FLOW.

Do you believe that happiness is a positive cash flow in a business? I believe it! If you don't have a positive cash flow, then most likely you're depressed and stressed out. To make sure you manage your cash flow and track your business finances, the most important tool to have is a good accounting system. There are many accounting solutions available to businesses, including SAGE, Microsoft Dynamics (formerly known as Great Plains), and the one that might be the most popular, Quick-Books. It's important to keep abreast of your business finances using an accounting system to track revenues, assets, investments and expenses.

Along with a good accounting system, you must have a credit card processing system or PayPal to make it easy for your customers to pay you. A payment processing system will help you collect payments quicker. Once payment is processed through your credit card processor of choice, you can easily track it with an accounting system. In business, happiness is a positive cash flow, so make sure you track it. Your accounting software will help show you the money!

5 - CLOUDING AROUND *GET FORTUNE 500 TECHNOLOGIES AT A FRACTION OF THE COST.*

Do you know that you can set up your company to function like a Fortune 500 company using hosted cloud services? As long as you have Internet access and a computer, you can quickly have a network infrastructure in place, with robust services. Using hosted cloud services is a business technology "must have."

One of the most popular hosted cloud services is hosted email, which helps increase the efficiency of your business through its many new features; employees can boost their productivity by having access to a consistent inbox, calendaring, and contacts experience across PC, browser, and mobile phone platforms. Hosted Exchange offers an enhanced Outlook web app that can be accessed from any browser. Plus, enhancements to mobile access allow you to extend the productivity benefits of Exchange to employees even when they're away from their PC.

Another popular hosted service is SharePoint. Hosted Windows SharePoint is a powerful platform for building shared document repositories, corporate Intranets, and project-specific websites. There's no hardware or software to manage. Windows SharePoint is designed to increase productivity; businesses of any size can leverage it to create document storehouses that increase collaboration within a company, and with its partners, vendors and customers. With Windows SharePoint, you can share documents, calendars, contacts, links, ideas and more without wasting time exchanging inefficient emails.

Most software solutions now are available as a service over the Internet. Accounting software, PSA, ERP, productivity software, and phone system solutions are now available in the cloud. These technologies allow you to operate like a Fortune 500 company...even if you're not close to making that list. With cloud services, the sky's the limit!

6 - VIDEO CONFERENCING *GO GLOBAL FROM THE SEAT OF YOUR OFFICE.*

Gas prices and travel costs are expensive. Having a video conferencing solution will help you connect with people globally without leaving your office. Most video conferencing solutions are available online for free. There are many online video conferencing solutions available, in-

cluding Skype, WebEx, Google Hangout, and Face Time (for Apple users). If you have a mobile phone, you probably have access to a free app
you can use for video conferencing. You can also buy a computer with a
built-in camera or a USB webcam to use with your computer hardware.

If you need a sophisticated solution to use for board meetings or meetings with international clients and/or your global team, investing in a
video conferencing solution is a "must have." Video conferencing gives
you the ability to collaborate in real-time without needing to travel.
Connect with people fast to tackle mission-critical communications for
your organization.

7 - THE LATEST AND THE GREATEST!
MOVE FASTER WITH MOBILE COMPUTING.

The most important I.T. "must have" to run your business efficiently
and successfully is reliable and up-to-date hardware with the latest software operating system installed. Technology is rapidly changing on a
yearly basis (or less), and having the right technology tools in place is
essential to operating your business.

Mobility is a big factor in end-user computing. Mobile computing and
being able to access information for work – using phones, laptops, or
tablet devices – is the new standard in enterprise computing. Desktop
computers are still commonly used, but typical computer users have at
least two other devices they use to access the Internet and work elec-
tronically.

For me, I have a total of four devices I use for work: a desktop, laptop,
tablet, and mobile phone. This may seem like overkill, but it's not for a
busy and mobile professional like me. It's essential that I have access to
my company information regardless of where I am. When I'm in my office, I use my desktop. When I'm working from home, I use my laptop,
and when I'm meeting with clients on the road, I use my tablet because
it's lightweight and I can easily carry it with me everywhere I go. Then,
of course, I have my phone for easy access to my email and the ability
to handle important communications while I'm on the go.

Professionals today are much more demanding with what hardware they
want to use for work. They also often demand to use their own equipment instead of company-owned equipment. Most companies can't

keep up with the rapid changes and still have old, outdated systems. It's typically too costly for organizations to upgrade systems when newer technologies become available. The recent movement to accommodate the demands of employees who want to use their own devices to work is called BYOD (Bring Your Own Device). There are security concerns with BYOD, but if it's implemented correctly, it creates a win-win for employees and employers. Employers benefit from the annual savings per employee, and employees use newer and better equipment to do their work. Everyone is happy! Also, make sure to replace old hardware. Make the investment and replace old legacy systems to improve your employees' and organization's productivity.

BONUS! Extra IT "Must Have" to Run A Successful Business

It's the "It" Girl of I.T.™ *Need I say more?*

This is a bonus tip! The bonus I.T. "must have" for your business is me, the "It" Girl of I.T.™! [giggling]. This might sound corny to you, but I'm really serious. I am! Are you getting a kick out of this yet? Yeah, I know [grinning from ear to ear]. I couldn't help it. I try to inject a bit of my cheesy humor here and there to make things a little more interesting.

In all seriousness, one of the most important I.T. "must haves" for your company is a reliable and dependable I.T. support and service provider. Technology is just a tool to run a business; you've got to leave its management to the experts.

Most computer users I know have a love-hate relationship with their computers. I've had someone tell me that computers are a necessary evil. I know this is a harsh statement, but to most people, there's some truth in it. When you're running a business, the last thing you want to worry about is for your organization to be dealing with computer issues. Successful companies rely on I.T.-managed service providers to manage their whole network infrastructure. Find a dependable and reputable I.T. service provider to help you with this. Regardless of what business you're in, leveraging technology tools to operate your business is necessary; it's essential to the success of your company's operation.

About Kathy

Kathy David, CEO and President of IT Tech Pros, Inc., is known as The "It" Girl of I.T. ™ Since 2006, her company has supported small to medium-size businesses by providing their own brand of managed services, overseeing their unique computing, networking and applications needs. Kathy prides herself on providing scalable and customized IT solutions that are proven, cost-effective and flexible.

Kathy has an extensive background in information technology, business management, business development and entrepreneurship, and she's also a published author. She contributed to the book, *The Power of Leadership – Finding the Leader Within,* and published a how-to manual, *Do I.T. Yourself – Insider Tips to PC Tune-Ups.* Currently, she writes about IT-related topics on her company's blog at: www. it-techpros.com/blog .

Kathy is active in the San Diego community, and her involvement hasn't gone unnoticed. The *San Diego Business Journal* honored her as a Woman Who Means Business in 2006. She won the Asian Heritage Award for excellence in entrepreneurship in 2010, and in 2012 she was a nominee for the *San Diego Magazine* Woman of the Year award, receiving recognition for her diligent and hardworking efforts to promote positive growth and vibrancy in her local community.

To learn more about Kathy, and how you can receive a copy of her how-to manual for free, visit www.it-techpros.com. You can also follow Kathy on Twitter at @kathydavidittp and subscribe to her blog at: www.it-techpros.com/blog . For more information about Kathy or her company, call 888-484-7767.

www.it-techpros.com

CHAPTER 18

DON'T BE AN OSTRICH, BE A SWAN

BY KATHY NOLAN

Women......

Picture this. You are gliding through life, head held high, poised and confident. You have a definitive purpose. Every part of your being is relaxed and at peace – mind, body, and spirit. You are secure and quite comfortable being on your own. In fact, you relish the simplicity. ...Accountable to no one other than yourself. ...Easy.

Well, I'm sorry to disturb the reverie, but for most women this is not reality. Well, why can't it be? I'm here to show you how.

First, a little background.

Our societal roles as nurturers and caregivers have overshadowed our financial proclivity – to women's own detriment, I might add. With over 65% of women controlling the wealth in our country, why is it that most women feel like the ostrich, hiding our heads in the sand, when it comes to managing our finances?

For over three decades, it has pained me to see women crushed by their own admitted lack of knowledge, confidence and planning for financial security. I would like to share three of my most poignant stories. Perhaps one may sound familiar to you or someone you know.

Penny had six children. She was a dedicated and loving wife and a "super" mom, with her family being the center of her universe. Her husband John was one of the hardest working men I had ever known. One day, as darkness descended on the jobsite, he decided to take a short nap in his van before working into the night. Since it was January, and quite cold outside, he left the engine running to keep it warm inside. He must have fallen into a deep sleep and did not notice that the van had run out of gas. In the morning, Penny was frantic that he had not come home the night before. When the police found the van, it was determined that John had died of carbon monoxide poisoning from a leaky gas line. It was New Year's Day. There was no life insurance. Six months later, their home was foreclosed. All karate, dance lessons, and soccer camps were done, too. The oldest had to drop out of college to help support the family. If only I had convinced them to purchase that life insurance policy, instead of letting them procrastinate. John had said they could not afford it, and besides he was as healthy as an ox and "not going anywhere" for a very longtime. Life has a way of throwing you a curve ball when you least expect it, just the same.

After several very difficult years, Penny had the courage and tenacity to go back to school at age 42 and became a Licensed Nurse Practitioner. She now has great medical benefits, a retirement account, and weekends off to go to baseball and soccer games. Her oldest son is doing well as a licensed electrician and is about to bless Penny with her first grandchild. She insisted that he and his wife purchase term life policies while they were still young; ones that were affordable and could be converted to permanent insurance later on if they wanted. After all his mom had endured, he understood the value and immediacy of having life insurance. There was no resistance from the expectant parents whatsoever.

Lori was a kind, intelligent, divorced woman whose mom had left her a substantial inheritance from their family business. Since Lori was never really into learning about investments, she decided to go with a broker who convinced her he would take care of everything, and that she didn't have to worry. When she would ask questions and try to learn about her investments, he would respond in a condescending tone that she wouldn't understand and that it was probably over her head anyway. When she came to me from a referral, I was appalled hearing about how she was treated, and thoroughly disgusted to learn she had lost over half of her inheritance in two short years. She had told her broker she was very conservative and did not want to lose what her parents had worked their whole lives to save. Unfortunately, he did not listen to what she wanted, and instead invested much more aggressively. It was hard for her to learn to trust a financial advisor again, but after three meetings of just getting to know each other, we were both confident that we would be a good fit. After encouraging Lori to attend my Savvy Women's Club Class Series, she is much more confident and not at all afraid to ask lots of questions before she makes any financial decisions. She has become a great role model to her daughters who have now graduated college with no school loans and have begun successful careers of their own. Liz is a graphic designer and Kari is a psychologist. Lori and I have encouraged them to learn about their investments and to spend less and save more. They are well on their way to becoming Smart Savvy Women.

Diane and Bill were married for 24 years. They were blessed with three great kids, two sons and one daughter. After years of study and clawing her way up the corporate ladder, Diane continued working long hours after Will was born so that Bill could finish his law degree. Life was hectic, but good for many years. She managed to attend most of the school functions, get the kids to their various sports, and even serve as a group leader for Kacie's Girl Scout troop. Since Bill usually worked late, she was also responsible for arranging home repairs, car mainte-nance, planning family vacations and juggling the monthly expenses. After Bill's Dad passed away, Diane also looked in on her mother-in-law several times a week and arranged her doctor's appointments and trips to the grocery store and hairdresser. What an incredible woman! Totally selfless, she dedicated herself to serving everyone in her life with love and grace.

She admits she was probably too busy to notice, but Bill had been spend-ing more and more time at the office – late nights and even weekends and the occasional conference out of town. She really thought he was just working hard for the family. Shortly before their 24th wedding an-niversary, Bill announced that he didn't want to be married anymore – just like that! Diane was a mess, the kids were acting out, and their son Will even blamed her for driving Dad away. Bill, on the other hand, got himself a new Harley, took skydiving lessons, and purchased a very expensive Rolex watch. He had a new girlfriend 15 years younger with two small children.

You can probably imagine how the rest of the story goes, but when it came to the divorce, it was the war of the roses.

Diane had not contributed much to her retirement plan because Bill had said that his plan was better, so they maxed out contributions to his. A forensic accounting of their finances uncovered two separate bank and investment accounts that Bill had apparently set up to receive the yearly bonuses he had gotten from the firm. A tidy sum for sure. The credit cards were nearly maxed out with all the recent purchases and trips to the Caribbean and Las Vegas, dinners out and lavish gifts to the girlfriend and her kids. He had also convinced her that they should take a home equity loan on the house so that "they" could buy that sailboat they always wanted. It was not a pretty picture at all. To make matters worse, he was very aggressive with their investments and the last two market declines had really put a huge dent in their accounts.

Like many women, she opted for the family home in the divorce settlement instead of the investments. He had a great lawyer, who managed to leave Diane with a great deal less than she probably should have received, and her lawyer didn't fight too hard on her behalf. Once the real estate market took a major downturn, Diane lost most of the equity that was left and found it harder and harder to keep up with the increase in property taxes and cost of home repairs. She is now 57, still has one child attending a community college and living at home. She sold the house, but barely came out with enough to purchase a townhome with a 30-year mortgage, closer to her job. Fortunately, she earns a pretty decent salary, so she is trying to contribute a good amount to her 401k. Most of the friends she once had have moved on – since she couldn't afford to keep up with the lifestyle. Bill married the girlfriend, is now raising her two kids and they live in a brand new 5000 square foot home in her old hometown. Last time I ran into him, he looked old, bald and fat!

Through all of this heartache and pain, one of the good things that came out of it is that she came to me. Once devastated and broken, she is now strong, very knowledgeable about her investments, and confident that she will be ok.

We made sure that Bill had to purchase enough life insurance to leave something for her and the kids if he partied himself to death, and we set Diane up with a systematic and structured savings plan. In addition, we rolled over her old retirement accounts into a fixed indexed annuity, so she'll receive a guaranteed income for life to supplement her social security when she retires. Good things do come to good people; a modest inheritance from an aunt allowed us to create a conservative managed portfolio of income-generating investments – which we earmarked for Long Term Care insurance. After refinancing the mortgage for a lower interest rate, she is able to pay down the balance much faster. Oh, did I forget to mention....she sold the engagement ring and gaudy necklace he had given her after a "business trip" and used the money to upgrade her life insurance so she would have something to leave the kids. One of the most touching compliments I have ever received as a financial advisor is when she told me that it was like God had sent her a Guardian Angel – and it was me! She was a new woman, and would be just fine.

There are many more stories that I can share, but I think you get the idea.

Women tend to put themselves last before family, friends and even co-workers. We are great at multi-tasking, but our financial health is usually way down on the to-do list. When a transitional life event occurs like a divorce, a death, an illness, or a job loss, this behavior can be a recipe for disaster.

Fortunately or not, more and more women are having to learn this lesson the hard way. You can change that. Here are some ways to become a Smart Savvy Woman.

Become a SWAN...

1. **Know your numbers:** You have to do the work. How much do you need to meet your monthly living expenses? Be thorough. Include the usual stuff like mortgage or rent, property taxes, insurances (home, car, life, and health), utilities, cell phone and Internet. Don't forget cosmetics and beauty care (haircuts, nails, etc.), food and grocery, car payments, credit cards (hopefully not too much), gym memberships, subscriptions to magazines & newsletters, travel expense (gas, tolls, trains or buses). Don't forget gifts for birthdays, weddings, showers and holidays, clothing, shoes, accessories. What about that daily Starbucks? Then there are bottles of wine or cocktails, ...and entertainment expenses: meals out, movies, etc. It all adds up.

This is probably the BEST exercise for learning about your spending habits. It will probably shock you and also help you to decide what you really NEED, and what you just WANT. Maybe some compromise is needed to reach your financial goals?

2. **Trim the FAT:** I know it sounds like we are always dieting, but this can actually be fun. If you really enjoy that daily latte or a girl's night out, then you should have it. Just like a food diet, total deprivation will surely leave you depressed and result in a binge-spending spree you'll feel guilty about.

This is about moderation and self-control. You write your own rules. Just be sure to follow them as best as possible and be willing to adjust them if necessary.

3. **Know your purpose:** What drives you? Take some alone time to really think about this. What do you want to accomplish? What is extremely important to you? Is there something that really excites you every time you think about it? Start a charitable foundation, write a book, change careers, learn Italian, travel to Tahiti, start a business, secure a family legacy? Whatever it is, how would you feel when you achieve it? Proud... successful...confident...complete?

4. **Be your own GPS:** Know where you are going by knowing where you are. Once you know your "number" ...your needs, you can work towards your goals ...your "wants." Having and establishing goals are great, but unless you know where you are, how can you hope to get there?

5. **Work with an advisor who "gets" you:** Having the right chemistry is extremely important to your success. A good advisor will listen and nod. A great advisor will ask you lots of questions and help you to "know your numbers," encourage you to find your "purpose," and collaborate with you to set short, medium, and long term goals that are achievable and realistic. She will also facilitate open and honest communication. No sugar coating here. It does not serve you or your advisor very well.

6. **Realize that you are unique:** Even though we often look to friends and family for their support or approval, everyone's

personal and financial situation are different. We don't all look great in the same colors or styles, no matter how designer chic they might be. Well, the best financial plan for you is not a one-size-fits-all either. Again, working with the right financial advisor will enable you to design a custom fit that will feel comfortable and appropriate.

7. **Cover all the bases:** A custom-tailored financial plan will be well complemented by having the proper legal documents in place. A caring and knowledgeable attorney will have no problem teaming up with your financial and tax advisor to make sure you and your loved ones are protected. Be sure to have periodic reviews to make sure your documents are current – as laws do change as well as family circumstances.

8. **Get a Financial Physical at least once a year:** Sooner if you are in transition due to a life-changing event like separation, divorce, widowhood, or RETIREMENT.

9. **Continue to seek knowledge:** You do not have to be an expert, but it helps to have a basic understanding so you know the right questions to ask, and to know if you are being heard and not dismissed.

10. **Plan to live a long time:** Just as a man, your family, or the government is NOT a retirement plan, working forever is probably not a viable option either. Who will want to hire you when you're 90? Women live a LONG time. Keep income streams substantial and plan for long term health care.

11. **Encourage a friend not to be an ostrich:** Be a SWAN.

It's never too late to start. Just do the best you can and have a great life!

Visit our website at **www.FFFGonline.com** to request information, receive a complimentary Financial Physical, or learn about our unique Savvy Women's Club.

The life you have led doesn't need to be the only life you'll have.

~ Anna Quindlen

About Kathy

Kathy Nolan is President and Founder of Family Focus Financial Group.As a 37-year veteran of the financial industry, Kathy has had a career that spans many areas of finance. Early in her career, she held positions with multiple prominent Wall Street firms including Oppenheimer, Janney Montgomery Scott and RC Stamm and Company. After her son Sean was born, she left Wall Street to have more flexibility in her career and family life. Kathy then expanded her financial knowledge to include Insurance and Real Estate and worked for Met Life, with a focus on helping small business owners provide health insurance coverage, retirement planning, succession planning and estate preservation. Kathy also worked as the East Coast and Midwest Regional Director for several Insurance Marketing Organizations—recruiting and training agents—before becoming totally independent. In 2007, she formed Family Focus Financial Group with her son Sean. Together they serve all of Central and Northern New Jersey, as well as others throughout the State. Kathy is also licensed in several additional states so that she may service referrals as well as clients who have moved.

Kathy is committed to listening first, then guiding her clients to a financial plan that matches their objectives and family values. As the president of Family Focus Financial Group, and an Investment Advisor Representative with Global Financial Private Capital, LLC*, her well-rounded knowledge base affords her clients a reputable and competent professional that they can count on. She is a registered member of the National Ethics Bureau, and an active member of NAIFA (National Association of Insurance and Financial Advisors). Kathy serves on the Board of Directors and acts as Fundraising Chair for C.A.S.A., a 501c3 organization that serves children and families in the Foster Care system who have been victims of abuse and neglect. She is also a member of Soroptimist International - Jersey Shore, a 501c3 organization whose mission is to help women and children in need.

Kathy is dedicated to helping families become successful at managing, saving, and protecting their assets. She is especially passionate about empowering women to become engaged in their financial lives through knowledge and planning.

Kathy has been a lifelong resident of New Jersey. She has been married for over 35 years and has two sons.

Contact Kathy at: Kathy@FFFGonline.com

*Kathleen A. Nolan is an Investment Advisor Representative. Investment Advisory Services offered through Global Financial Private Capital, LLC, an SEC Registered Investment Advisor. Neither Kathleen A. Nolan nor Global Financial Private Capital gives tax or legal advice.

CHAPTER 19

THE FIVE DO'S AND DON'TS FOR THE LIFE INSURANCE BUYER

BY KYLE BLACKBURN

The most important thing to consider when buying life insurance is to determine what your need is and for how long.

When people come in my office I always ask the question "how did you decide how much insurance you need?" Usually the answer I get is a blank stare or "I don't know."

Mistake number one is buying the wrong kind of coverage. When you sit down with your insurance professional, if he starts off asking you how much do you have to spend as a starting point, you probably need a new advisor. Your needs and concerns should be the first thing discussed not how much money you have to spend.

Some interesting facts: most term insurance policies never end up in a death claim. Less than ½ of 1% of all term policies issued end up in a death claim. This is not because the insurance company will not pay, they most certainly will…if you die. The problem is that you probably will not die during the specified time period, and when your policy is up for renewal, the premium will likely increase to a price you can't, or do not want, to pay.

Term policies are just that, a policy for a specified term. If you have a short term need like a loan or something of that nature, term is perfect, or if you simply do not have the financial capability to pay for something more permanent.

Most of our clients need a long-term solution. There are many choices out there for "permanent" insurance. We feel like the best two choices are universal life and index universal life.

Universal life is a permanent product with a flexible premium and death benefit with a projected interest crediting rate determined by the company. It also has a guaranteed rate. Most "guaranteed" interest rates are in the 2%-3% range.

Index Universal is similar in that it also is a flexible premium and face amount product. The difference is that the interest credited is based on some index. Usually this is the S&P, but there are many choices available. The crediting on index products is usually limited by some kind of a "cap". This determines the maximum return you could have in any one given year.

If you are buying permanent coverage, ALWAYS buy a guaranteed product if you are buying it for the death benefit.

If you are trying to decide if you should buy index universal or regular universal life for long term insurance coverage, always look at the GUARANTEE not the projection! I have been in this business for over 27 years. I have seen several thousand life insurance statements over that period of time. I have never seen a statement on an existing policy more than a few years old that matched the original projection shown at the time of sale. That's right, never.

I am not saying that somewhere they don't exist, all I am saying is in 28 years and after looking at several thousand, I have never seen one (kind of like a unicorn or bigfoot).

If you are trying to decide what policy is better between regular universal and index universal and they both have the same guarantee to age 120 (most permanent policies today project to age 120) pick the index product. Since they both guarantee to age 120 the index product has a much better chance of producing a greater cash value. This can be handy later down the road for various reasons.

One of those is if you become sick. If your health takes a significant turn for the worse and you have cash value in your policy, it is possible that you may want to suspend your premium and let the policy "feed" off of the existing cash inside.

For example if you have $50,000 in cash value in your policy and your premium is $15,000 your policy would last about 3 years without you paying any more in premium.

There is no reason to give the company more premium than necessary to achieve the ultimate result. We often have our clients suspend their premiums when their health takes a turn for the worse since you do not get both the cash value and the death benefit (unless you buy something called Option B – which is not a good buy in my opinion).

Ok, now you have decided what type of policy you want to buy, but how much should you buy?

Most companies will issue 20 times income on a younger person and 10 times income on someone older. They will also issue more than that if you can show a reason you need the coverage. Like if you have 20 children, or large loans to cover a buy-sell agreement with a business partner, large estate taxes, or you just really love buying life insurance (just kidding on that last one).

When a customer comes into my office, we have a discussion about their needs and goals. After that, they always ask me how much insurance do I think they need. I could spend the next 5000 pages telling you stories about people I know that actually had some insurance on the spouse, the spouse died, and within 5 years or less they were out of money. This is because they either spent the money foolishly, or more likely, they were woefully under-insured.

People think that $250,000 sounds like a lot of money and it is. However, if your spouse makes $100,000 a year and you need that to continue your current standard of living it will not take long to deplete your $250,000 worth of insurance money.

I have seen many wives have to go back to work, move out of their house, take their kids out of the school they were in, and struggle, because they thought that they had plenty of insurance.

What I am saying is to give serious consideration to what the economic loss would be if one of the spouses were to die. I like the idea of buying enough insurance so the remaining spouse could live off the interest from the death benefit while leaving the corpus alone. Also, you would want to take into consideration any other income that the survivor would have, like pension money, social security, or interest from other accumulated assets.

So, to summarize:

If you are young and do not have much money, buy term and buy as much as you can afford. Hope you make more money as you get older or have a lesser need for insurance in the future.

If you have a short-term need like a loan or you just want to get your kids through college, term may also be fine for you. If you have a long term need like taking care of your spouse, income replacement, estate taxes or a buy-sell agreement, then permanent insurance is probably more of a fit for you.

The next question is one I often hear. "What company should I buy?" This is a very important question. Lets start with term insurance.

If you need term only for a short-term need, it doesn't really matter what company you buy from. Buy the one that is the least expensive since they will all pay the same if something were to happen. I would always buy from a company that has a rating of at least "A" from one of the reputable rating agencies. Standard and Poor's is the best rating agency in my personal opinion. Prices on term insurance vary wildly between companies for the exact same coverage. For example, take a male of 50 who wants to buy $1,000,000 of 20-year term. Assuming he is a standard rate, based on todays rates the least expensive company would be about $3,300 per year. Or you could buy the exact same coverage from a different company and pay $5,590! It pays to shop around.

I know what you really like is going from insurance salesman to insurance salesman day after day to shop rates, because you have nothing better to do and this is how you get your kicks. Ha-ha!

Seriously, there is an easier way. You can go to the Internet and go to: www.term4sale.com. This is a site that has most of the available companies all in one single grid sheet. It will show you just about every company you would want to consider on a page or two sorted by cost. This same resource can also be used for permanent insurance. However, there are many variables that it will not show you. It will not show all the different riders that you may or may not be interested in.

You may want to show a cash rollover from an existing policy that is outdated and not guaranteed, you may want a long term care rider of some kind, you may want a critical illness rider, you may want a 'waiver of premium' rider or many other choices that you really would need to discuss with an agent familiar with various companies and choices, since every company is different as to what they offer and how the various choices work.

I said earlier that I have seen many thousands of existing policy statements. It is my opinion that a lot of the policies already in existence need to be reviewed and replaced with new coverage. If your policy was not very recently issued then you should have someone with vast knowledge of companies and products take a look at what you have – to make sure it is the best fit for your needs.

A lot of existing policies that I see are not guaranteed or the premium being paid is too much for the coverage. Most of the time you can buy a new policy that is guaranteed and pay a lower premium than you are paying currently. I strongly suggest if you have existing coverage, especially permanent coverage, that you review what you have to make sure you are getting the biggest bang for your hard-earned buck.

With the explosion of long term care cost in the last few years, and the huge cost increase for stand-alone policies to pay for this cost, some life insurance companies have developed some very nice riders you can purchase that are very affordable to help with this huge risk most people have.

In America, 1 out of 2 people will need some kind of long term care assistance in their lifetime. But the cost of stand-alone policies has skyrocketed and some companies have even completely stopped offering policies at any cost. The companies that remain are no longer offering guaranteed premium policies. It is my opinion that the cost of care will continue to escalate at an alarming rate, and the companies that remain for stand-alone coverage will be forced to raise their premiums to a point that most people will have to cancel their coverage – because they will no longer be able to afford it.

If you look at the various riders available for your life insurance you will see that these riders are very affordable and are guaranteed, unlike stand-alone policies. Everyone knows somebody that has had to pay for a long-term care situation. Most people have experienced this with someone in their own family. This cost can literally wipe you out. It breaks my heart to see someone that has skimped and saved their whole life to build up a nest egg to leave to their heirs only to see it completely wiped out in a very short amount of time due to a long-term care issue. I am not only talking about nursing home stays here. I am talking about assisted living, home health care and nursing home stays.

When I discuss this risk with clients, they are all very aware of the cost and the destruction that this can cause to their finances. Many times one spouse will need the coverage and it will wipe out all of their savings - leaving the surviving spouse destitute. So much for the "golden years."

The objections that our ciients have to purchasing stand-alone coverage are that the cost is too high, the premium is not guaranteed and if they don't use it they have wasted their money. I do agree with this assess-ment. But if you buy a rider on your life policy, the premium is guaran-teed, the cost is not prohibitive, and if you never use the coverage your heirs will get the death benefit.

I strongly recommend that anyone buying permanent coverage today look at these fantastic riders. The good ones pay for all levels of care. In other words no matter what level of care you need, it will cover it.

The three levels are home health care, assisted living and nursing home. I had a client the other day say "the government will pay for it." I told them that is true. However, the downside to that is you have to be desti-tute before that takes place, and they only pay in a nursing home of their choice not yours, not to mention the problem of the surviving spouse and his or her needs. And of course, the heirs would receive nothing because it was all eaten up by the cost of care.

No more than these riders cost, they should seriously be considered. Make sure you buy a policy that is an "indemnity" policy. In other words, when you qualify for the benefit (this is usually triggered by not being able to perform 2 of the 6 activities of daily living), the benefit is paid directly to you. You do not want to buy one where the benefit is paid to the facility. Also, look for one that has a waiver of premium when you go on claim. Wouldn't it be nice not to have to pay for your life insurance anymore during this time of need?

There are so many different uses for life insurance too numerous to mention here. I have tried to give you a general overview of some of the topics I think are of the most value, and I am asked about the most. If you are considering buying some life insurance, or you have not had your current coverage reviewed in the last year, I strongly recommend you go to see an independent agent that can represent a variety of different companies.

I hope this was informative and useful to you. If you have any questions and would like to contact me, my information is contained in the bio section.

About Kyle

Kyle Blackburn is a well-known speaker, trainer and financial advisor. He has been in the financial services industry for over 27 years. He has won numerous awards and distinctions over this time. His firm has been the top producer for many companies over the years.

He works with a team of attorneys, accountants, and other financial experts to design and implement financial plans and strategies to maximize clients' income and estate maximization and preservation. Kyle and his team specialize in conservative strategies to accomplish the specific goals their clients need and desire.

Kyle can be reached at:
- Office: 405-721-3512 ex 225
- Email: kyle@blackburnfinancial.com
- Mailing address: 4901 NW Expressway, Oklahoma City, OK 73132

CHAPTER 20

THE "ENHANCED PROCESS" OF SELLING HEALTHCARE SERVICE COMPANIES

BY PAUL MARTIN

The sale of your healthcare services business will probably represent one of the most important financial decisions of your entire life, and, if properly structured, will allow you to achieve financial freedom for you and your family. The "sale" process is extremely complex and is filled with major decisions and roadblocks. I firmly believe that you as the business owner need professional guidance, and the process should be what we consider, an "Enhanced Process." An Enhanced Process for the sale of your company will ensure that your business has been confidentially exposed to all potential acquirers; it will leverage the specific values that the acquirer will receive; and it will promote structure over simply price. This process will get you the business owner, more money for your business than simply finding a single buyer and selling your business. Why is this process absolutely necessary and so successful?

1. Buyers in the healthcare services industry are "pros" at buying companies; you, as a business owner, are not. They buy multiple companies per year; you will do this once in a lifetime. You must put a "pro" on your side and apply a process and systems to your approach.

2. Price is not nearly as important as structure and this is where an Enhanced Process will assist you to objectively and analytically choose the best structure to get you the most money in the end.

3. A normal transaction process will discover one or maybe two acquirers; an Enhanced Process contemplates ALL potential qualified acquirers, creating a bidding process that will give you leverage with the buyers.

4. In a normal transaction the acquirer is typically in control of the process, timing, etc.; in an Enhanced Process, you the seller are in control.

In order to help you understand the Enhanced Sale Process we will describe an actual client transaction, keeping confidential the "real" numbers while providing you with numbers that mirror the transaction and describe the value of the Enhanced Process.

A successful transaction has four basic phases, with each phase having specific strategies that will yield the greatest value. The four phases are Preparation, Marketing, Negotiation, and Due Diligence and Legal. We will describe each phase and outline specific strategies in order to enhance value and deal structure.

PHASE ONE - PREPARATION

The Preparation phase is integral to a successful transaction as the information that is developed will be what the buyers will utilize to determine an initial price for the business. The first step of the Preparation phase is the development of a Confidential Business Profile (CBP). The CBP provides a clear picture of the financial and operations performance of the business, highlights the staff and management of the business, and provides an overview of the current specific industry conditions. The most important aspect of the CBP is to clearly highlight the target company's growth opportunities, how the leadership and staff will execute on those opportunities, and the operations and financial outcome of executing on the growth plan. Acquirers are buying the growth and the better you can describe and objectively show that the business and management team can execute on a growth strategy, the more a buyer will pay.

Another important element of the CBP is the calculation of the company's EBITDA (earnings before interest, taxes, depreciation and amortization). This re-cast of your financial statement shows the true earnings of the business as though it were already acquired by the purchaser. It is imperative to make all "reasonable" adjustments to your expenses while not being aggressive to the point of losing credibility with an acquirer. This process is much more of an art than a science and will become a key element in the negotiation of price and terms.

Our example business was a rehabilitation company with nine clinics, approximately $7 million in revenue, and EBITDA of $1.75 million. We showed a clear strategy for the business to grow by two to three clinics per year over the next five years, creating a twenty-plus clinic company that would eventually have revenues of $15 million and an EBITDA of $3 million. The CBP was very specific in describing how and where the growth strategy would be executed, with full buy-in from the owners that the growth strategy was in fact a reality.

> *Acquirers are buying the growth, and the better you can describe and objectively show that the business can execute on a growth strategy, the more a buyer will pay.*

The next step of the Preparation Phase is to create a single page Fact Sheet and a comprehensive Non-Disclosure Agreement (NDA). The Fact Sheet displays the basic financial and operating data with a few basic highlights of the business, without revealing the name of the business. The NDA is tied to the specific Fact Sheet with a reference number.

Next, develop a complete list of all possible acquirers to include strategic and financial acquirers. The list can be developed by your current database, as well as research in the particular industry. An expert in the industry guiding you in this process should have a fully developed list of all acquirers within the industry, and this list will add enormous value to the process.

For our sample company, a Fact Sheet and NDA were developed and a list of ninety possible acquirers was prepared.

PHASE TWO - MARKETING PHASE

The objective of the Marketing Phase is to confidentially expose the business to all qualified acquirers, with the result of selling the business to the acquirer that is the best fit for you and your company. This is the phase where you must take charge of the process by providing the same information and opportunities to all acquirers. This establishes a competitive process (or professional auction) which will always result in a higher price. Transmit a Fact Sheet and referenced NDA to all qualified acquirers with a return receipt to ensure all are opened and viewed. We actually make a personal call to at least 20 of the "key buyers" to ensure that they are invited to the process. This is another area of the process where an industry expert should have those relationships and trust of the acquirers.

> *This is the phase where you must take charge of the process by providing the same information and opportunities to all acquirers. This establishes a competitive process (or professional auction) which will always result in a higher price*

Typically within two to three days, NDA's are executed and sent back to our offices either scanned or via fax. A spreadsheet is developed keeping track of those companies that have formally entered into the process. We typically will give acquirers one week to respond to the Fact Sheet and then we make contact with all companies that are now under confidentiality to discuss the process in greater detail. During that contact, we will outline the timing of the potential transaction, typically giving acquirers two weeks to review the CBP and make an offer in the form of an Indication of Interest or a Term Sheet. A Term Sheet outlines the basic price, terms, and major events to a transaction.

For our sample company, thirteen NDA's were returned within one week, and within three weeks, seven Term Sheets were sent to us, four from strategic acquirers and three from financial acquirers.

PHASE THREE - NEGOTIATION PHASE

Phase three is where the Enhanced Process begins to truly separate from the traditional investment banking auction process. A full analysis of all offers is performed, paying close attention to the "real" value of each offer. This analysis requires a spreadsheet tool that will clearly display and compare each component of the transaction, i.e. cash, notes, equity, salaries, etc. In addition, we rank the "execution risk." Execution risk is the level of confidence we have that an acquirer will actually close the deal. This somewhat subjective criteria is based on the history of the particular acquirer, capital sources, the description of the due diligence process and the depth of the team performing the acquisition. This analysis typically will eliminate certain buyers based on an overall ranking of their initial offers. This step requires professional assistance and is critical as it streamlines the process to focus on the best acquirers, not wasting any time with the "also rans." We have found that this step also creates a dynamic that results in buyers giving a better offer first, which starts the negotiation at a higher level than if an acquirer knows they are the only buyer. We firmly believe and have clear evidence to suggest that this aspect of the overall process will increase values by greater than twenty five percent as compared to a typical sale process.

For our sample company, we narrowed the field from seven that made offers to three that would move to the next step in the process, the management meetings.

The three or so finalists are then invited to meet face-to-face with the owners of the company. These meetings typically will take place near the seller's business, but not on-site so as to avoid any breach of confidentiality. Typically a hotel, or at the sellers accounting or legal firm works well. We spend hours preparing sellers to formally present their company to the acquiring companies, including a custom presentation to educate the acquirer on the operations and financial results of the business, the management structure, the marketing and development systems, and opportunities and specific plans for growth. These meetings are critical, as the next step will be to request the acquirers to make their "best offer" in the form of a written Letter of Intent (LOI) within one week from the time of these meetings.

LOI's are then received, analyzed and compared. A negotiation will then be initiated with those companies that have been chosen based on a combination of the management meetings and their final offers. In some cases negotiations commence with all of the finalists, or sometimes, just one.

With our sample company, one of the acquiring companies stood out based on a Letter of Intent that showed a return to the sellers that was 20% higher than the other two offers. They also felt that they would work best with that company based on critical values that were a clear match.

The negotiating process has also been shown to increase price, but just as importantly, to improve the structure of the offers. It also ensures that you have truly chosen the best buyer that is available in the market, as no rocks are left unturned.

At this point, the seller's attorney will do a review of the Letter of Intent. A couple of the key items in the LOI that are somewhat legal in nature, but extremely important are the "non shop" provision and "access to employees and referrals sources." It is important to limit the "non shop" period to ninety days or less, as this will stipulate that you are no longer able to talk to any other buyer during that time period. In addition, be sure to stage any access to your employees and referral sources to the end of the due diligence period, as this can be highly sensitive to those sources and staff. In our sample company, we were able to limit the "non shop" period to 60 days, which was a huge plus for our client. If the process started to deteriorate for any reason with the chosen acquirer, they could go back to the other companies who had made offers, and they would still be fresh and ready to proceed. This is another major advantage to our Enhanced Process.

Negotiation requires professional assistance and is critical, as it streamlines the process to focus on the best acquirers, not wasting any time with the "also rans."

PHASE FOUR - THE DUE DILIGENCE AND LEGAL PHASE

The final phase of the transaction process is where the real work starts, as the legal process can be tedious and the initial purchase price must be protected. Typically the acquirer will take responsibility to provide a list of all due diligence information that they would like to review. I was told by a Financial Buyer many years ago that due diligence is similar to "a living autopsy." Our approach is to set up an electronic secure website that will organize and maintain all of the due diligence materials. We create a folder representing each request and scan and place the requested documents in those folders. If an item is unavailable or does not apply, we have the seller create a one page simple document that states just that, and is signed by the seller. This protects the seller if the buyer would ever come back later stating that they were not provided with all of the requested information.

Phase four will also initiate the legal work. We always recommend to our clients that they utilize an attorney with healthcare transaction experience and we mean <u>real</u> experience. If they do not have an attorney, we assist them in finding a well-qualified healthcare M&A attorney. The acquirer's attorney will typically draft the purchase and sale agreements and other related legal documents.

It is not uncommon for acquirers to review the due diligence information and attempt to "re-trade" the deal, meaning request a lower price based on the findings in due diligence. This is where you absolutely need to have an objective look at the buyer's recommended changes to the transaction by someone who "really" knows healthcare, as many times the purchase price changes are made based on operational or financial changes in the business. A highly skilled specialist will be able work through these negotiations and ultimately protect the initial price and terms.

> *Phase four is where you absolutely need to have an objective look at the buyers recommended changes to the transaction by someone who "really" knows healthcare, as many times the purchase price changes are made based on operational or financial changes in the business, and a highly-skilled specialist must work through these negotiations.*

For our sample company, there were some specific legal and due diligence items that caused our M&A professional to work closely with the seller's attorney and to provide specific information of the coding and metrics within the industry in order to keep the transaction as initially proposed. We are confident that without this skilled intervention this deal could have "blown up!"

The final stage of the Enhanced Process is the Closing. This is an exciting and rewarding time for all, including the acquirer, seller, and all professionals assisting in the transaction. This is typically the culmination of six or more months of work and is when the buyer and seller truly become one! The actual Closing in our current electronic environment will most typically occur at a distance with documents being scanned and sent by email and wire transfers for the exchange of monies.

SUMMARY

In summary, the owners of our sample company sold a majority portion of their business to a strategic acquirer, thereby creating a new company with the acquirer having a majority interest and the seller having a minority interest. The multiple of EBITDA was >5 and they were paid

95% of the majority portion that they sold in cash. The owners receive monthly distributions based on their equity position in the newly formed company and will have a built in sale mechanism in the future to sell their remaining interest to the acquiring entity, at the same multiple with which they bought the majority portion. The owners have five year employment agreements and will be a big part of the continued growth, utilizing the capital and resources of the acquiring company.

The sale of a business is a highly complex process that involves multiple steps and is performed by multiple people. In the life of most business owners, it is a one-time event that will be the single most important financial decision of their lives. The "Enhanced Process" of taking your company through this endeavor will ensure you that are receiving the best price and terms that the industry has to offer!

About Paul

Paul Martin, Martin Healthcare Advisors (MHA) founder and president, is a nationally-recognized expert on the development, management and eventual exit strategies for healthcare services businesses in the middle market. Since 2000, he has successfully assisted more than 500 healthcare businesses maximize value and profitably through the development and execution of strategic business and succession plans. As a consultant, mentor and speaker, Paul draws from his long history of success in healthcare mergers and acquisitions, business development, healthcare reimbursements and operations to show business owners how to create significant value throughout their entire organizations. Paul has authored more than 50 industry articles and publishes a weekly newsletter, *Paul Martin's Friday Morning Moment.*

Prior to MHA, Paul founded Physical Therapy and Sport Services, P.C., which he built to revenues of $15 million and personally negotiated the company's sale to NovaCare Inc. in 1996.

In addition to his master's degree in Physical Therapy from Hahnemann University, Paul earned the prestigious "Certified Business Intermediary" (CBI) and "Merger & Acquisition Master Intermediary" (M&AMI) certification designations by the International Business Brokers Association (IBBA). These internationally-recognized professional certifications are awarded to M&A Source and IBBA members who have completed coursework, and who have demonstrated proven professional excellence in M&A activity through verified transaction experience.

pmartin@martinhealthcareadvisors.com

CHAPTER 21

PERSONAL RESPONSIBILITY IS THE FOUNDATION OF SUCCESS

BY PETER NEEVES

I was electrocuted when I was eighteen. It was the summer between my freshman and sophomore years at college and I was doing a maintenance project on a building at work. Accidently my left hand came into contact with a one hundred amp main service into the building. The current caused the muscles to lock up and I could not let go. The electricity passed through my upper body and exited out my back which was in contact with a metal pole. I was stuck for about a minute, it seemed like hours. The near-death experience changed me. I became aware that we never know how much time we have; that we are responsible for what we do with our lives – *completely responsible; personally responsible.* Across the following years I thought a lot about that, and studied how others view personal responsibility as I explored this concept and what I was to do with my life, how I was to be my best.

Personal responsibility is about the choices we make. There is no other single factor which influences our success to a greater degree than personal responsibility. We have varying degrees of talent and ability, but personal responsibility will beat talent every time. Success is ours if we own it, if we are responsible for it, personally responsible for it.

The study of personal responsibility is an investment into success. The more we are personally responsible the greater the success, and the greater the happiness. Knowing the common roadblocks and having a plan to develop the habits of personal responsibility will lead to greater success than any other change an individual can make in how they approach life.

THE FIVE ROADBLOCKS TO PERSONAL RESPONSIBILITY

There are five primary roadblocks to personal responsibility. These are the things that stand in our way of being personally responsible. Each of us will experience these obstacles at different levels, with some being more of an issue than others. Identifying the mechanisms by which we are not responsible is the first step toward assuming personal responsibility.

REACTING INSTEAD OF RESPONDING

Reacting instead of responding is an indication that we have failed to listen. Reacting removes our ability to choose our responses; reacting is automatic, generally based on emotion rather than reason. Emotional reaction can only occur when we have failed to fully consider what has been said to us; we have not considered the other person's statements from their perspective. Responding, on the other hand, is making a choice. In taking the seconds or moments to evaluate what we have heard we can select a reasoned response, one not based in fear or emotion. Even when we choose the same response as we would have chosen had we reacted there is an improvement. A response is based in conviction, and lacks the unreasoned emotion of a reaction. To be personally responsible we are responsible for always doing and being our best. Responding instead of reacting improves our communication, the quality of what we say, and helps us to be our more responsible best.

EXPECTATIONS

Expectations can be a major roadblock. We are not responsible for other people's expectations, yet frequently we expend much energy trying to meet them. Being personally responsible is effectively a contractual relationship. For work, the contract establishes that I do a fair day's work for a fair day's pay. In relationships, the contract establishes that I be open and honest. My responsibility for other people's expectations is limited to the extent that I created those expectations. If I said I was going to be somewhere, I need to be there. If, on the other hand, someone expects me to be somewhere and I never committed to being there, that is not my responsibility. That is their expectation, not mine. Any effort I put into honoring expectations that I did not help create detracts from my ability to meet my real responsibilities.

'SHOULDS'

Shoulds' are expectations placed on me by my subconscious. If I consciously placed these expectations then they would be in the form of I will, I do, etc. Should comes from my subconscious on the basis of perceived expectations of others. These are not commitments that I have made. If, for example, I find myself thinking I should keep my kitchen cleaner, I am living up to someone else's standard. If the standard were my own I would not procrastinate on it. There would be no *should*, there would just be *do*. The basis of our 'should' habit is deeply ingrained. Many of these subconscious expectations come from our childhood programming. For example, many of us work toward the idea that all our stuff should be neat and tidy, but that is not how we work best. The expectation is not my own, hence the procrastination, hence even when I do the 'should,' it doesn't stay that way. The word 'should' needs to raise a yellow flag. Any time I hear myself qualifying something with the word 'should,' I need to examine my motivation for undertaking that task.

BEING RIGHT

A famous question asks: "Would you rather be right or rather be happy?" Humans have a desire to always be right, to look good or to look smart. In any disagreement at least one person is wrong to some degree. By the law of averages this makes most of us wrong about one half of the time. As none of us are perfect, none of us are right all of the time. The problem is that we believe what we believe; we assume we are right and the other person is wrong. By questioning what we believe we become open-minded; open to the other person being right. This improves communication as we truly listen to the other person and consider their ideas. In doing so, we also learn and grow. Ceasing to be right all the time improves our relationships, makes us more trustworthy, and allows us to grow and achieve more.

FALSE PRIDE

False pride is arrogance, an overinflated sense of self-importance. There is no faster way to alienate those around you than by being arrogant. False pride manifests in a person's behavior. True pride is the opposite – it is internal and does not have a negative impact on behavior. True pride is a source of confidence, a recognition of one's true abilities and accomplishments. Being responsible as a person requires that we are confident in our abilities so we will step up and assume responsibility. False pride is rooted in insecurity; people lacking in security often boast and try to make themselves be seen as something they are not. False pride does not inspire the confidence of others and does not lead to lasting gains. In avoiding false pride we are seen by others as we truly are, and the congruence between our word and actions inspires others to have confidence in us.

THE FIVE KEYS TO MASTERY

There are five keys to the mastery of personal responsibility. Mastering these five key areas will lead to a high degree of personal responsibility, which will improve all of your relationships and lead to a greater degree of success and happiness. Mastery is difficult; it takes a concerted effort across a period of time. By working towards mastery, however, the benefits begin immediately. Each incremental improvement towards personal responsibility yields positive tangible results.

PUTTING YOURSELF FIRST

Putting yourself first as an essential ingredient for personal responsibility may seem counterintuitive. On the surface it may even appear rather selfish. It is, however, anything but selfish; anything less than putting yourself first will detract from your performance – which means you actually do less; less for others as well as for yourself. Putting yourself first is self caring, not selfish. You are the only adult you are responsible for. You may be responsible to others, but not for them. They are responsible for themselves. Putting yourself first means doing what is best for you. It does not mean doing anything at the expense of others – that would be selfish. Nor is the choice always easy or clear. If faced with the decision of meeting a deadline on an important work project or meeting a commitment to your spouse or significant other, which do you choose? The choice becomes one of self-interest – of finding the balance between competing areas of your life which will maximize your happiness and success. If we really think it through our relationships are probably at least as important as our careers. If we act in self-interest we will take care of both, as well as any other important areas, such as volunteering or service. Putting yourself first increases your productivity and accountability to others. It forces open communication as you let those close to you know why you make the choices you do – resulting in improved relationships. Putting yourself first, being self-caring but not selfish, is the first step on the journey to personal responsibility.

ALIGN WITH YOUR VALUES

Aligning with your values is essentially putting yourself first on a moral plane. To start, it will be far easier if you are very clear about your values. If you identify your top five values and stay in alignment with those you will find that you are in alignment with your values over 95% of the time. Values serve as our moral compass for our decisions and our actions. Making decisions and taking actions in alignment with our values causes congruence between our morals and our behaviors. This reduces stress and conflict and increases our performance. It can be challenging to be in alignment in some environments. Challenging, but not impossible. For many people, their work environment causes the greatest difficulty. It helps to remember that personal responsibility is about your behavior, not the behavior of others. The behavior of others is not your business unless it impacts you directly. One question I am frequently asked is what to do if you're asked to lie at work. My first question back is to ask if that is in alignment with your values. This is not to be smart, but to clarify consciously that it is not in alignment. This makes the decision about how to handle the problem easier. There is not one set answer, it depends on the circumstances. I once had a manager asked me to lie to a customer. I told him that I could not do that. I did not get fired, but immediately began seeking other employment. The choice I made was to not be in an environment where I had to choose my values or employment. I was perfectly willing to lose the job, my integrity was more important.

CHALLENGE YOUR PROGRAMMING

Much of what we know and believe does not belong to us, it is our programming. We were programmed by our parents, by our teachers, and by others we believed. Not only were they not always right, but also times have changed. Facts we know from the past may no longer be true. If we fail to challenge our beliefs and assumptions we make decisions based on false facts. Not for every decision, but for some, and any decision based on false premises is a less than optimal decision. Challenging our programming has additional benefits. In examining what we know and believe we gain faith in our core selves and at the same time we become more open-minded. We gain faith in our core selves as the process promotes growth, we learn, and we come to understand that we cannot know everything, but that our decisions are based on the best information available at the time. We become more open-minded as we realize that facts are temporary, they are subject to change as science and knowledge progress. Facts are not the same as truth; truth is not subject to change, it is absolute. There is no version of truth, truth stands alone. Beliefs are not the same as truths, they are our perspective of truth. Questioning our programming improves our perspective; our beliefs become closer to the truth. Personal responsibility requires that we be the best we can – challenging our programming helps us to become more personally responsible.

BE IN THE PRESENT

Life can only be lived in the present. All we have to work with, emotionally, intellectually, and spiritually is 100%. We cannot do more than that. Any dwelling on the past detracts from our putting 100% into the present. Any dreaming or fretting of the future likewise detracts from our putting 100% into the present. We cannot undo the past, but if we recognize that we did the best we could have with the knowledge, information, and awareness that we had, then we can let the past go. The only way we can ever alter the past is to do our best in the present, as that will soon be our past. The future will bring what it will bring; we cannot predict what that will be. The only thing we can do is to do our best in the present, that will have us best prepared for whatever the future brings. Note that planning for the future, in terms of budgeting, scheduling, or other such activities, are present activities and should be done. It is the abstract, the daydreaming and worrying about the future, that is a problem. It is only by being 100% in the present that we can give 100% to the present, and that is being personally responsible.

EVERYTHING MATTERS

One question I am asked nearly every time I speak on personal responsibility is about where does it end, where does one stop? The answer is really that we don't, not within the scope of what we are responsible for. Remember that we can only be responsible for people who are not capable of being responsible for themselves. We may be responsible to others, not for them. They need the dignity of being responsible for themselves; their success or failure is their responsibility. When I was younger I thought I wanted to change the world – really to save the world. As I matured I learned several things. One is that it is not up to me to determine that the world needs to be saved. Also, that I cannot change the world directly, but I can change my world. I change my world by being responsible. I cannot save the environment, but I can do my best by being a conscientious citizen, by recycling, reusing, and not contributing to environmental degradation. I can speak up, bringing problems to light. In doing my part, I can also serve as an example to others. Each of us is a role model and influences, for better or worse, those around us. Certainly some things are more important than others; what is most important to me may be less important to you. Whatever you are responsible for matters, and how you step up can change your world.

PERSONAL RESPONSIBILITY ACTION PLAN

To become as personally responsible as possible we must take action. These are the seven most important steps to take to become the most responsible, successful, happiest person you can be.

1. Where am I reacting instead of responding? What steps can I take immediately to make sure I do not react?

2. Where am I being influenced by the expectations of others? What can I do today to not get dragged into other people's expectations?

3. Where do I not put myself first? What can I do today to make my success my number one priority?

4. Where am I experiencing conflict with my values? What steps can I take today to move my actions in line with my values?

5. What beliefs of mine are limiting? What steps can I take today to challenge existing programming and become more open to new ideas?

6. What is preventing me from always being in the present? What steps can I take today to move towards being in the present at all times?

7. In what areas am I neglecting personal responsibility? What steps can I take today to take responsibility in additional areas of my life?

Review these steps often. By constantly challenging ourselves to be completely personally responsible in all areas of our lives, we can have greater success and happiness than we could ever have imagined.

About Peter

Peter Neeves has written hundreds of articles which have appeared on *eHow Business & Personal Finance, Answerbag, eHow, Essortment,* and *Soyouwanna.com.* In addition to extensive writing in the areas of personal finance and personal responsibility, Peter has spoken on these topics regularly at corporations of all sizes.

A former Director of Operations for a division of a Fortune 200 company and a Vice President of a regional company, Peter blends business experience with financial knowledge from 20 years in the personal finance field. His education background includes an MBA with a PhD expected in 2013. He has trained and developed hundreds of financial advisors to run successful practices.

To learn more about Peter, visit his website at: www.peterneeves.com

CHAPTER 22

HOW TO CREATE A SUCCESSFUL MARRIAGE

BY JOSE GOMEZ, M.D.

Joseph and Mary had been married for seven years. He has been working extremely hard and holds an important position in his company. Mary is spending a lot of time with her friends and relatives. She also has a problem controlling her appetite and is overweight.

Joseph's only source for feeling important is by achieving success at work, where he feels recognized and appreciated.

Joseph gets no appreciation or recognition at home from Mary, who is always busy outside with her friends and parents. At the same time, Mary can't connect with Joseph because he is always working and paying very little attention to her.

As the time passed, they continued to grow further apart from each other and when they started to consider the possibility of getting a divorce, they decided to come to my office and began my thirty-day program to help them improve the quality of their marriage.

I am now going to tell you the seven steps that I asked Joseph and Mary to take during my thirty-day coaching program, which I offered them in my office and now available online in my web site, and which completely turned around their marriage.

1. When they first came to my office, Mary was bitterly complaining that Joseph had a bad temper and that he frequently appeared

to be angry and irritated. Joseph admitted it, but blamed stress from working too hard at his job. He also added that the real problem was poor communication between them. They were provided with anger and communication management programs.

2. Another problem they complained about was not having an agreement on how to spend their money.

   Knowing that financial problems are one of the main causes for divorce in the United Sates, I immediately offered them a good financial planning course.

3. At one point, Joseph threatened not to come back to therapy anymore because he had no time to do it. So I also suggested a time management system to him to better manage the way he was spending his time.

   [All of this additional information is currently available as free bonuses to those following my 30-day on-line course.]

4. Joseph and Mary were made fully aware of all of the benefits of committing to work out their difficulties – such as having a happier, more supporting and loving married life and possibly even having children in the future and raising a happy family together.

5. It was also explained that the high cost of continuing to have a miserable life, devoid of love for each other, was likely going to end in a divorce.

6. But above all, it was explained to them, and this is the most important piece of information that I have for you too, was what seems to be the subconscious tendencies we all have, and which needed to be brought into their awareness in order to enjoy a happy marriage.

7. And finally, I explained to them what the changes were that they needed to implement on a daily basis to turn around their shaky marriage.

   Today, more than ten years later, Joseph and Mary are happily married with two beautiful children and enjoying a well-balanced and happy marital life.

THE SINGLE MOST IMPORTANT FACTOR

To have a successful marriage, you need to find out what the Drivers are (I will explain to you in the next paragraph what I mean by Drivers) that control and direct your relationship in your married life. These Drivers live in your subconscious mind. Most people are not aware of the existence of those Drivers; however, they are deeply rooted at a subconscious level and from there, they will control and direct your life in general, and your relationships in particular; especially powerfully impacting the way you behave in your marriage.

WHAT ARE THE DRIVERS?

What I call the Drivers are the "I want" and the "I need" forces that we all have operating in our subconscious mind. According to the renowned psychologist Abraham Maslow, there are six needs or Drivers. Some of them have to do with the protection and preservation of your physical body, such as the urge to drink or eat when we are thirsty or hungry; other Drivers are involved in maintaining your personal growth as well as contributing to helping others. But only four of all of the Drivers, which I call the Psychological Drivers, are important to be understood by you in order to have a good relationship in your marital life.

THE NAMES OF THE DRIVERS

I have created names for each of the four Psychological Drivers. Those names closely resemble the way they influence our behavior.

These four Drivers are:

- The "Gregarious"
- The "Unique"
- The "Diversifier"
- The "Cautious"

We all are influenced by each one of these four Drivers; some of them tend to be very strong in your life, while others are rather weak in directing your behavior.

The two strongest Drivers are the ones that will most impact the way you think, the way you speak and the way you conduct yourself in your marriage.

HOW DO THE DRIVERS WORK?

The Gregarious operates by driving you to seeking connection and bonding with other people, ideas or groups.

The Unique controls you by pushing you to achieving recognition and significance.

The Diversifier impacts you by directing your behavior to seeking variety and changes.

The Cautious influences you by making you live in your comfort zone where you can feel safe and secure.

ROLES OF THE DRIVERS IN A RELATIONSHIP

The four Psychological Drivers can impact your behavior in an acceptable and positive way or, to the contrary, they can do it in a negative and destructive manner.

(A) The Gregarious

In its positive expression, when you are heavily influenced by the Gregarious, you will seek in your marriage to experience the feeling of being liked, accepted and loved by your spouse. Typically you will be close to your mates, relatives, friends, co-workers or classmates. Gregarious typically become members of a church, a club or join a team. They also like the outdoors, connecting with nature.

On the other hand, when a Gregarious is impacting in a negative way your relationships, you tend to abuse food, alcohol or drugs in order to get negative attention and connect with your spouse. Therefore, you easily become overweight, or addicted to chemicals. In the story, at the beginning of this chapter, you will find that Mary was a typical Gregarious.

(B) The Unique

When expressing positive aspects, the Unique have a need for recognition. They want to feel important and significant in their marriage. They feel that they are different, and to a certain extent separated and not truly connected with their spouse because they are mostly self-centered; the focus of their attention is on what they want to become and what they want to accomplish; therefore, typically, the Unique work very hard at any task and become high achievers in their jobs, profession or studies.

In the story, at the beginning of this chapter, you will find that Joseph was a typical Unique.

When the Unique is expressing its more unconventional side, they often will wear unusual clothes that set them apart, or they will show rings or other pieces of jewelry on uncommon places on their body; or they will have flashy artificially colored hair; or they may display distinctive tattoos that make them look different to everyone else.

If the negative expression is taken to an extreme, the Unique can become terrorists or serial killers, in order to achieve recognition in a negative and destructive way and thus be always remembered as special and different from everyone else.

(C) The Diversifier

When influencing lives in a positive way, the Diversifier will show a fast-paced living style, with many changes and uncertainties about the future. They typically love variety and surprises when interacting with their spouse and they will feel easily bored in a marriage surviving on an automatic pilot, full of routines which are not exciting. They love the thrill of living on the edge. They look for constant stimulation and changes. Diversifiers are also inclined to get involved in physical. They are very intimate in their married life and can be very good lovers.

When Diversifiers are exhibiting their more negative characteristics, they become very emotionally driven, easily irritated and frustrated, because they tend to live more in their ever-changing variety of emotions than in their cool stable head. They can be unpredictable, moody and at times even rude or aggressive with their spouse.

(D) The Cautious

In the positive expression, the Cautious typically look for security and safety in their marriage. Contrary to Diversifiers, they live a slow-paced life, full of routines and repetitions. They like to live in their comfort zone, without too many changes or unpredictable consequences from their actions. They dislike uncertainties, variety and surprises.

When Cautious are expressing their negative influence, growth will be impaired because of their resistance to changes and the discomfort of accepting new and different ideas in their marriage.

THE DRIVERS TEST

To have a successful marriage, you need to find out what are the forces controlling and directing your spouse's behavior in your marriage. These forces that I have called the Drivers are: the Gregarious, the Unique, the Diversifier and the Cautious.

They represent the "needs" and "wants" that we all have in our subconscious mind. Most people are not aware of the existence of those Drivers, however they are deeply rooted at a subconscious level and from there, they will control and direct life in general, and in particular your spouse's way of relating to you in your marriage.

Therefore, it is of an utmost importance that you discover which ones are your spouse's two strongest Drivers amongst the four. In order to find out what are the two most influential Drivers impacting your spouse's behavior in your marriage, you can ask him or her to take the following copyrighted Drivers Test that I have created:

Directions: In the four tables shown below and in the column to the right give a rating in points to each statement according to the Rating Guidelines. Then, add all the points for each Driver and determine which ones are the two Drivers that have the highest scores.

RATING GUIDELINES:

NEVER .... 0 POINTS

RARELY .... 1 POINT

OFTEN .... 2 POINTS

ALWAYS .... 3 POINTS

GREGARIOUS

1	I AM MOSTLY A GIVER IN MY RELATIONSHIPS	
2	I CAN BE ROMANTIC WITH MY SPOUSE OR PARTNER	
3	FEELING ONENESS AND UNITY IS IMPORTANT TO ME	
4	I CAN CONNECT EASILY WITH OTHERS	
5	I LIKE TO LOVE OTHERS AND FEEL LOVED	
6	I DON'T ACT IN A SELFISH WAY TOWARDS OTHERS	
7	I ENJOY BELONGING TO A CHURCH, CLUB OR TEAM	
8	I GIVE GENEROUSLY OF MY TIME, MONEY AND SKILLS	
9	I LOVE TO HELP AND SERVE PEOPLE	
10	I WILL DO WHATEVER IT TAKES TO CARE OF OTHERS	
	TOTAL NUMBER OF POINTS FOR GREGARIOUS:	

UNIQUE

1	I LIKE TO IMPRESS OTHERS WITH WHAT I AM AND DO	
2	I LIKE TO EARN PRESTIGE AND FAME IN MY LIFE	
3	I WANT TO BE RECOGNIZED AND APPRECIATED	
4	I LIKE TO BE CONSIDERED UNIQUE AND SPECIAL	
5	IT IS IMPORTANT WHAT PEOPLE THINK ABOUT ME	
6	I FEEL GOOD WHEN PEOPLE RESPECT ME	
7	I FEEL PROUD OF MYSELF AND MY ACHIEVEMENTS	
8	I TRY HARD TO BE SUCCESSFUL IN WHATEVER I DO	
9	I THINK, FEEL AND ACT AS SOMEONE IMPORTANT	
10	I SEE LIFE AS A PLACE TO COMPETE AND WIN	
	TOTAL NUMBER OF POINTS FOR UNIQUE:	

DIVERSIFIER

1	I LIKE TO ENGAGE MYSELF IN MULTIPLE TASKS	
2	I LIKE TO LEARN NEW THINGS	
3	TAKING ON A NEW PROJECT OR CHALLENGE IS FUN/EXCITING	
4	I LOVE TO HAVE FUN AND ENTERTAINMENT IN MY LIFE	
5	I LIKE TO LIVE MY LIFE WITH CONSTANT CHANGES	
6	ROUTINES AND REPETITION ARE BORING TO ME	
7	SUSPENSE AND THE UNKNOWN APPEALS TO ME	
8	I LOVE THE THRILL OF RISK-TAKING	
9	I CAN BE INTIMATE AND A GREAT LOVER	
10	I LIKE TO MOVE AND ENGAGE IN PHYSICAL ACTIVITIES	
	TOTAL NUMBER OF POINTS FOR DIVERSIFIER:	

CAUTIOUS

1	I LIKE WHEN THINGS ARE PREDICTABLE	
2	I LIVE MY LIFE IN MY COMFORT ZONE	
3	I AVOID SITUATIONS CONSIDERED DANGEROUS	
4	IT IS IMPORTANT TO HAVE STABILITY IN MY LIFE	
5	I LIKE TO THINK FIRST AND THEN DO	
6	I LIKE TO PLAY SAFE AND NOT TAKE RISKS	
7	I TEND TO BE PRECISE AND ACCURATE	
8	NOT BEING GROUNDED IS UNCOMFORTABLE TO ME	
9	I DO THINGS ONLY IF I KNOW ALL THE CONSEQUENCES	
10	FINANCIAL SECURITY IS VERY IMPORTANT TO ME	
	TOTAL NUMBER OF POINTS FOR CAUTIOUS:	

MY DRIVERS SCORES ARE:

1. GREGARIOUS: _____ POINTS

2. UNIQUE: _____ POINTS

3. DIVERSIFIER: _____ POINTS

4. CAUTIOUS: _____ POINTS

HOW CAN WE HELP YOU?

Finally, I am going to share with you one tip for each Driver that will greatly help you when put them into practice in your marriage. The full program with a comprehensive practical approach is available on my web site.

If you are married to a:

Gregarious: Knowing that gregarious need to feel connected and bonded; that they seek the feeling of being loved, liked and accepted, I suggest to you to write a list of all of the things that you like and love about your gregarious spouse, and then, tell him or her from the bottom of your heart, what is on that list. Also, for positive reinforcement, keep frequently mentioning the same things on your list when having a conversation with your spouse.

Unique: Since Unique likes to feel acknowledged and recognized, don't let your Unique spouse leave or return home without always going to the door and, after hugging and kissing, saying in a loving way something like this: "Have a great day at work" or "I am so happy to see you back."

Diversifier: Because a Diversifier loves surprises, write a love note to your Diversifier spouse and hide it in a place such as her purse, his or her pocket, wallet, kitchen drawer, lunch bag, etc., where he or she will be totally and pleasantly surprised when finding it.

Cautious: Give your Cautious spouse the predictability, security and safety he or she needs to relate to you in a trusting and comfortable way.

Every week on the same day and for as long as needed, hold a planning meeting, where you and your spouse will come with a list of issues that have been a source of disagreement and argument in the past.

Small or important issues, such as: How do we budget our income and spend our money? Who is doing the dishes or taking the garbage out? Who is picking up the children? How are we going to fix the broken faucet? etc.

You and your spouse will agree for one week who is going to be doing what, and by when, and how it will be accomplished. During that week you and your spouse agree not to argue about those specific issues. If someone is breaking the agreement, then the other spouse says in a non-argumentative way and without getting into a fight something like, "Do you remember you agreed to do…" then the same issue is brought back to the next planning meeting and renegotiated again for the next week.

In closing, remember that what matters in turning around your marriage is not what you are going to get from your spouse, but what you are going to give to satisfy your spouse's subconscious needs or Drivers.

About Dr. Jose Gomez

Awarded for the past four consecutive years since 2009 the qualification of one of the top Psychiatrists in America, Dr. Jose Gomez has been an extremely successful professional helping people to enjoy happier and successful lives.

He is a brilliant teacher who has been a former professor of Psychiatry and Director of the Medical School at the Technological Institute of Santo Domingo in the Dominican Republic.

His extensive work in helping couples to live fulfilling marriages began over forty years ago, when he was appointed Medical Director of a community mental health center in Louisville, Kentucky. Since that time, he has developed his own coaching system called The Drivers, which he uses to teach spouses how to learn to meet each other's needs in their marital relationships.

Dr. Gomez is the author of the book *THE DRIVERS – Turn Your Marriage Around In 30 Days* and also the creator of an on-line 30-day course with the same title. He is a dynamic motivational speaker who had delivered many talks in the United States of America and other foreign countries, including India and the Caribbean.

He is a distinguished member of the Royal Society of Medicine in England and a Founding Fellow of the Institute for Coaching at the prestigious Harvard University Medical School. He is also a member of the Harvard Business Review Advisory Council.

Dr. Gomez can be contacted by accessing his web site at:
www.MarriageAcademy.us

CHAPTER 23

HOW TO CREATE AN INCOME YOU CAN NEVER OUTLIVE

BY KEN AND LORI HEISE

Just because we're safe money people doesn't mean we can't have fun. Just ask Daniel, who wanted to find a way to keep his money secure after spending his career trading volatile stocks.

After a few too many losses, he came to speak with us. Once we told him what we could do, he pushed his paperwork across our desk like a stack of poker chips. "I'm all in!" he said.

Fast forward a few months, and Daniel began spending more time on the golf course and less time in front of the TV, where he used to stare at the stock ticker. "You gave me my husband back," his wife told us. He was having fun again, and she was too.

As safe money people, we don't just work to make sure your money stays safe throughout retirement. We work to help ease your stress. We work to get you back on the golf course. We work to get you back living life, not afraid of it.

We're Ken and Lori Heise, a husband and wife financial team. We work with retirees and those approaching retirement to make sure their savings and income remain a constant in their twilight years. We also help them leave something to future generations.

Our clients want to look out for their family. We look out for them. We hug them like family, and protect their money like family. This is not just a business to us and we know our clients feel that too!

IT'S ABOUT FINDING STABILITY

With 45 years of combined experience, we like to think we know what most people want out of their retirement. They want stability and cash flow they don't have to worry about. They want something that won't go away.

These days, that's an increasingly difficult thing to get. Everything is changing – the global market is a different place everyday, and no one knows where the next disaster will be.

Our approach is simple. We want to build a solid foundation and create a strong financial home for our clients. That way, when the next financial storm comes through, the savings they worked so hard for won't blow away.

UNDERSTANDING RETIREMENT

How do we do it? We start by helping clients understand what retirement life really is. It won't be like the life they lived when they had a full-time career. As career people, our clients were in accumulation mode. They accumulated wealth over 30, 40 years.

They were their own assets – they used their experience, personality, and professional community to get ahead. They relied on themselves and their skills for their livelihood.

While that's easy to grasp, it's hard for most clients to understand what to do when that ends. After your career, you are no longer your own asset. Your assets are the wealth you've accumulated over a successful career.

We say it over and over. Once you're retired, one big thing changes. Your income no longer comes from a boss, it comes from what you've saved and accumulated. You have to protect it!

Instead of investing your money the way you're used to investing it – for growth, maybe making risky investments, because there will be more coming with the next paycheck – you have to understand that your priorities have changed to preserving and creating cash flow (income).

This scares most people, but it shouldn't. Not with us.

FINDING THE ANSWER: ANNUITIES

We'll put your money where it can provide you with secure, steady income for as long as you need. We'll ensure that your income will survive whatever happens in the market. We'll place some of your retirement principal in annuities. There are a few different kinds that we'll go through in detail.

If you have become uncomfortable weathering the ups-and-downs of the stock market, and who isn't, then we are your people. We are the ones you should work with.

With **Fixed Index Annuities**, you get what you ask for – peace of mind that you will never experience a market loss. If you're already familiar with savings accounts and CDs and their purpose, then you can begin to understand a fixed index annuity. They are taxed deferred savings vehicles that provide safety of principal and a potentially higher interest rate that is linked to the performance of a stock market index.

By linking the interest to a stock market index, there's always the opportunity for growth. We get some of that growth, and in return we never lose anything when the market takes a dive.

Many people suffer from sleepless nights. In fact, for much of their working lives, people worry about money in that classic way. They lie in bed and stare at the ceiling when they should be dreaming peacefully. When they enter retirement, those sleepless nights often become more frequent. People realize that money won't flow in as it did when they worked full time, and suddenly they're afraid to spend a dime.

That's not how it should be.

ENJOYING GROWTH, AVOIDING LOSS: HYBRID ANNUITIES AND YOUR WEALTH

We hold seminars regularly that teach members of our community how to handle their money. We meet many future clients this way. One couple in particular, Bob and Mary, came to us after spending most of their lives risking their money in volatile markets. They wanted a secure place to keep their savings as they entered retirement.

But that's not all they wanted. They also wanted to move closer to their grandkids, go on annual cruises, and take up tennis and painting. They not only wanted to save their money from market woes, they wanted to enjoy market growth.

Hybrid Annuities work much like fixed index annuities; only they are more dynamic and customizable to each client's personal preferences and plans. If you have big goals for your retirement life, this may be a good solution.

We can work together to secure an income that you can take every month without wondering if it's too much, or whether you will outlive it. With our chosen annuities, there's no more uncertainty..

Hybrid annuities have some of the highest percentages of cash flow per dollar of asset that you can get anywhere. That way, you'll be moving near your grandkids – not moving in with them.

By using the best features of the fixed index annuity (safety of principal and upside interest rate potential) and the best feature of an immediate annuity (lifetime income) a hybrid income annuity can give you the best of both worlds without market risk.

STOP FIGHTING, SPEND CONFIDENTLY AND TAKE THAT VACATION, ALREADY!

Our favorite part about working with retirees and those nearing retirement is seeing their lives change before our eyes. Too often, retirees come to us with a great deal of stress and financial uncertainty about outliving their money. We try to set them straight.

With our help, there's no more uncertainty. There's a cash flow guaranteed for life. And in our experience, that **reaps much more than just financial benefit,** it provides our clients peace of mind, and allows them to sleep well at night.

Our clients are almost always happier people when they come in for a review than when they came in for their first consultation. One of our favorite client stories involves a couple that came to us very worried at first. We worked closely with them, and began to notice a change. They were in better moods each time they came into the office.

The next year when they came in for their review, the suntans were evident, and they obviously were getting to the beach. They said they had stopped arguing about money. In fact, they had stopped arguing all together. They slept better, planned more trips, and genuinely enjoyed their post-working lives. That's how it should be.

We don't believe that anyone, after working for three or four decades, should suffer through financial uncertainty. Annuities are our way of helping wean them off of old habits and financial psyches.

No more spending breakfast reading about the market, or leaving the TV blaring with stock reports. When you're retired and at ease, you shouldn't care what the traders are doing on Wall Street. You should care about your passions, your family, and your overall wellbeing.

PLANNING *NOW* FOR THE FUTURE

For many, there are future generations to consider. We help in that direction as well. Plans for helping future generations are always personal matters, and we cater to each clients needs. We'll work with you to provide peace of mind for both you and your children, and their children too.

What's needed is to take care of you – Mom and Dad – first. Think about what you need, besides what we've already discussed. You'll get a steady savings and a steady cash flow. But you'll need a little more when you begin long-term planning.

There's healthcare to consider. There has to be emergency money set aside. After all, there are other kinds of emergencies besides market drops. You'll also want money to spend on non-essentials. There are hobbies to take on, flights to enjoy, and suites to lounge in.

After you know how to cover the above essentials, you'll want to know how to pass your savings along when the time comes. Like annuities, the answer may be simpler than you imagined. Just because you should be careful doesn't mean the job is complicated.

It's a good idea, though, to plan ahead. If transferring money to another generation is important to you, then one option might be establishing an irrevocable life insurance trust set up according to your lawyer's legal specifications.

Using our "IRA Total Return Plan," we'll show you how to transfer money using the hybrid income annuities we already talked about. By setting up an irrevocable life insurance trust, you'll have the safety and security we provide all our clients, boosted by the number one way to transfer money to your children: life insurance.

Life insurance is the best way to move money cross generationally. Why? Because they have a leveraged tax-free nature that's impossible to find anywhere else.

If you have money to move into inheritance for future generations, be sure as much of it as possible goes to those you love. If you can avoid paying unnecessary taxes, which are often painfully high, why not do so? We know how.

We like to think of this method as a "Supercharged Roth IRA Conversion." Of course, it's not an IRA. But, like Roth IRA conversions, they guarantee a tax-free return. It's too good to resist, because it makes sure your loved ones are taken care of in the right way.

It's much like planning for other parts of your financial life. You worked hard for the money you'll now use to enjoy in your retirement. You should enjoy it. In the same way, you worked hard for the money you'll pass on to your children's families. You should make sure it gets there in the appropriate way.

FINAL THOUGHTS

In your financial life you've no doubt suffered from ups-and-downs, and good times and bad. That's a given in life. Retirement, however, ushers in a new stage of a person's life, one that is meant to be enjoyed, savored, and as carefree as possible.

As a retiree, you should enjoy the time you spend with your family, see parts of the world you may not have had time to see, and follow your passions to the next logical step with the free time you now have. Spend with confidence! Live the life you worked so hard for.

And you can do all these things quite simply. We'll help you do it.

About Ken and Lori

Ken and Lori Heise are a husband-wife financial team focusing on safe money for their clients. They are co-founders of the Heise Advisory Group in St. Louis, MO. They like to call themselves "Geriatric Specialists of Retirement Income Planning."

They met as they both became interested in helping those in retirement achieve complete financial security. Lori, from St. Louis, MO, spent 18 years in insurance before deciding to help those reaching the end of their careers. Ken is from Milwaukee, WI, and spent nearly 17 years working with insurance and securities. Together they help retirees create a steady income stream that they can never outlive. Ken and Lori run their practice like they run their family, with passion and love.

Driven by a meaningful quest to help those who aren't sure how to move forward, Ken and Lori hold regular evening seminars to inform their community. They are available and willing to help anyone ensure their future is as bright as possible. The accolades that Ken and Lori have earned over the years are staggering.

Ken is a Registered Financial Consultant, a professional designation awarded by the International Association of Registered Financial Consultants. Ken is a Top of the Table member of the Million Dollar Round Table, placing him among the top one-half of one percent of financial and insurance professionals worldwide.

Lori is an approved member of the National Ethics Bureau (NEB), an independent organization of insurance and financial advisors who have maintained an exemplary record of business ethics. Lori is also a past member of the Million Dollar Round Table.

For more information or to reach out to Heise Advisory Group, visit:
www.heiseadvisorygroup.com
Or call the office at 314-909-1116
Or toll-free at 888-414-1116.

CHAPTER 24

HOW TO CHOOSE AN EXPERT ADVISER –
FIVE QUESTIONS TO ASK YOUR FINANCIAL ADVISER

BY MATT DICKEN

(1) WHAT MAKES YOU AN EXPERT? HOW SUCCESSFUL ARE YOU?

You have to ask your adviser how they think they'll be able to help you and how successful they are at their job. You might have an adviser with an alphabet of letters behind his or her name, but you need to find out how much real world experience he has in helping retirees and pre-re-tirees. There's a big difference between studying in a book how to be a financial adviser and actually applying those methods and experiencing what works and what doesn't work. It's kind of like a doctor who reads all the medical books and knows how to perform the surgery but hasn't actually done it. You want to find out what makes your current adviser an expert and how successful they are.

The second part of that question is obviously very important. You want to find out how many clients the adviser has, how much experience he has in dealing with bull markets and bear markets, and how many clients he has helped transition from the working world into retirement.

(2) ARE YOU A REGISTERED REPRESENTATIVE, OR A REGISTERED INVESTMENT ADVISER?

Those two titles might sound similar, but there's a big difference in the type of advice you're going to get. Many people think all advisers do what's in the best interest of their clients. I certainly wish it was that way, but it's not.

This is a question of to whom or what the adviser has a fiduciary responsibility. It's an important concept to understand. Not all financial advisers have an obligation—a fiduciary responsibility—to look out for you and do what's best for your investments and your retirement.

If you currently work with an adviser from one of the large firms, and on his or her business card it says "registered representative," that means the adviser has a fiduciary responsibility to the firm. It could be any of the big firms, Merrill Lynch, UBS, Hilliard Lyons, Ameriprise—they all pretty much work the same. A registered representative is an employee of a firm and has a fiduciary responsibility to the firm, not the clients.

To emphasize the fact that they work in the firm's best interest, not the client's, let me give you an example of what would happen if an investor gets into some sort of conflict with a registered representative and they end up in court. Let's say the judge asks the adviser, "Why did you recommend this product when this other product would have been better for your client?" A legitimate response for a registered representative would be, "I sold this other product because that's what makes my firm the most money. I'm a W2 employee of that firm, and that's what I have to do." That's a fully acceptable answer in that situation. Why? It's acceptable because, as a paid employee of the firm, the adviser's obligation is to sell products and make money for the firm. That's what he or she is legally contracted to do. Registered representatives are not legally obligated to save money for investors at the expense of their employer. The firm dictates what products, services and strategies a registered representative can and can't recommend to clients. That's why these firms can have quotas for a certain amount of mutual funds or certain products that the advisers have to sell, regardless of whether it's in the client's best interest. How do I know this? I used to be a registered representative at one of the large firms. Once I realized how things operated there, I left to start my own company. Now, I don't have quotas or a manager looking over my shoulder telling me to sell products instead of helping people build and enjoy their retirement.

On the other hand, you could work with someone like me, who is part of a registered investment advisory firm. We are known as registered investment advisers (RIAs) or investment adviser representatives (IARs). We, unlike registered representatives, have a fiduciary responsibility to our clients. Let's go back to the same scenario I used a moment ago, but instead of a registered representative, we have an adviser who is an IAR and registered with a registered investment advisory firm. If that adviser were to recommend a product that was not in the best interest of the client—let's say he sold a product that would line his pockets with additional compensation and commission, but not necessarily improve the retirement portfolio of the client—he could potentially lose his license, have to pay fines, and, depending on how severe the offense, go to jail.

The good news is that Congress is working on financial reform regulations. The legislation would require stockbrokers, insurance agents, and other financial advisers to have the same fiduciary responsibility standard that RIAs have. All of the big brokerage firms are fighting this, and they have a lot of money and some powerful lobbyists with which to do so. They don't want the laws to change, because if they do, their advisers are going to have to start acting in the clients' best interest, not in the firms' best interest. And, of course, that would bring down their profits and revenue.

(3) ARE YOU A MEMBER OF THE NATIONAL ETHICS ASSOCIATION?

What's with all those letters after the adviser's name? You may see certified financial planners (CFPs), personal financial specialists (PFSs), chartered financial analysts (CFAs), registered investment advisers (RIAs), registered financial consultants (RFCs), wealth management specialists (WMSs), or any one of many, many other designations. Most investors don't know the difference between these letters and licenses.

It can be difficult to sift through all the different licenses, firms, and titles. The first thing I usually recommend is that investors work with a member of the National Ethics Association (NEA). Every NEA member has gone through an extensive background check. Before I became a member, the bureau looked extensively into my background, including whether I'd had client complaints, whether I'd ever been sued by a client, and whether regulators had audited, fined or sanctioned me. If anything undesirable had been found in my background, I would have been barred from membership. And the NEA takes it a step further by looking into an adviser's personal life. If an adviser has any DUIs or judgments, liens, bankruptcies or the like, then he can't be a member of the NEA. The association does spot checks throughout the year and a full-blown background check annually. If an adviser is sued, or if anything else changes, membership is denied. Here in the greater Louisville area, there are more than 1,000 financial professionals, including bankers and insurance agents. Over the years, the NEA has tightened standards, and each time we have lost members. At the time of this writing, I am one of the members. Membership in the NEA is taken very seriously, and we're all proud to belong to that organization.

(4) HOW HAVE YOU PERFORMED OVER THE LAST 10 YEARS?

I've been in the industry since 1997, but I've also been a student of the markets, and it is very important to find out how an adviser has performed over the last 10 years.

When the stock market is growing, it's very easy for an adviser to make his clients' money; but making money even when the stock market is going down is what separates the professionals from the amateurs.

It is common for me to meet people whose investments haven't gone anywhere for eight, nine, even a dozen years. Almost every day, people tell me they've watched an investment go up and down for a decade without earning anything. If it takes you 5, 10, or 15 years to recover from a bear market, you have never really recovered, because you have wasted all that time making your money back when you could have been building upon it from the start. You are that many years older and closer to retirement, if you're not already in it, and inflation has rendered your money unable to purchase what it would have bought when the bear market began.

In 2008, a lot of investors lost money. When they called their advisers, they heard this line: "Everybody's losing money. Nobody saw this coming." I don't buy that. You don't care about everybody else losing money; you care about your own money and your retirement. A good adviser who was paying attention to what was happening in the U.S. economy should have seen it coming. After all, it is the adviser's job to see it coming. When the stock market is growing, it's very easy for an adviser to make his clients' money; but making your clients money even when the stock market is going down is what separates the professionals from the amateurs.

(5) ARE YOU OPEN TO CHANGE? HOW DO YOU KEEP UP ON NEW STRATEGIES?

There are advisers out there who still follow strategies that worked very well back in the 1980s and '90s. Unfortunately, the economy we're in now is not the '80s or '90s, and it's not going to be that way again anytime soon. Find out what your adviser is doing to stay abreast of the changes that are going on in the industry and economy. Are they well-versed, or do they use a cookie-cutter approach?

Some advisers are trained to do only mutual funds all the time, or maybe they take the approach that life insurance is best all the time. It might be good for them, if they only need to know one product or two products. They can talk about them and sound well educated, but that's not going to be good enough. They have to recognize and adapt to change. If an adviser hasn't changed his approach in the past three to five years, chances are he is going to lose a lot of clients, or a lot of those clients are going to struggle during retirement.

PROTECTING YOURSELF FROM THE NEXT BERNIE MADOFF

"So how do we know you're not another Bernie Madoff?" people have sometimes asked me. Others, less blunt, just want to know: "How do I protect myself from a Bernie Madoff or a Ponzi scheme? How do I protect myself from getting ripped off?"

One layer of protection is to work with a member of the National Ethics Association. Another way you can protect yourself is to not work with advisers who take custody of your funds. If we use Bernie Madoff as an example, he owned the company that held the assets. People wrote personal checks made out to him and asked him to invest that money. He was not honest or ethical, and he ran off with it. Try to stick with advisers who use LPL, TD Ameritrade, or some other outside firm. At Strategic Wealth Designers, we don't take custody of the assets. Our clients' statements don't have Strategic Wealth Designers on the letterhead. I'm not saying every adviser or firm that takes custody of assets is operating a Ponzi scheme, but avoiding such a situation is one way investors can protect themselves.

About Matt

Matt Dicken is the Founder of Strategic Wealth Designers, a financial planning firm working to help both retirees and pre-retirees secure their financial futures. He is a national coach and mentor for financial advisors and CPAs. His "safer money" approach to investing, coupled with his track record of success, has made him a prominent authority on television, radio and many publications.

Matt's TV Show, *Strategic Wealth with Matt Dicken* is a 30-minute television news magazine covering all things financial. Since 2012, Matt has been bringing Kentuckians the essential financial strategies for the new economy that every retiree and pre-retiree needs to know. With segments like *Man On The Street, X's and O's with Coach Matt and The Money Minute,* Matt gives important information you need to make prudent decisions with your hard-earned money. The show airs every Sunday Morning at 10 a.m. on WHAS 11 (ABC).

Matt's Radio Show, *The Matt Dicken Show,* is your home for America's best financial talk radio. Matt educates and entertains thousands of listeners every week with useful financial strategies, guidance and an array of special guests from the financial industry. *The Matt Dicken Show* airs every Saturday morning from 11:05 a.m. to Noon on NEWSTALK 1570 AM WNDA.

In addition to being a television and radio talk show host, Matt is an active member of the financial/retirement speaking circuit. Since 2007, over 10,000 people have attended his seminars. These workshops offer insight on how to preserve and protect your assets, increase your retirement income and potentially reduce your taxes.

Over the years, Matt has authored several financial articles for both the public and the financial services industry. His new book, *"Retirement Planning in a New Direction, A Return to Common Sense"* was released in 2012 and can be found at BarnesAndNoble.com, Amazon.com and other fine bookstores. You can also find out more info on the website: AskMattDicken.com.

In his personal time, Matt likes to be an involved member of his community. In addition to being a member of the Animal Care Society and Northeast Christian Church, Matt is the owner, lead driver and instructor of Dicken Performance, an auto racing team. Matt and his wife Colleen were born and raised in Louisville, KY and they reside in Goshen, KY.

CHAPTER 25

WORDS OF WISDOM FROM THE KING OF POP ON WINNING CLIENTS OVER EVERY TIME!

BY PATRICIA DELINOIS

From the regal Medieval style doors to the light wood-laced Great Hall and Belvedere Room designed for entertaining guests, the South Florida castle known as "Tyecliffe" was a home truly fit for a king – the "King of Pop" that is.

From the moment I met Michael Jackson, I knew he was all that I imagined him to be! He was a musical icon and wouldn't settle for anything less than an iconic mansion. It was natural that he wanted to come and see the 24,000-square-foot, five-story castle that I was beyond proud to represent.

As Michael entered through the massive castle doors, you could just feel the aura of his presence fill the room. There he was - he had that gentle spirit, yet was also just larger than life!

Growing up, I had always admired Michael Jackson, following his life and his career. There was just no one else like him. He was the most successful entertainer of all time and a dynamic international legend.

His creativity never ended – his inspirational music and his dancing was like nothing ever seen before. This was the man that created the "moon walk"!!! He transformed the face of pop music and pop culture.

Michael arrived with his Nanny, his bodyguard Henry Aubrey, whom I became friends with, and the most gorgeous kids I had ever laid my eyes on! Paris his daughter looked like a porcelain doll with beautiful brown curls.

Prince was so blond at that age (his hair got darker later) and handsome, he looked like a real prince! They both looked like top model children.

It was January 2002, so they must have been 4 and 5 years old. They were both absolutely beautiful, well-behaved children, especially when they saw the castle's theater with a special drawbridge platform. To put it simply, the kids were in awe. I could tell they loved the estate instantly.

They were so beautiful they almost did not seem real. Michael was a very thoughtful, kind father; you could easily see the bond he had with his children. He was a very attentive, loving father and it showed that his kids were his world. All he wanted was something his children loved and could call their home.

As I followed him through Tyecliffe, the music icon wandered through the Estate, as he danced, glided, sang and entertained me in each room. We chatted in the main sitting room, designed like a tavern, then took in the beauty of sunny South Florida weather by the rock-lined pool. Michael was so full of energy and enthusiastic! It was quite magical to watch Michael so full of spirit and joy.

This was the most memorable experience I have ever had in my career of Real Estate! I can only hope for another experience half as special in the future.

This castle had been built by the Wackenhut's, a prestigious, well-known family that had founded Wackenhut Security. The Wackenhut's built this estate modeled after a castle they fell in love with while traveling in Europe. It was a very romantic story, in which George Wackenhut built a castle for the love of his life, Ruth. I am waiting for my prince charming to do that for me!

This mystical castle, sitting on three acres of waterfront property, was one of the most prestigious mansions at Gables Estates in Miami,

Fl. People would drive by the estate all the time, and it was almost a tourist attraction. This landmark Tyecliffe offered a unique royal ambience with majestic surroundings in South Florida's best area.

Tyecliffe was a true masterpiece, a real visual work of art, combining the splendor of the past with luxury and total comfort. Tyecliffe had Disneyland-esque grounds and a Disney-style pool with a bridge, waterfalls and all!

A child at heart, Michael immediately fell in love with the grounds, caves, the wine cellar, tennis court and more! I could not believe the Wine Cellar's walls, ceiling and floors were constructed of hand-cut solid granite to keep the area at a constant, cool temperature. There were at least six different themed bars or pubs throughout the house. Even the toilets in the castle were thrones!

The lighting in the ladies master bath used custom-made Harry Winston crystals! Every detail was done with so much imagination. The same type of imagination and detail Michael had always put into his music. It was a match made in Heaven.

After his tour through the dramatic, yet comfortable grounds, Michael said, "I want to thank you for making me feel so at ease and comfortable. This house has such great energy, and you have made me feel safe and warm. I really mean that. I have seen so many homes, but I feel so good here." As someone who has been a professional in real estate for as long as I have, that was the ultimate compliment from the ultimate legend.

We spoke for a while and he added, "Really, I have seen countless homes all over the world. You have been great!" I could have listened to him for hours. I absolutely hung on every word this man said. Who wouldn't?

He was definitely an old soul from whom I felt I could learn so much. Michael was a spiritual person, the way he connected with people was very important to him. He definitely made a strong connection with me that day.

After further conversations, I learned it really is all about how you make a client feel. It's all about how I made Michael feel that day, and no matter if you are the "King of Pop" or someone's grand-pop, you need to make them feel special at all times. The key to success in sales is having your clients like you. It is all about having them feel comfortable and feel safe with you. Your clients want to know they can relax with your guidance.

There are seven simple steps to break the ice and make people you meet feel comfortable with you and win them over forever! Just like I did with Michael.

1. **Smile** - It seems like such an easy thing to do, but then why doesn't everyone do it? Such a simple thing makes a huge difference when you meet with someone. Your first impression is always the most important impression. You can never get that first meeting back, and there are no do overs, so smile often to make a positive impact.

2. **Listen** - We all love to talk, but do we ever listen? It is amazing what you learn when you sit back and just LISTEN. Be considerate and willing to listen to what the client has to say. It is very important to clearly understand the client's values and needs. It is all about what makes your client happy. You might also come up with a great idea to make the deal work as you listen to the clients concerns. When you listen like you care, it is really the kind of attention every client wants. These days, people love to talk, especially when they are nervous or anxious during a first meeting. Always remember, just sit back and listen when you feel this coming on.

3. **Body Language** - Reflect and mirror the body language of your client. This again makes them feel more at ease and more at home with you. People feel more comfortable being near you when you have similar body language. Try it! We all have the ability to read body language, we just need to take the time and pay attention. Also make sure your body language is open and positive. Try not to cross or fold your arms. This conveys you are closed off and not open to communicating.

4. **Look Your Client In The Eyes** - Absolutely a must and a sign of respect. You have to look someone in the eyes when you talk to them. Always try to connect on a personal level and make eye contact to build trust and rapport. Wouldn't it be strange if

you were talking to someone and they never looked you in the eyes? It would definitely make me feel uncomfortable, and I would start to wonder what is this person so nervous about? As simple as this may seem, it is a social skill a lot of people struggle with! Good eye contact develops a more personable and sincere connection. It also let's them know you are not thinking about anything else but their happiness.

5. **Build Rapport** - Transition to a place of trust and comfort; people work with people they like. You want your client to experience the value in what you have to give. You want to create loyalty for life. Your clients will buy on how they feel with you assisting them. Show you care about how they feel.

6. **Believe** - Believe in what you are selling. Believe in what you are doing. Be inspired and let them know you are inspired. Sell what you believe in and are inspired to sell! This will make you trustworthy and authentic. So many people today are lost and it shows. If you don't believe in your work, you will never excel.

7. **Be prepared** - To gain your clients confidence, it is important that you have done your homework. Show them you are competent and knowledgeable. In the end, you will always get the largest percentage of business from repeat customers, so you want to build those lasting relationships. The main key to your success is your integrity and how you treat your clients. A prepared professional will ALWAYS outsell someone who is just 'winging' it.

Back to my brush with destiny, Michael did make an offer on Tyecliffe, but it was a period in his life, where his cash was tied up, so he made an offer as a lease purchase.

In the end, the sellers decided to go another way, one that resulted in a sale, not a lease. But that is not what I focus on with this story. I focus on the fact that my ability to connect with clients resulted in an offer most realtors dream of but never get – an offer from an icon.

Sadly today, we no longer have Tyecliffe, which was bulldozed by the last buyer, and we no longer have Michael. On June 25, 2009 Michael Jackson died at the age of 50.

It is so sad that we lost such a powerful, creative, and special person at such a young age. I feel Michael had so much more to give - but yet, his legacy lives on! He taught me the importance of how you make others feel! I will never forget the lessons Michael taught me that day. Michael had such an undeniable and authentic spirit that will live on forever.

When the movie "This is it" came out, I went to see it with friends. I cried throughout the entire movie! It was an amazing film - a positive, electrifying celebration of his life. If the planned concert had happened, it would have been a huge success! But his life will forever be a huge success – to his millions of fans and even to the South Florida Real Estate Broker that he inspired during a meeting, even if he never knew it.

I will always remember my moment with the "King of Pop!"

About Patricia

Patricia Delinois is one of the most successful and powerful professionals in real estate today – hands down. But you wouldn't know it by talking with the ever sweet, soft-spoken woman, who makes you feel as though you are the absolute center of attention. And that's exactly how she wants it.

Patricia is the CEO of Century 21 Premier Elite Realty, with over 175 agents and offices in Miami Beach, South Miami and Coral Gables. Premier Elite Realty focuses its efforts on luxury residential and commercial complexes. If that is not impressive enough, she is also the 2012 President of the MIAMI Association of Realtors with over 27,000 plus members and the largest international council in the world.

Patricia started in real estate at the age of 18. She admired her grandfather's work in New York and California, buying these old hotels to rehabilitate, then turning them into these trendy, boutique resorts that became a haven for celebrities and those in "the know."

An artist at heart, Patricia loves the feeling of being able to create living art in the form of a residence. She also loves meeting people and dealing with all different kinds of personalities and cultures. This passion for working with and satisfying her clients has earned her a prestigious reputation in the field, such accolades that other realtors seek her communication advice on a daily basis.

Patricia has served as a speaker on numerous Real Estate topics, lobbied for the industry on Capitol Hill, and is very involved politically in RPAC. Patricia is a Real Estate TV Correspondent and recently filmed a segment on the soon-to-be released TV show: *www.THEREOSHOW.com*, an interactive program featuring Florida Real Estate opportunities. In addition, Patricia is going to be on a Real Estate TV Show called *Luxe Life Miami* being filmed in Miami mid-March 2013 by NBC/Style Network with 80 million viewers.

Patricia loves that Miami is a global city, where speaking French, Spanish, Creole, and English has served her well. She was named Broker of the Year in the South Florida BEST Awards, overseen by the BEST Board of Governors, comprised of representatives from the Builders Association of South Florida and The Miami Herald.

To say Patricia's impact has been positively felt in the South Florida community would be the understatement of the century. She is a registered lobbyist, has been a trustee member of the Greater Miami Chamber of Commerce, and served as a Real Estate delegate with Enterprise Florida, traveling on trade missions with Governor Jeb Bush to Brazil, Argentina, and Chile.

Patricia has three offices in Miami Beach, South Miami and Coral Gables in efforts to make all her clients happy and their process as convenient as possible.

For more information, call her at: 786-252-6288
Email at: patriciadelinois@gmail.com
Or visit: www.patriciadelinois.com and www.premiermiami.com.

CHAPTER 26

F4 LIFESTYLE

BY REGAN S. KUJA

FAITH ... FUN ... FREEDOM ... FULFILLMENT

Faith

Napoleon Hill noted that God gave us control of but one thing; our mental attitude, our mind. And he went on to say that if we have control of just that one thing, it must be important. It must be the key to all else.

To accomplish a dream lifestyle, my friend Ed Blunt says you need to live in the future, not in your past and not even the precious present. At the same time, my friend Steve Jones says you need to get off the sofa and out the door or you're just gonna leave a legacy of butt marks!

I remember my first obsession as a child: a motorcycle! My friend Louis Provost first bought a beautiful 50cc red Honda! It symbolized fun, freedom and fulfillment to me! I remember buying motorcross posters, drawing pictures on any surface I could find, riding an imaginary dirtbike any time I was walking or riding my bicycle, buying racing jerseys (and being ridiculed by classmates who knew I didn't own or even ride a motorcycle). Several years later my friend Kenny Levesque had the same 50cc Honda and a 100cc trailbike. One day Kenny invited me over and my Dad had just one condition: no riding motorcycles. "Okay Dad." I was on my way. When I arrived, Kenny came riding up on his 100 and I was in awe! Said bye to my Dad and Kenny began to ride around his yard. He came back and asked me if I wanted to ride his old minibike, since I had never ridden before. I was nervously excited beyond my dreams! He gave me some quick pointers, demonstrated it and handed it over.

Oh Lord! As I sat on the seat, a rush of the greatest emotions came over me! I was riding for my first time! I took off and, wow, what a feeling! Everything was going great until…the front tire slipped down the edge of the paved driveway, into the soft dirt, and the bike toppled as I lost control. No big deal except that I got a nice road rash on my arm and now I was going to have to explain it to my Dad! The inevitable conclusion was my telling the truth and getting grounded for what seemed like forever. But, and a big but, my fire was lit and not long after that I purchased my first motorcycle with my Brother Shane. It is still one of my fondest memories. I had accomplished what seemed like only a dream as a mere child.

Belief was born in me the day I got that bike! I now knew that when I dreamed, held that dream long enough, and earned what it took to acquire the object of my dream, that my dreams would come true! I had discovered for myself what it took to design my ideal lifestyle: clarity, focus, persistence and faith.

So first clearly define what you want, and then surround your senses with as much reinforcement as possible. Imagine the things that just bring absolute joy to your day. Make an inventory or bucket list, but one you begin acting on today! Take photos of yourself, if possible, in the setting or with the object of your desire, and place them all around your home, business and vehicle. Cut our colorful pictures of the object of your desire to add to the mix. Visit the location(s) and take in the smells, sounds and textures. Listen to music that, as Tony Robbins says, will put you "in state." Talk to people who have been there, done that, or have it. Write your stated desires in permanent marker on your mirrors and windows. Obsess on it; see yourself having attained it and how you will feel. Think constantly about your attainment of it. Share only with positive supportive people what your goal is, but when the naysayers get wind of your "crazy" notion (because they will) and try in many ways to keep you from it's attainment, stop them before they finish the thought and just remember it's water off a ducks back.

You must be confident in living life on your terms if you wish to live an outstanding life. You get but one life, which soon is past! Pray earnestly for the elements and people necessary for all the steps along the way to your ultimate goal. Read daily on the topic of your obsession. Participate in teleseminars and webinars which are so abundantly available. Watch videos online. Join groups or associations related to your desire.

VOLUNTEER somewhere either related to your desire or with people who can help you with the attainment of it. I can't stress how HUGE a benefit volunteering can be to your future lifestyle attainment. You will have some great experiences and meet some of the best quality people you will ever meet! One of many life-changing, belief-changing experiences I had was when I registered for a seminar somewhere around 2001; my business partner and I just asked at the door if the promoter needed any help. As it turns out, he needed 2 people at the door so we said sure. It was cool to be able to meet all the motivated people attending the event. We didn't get to attend all the minutes of the event, but it was easily offset by the thrill of being part of such an event and being able to serve others. At the end, as the event completely wound down and even the help was leaving, we just asked one more time, "Does the speaker need a ride to the airport?" We were beside ourselves with joy and excitement when the promoter said yes! So my friend Tom Hood and I got to spend 15 minutes of face-time with the legend, Brian Tracy!

Buy every pertinent course to learn what you don't know yet. As you flood your mind with this input, many times just one thing you read, hear, watch or are told will send you spinning off in a direction you would have never conceived, and that can often be the key that unlocks the door of success to achieving the lifestyle of your dreams. Keep in mind it is extremely easy to end up in information overload today, resulting in procrastination; don't get caught in that trap! When you uncover new info, put it to work or to the test. You should expect failure and more of it than success, but you only need to uncover that winning strategy once, so stay with it!

Fun

You deserve to enjoy your time here on earth, and since excitement sells your dream, be sure you do what you love, so you will be fun to be around. All men are self made even though only the successful ones admit it; however, many people are necessary for each individual's success, so be magnetic and attractive in order that you can draw the best quality people to your team. Remember, this life is not a dress rehearsal;

you don't get a do-over. Give and live with passion and do it on your terms! Don't be swayed by what others think you should or should not do; be guided by your conscience. You are made in the image of God, so among many attributes, you are a creative being designed to express that to your utmost capacity! Get out and do what He designed you for! As you live out your potential, your energy will radiate and excite those around you.

Freedom

One of the greatest, most attractive aspects of the USA is our unprecedented freedom! It is both a blessing and a responsibility bestowed on us. First, it was fought for and died for; "freedom isn't free" as the lyrics of the song we sang in elementary school say. We now need to continue fighting and dying for the freedom of posterity. Second, we need to maximize our use of our freedoms and live lustrous lives for the sake of our Creator, our loved ones, the world and ourselves. It is actually irresponsible to waste our lives underperforming when we have the unlimited creative capacity of our mind, and total control of that one thing.

I was startled by this realization around 2006 when an addict living on the street berated me saying I owed him! What? I didn't owe him what he suggested, but I realized at that point, we all do need each other, and as such owe each other considerations as an integrated society. I recall servicing the home of a Silicon Valley Executive and founder of a major corporation here. We were standing in his driveway just talking and he paused and said, "You know Regan, we are all valuable; I can't do what you do and my wife was not sleeping due to this problem." I replied, "Thanks. I can't do what you do either." No matter what your skills and dreams, you have an integral and important role in this life; dare to dream!

The USA is founded on the belief that *all* men are created equal and endowed with certain unalienable rights. With each right is an equal and opposite responsibility. We have great freedom and pleasure from that and responsibility to share and spread it to *all* mankind. We must press beyond our borders and particularly beyond the walls in our minds. Just today I read a great Facebook post from a photo someone took of a marquee, which said, "Don't believe everything you think." One of my favorite mentors, Tim Ferriss (Author of what I call the 4 hour Trilogy: *The 4 Hour Work Week, The 4 Hour Body, & The 4 Hour Chef*) spurred me on to test my assumptions which directly resulted in my inclusion in this great book with my longest time teacher, trainer and mentor Brian Tracy. Do not accept the limitations that society or your peer group *will* place on you. You can become world class in your chosen field! Free your mind!

Fulfillment

In the event that no one in your life has already done so, I tell you now that you are valuable, you are worthy of attaining your dreams and goals and I hereby give you not only permission, but also a commission to go out and live your passion and thereby enrich the world!

Mike Dillard, another recent mentor of mine, advises you to declare yourself a leader and then begin to act as one. It really is as simple as that! People want to follow someone with definiteness-of-purpose as outlined by Napoleon Hill! I went from being a long-haired boy from Boston to an entrepreneur in California and I am able to offer people from 21 countries (and growing) around the globe the opportunity to establish financial freedom for themselves and for their loved ones. It is most satisfying to be able to extend to people opportunity from this great land where we are so blessed by God's provision and mentor them through challenges to their own great success. And with the ease of technology today, to be able to bring our success to mankind throughout the world is just humbling and inspiring! Each of us is but a tiny speck in an incredibly vast plan and simultaneously affecting every other speck in ways you cannot even imagine.

We are an intricately woven fabric and each essential for the greater good. The impact you have from each of your actions, however seemingly good, bad or insignificant, ripples throughout the world, so decide today to predetermine what initial splash you will make and watch the ripples turn into waves that others can catch and ride to their destiny!

About Regan

Regan Kuja has worked extensively in Health and Fitness, Termite and Pest Control, and Network Marketing and was first turned on to the world of sales and the need to become good at it through an audio training program by Brian Tracy.

With a passion for entrepreneurism inspired by his father Larry, and the love and support of his mother Sheila, he started working as a child around his neighborhood as well as delivering newspapers. Thrilled with business he studied Business Administration and Management at U Mass Lowell and moved to CA to pursue a Health and Fitness career at Gold's Gym. Training and working there as well as many other gyms led to his founding Phys-Cal Fitness, a personal training and nutrition consulting business.

Following that were many years honing sales, management and leadership skills in the termite and pest control industry, breaking and setting sales and service records at a number of companies including the largest in the world, Terminix International; ultimately culminating in the founding of Kuja Pest Management and Animal Abatement Specialists. He can be seen on Discovery Channel: Mythbusters – Home remedies for skunk odor removal.

He also co-authored the following books:

- *HOME SWEET HOME: Tips from industry experts on maintaining the value of your property* by Ocean Blue Publishing.
- *MAXIMIZE THE VALUE OF YOUR HOME: Featuring interviews with 16 Real Estate and Home Improvement Experts* by Ocean Blue Publishing.

As an evergreen entrepreneur, he was introduced to network marketing and instantly "fell in love" with the concept. Due to the changing economy and the new rules of business and under the advice of Warren Buffet, Donald Trump and Robert Kiyosaki he made the transition to become a Professional Network Marketer.

He currently resides in the Silicon Valley with his Bride Rhoza - the love of his life, and his three children McKenzey, Lauren and Preston.

For more information, special offers, speaking engagements and to contact Regan Kuja please visit: www.ReganKuja.com

CHAPTER 27

TRUST BUILDS SUCCESS

BY RUSSELL KEENER

This isn't going to be one of those typical Success stories that you read in books like this, I'm not going to talk to you about working hard, I'm not going to talk to you about taking risks or innovating a new product. These can be great vehicles for obtaining success, but not everyone is a Mark Zuckerberg. I am going to talk with you about being successful as an everyday person in an everyday business.

You see, I believe success starts at a more fundamental level, and while everyone has a different vehicle for obtaining success, the right principles need to be in place as a foundation. Without these principles, true lasting success cannot be obtained, as you will lose motivation and your drive to success (not to mention clients and customers), because despite what you'd like to believe, true lasting success doesn't just happen, it's earned.

Now I know some of what I've already said isn't what you may want to hear, and in this, you should learn your first lesson about me. One of the reasons that I've been able to achieve business and professional success in my life is that I tell the unvarnished truth to my clients, whether they like it or not. I find they like and respect that. Now, that doesn't mean I'm tactless with the words I choose. I like to think I'm direct, but tactful.

So, as we progress through this chapter and I share with you some of my other secrets of success, it's important to keep in mind that you may not like some of them. But, I want you to know the full truth so you are equipped to obtain real, lasting success.

Let me explain…

…In my business as an injury lawyer, my number one source of new clients is word of mouth and referrals from previously satisfied clients. The reason these clients are satisfied is because I deliver what I promise. Now, not all these clients get the payout they may have initially expected. Sometimes a client has a higher (or lower) expectation of their claim than is realistic, and it's my job and responsibility as a lawyer to help them understand the true value of their claim.

This honesty and direct talk has allowed me to build a strong bond and relationship with my clients, which lead to referrals. Direct talk is one of the pillars of my success. My experience is that clients want the truth about their case. And when they know they have a lawyer who tells them the truth, they like and trust that lawyer and will refer their friends and family.

I could have, like some other lawyers, told a half-truth in the initial client interview and promised a bigger case value than could possibly be achieved. This may have made them sign up with me immediately, but, in the end, when they didn't get that value they were promised, they would not be satisfied with the result or with me. A lawyer who over-promises results will soon be found out and their business will suffer.

It's important in all actions you take within your business, financial and personal life that you act with honesty and integrity. Tell the truth and build trust. It will result in clients who trust you, and refer others to you.

So your first pillar of success is:

I. ACT WITH HONESTY AND INTEGRITY AT ALL TIMES, UNDER ALL CIRCUMSTANCES

I know this sounds simple and most folks probably already believe that it is a core value within their business. But, the problem is, as economic times get difficult, and in an effort to "get the sale" the line between honesty and integrity can become blurred if you don't vigilantly practice honesty and integrity in all areas of your life.

Your mom was right. Always tell the truth. The future success you create for yourself by acting honestly and with integrity is far greater than any short-term gain from a sale made by compromising your values.

The second pillar of success builds on the first pillar as it allows you to leverage your honesty and integrity to develop trust. One of the most underrated aspects of business relationships is trust, if you can build a strong, trusting relationship with folks, you can build life-long clients.

There's a saying in marketing circles and among business owners that clients like to buy from people that they KNOW, LIKE, and TRUST. During my years as a lawyer and small business owner, I've seen this ring true time and again.

If I can establish a strong foundation of trust with my client, they will allow me the freedom to do my job WELL. An over-bearing client who lacks trust in me will have a negative impact on the outcome of their case. A client who trusts me to do my job well will not second-guess my decisions and do themselves a favor.

It is easy to build trust by conducting your affairs with honesty and integrity. Let me give you an example…

A few years ago, I had a job injury case in which my client was seriously injured. In order to try to get his case resolved, we scheduled the case for mediation. At the mediation, the insurance company offered to settle his case for $800,000. I have to tell you, although that was a lot of money, this man was seriously injured and I knew it was not enough to cover his medical bills and lost income.

I recommended that my client not accept the settlement, despite the fact that it would have generated a sizeable fee for me. I thought it was in the client's best interest to reject the settlement and move forward with his claim. The case continued for several more years and during that time the insurance company spent over $2 million on his ongoing medical expenses, well over the $800,000 they had offered.

Eventually, once again, we went to mediation and the case was settled for $500,000. While that was less than the $800,000 originally offered, when you combine it with the $2,000,000 of additional medical bills they paid in the interim, it was a much better result for the client.

So, by passing up the initial $800,000 the client actually received $2.5 Million of benefits for his claim. Sure my fee was less, and some business school professors would think it was a bad choice for me, but I didn't mind. I did what was best for my client and I'm glad I did. That's the way I do business. When the case was over, my client had every reason to like and trust me. Because I act with honesty and integrity, I sleep better at night and my client has someone he knows he can trust to make future referrals for the future legal needs of his friends and family. This is an example of a short-term financial hit that generated big gains for me in the future through the trust principal.

Now because my client trusted me, I was better able to do my job, which is to get my client the best overall settlement. In the end the client won and I didn't get as high a fee, but JUSTICE was served, and I gained a lifelong referral source. I realized that the needs of my client were met far better than if I had (like many would have), taken the path of least resistance.

You obtain trust from clients and customers because you are worthy of trust. You become worthy of trust when you act with honesty and integrity and are actually trustworthy.

And the second pillar of success is:

II. DEVELOP TRUSTING RELATIONSHIPS WITH CLIENTS AND CUSTOMERS

This now brings me to the third pillar of my success, and I touched on it briefly earlier…

…I believe that one of the major reasons that I have achieved personal and business success is because I am living my purpose. Now, I know, this may sound strange coming from a lawyer, but I honestly believe that purpose is a key determinant in success.

If you are in an industry, running a business, or trying to achieve success in life, it's easier to do so if your work is in line with your overall life-purpose. When you align your purpose with your business or career you fully ignite a previously slow-burning ember of passion deep inside you. When that passion comes to full flame, your motivation, your level of intensity and focus is SO much greater, that success follows naturally.

This passion motivates you; it inspires you and pushes you to achieve excellence in your field no matter the cost. Now, this is probably the part you're not going to like but I'm going to tell you anyway. My success as a lawyer was not overnight, I struggled for years to get clients, but unlike other lawyers who give up and joined other firms, I struggled on. I fought through those hard times and created success for myself. I stuck it out.

The reason why I was able to fight on and achieve success was because I was passionate about what I was doing, I was living my PURPOSE. This is not something which I regularly share, in fact it almost makes me uncomfortable to open up so much but I want you to know the TRUTH about my success.

You see, I'm not saying that being a LAWYER is my purpose, being a lawyer is merely a vehicle used to achieve my purpose. I believe that my purpose is to fight for, and achieve, FULL JUSTICE for those in need.

My clients are often people who couldn't help themselves, people who were being taken advantage of, people who were living with physical and emotional pain and DESERVED JUSTICE in their lives. This is my purpose and EVERY SINGLE DAY I live my purpose. And, because I live my purpose, I attract into my life the people, the resources and the opportunities that cause me to succeed.

Then the third pillar of success is:

III. LIVE YOUR PURPOSE AND USE THE PASSION IT GIVES YOU TO SUCCEED

Just a quick point I would like to make here before I move to the fourth pillar. You are already starting to see that SUCCESS has very little to do with the VEHICLE you choose for success, but is based on the fundamental principles behind success.

I personally believe that EVERY PERSON can live these fundamental principles and that's why I believe that success is something that everyone can achieve. If you can align yourself with these principles, success may not be instant but it most certainly will be forthcoming.

With that said let's move to the fourth pillar of my success, which again, just like the other three pillars, is a principle rather than a practical vehicle. The fourth pillar is to understand the value and worth of your product or service.

Often I meet folks who have issues with selling their products or services because they are not comfortable with the value they are delivering. The problem is they believe their service or product is not worth the price tag they are asking, and they may be right. But, if you are truly living your PURPOSE in an ethical way, you can provide products and services that bring real value to your customers and clients.

Give yourself permission to financially prosper. There is nothing wrong with profit. So long as the profit is based on real value you are able to promise and deliver. If you are living your purpose in an ethical way, you will naturally provide real value to your clients and customers. You can't do otherwise. You are not asking for something for nothing. But, rather, a fair exchange of value for the product or service you deliver. If your product or service is not worth the value you are charging, living an ethical purpose cannot allow you to stay in that industry.

Money is not the root of all evil; it's the love of money that is the root of all evil. If you love money so much that you are willing to compromise your ethics and values just to get it, you are on the road to certain, eventual failure. So long as your prices and billing practices are consistent with the true value you bring to your clients and customers, a reasonable profit is not only acceptable, it's expected.

Whether you bring value to your customer or client by zealous representation or by providing a valuable product, you have the right to charge a fair profit. So don't let the emotional satisfaction you get for living your PURPOSE outweigh the satisfaction you are entitled to by earning a profit for delivering on promises you can make and keep.

The good news for your clients and customers is that because you are living in line with your purpose, and passionate about your business or profession, you will deliver a higher level of service than anyone else you are competing with. If you earned a profit by adding value, don't apologize, you earned it.

And the fourth pillar of success is:

IV. UNDERSTAND THE VALUE OF YOUR PRODUCT OR SERVICE

Now these 4 pillars should serve you well in pursuit of success no matter what vehicle you choose. If you choose to be a lawyer, construction worker, business owner or engineer, these pillars will transcend industries.

Before you start living these 4 pillars in your life though, there is one thing that you need to do, and this could be most difficult part of discovering your path to success.

I know people who have been searching for this one thing their whole life and never found it, I also know children as young as 3 or 4 who found it instantly. In my opinion, for you to achieve success you need to focus on this ONE THING, and then the four pillars will be easy to live by.

DISCOVER YOUR PURPOSE

In my opinion the number one thing stopping you from achieving the success that you deserve in your life is that you haven't discovered your purpose. You need to commit your time, energy, and focus to discovering your purpose so that you can succeed.

Now, I'm going to be straight with you, discovering your purpose for some people is easy and for others it's difficult. The reality is that once you've discovered your purpose, and you start ethically living it, success is sure to follow. Unfortunately there's not a one size fits all when it comes to discovering your purpose, I can't tell you to sit in a quiet room and think, or go for a walk and it will just come to you.

Each of us needs to make the journey to discovering our purpose differently, but the one piece of advice that I can give you is that when you make discovering your purpose the number one priority in your life, you will discover it, without question.

So stop focusing on just surviving, stop focusing on the economy, stop focusing on less meaningful areas of your life and focus on discovering your purpose. When you have done this, you are well on your way.

I know that this chapter may have been COMPLETELY different than what you may have expected from a lawyer. I'm sure you were expecting logical and persuasive arguments, but understanding that all relationships (which is what business is all about), and all trust-based decisions, flow from the heart and not the head; I thought it important to share this with you. The understanding and applying these pillars have been an important component in achieving my personal and business success.

I don't merely try to do what others expect me to do, I do what is right, no matter the circumstances, and in this case, in this book, the right thing to do was to tell you the plain truth to help you achieve true, lasting success.

About Russell

Russell Keener is one of metro Atlanta's leading personal injury attorneys, specializing in worker's compensation, accident injury and Social Security disability claims. For more than 20 years, Russell has dedicated his life and law practice to helping ordinary people achieve justice. He is passionate in his belief that everyone deserves full justice, and to him, no case is too small or too large as long as justice can be served. Russell knows that when clients enter his office they have possibly just been through the worst experience of their lives. His commitment to 100 percent satisfaction and personal attention to oversee each case makes Russell, and Keener Law, stand above the rest.

Russell earned a business degree from the University of Georgia and later a dual law degree and MBA from Georgia State University in Atlanta. He has been featured in USA Today as an expert in the area of personal injury and has recovered millions for his clients. Russell has also earned high recognition from his peers and industry associations. He has received a 10.0 Avvo rating (superb) in the top attorney rating for Georgia Workers' Compensation, car accidents and social security. His success has earned him a spot in the coveted Million Dollar Advocates Forum and the Multi-Million Dollar Advocates Forum. Other lawyers recognize Russell as an expert, and his expertise and high ethics have earned him the AV rating by Martindale-Hubbell, which is reserved for the top 3% of lawyers. Russell is also a featured lawyer on LawyerCentral.com. He is a member of the State Bar of Georgia Association, Atlanta Bar Association, American Association of Justice and Georgia Trial Lawyers Association.

These years of work experiences and association memberships have given Russell the knowledge to know what it takes to be successful in not only a professional manner, but also a personal one.

Russell has owned his own legal practice for more than 20 years, has been a successful small business owner for more than 30 years and has been married to his wife, Angie, for 26 years. Russell is the proud father of three young men, and he believes their successes in life are by far his greatest achievements.

To learn more about Russell Keener and how you can receive a free special report, contact: www.keenerfreereport.com
Visit: www.KeenerLaw.com
Or call him at 1-800-900-2400.

CHAPTER 28

MAKE LIFE HAPPEN FOR SUCCESS

BY SETH PRICE

What if you could write to a younger you and share the most valuable lessons you have learned through grit and determination? I have always thought I might have a guardian angel, for why else would I have survived some of the mistakes I have made, the careless risks I have taken and even thrived in less than optimal circumstances. We all occupy diverse interpersonal worlds, self, spouse, family, extended family, friends, work, and community. The tools of living are mostly lacking from early education and we must rely on personal fortitude, luck, trial and error. Life is an amazing journey that never ceases to amaze me. Buckle up and enjoy the ride.

My path to self empowerment came from my upbringing. I grew up as an only child to teen parents. Kids basically, exploring their teenage lives in the early sixties – bi-racial, multicultural and certainly questioning the structure of the time. You name it, they were as different as you could imagine, yet at that moment they were intimately bound, aspiring basketball star and enthusiastic cheerleader from another side of the tracks figuring it out in New York City. Now that I am a parent of four, I think about them reeling at the tender age of 17 when they discovered my mother was pregnant, I can only image their fear and commitment to carry on as some sort of rebellion. Their defiance may not have turned out how they originally imagined, but as far as I can see, life is not an exact science.

Fast forward a few years and I became the ultimate vagabond, moving from one family home to another, a grandmother here, an uncle or auntie there, being an optimist has it's benefits, I buried myself in books and have successfully blocked out any real negative feelings I have about that time. I do remember being deeply loved by my grandparents, parents, aunts and uncles who cared for me and cared for my parents. My recollection of hushed conversations and adult discussions are a bit blurry. It wasn't until 3rd grade that my world of collective upbringing came to a screeching halt. My father, who was in university 3000 miles away, was finally graduating, and unbeknownst to me, I was going to live with him. At the time, I barely knew him, he was the cool guy that came to visit a few times a year on his motorcycle.

When I arrived in San Francisco, I had no idea that the visit would be permanent. It was quite a shock, insta-dad. Even I knew he was barely a kid. I must have complained for the first few years straight. In retrospect, he did a fantastic job, never throttled me, and somehow made me a priority in his life. I used to think that my experience of change was unique; I was the only one reinventing myself every day, learning to pay attention to the nuance of communication. Now that I am older, I know that everyone has some unique story unique to them. That experience taught me some crucial lessons.

I was given an amazing amount of freedom, had very little oversight and was instilled with the notion that if you wanted to do anything in life, you had to take complete responsibility for it. I learned to value apprenticeship, learning from others mistakes and successes, I discovered some false gods – those who professed to know it all yet were human and fallible as we all are. I learned of craft, artistic expression and expertise acquired through years of hard work. I learned the art of listening, a chess game of discovery that is multilayered. I also learned to befriend others, to choose my friends wisely, but be accepting of those that are different than me. The lessons in this book are as reflections on a younger me and letters to my children, tools for success in a world a constant change.

DEFINE YOUR OWN SELF WORTH

We all get bombarded with ideas about what it is to be special, from parents, friends, family, outside influences. What I've learned is that others will never know exactly what goes on in your head. True self worth has to come from within. Allowing others to dictate your value gives them control over your emotions, and power to influence your destiny. I have yet to meet an individual that didn't have some thoughts of insecurity. It's human. Just remember that when someone else is looking to put constraints on your potential.

LEARNING IS A STATE OF MIND NOT A PIECE OF PAPER

The idea of a 4 year program being a guaranteed path to success has had a short-lived run in the scheme of things. That everyone should jump at the opportunity of having uninterrupted time to pursue intellectual curiosities is rare in life. But most importantly, learning how to learn will serve you forever. Learn to sort through the massive amount of learning options out there to acquire knowledge and skills in a way that you can digest. This mindset of learning will allow you to grow throughout your entire life, not just while in school. Learn to embrace the unknown with curiosity and study.

CONNECT WITH OTHERS ON THEIR TURF

The people you interact with aren't really thinking about you, their priorities are personal, having to do with their own entertainment, survival and self-preservation. Don't take it personally, being self-centered is part of human nature and has allowed us to survive as long as we have on this planet, it's not about you. To connect, you need to tap into your audience, find out what makes them tick, what's important from their perspective, what makes them laugh, cry or scream. Start by really listening to someone speak, ask questions, give them your complete attention, use eye contact, physical touch, shaking hands, touch of the shoulder. Your job when you are trying to connect is to make others feel comfortable and understood. This will allow you the opportunity to connect past the noise.

SPEAK WITH CLARITY SO YOU CAN BE HEARD

Having your ideas and feeling understood requires the ability to speak in a way your audience can understand. Not everyone hears the same way. Each person that you communicate with speaks a different language, and your job is to translate accordingly so you can hear and be heard. You don't walk into a bank and chat like you are at a football game. Situational appropriateness will help get your message heard.

Don't speak to a truck driver in the King's English, and definitely don't speak to your wife like you speak to employees.

LEARN TO RESPECT YOUR BODY

Fortunately and unfortunate the body you were born with is the only one you get. While genetics have a say in the cards you were given, you have an amazing amount of control over how you can support, accept and enjoy your body. There is a saying that I heard often as a young man, that youth was wasted on the young. I have come to disagree with this point of view. I have met the most depressing young people as well as octogenarians more vibrant and curious than teenagers. Take care of your body, push it beyond it's comfort zone and be conscious of the fuel you feed it. Each body seems to be somewhat unique; the rules that apply to one do not apply to all. Find what works for you and embrace it.

SEX IS A GIFT

Our culture has made the discussion of sex a taboo conversation, either denigrated by the topic of pornography or solely for the purpose of procreation. Sex is as natural as life itself, and presents an opportunity to embrace another human being in ways that transform your experience of the world. Be respectful of your body and the body of others. Demand that from your mates and never give up on engaging the sexual aspect of who you are.

FIND YOUR OUTLET OR IT WILL FIND YOU

Everyone experiences fear, anxiety, pain or just plain old stress. How you deal with it will serve you and those around you, or it will be weight on your shoulders. There is no set rule on how to handle the discomfort in life – exercise, meditation, therapy, conversation, reading, or some other activity. Just know that challenges will happen. If you avoid finding ways for you to process the pain, your stress will find a way to manifest itself in your life.

STRIVE FOR MASTERY IN WHAT YOU DO

Having skills and understanding in the top 10% on any one subject is not rocket science. Most people are not motivated. By reading as much as you can on a subject and applying yourself with some thoughtful consistency, you can gain an understanding greater than 90% of the people in the world. This understanding will provide greater opportunity, allow you to view your subject from multiple perspectives, past and future, local and global. It will help you create your own perspective. The more you know, the more you can play jazz.

CHOOSE WORK WISELY

Just because you like a subject or industry, it doesn't mean it's a good business idea. It's a lot more fun working on a successful business than a failing business in an industry that you like. Give real thought to the directions that you choose, as it will impact your life profoundly. Find mentors, interview people in the field, study market trends. Don't be afraid to change course.

UNDERSTAND HOW WE SELL EVERY DAY

Selling is not about the object or even money, selling is about the exchange of ideas. You see value in an idea and you must present a case to another human being that your idea should be adopted. We sell all the time. As babies, we are cute to survive; as we get older we sell to make friends, to get a date, a job, a raise, or better service. The misconception is that selling and buying is about the item. When we buy, we are not buying the item, we are buying the feeling that we perceive the item will give us. Selling is a skill that becomes easier when you start to understand it. The only way to live in this world without selling is to be in a coma. And then again, you will have sold the world on the idea that you are immobile, still alive and requiring care.

WORK HARDER THAN ANYONE ELSE

Coasting at work is a recipe for disaster, and mostly a sign that you are doing something that you don't really want to do. Your employers can sense your lack of interest and will either ignore you or place you on the bottom of their plans for advancement. We all end up in situations where the job isn't perfectly suited to our long-term goals and expectations; don't let it be a total waste of time. Doing your best and working harder than your peers creates amazing opportunity and helps you get the best out of sub-par work situations. Most people are lazy – which presents an amazing opportunity to be exceptional.

FEAR IS JUST AN EMOTION

Fear ebbs and flows, don't be shocked when it surfaces. Learn to acknowledge its existence, do a gut check for your personal safety then push your limits as much as you can. Once you learn to act even when you are fearful, you begin to have power over your fears.

SURROUND YOURSELF WITH A SUPPORTIVE SPHERE

Truth, Comfort, Inspiration and Intelligence – We need supportive people around us to thrive. When I was young, my father used to say "choose your friends wisely as they will support you the only way they know how." I choose to surround myself with positive people, people who are smarter than I am, have different interests, ones that will push me to be better, comfort me when I need it and above all, people that I can respect. Who will you surround yourself with?

Create a digital footprint that you can be proud of and that supports who you are.

It's not what you say, it's what's found via search – just make sure your footprint doesn't come back 'to bite you in the ass.' There is no such thing as privacy in the digital world. Your online world is your resume, a representation of your influence and a connector to friends, family, work and those unknown. Treat it as such.

DRESS BETTER, EAT BETTER AND KEEP YOURSELF CLEAN

Unfortunately, we are vain and visual creatures that make snap decisions upon what we first process. Your outside presentation has an impact on how others view you and your ability to be heard. Make sure the decision that you make regarding your appearance matches your desired outcome.

BE RESPECTFUL, MANNERS ARE A LANGUAGE TO COMMUNICATE

Small gestures can have a huge impact on those around you. Opening a door for another, lending an extra hand, learning to say please, thank you and I'm sorry. There is a fine line between civility and complete chaos. These five words can change the thoughts of those around you. Pay it forward, be helpful and kind without the promise of personal gain and you will be repaid many times over.

I have found that there is no "one" way to be in the world nor can you control all of the circumstances that surround you. *What you do have sway over is how you respond to the world around you.* Don't wait for life to happen to you, dream it and go for it.

About Seth

Seth Price is a 14-year veteran Internet marketer. He has consulted for leading B2B and B2C brands including: MetLife, BMW, Sony, Nationwide Financial, AAI, Foster Grant, Toys R Us and Conde Nast. He is a master relationship builder, innovator and thought leader. In particular, his experience integrating new technologies and thinking across a variety of industries allows him to uniquely navigate the rapid state of flux that challenges marketers today.

Currently, Seth is Director of Sales and Real Estate Marketing at Placester, a Cambridge-based technology company that is transforming online marketing for the real estate industry.

He resides in Rhode Island with his beautiful wife Catherine and four boisterous kids. He is an avid martial artist, accomplished cook and self-proclaimed gadget junkie. Connect with Seth on Facebook at: www.facebook.com/sethkprice, and Twitter: @ sethstuff and on his blog: http://sethkprice.com

CHAPTER 29

BUILDING WEALTH VS. FINANCIAL PLANNING …SUCCESS BY ASSOCIATION

BY STEVE GOLDBLOOM

ON TOP OF THE WORLD

I am finishing this chapter the night before my 55th Birthday. In my late thirties, my family and I were blessed to be living a lifestyle that had us living in a neighborhood where superstars such as Rosie O'Donnell called home. I had just finalized the sale/merger (pre-dotcom explosion) of Bay Area & Hawaii Barter Exchange Inc., the San Francisco-based, barter and trade company I had founded and built over 14 years.

My ties in this unique industry were strong. I served on the industry association's BOD and came to know two men on the same BOD, the President and CEO of Active International, the then (and I believe still now) undisputed Industry leader. When they learned of my transaction, they "made me an offer I could not refuse," which soon was titled Senior Vice President of worldwide, non-media trading, which is what brought my family from San Francisco to New York.

Three years later, after achieving more success than we all anticipated (and even more learning for me from two brilliant men and their incredible team), I was recruited by a venture capitalist firm to lead a technology company, a dotcom to which I lent my financial and barter experience. Reading about admin assistants who made 8 million due to IPO's,

I took the offer, despite enjoying my work and the genuine respect and admiration for my "recent" employers.

I commuted from my New York home to San Francisco each week. I was continuing to be highly compensated for solving complicated financial problems and creating large profitable opportunities for clients, both American and international corporations, something I'm good at and enjoy; my family and I wanted for nothing.

A BABY GIRL IN A CELL

In 1997, during the time period I sold my company, my son Sam was born. Sam is a gift from God in many ways. His birth nearly cost his mother her life. It was time for adoption, what we had already agreed as an option before Sam was conceived. Sam was about a year old when we started the international adoption process, which we learned was a true exercise in patience and stamina.

Around that time, an advertising transaction with one of my more famous corporate barter clients, Anthony Robbins allowed for tuition for my staff and me to attend his various events and have ongoing access to his numerous materials and trainings. One of many tools I internalized while attending trainings leading to the weeklong Mastery Series event was the Triad. The Triad was a seemingly simple tool that really resonated with me, as I realized I had unconsciously used similar components of it in my earlier years in swim competition. I saw clearly by Anthony Robbins clear documentation of the concept how it could easily and effectively apply to many aspects of life. It was a tool we used daily during the adoption process, and continues to be useful and I pass it to others who are open to personal growth.

The adoption process went on for quite some time. We had doors close in our faces after weeks and months of effort on multiple occasions. In 5/2001 we received a photo, a little girl approaching a year old in Vietnam from the agency we were working with. When we arrived in Vietnam, we saw our little girl, whom we had already named Zoe through the narrow strip of glass in the door at the orphanage. In a large room with dozens of other babies, she sat in a crib constructed of metal bars with a net over the top like a cell.

The plan, Zoe was to be in our arms the very next day. We could see an infected scab the size of a silver dollar atop her head, which of course made the delays even worse. We kept our heads up and our language positive, always believing the dream would come true this time; without allowing doubt from past false starts. The Triad is a powerful tool.

After what was already almost a 3-year period, two days later Zoe was in our arms, and soon after we were able to fly home. When Zoe's feet touched US soil she was officially a family member, and an American citizen. The joy was overwhelming.

THE INCREDIBLE, BLOOMING BABY

The days that followed Zoe's adoption were some of the most miraculous I've known. Like the video clips of a flower blooming in time lapse, Zoe's progress was stunning.

She was a lifeless, unresponsive child when we received her. Just three days later, after a "complete family love immersion," she was laughing and giggling as we played in the pool. The transformation was unbelievable, really. I promised myself and Zoe then that we would return to Vietnam for her tenth birthday – for her to see her beginnings and understand all that it entailed.

Not uncommon, becoming a father was a turning point in my life. A difference for me; I had accumulated enough wealth to where I really did not have to be concerned about money. With Zoe's adoption, the decision became clear; I resigned from the dotcom to once again be self-employed, really to be a stay-at-home dad, to prioritize building and growing what was surely my most valuable asset: my family. Eleven years later, many things have changed in our family but much also remains the same. Zoe is twelve at the time that I write this, very close to straight A's, and is determined to achieve them. She is doing back handsprings at gymnastics practice, planning to go to her first Junior High school dance with two girlfriends; and I am confident she will make the right decisions.

EXPERIENCE ASSETS GALORE!

The part of the story I've left out were the severe challenges which I hit sometime in 2002-2003, just before and after my family's relocation to Seattle, during the messy dissolution of the marriage between my children's mother and me. Now a single dad, I found myself living in a series of modest apartments, sleeping on the floor on air mattresses near my kids during the seemingly rare times I saw them. Once again, I leaned on the tools I acquired through the years of association with great mentors, including but not limited to Tony Robbins' Triad; I remember thinking, "Gratitude is the key, we're all healthy…things could be worse and they're bound to get better."

How did I go from a millionaire to not being able to afford beds for my kids and I? …It doesn't matter. What matters is the promise I made to myself and my daughter that I was determined to keep, even at a time when the financial hole seemed very deep.

In my mid 40's, I was essentially starting over. In the process of beginning a new career, different from what I had been doing (I had to get off airplanes as part of my work) but still in the world of finance. I was significantly in debt to a handful of my closest friends who "knew" I would succeed …to them I am eternally grateful. An international trip in a few years with my kids seemed logically out of reach. We were just gathering the basics, but I soldiered on.

In 2010, I more than delivered on that promise. By that time, I was remarried to the love of my life, Eden, an American Filipino widow with two sons, Chris and Tony which completes my current, blended family (who I lovingly refer to as "The UN"). I had been in the insurance industry for some time, helping those approaching retirement or retired move from risk to safety. We were doing very well at meeting our clients' objectives. The crash of 2008 took its toll, causing insurance companies to significantly reduce commissions in the "safe money" areas. My company's dynamics would have to change to continue to meet client objectives and prosper. While many people were losing significant portions of their retirement and net worth, I am proud to say that the money we had taken care of for the 200 client families we served remained 100% unscathed. Today, both of our institutional money managers show that same past 10-year audited track record.

The events of 2008 shone a spotlight on the financial services industry I was already witnessing, and as a result was preparing for. An added path to our plan that would serve two purposes became very clear to me. Many people I was meeting were in a place where much of their retirement savings was just gone, as the person who gained from serving them was not "watching their back." Many were dealing with brokerage firms who have no legal responsibility to be transparent and put their clients objectives as #1. I saw a better way through forming a Registered Investment Advisory Firm (RIA). I felt a more robust securities licensing that would have my team and I working under a fiduciary responsibility which legally bound us to 100% transparency, no hidden fees, and to use the best interest of the client as the goal. The RIA (not the majority choice today) requires the advisor to give up the right to make commissions on transactions and make client objectives the goal. Wanting to be paid only for advice, and not from sharing the profit margins hidden in the brokerage world's manufactured financial products at the expense of the client, it was clear the RIA was the road less traveled, but perfect for us, as it was best for our clients.

So there I was, my company and industry experiencing changes, plans to add licenses, to add another location, to add staff. I had just paid for our wedding, the purchase of a larger Sammamish home for my newly-blended family, and was experiencing real estate value declines – causing poor timing to choose selling the homes my wife and I owned prior. Not exactly a time you'd think that I, someone who gives financial advice for a living would choose to spend five figures on a family l trip to Vietnam and to meet my new extended family in the Philippines.

I THOUGHT THIS CHAPTER WAS
ABOUT BUILDING WEALTH!

Are you wondering? What does it all have to do with Building Wealth vs. Financial Planning?" Great question. Here it goes.

I was just interviewed and taped a show that I was invited to be an "expert" financial commentator on that will air soon sometime in 2013 on NBC, ABC, CBS, and Fox and affiliates, and I explained we all live our own story, have our own struggles, our own wins, all of which amount to a type of asset. I'm not talking about money, although financial assets are certainly important, but one of a set of four assets defined by entrepreneur and author Lee Brower (also featured on Oprah). Lee has become a mentor of mine over the years as I've invested time regularly in an exclusive Strategic coach program he leads quarterly to continue to improve my service to my clients. In his book, Brower discusses

"True Wealth" consisting of a person's collective assets: Core Assets, Experience Assets, Contributory Assets AND Financial assets.

Through the recognition and acknowledgement of all of one's assets, Lee suggests that we all "live life deliberately." What you have is not about doing more with less, but doing more with more in all areas of your life!"

Related are the many success principles Anthony Robbins identifies, who I mentioned earlier in the context of my daughter's adoption. The Triad - comprised of three elements: Beliefs, Language and Physiology, each of which affects how you feel; if you start with the end in mind, "I want to feel happy" then adjust each of the triad elements to suit and happiness will ensue. It may sound simple, but implementation is key. My experience and the ongoing feedback I receive is that it really works.

I've also found that the concepts of The Brower Quadrant blend synergistically with those of entrepreneur and author Bill Bachrach, another mentor of mine whom I've spent weeks with in recent years studying at his San Diego Academy sessions. Bill is the author of "Values Based Financial Planning: *The Art of Creating an Inspiring financial Strategy.*" Bill says, "In the grand scheme of things, money's not that important. It's important only to the extent that it allows you to enjoy what's important to you. And not worrying about your finances is critical to having a life that excites you, nurtures those you love and fulfills your highest aspirations." In other words, money is just money... it has no intrinsic value. Money only has value when it's put to work towards what you value in life.

I recently met Don Yaeger, who spent 30 years interviewing star athletes for Sports Illustrated, and he spoke of "success by association." He hit the nail on the head!

For over 35 years I've studied with and learned from many brilliant mentors, recent examples I've mentioned already, and many more, in an effort to glean their experience. Not only to achieve personal growth, but as important, improve my ability to best or better serve my ideal client. I'm grateful for the association and knowledge I've received from each one. Each has various tools, tips and repeatable methodologies to achieve success that I draw from regularly and use to help others.

The Brower Quadrant and Values-Based Financial Planning help to define a part of the difference between Building Wealth vs. Financial Planning. Building wealth encompasses all your assets, not just your financial assets. It acknowledges that things like the adoption of a baby girl from Vietnam, and the journey back with your kids to deliver gifts to others, when its easier to be financially practical and "put it off," from being somewhat wealthy one month to finding yourself sleeping on the floor on air mattresses with your kids the next, are ASSETS - MY Experience Assets. Like a bank account, a life insurance policy, or a market account, Experience Assets such as education, career, life experiences, etc. are also passed down through the generations, ... back to the trip I took my family on in 2010...

At a time where the trip meant raiding some of my cash reserves, at the age of 53, when I would advise most people to simply put the trip off for a few years, I knew it had to be done then to increase my families overall assets most significantly. The trading of some Financial Assets, for the value that came from this trip was simply trading one asset for another that I believe is a greater value.

I understood making that promise back in 2001, that the experience of visiting the orphanage Zoe came from in Ho Chi Minh City, after ten years of a typical, American childhood filled with iPods, flat screens, and gymnastics lessons would become Zoe's Experience Asset (although it was 3 months prior to my meeting Lee, and I did not yet have this term). Our children handing out $400 worth of simple toys such as balls and puzzles from the dollar store, one at a time to each child at that orphanage and seeing them react as if they had been handed solid gold, would be a valued asset that Zoe, Sam, and Chris would carry with them forever. The realization on our kids' faces as they saw kids Zoe's age at the orphanage, and understood that they were "her" nine years prior, is an Experience Asset that we all gained that day. All three kids realized how very fortunate our family is, and the gratitude I feel to see my children grow in a way that's hard to put into words. Deliberately living life comes to mind.

I believe the experience we gained on that trip will lead to the increase in their Contributory Assets as they grow. I have been fortunate enough in my life to be able to accumulate Contributory Assets; giving has become part of who I am. I believe that asset too, is passed down through generations of my family by deliberately "Building Wealth vs. Financial Planning."

BUILDING WEALTH VS. FINANCIAL PLANNING: SUCCESS BY ASSOCIATION

The term "financial planning" is often used interchangeably with other related terms such as "wealth management," "asset management," "retirement planning," etc. No semantics lesson here, but I do want to make clear that all financial services approaches are not created equally. Financial planning sounds good; so does Wealth management, and they are. I use a team of subject matter experts in tax, legal, insurance and securities to name a few to financially plan – using our clients' goals. Retirement planning, income planning, wealth distribution and wealth preservation in a tax effective manner are important, and my team and I excel on these subjects. It does not stop there, for those I work with directly in an ongoing manner.

The problem with financial planning is that, by definition, it only deals with financial assets. What I've learned through life experiences, and what we've learned from Lee Brower is that financial assets are not our only assets. What we've learned from Bill Bachrach is that our financial assets are meaningless unless they're supporting the rest of our assets, which really represent our values. Financial planning often does not take into account the whole picture of our lives. Often it results in a "set-and-forget" type thing, which for many reasons doesn't work in the dynamic setting of our ever-changing lives. Those referred to me to give a second opinion on, who have worked with their advisor for years "accumulating wealth, often do not take into account critical aspects of their "grand plan" and actual objectives today. They are not "bad advisors," they just have different "non-fiduciary" tools. The terms I prefer to use when working with my ideal client, who typically would be "the millionaire next door": a professional, a business owner, or corporate executive nearing retirement with between $2 and $25 million of investable assets are "building wealth" and "wealth management" (and the same holds true for the people with less than $2 million who I refer to my associates and direct relationships for). Both are dynamic terms implying ongoing attention and action. You spend the entirety of your life, before and beyond retirement building wealth, represented by the accumulation of your quadrant of assets. Wealth management at Goldbloom Wealth Management LLC (GWM) is the process by which you are asked, "What is important about money to you?" Your cumulative assets are dynamically managed and allocated. It includes financial planning, but is entirely more robust, encompassing your own set of values, what you want your money to do for your family, what you want passed down through generations of your family and how. At GWM, Wealth management considers the whole ball of wax, core assets, experience assets, contributory assets, and financial assets which includes advanced estate planning, legacy planning, with focus on not only securities, but insurance, legal and tax planning. A wealth management plan is a living thing, regularly reviewed and scalable and flexible to your life.

The collective tools of my past experiences and the ideas and strategies of the brilliant minds I've had the incredible fortune to associate with (Don Yaeger most recently), such as the few examples I've included here, are what I bring to the wealth management table in addition to my education, and securities and insurance licenses.

While I continue to learn, I can pay it forward by sharing with families who really want to pass on their collective assets. Beyond financial planning, beyond even wealth management is a relationship between me as an advisor and my ideal client that borders on, and often extends into, friendship. For those referred to us who need less of my services, I act as the initial "direction" setter and one of my associates takes the ongoing relationship management role, bringing me in as needed. I sit with people and I learn not just about their money, which is why they're there in the first place, but also about their problems, about their kids and grandkids, and about their passions and dreams. I use the many tools I've learned and applied to my own life and ongoing self-improvement journey to help people grow and get clear, so they can make decisions that allow more comfort, enjoyment and pleasure into their lives. It's a pleasure and an honor to help guide people using their own values and dreams, focusing on what is most important to them; it's the whole idea behind my being a fiduciary, to make sure it's all about the client. It's my job to "watch their back" so they can spend their time doing what is important to them.

Success in life can be measured any number of ways, as can happiness. Everyone has different ways of moving through life, tackling challenges and celebrating wins. I've had many blessings in my life, ...many gifts.

I've also, like everyone, had many challenges and made my own share of mistakes. The learning I've acquired I feel honored to share with those I come in contact with, just as I hope to continue learning from the rest of the citizens of this world (Don Yaeger -"success by association"). I've shared a few of my big takeaways with you here, among them Tony Robbins "Triad," the Lee's "Brower Quadrant," and Bill Bachrach's "Values-Based Financial Planning." I am lucky to say these gentlemen are just the tip of the iceberg.

About Steve

Steve Goldbloom has been championing entrepreneurs, executives, professionals and their families for over 30 years in the world of money. Utilizing the same "value-for-value" fair business approach that made him a front-runner in the Barter & Trade industry, Steve now helps clients optimize, preserve and effectively pass on their financial assets through generations. An expert problem solver, Steve negotiates complex financial problems on the client's behalf according to their values, creating big wins for the client and their family that wouldn't be possible with just any financial planner.

Through client education, transparency and fiduciary behavior, Steve and his team of "best in class" professionals offer a better, honest approach that is refreshing in today's world. As an Investment Advisory Representative (IAR) of Goldbloom Wealth Management LLC (GWM), Steve's status as a Fiduciary legally binds him to 100% transparency, no hidden fees, and to always do what's best for the client – which really sets him apart from many financial professionals. Between the fiduciary standard and complete, professional independence from any one insurance company or brokerage firm, Steve and his team are truly able to offer clients a plan that's best for them and their particular individual situation.

Utilizing a Values-Based Financial Services model, Steve gets to the heart of what people value most and then puts their assets to work towards those values. Steve addresses his clients' entire financial house, getting it in order, the goal being wealth preservation through generations. His clients' delegation of that responsibility to Steve and his team allows them to better enjoy spending their time in the way that they choose and sleep easy, knowing their financial house is in order, constantly monitored, and tended to from a fiduciary standpoint, and being cared for generations to come.

In addition to what Steve considers to be his most important role of father, husband, family member and friend, Steve has been seen in the public domain. Steve has been seen in *Newsweek* magazine as a Financial Trendsetter, as well as on America's Premiere Experts/Consumer's Advocate TV Show on Fox, NBC, ABC, CBS, and affiliates. He has been regularly heard Sunday mornings at 10 am on Fox News' station 770AM in Seattle, WA as a local guest expert on the nationally-syndicated *Financial Safari* Radio Show. Steve has been featured on the CBS evening news hosted by Dan Rather as well as on KTVU, the Fox affiliate on *Mornings on 2* interviewed by Ross McGowan. Steve earned a spot in the IRTA's Hall of Fame as one of the youngest members inducted for his efforts in helping to shape the barter industry through his involvement with the International Reciprocal Trade Association (IRTA). Steve has also been featured in many periodicals including the *San Francisco Chronicle, Nations Business, San Francisco Business Times,* radio interviews, and as a guest lecturer in the MBA program at the San Francisco School of Business among hundreds of other speaking engagements.

CHAPTER 30

BUILDING YOUR RETIREMENT PLAN FROM THE FOUNDATION UP

BY TAD HILL

Here's a thought to keep you awake at night: once you retire, you have amassed all of the wealth that you are ever going to have. Poof! Earning game over. You are through earning and growing and must now rely on whatever money you saved, or did not save, for retirement. To avoid retirement planning nightmares, an investor should consider working with a Chartered Retirement Planning Counselor (CRPC®). A chartered retirement planning counselor is the architect who will guide you to create a retirement blueprint for what your retirement plan should consist of.

In order to design the blueprint, however, there are many questions that need to be answered BEFORE the design can be finalized. I call these answers the MUST-KNOW FACTS of retirement planning. Here are a few of the most important questions that you need to answer:

A. *What matters to you the most in retirement?*
We have to get really clear on what we want out of our retirement years. Is travel a priority? Do you want to move closer to your grandchildren? Is it ok to sell the McMansion and buy a smaller house you can pay cash for and invest the difference? The goal that I hear the most from my clients is that they want to maintain their current lifestyle while having some assurances that they won't run out of money, but also be able to sleep at

night! You don't want to be breaking out in a cold sweat every time the stock market drops 100 points.

One of the biggest mistakes I see retirees make is taking more risk than they are really comfortable with because they think it's necessary for their long-term success. So when we are asking ourselves what matters most, we really should give some thought to how important having a sense of security is to us during our retirement years. It's one thing to see our portfolio cut in half in a market crash when we are 30 years old and still have 35 more years to work and make it back. It's another thing entirely when we have quit working and we are now counting on that same portfolio to pay the bills!

B. *What are the things that could impede you from having the retirement you've always dreamed of?*

Retirement planning is much more complex than growth and accumulation planning. Mistakes are magnified by the fact that we don't have the time to correct them that we used to have. We also have to concern ourselves with issues that we didn't have to before. A few examples are: healthcare planning, long term care needs, when to take social security, longevity, legacy concerns...these are just a few. It's also important that we reduce the risk of market volatility hurting us right when we need our savings the most. Good retirement planning is about identifying all of the risks to our lifestyle in retirement, and creating solutions for them so that we can live the life we want and have a sense of security while we do it. The best way to do this is to pay attention to the four key areas of retirement planning that I will describe later in this chapter.

C. *Are you and your advisor speaking the same language?*

Let me give you an example of what I mean here. I had a very nice widow (I'll call her Mary) come to see me in early 2009 and when I asked her what was on her mind she said, "Well I've come to see if you can help me. I had over a million dollars just a few years ago and now I'm down to almost half of that. The thing that I don't understand is that I told my advisor I wanted to be very conservative with my investments and he assured me we were. He said that I was only in "safe" stocks that were stable and paid good dividends, and that we were diversified so that if any one particular stock had a problem it wouldn't have too much of an impact. That's why I don't understand how this could have happened?"

So, can you think of a few areas where she and her advisor weren't speaking the same language? The first thing is that they obviously have very different definitions of what "safe" means. The second is that there are many types of diversification. The type that she had will help against what is called *business risk.* Business risk is the risk of any one company having a problem and it causing their stock to take a hit. Unfortunately this type of diversification doesn't do anything to solve for what is called *systemic risk,* or "risk in the system." An example of systemic risk is the market crashes of 2001-2002 or the crash of 2008. It didn't matter what types of stocks you owned, if you owned stocks, you got clobbered! So we want to diversify in a way that protects us from both.

D. *How can we strategize to protect investments while still generating income and protecting against inflation all at the same time?*

In retirement, we need our savings to generate a paycheck since we are no longer earning an income. There is a shift from a growth strategy to a distribution strategy. I'm often asked "what are some good investments these days?" that's like going to the doctor and asking, "what are some good medicines I could be taking?" Investments are a lot like medicines in that they are designed to do different things.

So the types of investments that can generate a stable, predictable income may not be (and probably aren't) the best way to get maximum long-term gains. By the same token, if we are expecting our growth investments to generate an annual income, we had better have a constitution made of iron. That type of approach may appeal to mountain climbers, racecar drivers and cage fighters, but the people that become my clients are looking for stability. In order to accomplish that, we have to be very careful and deliberate about how we structure your income plan. It doesn't mean we don't want some growth investments in the portfolio, it just means we don't want to count on them to pay the bills every month. Going back to the medicine analogy, penicillin may be the miracle drug, but how well does it fix a broken leg? We want to pick the right medicine for the right ailment.

E. *How do you know if your advisor's advice is designed to benefit you or to benefit their pocketbook?*

There is a little known fact in the world of investment advice about how we are governed. There are actually two different standards that people in my business are held to. One is a fiduciary standard and the other is a suitability standard. In layman's terms here is the difference. A suitability standard only requires that an investment be "suitable" for the person making the investment. One main way this is determined is whether it falls within your risk tolerance.

Your risk tolerance is typically defined by the answers you give to a questionnaire that you may have paid little attention to at the time you answered the questions. This will determine whether you are "conservative" "moderate" or "aggressive." As long as the investment falls within your category then chances are it's considered suitable. On the other hand, some people are held to a fiduciary standard. This means that we are required to actually do what is in your best interest, not just what is "suitable." This is a much higher standard of conduct and, as you may imagine, comes with considerably more liability on our part. We have to prove that what we recommended is actually best for you. If you don't know whether your advisor is a fiduciary or not, just ask. If they give you an answer that sounds like a politician running for office, then chances are they aren't!

F. *How can you keep your advisor from sailing to Bora Bora with all of your money? (Or "how not to get Madoffed!")*

There have been innumerable articles on this topic since the crash of 2008, but I'm constantly surprised that very few people actually understand how to protect themselves from this. It's really very simple. You must make sure that your advisor has a 3rd party custodian where your money is held. This means that your money isn't kept at an account in your advisor's name or the name of their company. Madoff's client wrote checks and had money wired to Bernard L. Madoff securities, this is a big NO NO! For example, the name of my company is Freedom Financial Group, and I've actually had many new clients ask if they should make checks out in the name of my company. DO NOT DO THIS!

Always make sure there is a 3rd party custodian where your money is being sent. A few examples of third party custodians are: Fidelity Investments, Charles Schwab, T.D. Ameritrade, Scottrade, etc. My company's custodian is Fidelity Investments, one of the most well-respected firms in the world. This assures our clients that if I woke up one morning and decided to become a mastermind criminal, I'd have to start by knocking off the gas station across the street from our office, because I couldn't get my hands on our client's money if I wanted to!

Now that we've discussed some (but by no means all) of the really important questions that must come first, let's dig a little deeper into the specifics of good retirement planning. I've listed below the *four main areas of retirement planning* and the key questions that should be answered before we can structure the best plan possible for your situation.

   1. Income Planning: Income planning is the foundation of a good retirement plan. The first thing we have to concern ourselves with in retirement is how we are are going to replace our paycheck. In order to do that we need to know the answers to the following questions: What does it take to support our lifestyle? In other words, how much do we spend every year? I normally insist our clients print the previous twelve months of bank statements to use in determining how much actually goes out the door every year. This is quick and accurate because the bank statement will catch every dollar that was spent. This gives us a basis for how much will be required in retirement. Without bank statements to eliminate the guesswork, I've frequently had people report expenses of 20-30% less than the actual amount spent annually. A foundation that is off by 20% is not stable and could very easily cause your plan to be unsustainable. The next question is, what sources of income can we count on? These are usually things like Social Security or a pension. It's also important to understand how the death of your spouse would affect these income sources. Once your spouse passes away, the smaller of your two social security checks will go away and if a pension income only has a 50% or 75% spousal option, the combination of both reductions could have a big impact on the person left behind. Once we have a clear picture of these areas, this will tell us if we are going to need to generate income from our investments or not. For most people the answer is that we will need to do that, which leads us to.....

2. *Investment Planning*: Investment planning should first and foremost be structured in a way to support your income plan. If we are going to need income from our savings in retirement it is critical that the income have three main characteristics: (i) Be Secure, (ii) Be Predictable and (iii) Last for both lifetimes. I have met with countless people who have had to reduce their lifestyle or even go back to work, because they didn't under-stand this core principle. The good news is that rarely is it nec-essary to commit all or even most of your retirement savings to your income plan. Often we can create a secure income plan with less than half of your savings and at that point we can in-vest other dollars for long term growth, inflation protection, etc. So the main question to answer when doing income planning is what job are we asking different pieces of our portfolio to do? Because, as I said earlier, the types of investments that will do really well for income planning aren't usually the best for long term growth and *vice versa*. When investment planning is done correctly, it is one of the last pieces of the retirement planning process. This is because we must know the answers to all of the other questions before we chose the investments. For many people in my field, it seems to me that it's all about picking the investments. I have no idea how you can do a good job of that, if you haven't answered all of the other questions first.

3. *Legacy Planning*: Legacy Planning is about what you will leave, to whom, and how you can avoid leaving most of it to Uncle Sam. A common misconception here is that a trust will take care of all of your legacy planning tax problems. It is true that certain types of trusts will help you minimize estate taxes, but the bigger problem for most of us is going to be how to deal with income taxes that our loved ones may be hit with once the

money is left to them. Money that is currently in tax deferred accounts like 401k's or IRA's are especially vulnerable to income taxation since no taxes have ever been taken out of these accounts. These dollars will be taxed at the beneficiaries highest tax rate when they distribute it from these types of accounts. The main question to know the answer to here is: What types of taxes are your savings exposed to once you pass them on and at what tax rates? Once we are clear on that we can begin to devise strategies to offset the tax burden on your loved ones. A good vehicle to do this with is life insurance. You can pay a relatively small premium and leverage the money many times over as a tax free benefit to your heirs.

4. *Tax Planning*: We know that taxes will probably be going up in the future. In fact, as of the writing of this book, they are slated to go way up very soon. Income tax rates, capital gains tax rates, taxes on qualified dividends, the whole shebang! If you're reading this and that has happened then we have to take a fresh look at how we structure withdrawals from our savings and investments. It may become more important than ever to find ways to defer our taxes or structure things in tax-free accounts like Roth IRA's or using investments like municipal bonds. Tax planning is an area that is constantly changing, so the most important thing is to work with an advisor that employs forward-looking tax reduction strategies.

Ultimately, the goal of retirement planning is to protect your golden years so that you have the lifestyle and a sense of security that you've always dreamed of. What this needs to look like for you personally will be dictated by your unique circumstances. That's why it is so important to have a defined decision-making process that uncovers the must know facts for your situation. We must take the time up front to do this right so you are as protected as possible from the many risks that may (and probably will) try to get in your way. The good news is that when done correctly, this process can give you a tremendous sense of security in knowing that you've planned and have a strategy for anything that may come your way.

About Tad

Tad Hill is the President of Freedom Financial Group. He founded Freedom Financial Group with his wife and business partner, Toni, in order to fill a niche they felt was not being addressed properly in the retirement planning environment —helping retirees and pre-retirees in Alabama find answers to issues that may affect their quality of life during retirement. They believe each investor is unique and no single strategy is right for everyone. In fact, the defining point that separates their process from other firms is that they carefully identify all of the "must-know facts" that are critical to the individual client's retirement success BEFORE they make investment decisions. This goes far beyond a "risk tolerance" questionnaire that is employed by typical firms. Eliminating potential risks for their clients' retirement success is done through a four-step process, including: Income Planning, Investment Planning, Legacy Planning and Tax Planning. This approach requires more effort on the part of Freedom Financial, but results in a roadmap that creates a sense of security for their clients.

Tad is a Chartered Retirement Planning Counselor (CRPC®), a Registered Financial Consultant (RFC) and holds a Series 65 License. He is an Investment Advisor Representative, offering advisory services through Global Financial Private Capital, LLC, an SEC Registered Investment Advisor, and he also holds insurance licenses in the state of Alabama. Tad is honored to be the co-host of the nationally syndicated television show "Retiring Well." He is also a frequent financial commentator on ABC's "Talk of Alabama" and Fox 6's "Good Day Alabama." You can also hear him weekly as the co-host of the Financial Safari Radio Show on 105.5 WERC, 101.5 WAPI, and 100.5 The Source. He was recently recognized in *Newsweek* as one of the nations "Financial Trendsetters" and has co-authored two books. The first book is an updated version of the Napoleon Hill classic *Think and Grow Rich* and the second is the *Ultimate Success Guide* with Brian Tracy.

Tad is a member of the Better Business Bureau, the National Ethics Bureau and the International Association of Registered Financial Consultants. He was awarded the Global Financial Fiduciary Excellence Award in 2011 & 2012, and he was featured on the cover of Advisors Excel's AE Insider magazine in 2012 as the leader of one of the fastest growing financial planning firms in the country. He and Toni are graduates of Auburn University and reside in Indian Springs with their three daughters: Peyton, Tyler and Shannon.

To schedule a time to discuss your financial future, contact us at: TadHill@FreedomFinGroup.com or call us at 205-988-0006 today!

Investment Advisory Services offered through Global Financial Private Capital, LLC, an SEC Registered Investment Advisor.

Insurance and Annuity product guarantees are subject to the claims-paying ability of the issuing company, and are not offered through Global Financial Private Capital.

CHAPTER 31

THE NINE GOLDEN RULES OF RETIREMENT PLANNING
— OR ALL I NEED TO KNOW ABOUT INVESTING I LEARNED FROM GOOFUS AND GALLANT

BY TOD LENHOFF

When I was young, my mom got us a monthly subscription to the magazine Highlights. The very same Highlights magazine that has adorned dentist's offices for years. In the magazine was a recurring cartoon about two brothers, called Goofus and Gallant. The tenor of the piece was to teach children, such as myself, the difference between right and wrong.

Goofus (wrong), and Gallant (right).

The cartoon always started with Goofus handling an everyday situation the wrong way, and then the identical situation was shown how to be handled correctly by Gallant. For example, at a birthday party Goofus might selfishly grab the last piece of cake for himself, whereas Gallant would be courteous and ask first if anyone else was interested in the last piece, before taking it for himself.

As silly as this illustration of morals and model of ethical behavior may seem, these same basic prudent principals, or common sense approaches, are a cornerstone of the **9 Golden Rules** for investing for a successful retirement.

First, a real life Goofus and Gallant illustration.

I had a client named Jack come into my office several years back. It was 2005 to be exact. Jack was gloating about all the money he stood to make in buying up houses in Phoenix, AZ. He already had successes in the real estate market to prove his point. We all know a Jack. Jack took every dollar he could muster up and bought real estate. Where possible he leveraged with 120% financing. Need I go on? You know the rest of the story. In 2012 Jack had already been through foreclosures, short sales, and is considering bankruptcy. Jack was enticed by greed and fast money. He was looking for the short cut to striking it rich in his investments. Unfortunately, his savings had been obliterated by investing like a Goofus.

Contrast Jack's approach to another client of mine, Bob and Mary. Bob and Mary had always followed the slow and steady approach in their investing. Their focus is always first and foremost on capital preservation. Sure it is kind of boring, and they often miss the big gains from run-ups in the stock market by not going "all in" when the market looks hot. Nonetheless they maintain a much more prudent approach to investing. A slow and steady approach, they never commit too many eggs to a high-risk basket. They enjoy a financial stress-free life and are able to live comfortably. They invest like a Gallant.

So let's explore the **Nine Golden Rules to successful retirement planning**. Things Gallant would do.

1. SLOW AND STEADY INVESTMENT PLANS WIN THE RACE

Like the concept of compound interest, a consistent, slow, boring approach to growing your investments usually works out best in the long run.

2. HAVE CLEAR OBJECTIVES OF WHAT IT IS YOU WANT

How can you know if your financial plan is moving you closer to your goals if you can't clearly define those goals? Take a look at what you are invested in today. If it is not clear exactly how those investments are moving you towards meeting your objectives, dump them and reinvest accordingly.

3. IF IT SOUNDS TOO GOOD TO BE TRUE...

Always remember that most investments are sold, not bought. That means your "advisor" is trying to find some way to entice you to make that certain investment. In Sales 101 you learn that people are easily motivated to invest by either fear or greed. Promising unrealistic returns simply whets your greed appetite. However, if someone implying a "safe" return of, say 10%, when you know the banks are safely paying only 2% on CD's...well, this just sounds too good to be true. It probably is. Trust your gut that something doesn't make sense. Ask lots of questions until it sounds more realistic. Learn all about the risks. Learn what is guaranteed, and what is not. Make an intelligent decision. Not a wishful one.

4. CASH (FLOW) IS KING!

Remember back in school when you could trade your peanut butter jelly sandwich for someone else's goodie in return? Well, in the grown up world you need cold hard cash to get the things you want. Accumulation plans are fine for theoretically growing your wealth, but income plans are king. *Make income the driver of your plan.* Consider staples such as bond interest, stock dividends, annuities, rental real estate. All these investments kick off cash flow you can then use to buy lots of life's goodies. Also, if income is the key, then as long as it is steady and reliable, the market fluctuations of the principal are secondary. Contrast this to a heavily-laden accumulation plan in things such as growth stocks and funds where if you take cash out on a regular basis, the potential erosion of principal through withdrawals and market fluctuations could have a significant negative impact on your ability to continue taking those withdrawals. What happens if the money runs out? With a reliable income plan, the money never runs out.

However, say you want some investments in a growth strategy to meet the objective of having cash available in the future, just not today. Perhaps you want to self-insure for a possible catastrophic illness, or leave the money to your heirs. Just remember that with ample cash flow, you can still fund things like long term care insurance, or life insurance that may more reliably grow your dollars and meet your objectives.

5. SIMPLICITY USUALLY WORKS BEST

If you are like many people your investments look like a Hodge-podge of things you picked up along the way. You may even be duplicating holdings in say your mutual funds and not even be aware of it. Well, it just may be time for spring cleaning. Take a fresh look and see if you can still justify why you still own a particular investment. Make sure it is consistent with meeting your current objectives. Remember, if you can consolidate your holdings wherever possible this will make things easier to measure, manage, and control. Just be careful not to put all of your eggs....

6. DON'T PUT ALL OF YOUR (MARKET RISK) EGGS IN ONE BASKET UNLESS YOU WANT TO MAKE OMELETTES

I purposely differentiate market risk investments from investments that simply grow with guaranteed interest.

With investments that have market fluctuation of their values, proper diversification can help to reduce the volatility, or risk. This is critical in controlling your risk of loss in investments such as stocks and bonds. That's one reason why mutual funds are very popular. They provide a diversified way of owning stocks and bonds, all in one neatly-packaged investment.

Although credit risk is also an issue, it can be more readily controlled by only investing in credit-worthy companies, or by understanding the regulations and insurance protection that may be in place to protect against defaults. For example, only investing in banks up to the FDIC insurance limits would be an example of controlling your credit risk.

My illustration above where Jack put all of his eggs into real estate is an example of not diversifying prudently, and in turn ending up with egg on his face.

7. FAILING TO PLAN FOR THE POSSIBILITY OF CATASTROPHIC ILLNESS, IS PLANNING TO FAIL

No matter whose statistics you believe, whether it be AARP, or the Department of the Aging; they all will tell you that if you live long enough you have a greater than 50% chance of not being able to live fully independently into your ripe old age. This means a strong possible need for long term care. This could mean help at home with an aide coming in occasionally, assisted living facility, or a nursing home.

Please don't be a Goofus here by doing nothing, or going into denial about it just happening to "the other guy." You need a plan. If you won't do it for yourself, then do it for your spouse, your children, and others you love. Don't be a burden and self-ishly dependent simply because you didn't want to face the truth and probability of it occurring.

Having a plan doesn't necessarily mean buying insurance – though that is certainly a good place to consider if you can af-ford it. It may be as simple as investing your extra savings in a guaranteed growth strategy, and reducing your market risk, so you will definitely have more dollars in the future.

8. DON'T DO FINANCIAL PLANNING IN A VACUUM, OR YOU JUST MIGHT BE EATING DUST

Ok. So you like a particular investment. Love the anticipated glorious returns! But have you considered the tax consequenc-es of the particular investment? What about the liquidity? Will this investment go through probate if you die? What is your exit strategy out of this investment? So many considerations, it makes your head spin. However, a good well-rounded and experienced advisor earns their keep here.

Of the many things you look for in an advisor, this may be one of the key things you want. *Look for advisors who have knowledge in many areas. Look for experienced advisors.*

For example, while recommending a mutual fund to a client, I am con-sidering the following:

1. What is the potential market risk of this fund and does it match well with my client's risk tolerance?

2. Is this fund consistent with their investing objectives? Are we investing for growth, income, or both?

3. Is it in an IRA? If it is, we don't care about how much capital gains are kicked off on a 1099 each year since we don't have

to pay the taxman until we take money out. If it is not in an IRA, what phantom income might be showing up on a 1099 each year?

4. Are we buying into a capital gain distribution problem by buying it too late in the year?

5. How liquid is the fund? If it is a REIT we are probably buying it through a fund just so we can have the liquidity feature. What share class should we be in? A, B, or C? This will definitely affect the fund fees and my client's ability to take money freely from the fund without penalty.

6. How is the fund to be owned? Does it go into the family trust? Should the family trust be the beneficiary? Is there a 100% step up at death?

And so on... *Don't you want your advisor to be thinking about all these things so you don't have to?* Well unfortunately, if your "advisor" is really just an investment product salesperson without a variety of investment and tax knowledge and experience, he or she probably is NOT considering these details. It's not their fault. They just don't know.

9. DO ALL YOU CAN TO SAVE TAXES, BECAUSE "IT'S NOT WHAT YOU EARN. IT'S WHAT YOU KEEP THAT MATTERS!"

"The only difference between a tax man and a taxidermist is that the taxidermist leaves the skin."

~Mark Twain

When was the last time your financial advisor talked to your CPA before recommending an investment strategy? Did you know there are specific tax-efficient investment strategies that might save you thousands in taxes? Are you confident you are paying the absolute minimum taxes possible?

Review your specific tax situation with your advisors during the year and make certain you utilize all of you exclusions, exemptions, deductions, and credits you are legally entitled to. Remember that saving $5000 in taxes is the same as earning an extra $5000 in your investments!

IN CONCLUSION

Successful retirement investing simply requires the reconnection to the prudent ethical behavior you were taught as a child. However, this isn't about morals. This is all about prudent "investment" behavior. Even if you are not skilled in understanding investment strategies, or not fully understanding the inner workings of the stock market, you can still trust your intuition between right and wrong. Just remember to trust your gut and not get caught up in the promise of short-term gains, or sales pitches. Follow these Nine Golden Rules previously discussed and enjoy a successful financial future.

Don't be a Goofus!

Registered Representative of and Securities offered through Capital Synergy Partners, member FINRA/SIPC. 4400 MacArthur Blvd, Ste. 230, Newport Beach, CA 92660 Phone: 888-277-1974. Lenhoff Financial Group and Capital Synergy Partners are unaffiliated entities.

About Tod

Tod Lenhoff is the Founder and President of Lenhoff Financial Group. Tod has *over 29 years* of professional experience providing financial advice to retired individuals. Tod has dedicated his entire professional career to this field and is passionate about helping senior clients meet their financial goals.

Tod was born in Chicago and grew up in Los Angeles. In 1982, he graduated from California State University, at Northridge. He started his financial career in Los Angeles working for the international financial accounting firm Ernst & Young, providing advice to high net worth individuals on tax strategies, investment choices, insurance options, and retirement planning.

Subsequently, Tod became a Certified Financial Trainer, teaching finance to top executives at *IBM, Kodak, Caterpillar, Ingersoll-Rand, Valvoline, Qualcomm, Shea Homes,* and many other Fortune 500 companies. Tod even travelled above the Arctic Circle to teach finance to the native Inupiat Eskimos of Kotzebue, Alaska!

In 1992, Tod made the quality of life choice to leave Los Angeles and head south to San Diego, where he opened his current tax and financial practice in Vista. Tod *specializes in financial planning for retirees* to invest prudently, save taxes, have a catastrophic illness game plan, and maximize the estate legacy.

Tod is fully credentialed in many financial arenas. Tod is a **CPA, Elder Planner, Securities Registered** (both Series 7 and Series 66), **Investment Advisor Representative, Insurance Licensed** (Lenhoff Senior Planning, Inc. California Life License #0D86642), and a **Certified Financial Trainer.**

CHAPTER 32

ACHIEVE ULTIMATE BUSINESS SUCCESS: WHY YOU NEED A MARKETING WEBSITE

BY LINDSAY DICKS

Many business owners have the misconception that, in order to take advantage of the power of the Internet, all they need to do is put up a basic website that gives some information about their business and maybe includes their phone number. Once they've done this, business will just roll in… or so they hope.

Unfortunately it's not quite that simple.

Your website needs to be more than just a "brochure" giving some basic information about your company. Your website needs to be a *marketing* website if you hope to achieve Ultimate Success. If generating leads and making sales are important to your business, your website needs to be set up to facilitate these goals.

It's interesting to watch the evolution of marketing throughout the years. While the methods have changed, the need to be marketing oriented has not changed. Some years ago we had the Yellow Pages as a main source to find businesses.

Today, we still have a "Yellow Pages" concept, but we call it Internet. When you stop to think about it, the Internet is just the Yellow Pages on hyper-steroids. The concept is basically the same, but the Internet is much more cost effective, much broader in its reach, and has a potential return on investment (ROI) that could never be reached a couple of short decades ago. Just as business owners in the 1980's depended on the Yellow Pages and other print media to market their product or service, today's business owner depends on the Internet to serve the same function.

Let's face it, in today's marketing world, if you don't have a marketing-oriented website, you won't be doing much business. A marketing website is your opportunity as a business owner to take control of your web presence and the opportunity to sell your product or services to those that are in the market to buy. Why do you need a marketing website? Probably the most obvious answer is that marketing drives sales, sales drives revenue, and revenue drives profit. I think we can all agree that is the reason we are in business, to make a profit. But, let's dive a bit deeper into why you need a top-notch marketing-oriented website.

YOU NEED TO BE VISIBLE

I recently heard about a business owner, a man in his late sixties, who did an outstanding business during the original "Yellow Pages" days. However, today his business is being run over by other businesses in his market sector even though his business has been around the longest.

His problem is not that his product and service is inferior, in fact, all of his customers have loved him and were very pleased with his product and the installation service he provided. His problem is that he refused to succumb to the Internet monster. He never took time to understand the Internet and refused to hire someone to help him. As a result, his sales began dropping year after year. His business is now perceived by others as non-existent because they can't find his business when searching the Internet.

While an anti-Internet attitude may be quite rare and at the extreme end of the spectrum, there are many business owners today that don't realize why they need to have a marketing- oriented web presence or their marketing website is quite weak. They may have a website, but they don't maximize search engine optimization (SEO) and, as a result, they are not visible if someone searches for their product or service online. SEO is not a one-time set up. You have to continuously monitor your SEO and make the necessary adjustments to maximize it. SEO is the key component to being visible on the Internet.

Consider this, on Google alone, there are nearly 700,000 searches conducted every second. Every second your website isn't indexed on Google you are missing out on hundreds, if not thousands of opportunities for someone to visit your website, be influenced by your content, and potentially buy your product or service.

You can pay to have your website at the top of the search page or you can make it happen organically. It is estimated that approximately 88% of search engine users never click on paid ads. So, you can get great visibility by maximizing your SEO to obtain organic placement in the top spot(s) on the search engines.

When a person uses a search engine, such as Google, they are searching you out and seeking what you have to offer. Much like how people would use the Yellow Pages in the past. It's a more pleasant sales experience for them. It doesn't feel intrusive like many other forms of advertising they are bombarded with day after day.

Just by being visible and always available on the Internet you are attracting a friendly buyer who is feeling good about the buying experience. You are able to sell what a buyer wants, when they want it. It's a win-win situation.

YOU NEED TO SHOWCASE YOUR PRODUCTS AND SERVICES

After you have made yourself visible, show your potential customer what they want to see by showcasing your products and services. People need to know what you offer and why your products and/or services are the ones they need to buy. How are you going to convince them?

What information can you supply through your website that will showcase those products and services and cause that website visitor to be convinced that if they don't buy from you that they are making a mistake. Your website must be visually desirable and easy to navigate. You aren't really "showcasing" your product if your website visitor has to click multiple times to get to the page you want them to see. Make your product easy for your customer to find and displayed in such a way that they can get as much information as they need to make an informed decision.

YOU NEED TO GENERATE LEADS

People come to your website for a reason. Typically, they don't just stumble upon your site. You need to capitalize on their visit by capturing their information so you can continue to stay in touch with them. Even if you have the greatest product or service and even if they are convinced that you are the business from which they want to make a purchase, they may not be ready to make the purchase at the time of their visit. There may be multiple reasons.

But, if you have their contact information, you can gently "drip" on them through various means so they don't forget you when they are ready to make their purchase. When I say, "drip," I'm referring to a "stay-in-touch" process whereby you send them follow up communication in various forms which will serve as consistent "touches" without them feeling like you are pestering them or trying to push your product or service on them.

Drip enough information on them to keep them interested and in the buying cycle without pushing them away. There is a fine balance to be achieved in this process and you will have to find that balance in your niche market.

YOU NEED TO ESTABLISH THOUGHT LEADERSHIP

Your website is the perfect place to establish yourself as a leading expert in your field. Of course, you can and should use other internet and non-internet means to establish yourself as a thought leader, but make sure you start with your website.

Your website can house white papers you have written, blog posts, Q and A, and the list can go on and on. If you are uncomfortable placing yourself out there as an authority and as a thought leader, then you need to read, research, and learn from others in your field so that you can feel comfortable referring to yourself as a thought leader in your field. People will gravitate to someone that can give them the information they are looking for and that's why your website needs to reflect you as a thought leader.

YOU NEED TO DRIVE VISITORS TO PURCHASE

Once you get customers to your website, you need to be able to drive them to purchase your product or service or the reason for your website is really in vain. Driving people to purchase will require you to understand your customer's needs, wants and desires.

What are their hot buttons and how can you use that information to push (or pull) them toward your product? Actually, there is overwhelming research to indicate customers don't want to be "pushed" into a purchase, but they are much more responsive to being "pulled" into a buying relationship with a business.

Pulling a client is accomplished by offering them something that attracts them to you. Your website is the mechanism. You need to provide the content on your website that will make you "attractive" to them. Understanding your clients and how to "pull" them toward a purchase will take time and a lot of trial and error. There isn't a "one size fits all" methodology when it comes to getting the customer to click the "buy" button. You will have to customize your method and strategy based on your unique customer and their unique buying practices.

YOU NEED A CALL TO ACTION (CTA)

Your CTA should be short and action oriented. Your visitors need to know exactly what you want them to do within seconds of arriving on your site. Your product or service will greatly influence the "Action" process that will best help you make your website visitor a buying customer.

EBay is a great example of simplified CTA. Have you seen their "Buy It Now" link? It is a very simple call to action and they make it very convenient by placing the link in a very visible spot in relation to the item being considered for purchase.

Keep in mind that not all your potential customers visiting your site will be at the same stage of the buying cycle. As a result, you will need a primary CTA, as well as a secondary CTA. As I alluded to earlier, you may want your client to buy, but they may not be ready to click the "add to cart" or "buy it now" button. They may be very interested, but still have reasons to wait.

Make sure you have a secondary CTA so you don't lose them. Give them the opportunity to sign up for a newsletter, be added to your mailing list, or maybe download a free white paper or e-book you have provided on your site. These are great ways to get your visitor to take one step closer to completing the buying cycle. Every visitor is a data-mining opportunity, so don't pass it up.

YOU NEED TO BE AVAILABLE AND RESPONSIVE

Have you ever called a company, only to be walked through what feels like an endless array of one phone prompt after another, and then you have to listen to the complete menu to determine which selection is the best for your particular need? Sometimes it's a guessing game.

Do you remember how frustrated you get when you go through that experience and you think, "Can I just please speak to a live person?" Well, your website customers are also looking for quick attention. That's one of the reasons people use the Internet, to get immediate information.

Your website enables you to be available to them even when you are sleeping. But, for those instances when there is a specific piece of information your website visitor cannot find, they may ask you for something via your "Contact Us" page.

While most website visitors will understand it may take a reasonable amount of time to respond to their specific inquiry, your prompt attention does make an impression. If they request more information, you will make a big impression on them if they receive the information within minutes or hours instead of days.

If they request to be contacted, you have the opportunity to "pull" them closer to completing the sales cycle by being available and responsive to their inquiries. There are also many auto-responders that you can include on your website that will make your response to their inquiry immediate. Customers like prompt attention and you can give it to them through your well- thought-out, marketing-oriented website.

The bottom line is that if sales are important to your business, you need to have a marketing- oriented website that creates a persuasive awareness of how you can benefit the potential customer who visits your site. If your site is weak or void of an effective marketing strategy, you are probably letting thousands of dollars slip away from you and into some-one else's bank account.

Your website has the potential to create a considerable ROI if it is done right. Creating an effective website begins with understanding "why" you need a marketing website. I encourage you to take the "why's" I have outlined above and apply them to your website. I'm confident they will make a difference... and that the process will lead you closer to the Ultimate Success of your business!

About Lindsay

Lindsay Dicks helps her clients tell their stories in the online world. Having been brought up around a family of marketers, but a product of Generation Y, Lindsay naturally gravitated to the new world of online marketing. Lindsay began freelance writing in 2000 and soon after launched her own PR firm that thrived by offering an in-your-face "Guaranteed PR" that was one of the first of its kind in the nation.

Lindsay's new media career is centered on her philosophy that "people buy people." Her goal is to help her clients build a relationship with their prospects and customers. Once that relationship is built and they learn to trust them as the expert in their field, then they will do business with them. Lindsay also built a patent-pending process that utilizes social media marketing, content marketing and search engine optimization to create online "buzz" for her clients to helps them to convey their business and personal stories. Lindsay's clientele span the entire business map and range from doctors and small business owners to Inc. 500 CEOs.

Lindsay is a graduate of the University of Florida. She is the CEO of CelebritySites, an online marketing company specializing in social media and online personal branding. Lindsay is also a multi-best-selling author whose titles include the best-selling book "Power Principles for Success" which she co-authored with Brian Tracy. She was also selected as one of America's PremierExperts and has been quoted in *Newsweek*, *The Wall Street Journal*, *USA Today,* and *Inc.,* as well as featured on NBC, ABC, and CBS television affiliates speaking on social media, search engine optimization and making more money online. Lindsay was also recently brought on FOX 35 News as their online marketing expert.

Lindsay, a national speaker, has shared the stage with some of the top speakers in the world such as Brian Tracy, Lee Milteer, Ron LeGrand, Arielle Ford, David Bullock, Brian Horn, Peter Shankman and many others. Lindsay was also a producer on the Emmy-nominated film "Jacob's Turn."

You can connect with Lindsay at:
Lindsay@CelebritySites.com
www.twitter.com/LindsayMDicks
www.facebook.com/LindsayDicks

CHAPTER 33

LEADERSHIP UNDER UNCERTAINTY

BY LUIS VICENTE GARCIA

Let me start this chapter with a question: What does it take to become a leader in a constantly changing world? To explain my views, I would like to write about the concept and insights of a new form of leadership that I think has developed in recent years: <u>leadership under uncertainty</u>. This is happening in many countries, but particularly in those where both the economy and the rules of the game are changing constantly. This is what we have in many developing countries and it adds turbulence to all of our actions and decisions. It also creates a sense of urgency that is not present in other regions: here you need to decide faster, with probably less information.

We think we all know about change, but are we really sure we know what it means if we live it almost daily? We hear that we live in changing times, and it has really been a changing world in recent decades. We have seen many examples since the 1960s and 1970s: a dramatic transformation in technology, such as the changes in computers, the creation of tablets and smartphones, improvements in medical equipment, or the creation of the Internet and Social Media, all of which give us greater mobility. These are examples that have impacted us in ways that will continue to change our present and our future, so just imagine where technological innovations will take us from here.

Look now at the changes that have occurred in societies and nations all over the world during the past half-century. For instance, the end of the cold war, the fall of the Berlin Wall, the real estate crisis in 2008, the Arab spring of 2011, the oil price increases of recent times, or the difficulties in some European countries; these are a few events that exemplify the magnitude of changes in our current world. These historical issues and times are having a profound impact in how societies behave, how world politics develops and how economies function and operate today. Changes have affected us in ways we still cannot imagine, and will for years to come. Realize now that it is under these uncertain realities that leaders have continued to emerge and grow, and are continuously exploring new frontiers. **Strong leaders emerge under the most critical circumstances.**

Now take a look at the changes in the cultural, economic or political systems that have taken place in most emerging markets, and realize that these are shaping the future of developing societies. Too many people in the emerging world are living under many difficulties, adapting to the daily challenges they bring us. Latin American economies and societies - all different in sizes, shapes, people, heritage, or political systems - have had to adapt to continuing evolving situations, but also live in the very different reality of uncertainty. The Merriam-Webster dictionary defines "uncertainty" as (a) *the quality or state of being uncertain* (as in a doubt) and (b) *likely to change*[1]. Now add turbulence to the equation and you have a very complex reality. So, under these definitions, how do you cope with uncertainty? And, what do all of these conditions have to do with leadership?

Change and uncertainty increase the challenges that a leader has to face, and it is not always easy. A person might live in a country that is worlds apart from the rapid changes in technology or scientific innovations; true we have large natural resources, but we are lacking in our educational systems, in the productivity of our factories, or in the ways our society is organized. But the biggest challenge of all is living in a world with an unclear and constantly changing set of rules, laws, and procedures – which affects the way people behave or businesses are run, working under the effects of large economic swings, with lower growth, higher inflation or unemployment rates, a legal system that does not promote free trade or real competition, not to mention the difficult political situations that exists in several countries. In other words, we do

1 http://www.learnersdictionary.com/search/uncertainty

not have real competitive advantages, not only of our nations, but also of our people, who lack or are behind the skills, knowledge, educational level, the technology-based industry, or the infrastructure that is needed to reach the level of real development that all nations need to grow and prosper, and set its people towards a higher standard of living.

These are the conditions under which leadership in this part of the world has to adapt to as we live in a *certain uncertainty*. We are regular people, living and performing under these conditions; going out to work daily because we also want to see and make a real change in our societies; but we have to start at the basics, with our families, at our schools, and in our jobs. We are the ones that have to manage these day-to-day issues, being the heroes of our daily lives, and in that way, becoming the real and true leaders of our societies.

Yes, we have seen these leaders of the uncertainty, as I call them. They are the leaders that help the poor in the slums of the cities or in the jungle; that defend the human rights of those less fortunate; that push our communities further to look for a brighter future; or who want political or economic change for our countries. We become the leaders of our day-to-day lives when we decide to guide our sons and daughters, the students in our classes or our coworkers, day after day under these changing and difficult situations. Truly, we are leaders in our own way.

These leaders have strong qualities and values, with an optimist's approach to life. These leaders have the characteristics of a strong performer, always working under pressure, having to demonstrate a sense of urgency. Even in an uncertain world, they would show most of the regular characteristics of the leader, but would also show other exceptional characteristics that flourish when needed to perform under the reality of uncertainty. Here I give you what I believe are the 10 characteristics of the leader in uncertain times, but approached from a different perspective:

1. **Commitment**: The leader has a commitment to his people, co-workers and the ones who follow him in order to continuously demonstrate that he is there with them in their own terrain. He shows responsibility above all.

2. **Understanding**: A leader is capable and needs to listen, watch and understand all changing and uncertain circumstances, even

when not all the information is present. He is in touch with the people and understands their necessities; he knows their needs by heart.

3. **Connectivity**: He is to be able to communicate, to create alliances and relationships with all kinds of people. The leader is in touch with the people on a daily basis, as he needs to be out there to explain the ideas, tasks, responsibilities and challenges to others.

4. **Vision**: Leaders have a strong and profound vision, believing in their own objectives, looking for opportunities where everybody else sees problems, because in all crises - as deep as they may be - there are always many opportunities to be found. They encourage the people making them stronger and better prepared for the challenge. They create a vision while setting the pace for others.

5. **Values**: A true leader believes that the best way to lead the people is by living the true values and principles that guide them, maintaining their human and spiritual qualities. In other words, he believes in building excellence.

6. **Knowledge**: A leader is constantly looking for knowledge, understanding the needs of the society, following the path of continuous education and learning. But the leader also needs to show that he knows, cares, and that he is able to demonstrate his true qualities.

7. **Creativity and Imagination**: Leaders are always implementing creative actions, breaking the rules of the traditional schemes. They anticipate the moment, making the changes they need to make in their thinking and in their plans, showing everyone that they can have better ideas and solutions to most problems.

8. **Motivation**: A leader understands what it means to live under always-changing rules, and adapting to the new and more demanding reality, so he continues to motivate himself as well as others. The leader inspires the ones that need his guidance by what he tells them and showing them his real actions. All people need motivation, some need to be encouraged, and this is the job of a leader.

9. **Competitive Attitude**: A leader is armed with a positive attitude and with the motivation to achieve the impossible. They are the

integrators and the unifiers of teams; they organize a better view of the future and unify their followers; they achieve it with a positive and a competitive attitude.

10. **Take Action:** Now that you know all the qualities that make you a real leader, you need to take action, to decide, make opinions, to go ahead under the real conditions, to be the best all the time, to bring out the best in all others, and to show the people what you are made of. In some instances, you will need to deliver under the most difficult circumstances, and this is what will make you a complete and a true leader.

Other qualities and skills are needed in a leader; he or she needs to be honest, intelligent, inspiring, courageous, and straightforward.

Many years ago, I was posed with the usual question about leadership: Are leaders born or made? After carefully thinking I answered, *"I believe that leaders are developed."* I strongly believe that leaders are nourished from within, grow and develop; a really true leader is an expert in changing circumstances and adapts to a turbulent and an uncertain reality. Some will be born with the necessary skills to become a leader, but you need to develop them to become a leader. You do not appoint a person to become a leader; it does not work that way. It is the people that will follow him or her who will decide who their leader will be, not the other way around. You have to demonstrate your values, beliefs and your true spirit. In this sense, people who are born with talents and skills need to prepare and be ready for the moment of truth, to become recognized by what they do, and thus will become the real leaders, anticipating the opportunities that arise. Leaders will show us a better way, or how we can attain a better life, and start to solve the issues and problems that we face daily, arising stronger under uncertain and turbulent times.

It is very easy to read about what I have just explained and not grasp the reality of what it means. In a sense I cannot express in just a few words what people have to do in order to live in a world where you are continuously faced with changing rules, or your dream of a free society, or that to be in a true democracy you even need to fight when all goes against you. But in that part of the world, people live most days without electricity, water or public services, do not have social welfare, quit school at early ages since they need to go out to work for food, do not have regular jobs and some will be unemployed most of their lives. We have new laws or changed ones every few months, which change the way businesses are run, and the way people and societies perform. It is not easy; be clear on that. In my opinion, it has been these harsh and difficult experiences in our lives that have shown the better qualities on a handful of people in our towns, cities, and countries. These experiences mold, define, and create your character, your personality and my belief is that it is under these circumstances that the true leader arises, that the true person transforms himself into a real leader.

Leadership is an art in itself. Leading others is gained by respect, by the trust you transmit, the integrity you show, and the way you decide to assist all others. **Leadership for me is the pursuit of excellence**. You become a leader, being worthy of the friendship and trust of the people that follow you. Latin America and other regions of the world are in need of excellent, well-prepared and dedicated people; the leaders who live in these regions will require integrity, dedication, trust, values, personal commitment, strength, endurance, excellence and even survival skills.

People come and go; **leaders are recognized forever**. People look for guidance, **leaders look for initiatives**; people look for someone to follow and **a true leader will assume the responsibility** of doing so. Many changes and particular situations over the years have taken their tolls in our societies, in our economic and political development; but leaders always come out and shine while looking for and learning new ways of making things better. A leader will be there, no matter what the situation is, or what the challenges are. A true leader will gain the respect he deserves just by the way he behaves and acts, and will come out stronger, with more desire and more willingness to lead.

Leaders might be born every day, but it takes time for them to grow and develop, and it will be our responsibility, our duty, to call upon these regular day-to-day people to become the leaders of our uncertain future. These will be the leaders who will help change our future, that will hopefully change the uncertainty into certainty, who will change a crisis situation into a growing and developing opportunity. They will be the ones who will lead the way for so many people in the uncertain world, so that we will all see a brighter future, simply because they are the leaders of our times.

"Leaders are always people who see beyond the moment, they are likely to excel in the midst of serious problems, creating a vision and motivating people to achieve it," as my father wrote me recently. This vision of leadership will make us understand the characteristics of a leader, but looking at them from the perspective of one who lives in a constant state of uncertainty. Many men and women in history have done just that: see beyond the moment, dream for excellence and search for the impossible to make their greatest achievements; and the leaders of today, particularly those who live in an uncertain world, will always do the impossible while looking for excellence.

About Luis

Luis Vicente García is a financial professional who has devoted many years to the study of how motivation and attitude affect regular day-to-day people. Married for 20+ years, with two sons, he started writing articles about finance, franchising, and motivation since the late 1990's. These articles in turn developed into a Spanish Language BLOG called *Motivando El Futuro* (http://motivandoel-futuro.blogspot.com), a Blog on Motivation and Personal Growth. An Economist with an MBA, and a Master's Degree in Service Enterprise Management among other studies, he is a firm believer in continuing education. He published a franchising book entitled *Motivando al Futuro Franquiciado* in 2010.

With the experience gained in different companies, having worked in the manufacturing and service industries, he has learned to work under pressure, in a business climate characterized by turbulence. He has worked in a wide variety of companies, from well-established enterprises to publicly traded companies, from start-ups to family-owned businesses. Luis has also been involved with consultants, advisors and legal counselors in Venezuela and the US. This has allowed him to fully understand and appreciate the importance of core values that people and businesses need to succeed. This means that Luis is used to working under volatile business environments, having had to adjust to continuously changing regulatory, business and legal conditions, while obtaining important international experience. Altogether, Luis has gained an overall knowledge of local and international markets, business deals and interpersonal relations.

All of these efforts have resulted in aligning employees to find better alternatives for making more effective and efficient operations, while at the same time obtaining better results for the organization. His approach is that of a "people-oriented" leader and manager. He believes in providing all people with the right tools and opportunities to learn, in motivating and coaching them to perform better, while at the same time being a promoter of continuous training and personal and professional improvement through self-education. *A team builder,* a *motivator* and a confidence generator, always with a positive attitude towards life, Luis Vicente believes in being a leader for the people that work with and surround him. He lives in Caracas, Venezuela.

Contacts: lvgarciag@gmail.com; motivandoelfuturo@gmail.com.

CHAPTER 34

WALL STREET AND RETIREMENT - A BIG DISCONNECT
–7 REASONS WHY WALL STREET AND RETIREMENT JUST DON'T GO TOGETHER

BY MICHAEL DAVIS

The last decade has been a real challenge for investors to navigate through the retirement years. Problems with two recessions have made it very difficult to maintain a stable portfolio while trying to provide a steady income that will keep up with inflation. Please understand that while I think some investment vehicles are better than others, I basically believe that all investments are good if used in the right situations. Whenever someone is unhappy with an investment I usually find that either they had the wrong expectations of how that investment was to work or that they had used it in the wrong situation. Unlike some pundits that say, for instance, that whole life insurance is bad, I find that if used in the right circumstances it is the best choice. The key to finding the right vehicle is to determine your goals and aspirations and find the investment best suited to help you accomplish those goals. Anyone who doesn't take the time to help you determine your goals is nothing more than a salesperson and not a planner. Run the other way quickly.

Let's take a look at some of the areas that WALL STREET would rather you not know.

THE 4% RULE

The Wall Street 4% rule basically states that if you have a balanced portfolio of say 50% stock and 50% bonds you should be able to live out your life and never run out of money. Well let me tell you, it works sometimes and sometimes it doesn't. It would work well if we were always in a rising market, but we all know that the market doesn't always go up. If history repeats itself, we will have a recession on the average of every five years. Most people in retirement will experience about six more recessions during their lifetime. So let's take an example of someone who has a $500,000 balanced portfolio of 50% stocks and 50% bonds. Their income would be $20,000 a year.

As long as the market stays stable that is fine, but what would happen if they experienced a market like we had in the last months of 2008 and the first few months of 2009. The S&P 500 was down approximately 40%. Their portfolio would have been reduced to approximately $300,000, which would reduce that income to $12,000 a year. How are you going to explain to your wife that you can't go see the grandkids this year because your income was just cut by 40%? How long do you think your nest egg would last you if you continued to take the $20,000 a year? That is now 6.7%. Worse than that, what if you were relying on that to pay your bills. Another problem with that is that it might not be just this year, it might be for the rest of your life. After the last recession of 08/09 the S&P 500 is still not back to its July 2007 high. Wall Street's answer is to cut back when markets aren't performing. I don't think that is the way most of us want to enjoy our GOLDEN YEARS.

BALANCED PORTFOLIO THEORY

We already mentioned this balanced portfolio theory in the 4% rule. A balanced portfolio worked well in the bull markets of the 80's and 90's but that was an unusual time in the history of the market. We could hope for that again, but that is not the way to design a portfolio. First of all, logical thinking tells me that if I have a portfolio of 50% stock &

50% bonds, and knowing that usually they work in opposite directions to each other, I will have 50% of my portfolio working against me at all times. When stocks are doing good, what happens to bonds? When bonds are doing good, what happens to stocks? According to a study done by the Putnam Institute, they suggest that for retirement portfolios whose primary goal is to minimize the risk of depletion and sustain withdrawals, optimal equity allocations range between 5% and 25%.

KEEP SIX MONTHS OF INCOME LIQUID

Keeping six months of income liquid is a good rule for some but not for a person to rely on for income in retirement. Their idea is to use that money in the times when the market is going down, so that you don't pull funds from a losing account and compound the problem. Six months worth of income won't work when some recessions last as long as five years before they ever get back to even. Six months worth of income might be a sufficient emergency fund for unexpected expenses but not as an income replacement or supplement for a bear market. You must have incomes that will be dependable even in the bad times.

DON'T WORRY - YOU ARE IN IT FOR THE LONG HAUL

Remember that we are entering our retirement years. I know that most folks call that middle age, but I don't really think our chances are really good to live until age 120 or 130. Most of my clients tell me they don't even buy green bananas anymore because they are not sure they will be around to eat them. Do we really have a long haul left? How long is a long haul? That is sort of like how long is a piece of string?

Be wary of the broker that tells you that you are in it for the long haul. That's just a bad answer for a bad situation you are experiencing.

RETIREMENT ACCOUNTS SHOULD NOT BE FUNDED WITH EQUITIES

Retirement accounts (such as 401k, IRA, 403b, 457, SEP-IRAs) are unique types of account and should be treated differently. One problem with using equities to fund your retirement account is the fact that when you are in a bear market and losing money, you can't even take a tax deduction for the loss. I feel that you should fund these accounts with conservative accounts that have little or no chance of loss because of the fact that they offer no tax deduction. Also when you reach 70-1/2, you must take money out of the account (which may be down at the time) and pay taxes whether you want to or not. That really puts the government in control of your account rather than yourself. You should be in control of your accounts.

DON'T COMMIT ANNUICIDE

If you mention to your broker that you are going to buy an annuity they will suggest to you that you are committing ANNUICIDE. Please remember that I said in the beginning that I believe that all investment vehicles have their own place in the investment world. Annuities are just another financial tool. Keep in mind that I am talking primarily about fixed annuities and not variable annuities. I am not a fan of variable annuities basically because their fees are generally high but that's not to say that they don't fit some circumstances. In fact I own one myself and it works well for the purpose I bought it for. They must be used in the proper situation and they are perfectly good. If you wanted to cut down a tree you wouldn't use a shovel. That doesn't make the shovel bad, it was just not made for that purpose. Annuities, in the beginning were designed to provide a stream of income. Today's annuities are not your grandfather's annuities, they have evolved over the years into a great tool to be used in retirement. Why? Clients that come to me usually are looking for a lifetime income that they cannot outlive. I know of no other vehicle that can help them achieve their goal better than annuities. It is like creating your own pension. ANNUITIES=INCOME. That is what they are designed to do. Some of the misconceptions brokers will tell you about annuities are that your money is tied up and when you die the insurance company will keep what's left. Those are absolutely FALSE. It is all a matter of working with a professional that that has a good knowledge of annuities and proper income planning. Please note that I did not say annuities are necessarily the best growth vehicle, but they are very good at providing income which is what they were designed to do. Used in a proper plan they can provide a guaranteed income that you cannot outlive and any remaining balance can be passed on to your heirs. Your money is not completely tied up because all of the annuities I offer have a 10% free withdrawal privilege and after the surrender period there is no penalty for a complete withdrawal.

Today's annuities are very flexible and offer many choices to people that are retired or retiring soon. One of the latest additions to annuities are the many different income riders that offer guaranteed growth for up to 20 years provided that the rider is used as income. Again this is income you can count on. Your retirement income no longer has to be base on HOPE but can be based on ASSURANCE. Which would you like in your retirement? HOPE that markets do well or an income that will be there regardless of what markets do. Life Insurance and annuities are the only vehicles that I know of that can do that. You cannot guarantee an account that is based on stock market performance. I have been planning retirement incomes for the last 17 years and now it has become fashionable for even some of the large companies like Schwab, Fidelity and Vanguard to recommend annuities.

Any comments regarding safe and secure investments, and guaranteed income streams refer only to fixed insurance products. They do not refer, in any way to securities or investment advisory products. Fixed Insurance and Annuity product guarantees are subject to the claims-paying ability of the issuing company and are not offered by Global Financial Private Capital.

STICKING WITH THE ADVISOR THAT BUILT YOUR NEST EGG

When we were born, we were brought into this world with usually an obstetrician or a pediatrician. As we grew older we went to our family doctor. Now as we enter retirement, many of us have our own specialists. As we enter different phases of our lives we must change as our circumstances change. Not that there was anything wrong with the doctor that brought us into this world, but it is just that we out grew his area of expertise. The same things apply in your financial lives. During the early stages of our financial life, we were in the accumulation phase of our lives. During that phase we used a stockbroker, investment adviser, banker, or life insurance agent to help us accumulate our retirement nest egg. We were able to take more risk because we were employed and would not need that money for many years to come. They have done a good job of building that nest egg, but now it is time for you to seek the help of a professional income specialist. You have now entered (whether you like it or not) the distribution and preservation phase of your lives. It is not personal, it is just that your current adviser probably doesn't have the specialized training to guide you through your retirement years. Retirement represents a significant change in your life.

You are no longer working. Your health is changing. You can no longer afford to take the risk you could when you were working. If retirement represents a significant change in you life, don't you think your portfolio should make some significant changes also? Most of my clients have one thing in common. They have enough money to live out the rest of their lives very comfortably as long as one thing doesn't happen. That is, THEY LOSE IT! Losing money at this stage of their life should not be an option for most folks. Keeping what you've worked all your life to build so that you and your spouse can live out the rest of your lives (and not have to move in with your kids) is far more important that taking unnecessary risks just to try and earn 2% or 3% more.

REMEMBER — ASSURANCE RATHER THAN HOPE.

SUCCESS IN RETIREMENT

Success in retirement is not about how much money you have or the next hot stock tip. It is more about having that piece of mind that you can enjoy the things you love to do. It can be about trips, grandkids, family and friends. The idea that you can do these things and not worry about running out of money and being a burden on your kids, is priceless. I have had clients that tried the Wall Street way of retirement, with all of its ups and downs, only to find out that if they had only taken a less risky approach they could have done as well with none of the anxiety and stress. I am a big believer in the old Tortoise and Hare story. Slow and steady will still get you to the end of the race without all of the stress. You are only at halftime in this game of life and you know that no one ever remembers the halftime score. It is the score at the end of the game and the winner that everyone remembers. It is of the utmost importance that you at least develop a game plan that will make you a WINNER.

I wish you a HAPPY RETIREMENT!!!

Michael A. Davis is an Investment Adviser Representative with Global Financial Private Capital, LLC, a SEC Registered Investment Adviser. Guarantees are not provided by Global Financial Private Capital but by the issuing insurance company and are based on the issuing company's financial strength.

About Michael

Michael A. Davis, ChFC®, RFC® is a Chartered Financial Consultant and owner of Davis Financial Services, Inc.

Michael is a well-known financial educator in the Northeast Florida area. His retirement planning workshops have been attended by hundreds of people seeking straight, no-nonsense advice on how to accumulate and protect wealth. His goal is to educate people on "How Money Works." He believes that education is **THE** answer, guiding people to make informed decisions.

Mike has been advising clients on how to avoid making costly mistakes for over 30 years. People who consult with him often find that they lower their tax bills, reduce taxes on social security income, increase their estates and obtain better protection for their financial future.

Mike Davis is often sought by local and national media for his extensive knowledge on long-term financial planning and retirement income strategies. He has appeared on CNBC, Fox News, CBS Action News 47, and has been quoted in *Smart Money* magazine, the *AARP Bulletin, Jacksonville Times Union* and various other publications.

Mike and his wife Linda have resided in Orange Park, FL since 1983. They stay busy with their two grown children and five grandchildren. Mike is involved in his local community supporting Toys for Tots, American Cancer Society, MS Society, and numerous other charities. He is a Vietnam Veteran and also an active member of his church. When Mike isn't working to improve his client's financial situations, he enjoys boating and golf.

Mike is an Investment Advisor Representative offering advisory services through Global Financial Private Capital, an SEC Registered Investment Advisor. Mike has achieved the prestigious ChFC® (Chartered Financial Consultant) designation from the American College. Mike is also a Registered Financial Consultant and a member of the International Association of Registered Financial Consultants. He has been a licensed insurance agent since 1980 and is licensed in several states. Davis Financial Services, Inc. is a member of the Clay County Chamber of Commerce and the Northeast Florida Better Business Bureau. Mike is also a Court of the Table member of the Million Dollar Round Table (MDRT), the Premier Association of Financial Professionals.

If you have been looking for straightforward advice and wondering who to talk to, you have come to the right place. Mike will be glad to meet with you.

Visit our website: www.davisfinancialservicesinc.com

Davis Financial Services, Inc.
(904) 276-3900
358A Stiles Ave.,
Orange Park, Fl. 32073

Investment advisory services offered through Global Financial Private Capital, LLC, an SEC Registered
Investment Advisor.

CHAPTER 35

BRANDING YOUR MULTI-MILLION DOLLAR CORPORATION

BY RICHARD ARISTARCHOVAS

Well you have grown this far and success is no longer a stranger. The brand is established in the eyes of your consumer group and things are going well. It is no time to relax however, as your key responsibility now is to at least stay at the top of your game and even move forward to other consumer groups because (and write this down):

Whether your consumer group is growing or shrinking is just a matter of time.

Going into the recession, Starbucks had an established brand geared to satisfy the average consumer with his or her coffee needs. When the recession (the trigger) hit and this average consumer needed just that, a cup of coffee to start their day, and realized how much they were paying, all *en masse* decided that MacDonald's $1 something 'cup of joe' was just as good.

I am pretty sure the demise of this consumer group wasn't a huge surprise for Starbucks, and that's why they so swiftly rebranded this corporation to fit their new main consumer group as well as diversify into retail sales. Still CEO Howard Shultz and the board must have had to make some serious decisions that in the end led to Starbucks riding out the storm and emerging better than ever.

So that would be the first point I'd like to address, you have to always keep an eye on and monitor your consumer group, investigating every possible trigger as if it was the one. In this case, a hugely important number is your market share.

Take the time to figure out your market share as often as possible. There's a lot at stake here so don't be lazy. Understandably, some industries are going to be easier to track than others, but the time invested in tracking your market share is well worth it. If you need help monitoring your market share you can find more information on the subject at: www.Stayfirst.com/market-share.

Tracking your market share is important for a number of reasons, but mainly it indicates when there is a need for some critical decision making. I can only speak with certainty of branding-related issues, but I suspect the formula I'm about to give you is universal:

> A move of 5% - 9% in your market share per fiscal year in either direction requires attention to either correct a mistake or adjust to this new level accordingly. A loss of 20% in the market share is not too late to take action and work out the issue at hand; but anything beyond 40% loss is too late for corrections and is time for a complete reinvention of the product or service.

That said, once you do determine a slump in your market share, go ahead and figure out what's causing it. It may well be something internal like a sales department having a passive-aggressive quarrel with your customer service department, or external like retailers placing your products in the wrong category. Either way you need to act and act quickly.

As an example, we had a prominent developer from central Russia approach us with declining market share for several consecutive years. During our research we found that new emerging developers and contractors were quickly saturating the market causing this developer some serious pain. In this case the branding was at fault. It was old and outdated, hadn't changed in over a decade and translated into a completely irrelevant and outdated message to the buyer. They had lost (in total) upwards of 20% by the time we heard their story.

We took on the challenge of full scale rebranding and even renaming the company. New, modern condominiums that the company was building appealed to modern thinkers and movers, thus the name we chose,

Metrum Group, clearly set this company apart from the competition 90% of which ended with "Build" or "Builder." A new modern logo and corporate style followed the name change and expanded across all four divisions of the company.

To this day, CEO Vadim Patapov in charge of the new Metrum Group keeps us current and happily shares their progress. The first fiscal year following rebranding, Metrum Group had more than doubled their sales and continues to grow at a more than healthy 50% a year rate. You can view and read more about Metrum Group on our website at: www.Stayfirst.com/work.

On the other hand, as of the writing of this chapter, the most recent story in the news was Hostess closing down their Twinkie factories and laying off 18,000 workers. Initially trying to blame the unions, CEO Brian Driscoll wrote in recent court filings that sales have been declining year after year since 2009, and further analysis by *Business Insider* magazine showed that even though knowing full well about the importance of reinvention, Hostess stubbornly kept manufacturing their obsolete products that brought them to their knees.

As sad as this Twinkie finale may sound, we need to move on to our next point – Brand Security. Contrary to European markets, in America we believe in proven systems vs. innovation (that could have been the reasoning behind Hostess decision-making that obviously didn't work, who knows). That is why this following simple exercise is so effective:

> When you have a moment, Google your competition plus the word "logo" at the end. Take the images and make a 4x4 grid with any image processing software including your brand logo in one of the spaces in the grid. Once done print it black and white.

Even without printing it in black and white, you'll be able to see a clear distinction between the market leaders and "others." Even without a trained eye, one can easily spot the unconventional font in the logos or some unique symbolism or even a whole hidden message. An argument can be made that this is "useless" or it serves no purpose, but if you're not familiar with this process of branding let me elaborate a little.

In reality, the message you see in the logo reflects the whole philosophy behind the company. This message is exported over to a corporate style that talks to employees, management and customers alike in one single voice. There are interior navigation systems made, communication systems made, building décor, clothes custom styled, marketing communications all made based on one corporate identity and collective philosophy. These colors turn into a message that communicates the philosophy of the brand, and when it becomes congruent all across the board, magic happens. A factory is no longer a boring company, it sprouts a personality that customers and employees alike align with, and it grows on them and it unites everyone and customer service turns happy and entitled (in a good way), and customers become loyal and refer their family and friends to your brand. It is called the art of open communication.

So the next time you look at a logo, keep in mind that it is never just a logo or just a brochure or even just a website, it all goes together – painting the big picture and actually showing these corporations visually for what they are. You know what they say - a picture is worth a thousand words.

Getting back to brand security, these companies are industry leaders for a reason and so before you go out experimenting trying to beat them while reinventing the wheel I urge you to slow down, take a deep breath and first try and get to their level, not beyond, stand on par with the leaders.

The reality is simple, if you want security, just follow the rest of the industry, do what they do, evolve when they evolve. Just don't sit still thinking that you've got here and what worked so far will work forever. Simply being in sync with the industry already requires about 5% - 10% of your time be dedicated to innovation. Whether you use it to monitor the marketplace, watch the trends, or work on your brand image is up to you, but do always compare your brand to the leaders and try getting some of their mentality transferred to your company.

On being a leader:

Before we go over the ways of how your company can be a successful industry leader, I'd like to take a moment and go over what not to do. Whatever you do and I want to make a point of this – **DO NOT try branding your company as the "cheaper" or "more affordable" solution, it will never work.**

Eventually an exact copy of your business model will appear with deeper pockets, right next door and you'll soon be forced into a miserable submission. It is a vicious cycle of selling at a discount when skimping on resources, which leads to future development that keeps delivering poorer materials every time resulting in fewer customers that exponentially keep getting worse. In all honesty, I am amazed at the companies being built on this philosophy.

The best shining example is of course the great American discounter, Walmart. As of this writing, Walmart had its employees walk out on them on black Friday demanding bigger wages and better benefits, but unfortunately I think Walmart cannot provide that as their business model doesn't allow for raises, because that would mean raising prices on products. Walmart is stuck with a "boatload" of discounted stuff that now they can't even move.

Being a real leader then, is a little more intense. Competitors and lawsuits constantly breathe down your neck and there's little room for error. In this position, taking an example from others is no longer an option and it is time to invent something other than the wheel.

Innovation is now the name of the game. Leaders are there for a reason - to lead the pack, and of course, are rewarded generously by the public for doing so. In the leader position, branding turns into a whole new department called "Brand Management." Every innovation, every great new idea needs to go through this department before getting into the hands of the public. It is very important that this department has a say in the launch of products, because otherwise there is no reason of having one, just get a designer to slap your logo on everything you make.

Brand management departments are like little full-fledged branding agencies within your company except that their job is not on demand, but ongoing. Monitoring industry trends, speaking to early adapters, organizing think-tank groups, testing and using your very own products is the daily routine of such departments. In essence they become your target market and if they find an issue with one of your products, it should ring a bell or two if not sound an alarm.

Branding therefore is an ongoing process. It requires ongoing attention and supervision. It is not superstition but instead a part of your success. If your marketing department can dream up a concept, then branding can enhance it, polish it and make it work better than your best expectations. Just make sure you find a specialist that fits your needs perfectly, because there are only two types of branding – excellent branding or no branding – and nothing in between.

About Richard

Richard Aristarchovas is a Lithuanian-born entrepreneur with a permanent residence in United States. Following in the footsteps of his father, who had an opportunity to work with the President of the Russian Federation Boris Yeltsin, Richard has throughout his career worked with Inc. 500 and publicly-traded multi-million dollar companies from all around the globe.

He is an introvert fascinated with marketing, systematization and financials – looking into every detail and leaving no stone unturned. He turns things upside down and inside out until they work, documenting step-by-step procedures and systematizing future encounters.

Richard is a co-owner of Stayfirst Branding Agency that is primarily operating in the European markets and Russian Federation, serving companies with over $10 million net worth and various government institutions. Serving as VP Business Development for the newly-opened United States branch of Stayfirst, Richard overlooks every project and venture coming from the Americas.

The best way to contact Richard is to go to: www.Stayfirst.com/contacts and fill out the form, or alternately by contacting the Stayfirst New York office by phone at: (646) 39 – STAY1 or (646) 397 – 8291.

www.Stayfirst.com

CHAPTER 36

THE ULTIMATE FINANCIAL STRATEGIES & SOLUTIONS — A PLANNING GUIDE WITH YOUR OWN WEALTH TEAM

BY ROGER A. REKATE CPA

In today's financial world, we need strategies for financial success. You can do this by plugging into a Team of Advisors who would create your own Wealth Team. This is the key to meeting your financial goals. The Wealth Team can keep the entire approach simple by focusing on three areas individually to *preserve your wealth, protect your assets, and save on taxes.*

We believe there are five areas of planning where your financial needs and goals will need to be focused – depending on what you own, your goals, and concerns. Our focus will be on personal and estate planning, business and succession planning, and real estate planning. It's our belief everyone will be exposed to market and tax risk in all of these areas of planning. Having your own wealth team planning for your unique situation is crucial not just for your estate, but for many generations to come!

The Ultimate Financial Plan solves your problems with strategies and solutions from a Wealth Team with Advisor Ink as the Wealth Coach leading the Team. First, you discuss your Ultimate Goals with the Wealth Team and gather all the information needed. The Team's Ultimate Goals for each and every client is to increase the client's overall net worth by tax, investment and real estate strategies.

Current income and estate taxes are seeing drastic changes. Everyone should be planning and reviewing for future financial decisions with our Wealth Team!

TRUSTING YOUR ADVISOR WHO HAS A PLANNING PROCESS

During a planning process, we will review all potential problems for the short term as well as long term planning. This is critical to know so you stay on track with your goals.

It will also allow for the realization of changes needed to be made much sooner. Has your financial advisor completed a *personal financial statement* to determine your true net worth? We do this to understand everything you own, including multiple entities, to focus on the five areas of planning. These planning areas include personal, estate, business, succession, and real estate planning.

In addition, we believe income planning for life and tax planning each year will reduce market and tax risks for your lifetime.

REVIEW RISK AND REWARD SCENARIOS

If you are 65 years old, it is well known to many advisors, as a rule of thumb, that if you take your age from 100, this will be the percentage you should be risking your investments and portfolio. Therefore,, 35% in the market is really the highest a 65 year old should invest unless their net worth is extremely high. Today, we see many brokerage firm advisors investing in just the opposite, and as high as 80% in many cases. This leaves portfolios with some serious 'downturn' in market exposure. That is 80% in growth-type investments without really knowing their positions in these investments.

KEEPING THE APPOINTMENT PROCESS SIMPLE

When you have a Team of Advisors who work together, most clients will be able to finish the planning process in two appointments. Exceptions will apply for higher net worth clients with needs for multiple strategies and solutions. We believe after two appointments, the prospective client and the advisor will have enough time to determine if it's a mutual fit for moving forward. If it's not a go for long term planning, then shake hands and wish each other the best of success.

PRESERVING WEALTH

If you have found someone you trust and who aims for you to have an income for the rest of your life, you're on the right road for a retirement. This is the key to everyone's portfolio of investments in the three phases of money. Each client should have their goals for income aligned first with the savings, income, and investments they desire.

PROTECTING ASSETS

We all have different needs for protecting our assets with multiple entities and goals for the future. An important decision is determining your estate planning needs during life and after death. Today, we can protect our estate from home health care and nursing home costs in new innovative ways. This avoids a huge risk for our financial longevity and lifestyle. We also need to protect our accumulated wealth from estate taxes. Simple key strategies can be put in place to protect your wealth for many generations.

SAVING ON TAXES

Strategies to save on *income taxes* can be implemented each year depending on a client's Taxable Income, and overall profits from businesses. The key to saving on taxes is having an advisor that communicates with the CPA for several reasons. These include trades on investment income, distributions, and taxable income. We have several clients taking advantage of one-time oil and gas tax deductions to offset gains from investment property and Roth conversions this year.

REAL STORIES

Estate taxes are another critical area for high net worth clients and opportunities.

Recently, the Ultimate Financial Plan for an $11 million net worth client solved several market and tax risks. A large trust company, brokerage firm, and small CPA firm *were not communicating,* causing my client to be unaware of current estate gifting rules. These gifting rules could protect their estate up to $5.2 million. Even more bizarre, the client discovered from our planning and completion of a personal financial statement that their true net worth was $5 million more than they thought. With 80% in stocks and mutual funds, the net worth of my client could fall significantly in a short period of time. Meaning if the market crashed, they would no longer have an estate planning need as long as the exemption was still available. Since the exemption is a moving target, especially with it set to be reduced, planning needed to be implemented immediately so that the single client would have the wealth protected while alive or if they passed away.

FIVE KEY PLANNING STRATEGIES WERE IMPLEMENTED.

1) Taking advantage of the gifting with a $3 million gift from three separate investment accounts.

2) Transferring $4.5 million to preserving wealth for income the rest of the clients life, including passing the entire amount on to beneficiaries in the future, based on income needs. $2 million was utilized to give a guaranteed income of $130,000 per year and $2.5 million was invested in a conservative portfolio of separately managed funds with a 1% management fee being the only cost.

3) Permanent indexed-based Life insurance was placed on the client for any estate taxes in the future after Gifting to pay any estate tax, and also on the children to guarantee large amounts of wealth passed onto the grandkids with legacy planning. A $5 million payout will follow on a guaranteed basis to the grandchildren.

4) A tax strategy was implemented to sell highly appreciated stocks and mutual funds at low capital gains rates with offsetting oil and gas tax deductions eliminating current year taxes. While the market was at the highest point in five years and before Obama-care taxes on investments, this strategy really worked for year-end.

5) Overall access to assets in tax-deferred and tax-free investments was formulated for the distribution phase of the client's retirement life with much less market exposure to risk.

OUTSOURCING PARTNERS

The Team of Wealth Advisors are a significant part of our planning and real life stories. Estate Planning Attorneys and tax planning CPA's are all being coordinated for the same game plan by the wealth coach, giving you the ultimate strategies and solutions. This includes lifetime income planning, legacy planning, and advance tax concepts in today's financial world.

IN CLOSING

I encourage you to *run, not walk,* to this type of planning. We have simplified the process for the highest of net worth clients in today's complex financial world.

Trust us for your long-term financial strategies and solutions. Isn't it time you preserved your wealth, protected your assets, and saved on taxes? We look forward to helping you soon!

About Roger

Roger A. Rekate, CPA is an Investment Advisor Representative. He has over seventeen years experience in the insurance and annuity industry and holds a Bachelor's degree in Accounting from Missouri State University.

Prior to establishing Advisor Ink, Roger managed his own CPA firm from 1991 to 2007, where he worked with small business owners with a focus on tax and succession planning strategies. Over time he realized that most of the individuals needed assistance with additional advanced planning, leading him to launch a full-time, comprehensive planning firm.

Advisor Ink's mission is *to increase their clients' overall net worth with tax, investment, and real estate strategies.* Their primary focus is the preservation of their client's wealth and to create a guaranteed income for life.

Mr. Rekate has been recognized in several areas over the years including a special recognition from Entaire Global for his service to small business owners - presented by Buzz Aldrin, the first astronaut on the moon. He has also been interviewed by *The Wall Street Journal* representing the Entaire Global group of companies.

Over the years, Mr. Rekate has served as managing partner for several commercial real estate projects. His experience in developing these projects has helped him first-hand advising his real estate clients for tax benefits and the bundled services program offered by Advisor Ink and its sister-entity, Advisor Solutions, LLC.

Roger and his wife Theresa have been blessed with a daughter together, and a total of five children and two grandchildren. Roger enjoys sports, hunting and riding his tractor on the farm.

To schedule a time to discuss your financial future and income planning needs, contact them at: (417) 881-2080 or toll free at: (855) 881-5440 today!

CHAPTER 37

POSITIONING DESTINY — TOWARDS YOUR ULTIMATE SUCCESS

BY SIOU FOON LEE

Life is like a journey that stretches for miles into the distance with views of distant hills, limitless sky and never-ending land.

Your life journey sees you at the helm, driving your car called 'Destiny.' You choose the speed you want to travel at. You choose the way you drive and how you drive.

Only you are in control. Ultimately, your destiny lies in your hands.

How well you live your life, which direction you are heading and what you want to do with your life are questions your loved ones, ask but only YOU have the answers to.

If you are happy and have found fulfillment, then it is truly certain you have lived life on your terms. You enjoy quality of life; lead a stress-free life and know where life will take you.

You enjoy peace of mind, contentment, prosperity, health and well-being. You are what others term as successful. As a successful person, you make informed decisions quickly.

But do you consider yourself as being successful?

- Does the above description suit you?

- How does this picture fit into your life?

If you hardly know where you are going or constantly change directions - you tend to be easily distracted.

- Do you lead your life on other peoples' terms?

You could be scared, living in a shadow, or not inspired to be what you really want to be.

But truth reveals itself.

You could be on the precipice of change. You should make change. You find it hard to change. Unless internal change occurs, nothing changes externally.

But what do you change?

People have been known to travel around the globe to hear new illuminating messages. They seek out visionaries to learn ancient wisdom as well as modern personal change methodologies.

Are you one of them ready to go down this path?

Before you begin - pause for a moment to hear me tell you that there is an alternative path in finding answers.

An ancient system of decoding your destiny gives you better understanding of your core values. Here, the art of decoding your destiny is personalized for you. Whether you are looking for personal change or changes in running your business or enterprise, you need a BaZi reading personalized for you.

Once you understand your *destiny,* you can then *design your life.*

With insightful information about career, business, and wealth or life situations - you can design the life you want to live, on your terms, not on other people's terms. You take full control. Ultimately, it is your destiny.

BaZi or Zi Peng astrology investigates your destiny based on your birth data. It helps you to position yourself well in your journey through life.

It is positioning your destiny towards your ultimate successful life.

WHAT IS BAZI?

BaZi provides insights into your mental, pyschological and emotional wellbeing. The information gained from these insights is applied when making choices and decisions. Making good choices has always been a difficult challenge in career, lifestyle, relationship, networking or business life.

BaZi is an ancient mindset and philosophy that has been used widely in Asian society. Interested enthusiasts following this complementary system to life management find that it gives them opportunity to overcome inherent weaknesses, confusion and indecision.

NOT A BELIEF SYSTEM

If you think it is a belief system that will take the joy out of living, let us examine the mindset of two people who want to enter a new territory. Both want to reach their destination. How will each one fare?

One desires to arrive safely, without getting lost or experiencing the unexpected. The other prefers to follow instincts, believing life has to be lived and experienced.

The second person sees the new territory as a new experience giving him a chance to learn from mistakes. He sees no need to live according to forward thinking that preparedness gives.

The first person however, gets a GPS to enter the new territory. With an aid to read the environment, the new place is not so daunting. He enjoys the experience being more prepared and knowing.

PERSONALISED BAZI GUIDANCE

If you want to know what lies ahead, you will definitely see the value of BaZi guidance. A personal consult gives you that GPS. Knowing about potholes and good roads along life's journey is about self-awareness and preparedness.

You are shown two choices - the path of least resistance and the path of great resistance. You are informed of both outcomes.

Further insights into events, timing and cycles of changes shows you what lies ahead. Plunging into the unknown can lead to being lost.

- Can you afford losing precious time?
- Do you need to do it tough?
- There is a better way.

Destiny well-designed improves the journey along a selected life path aimed at arriving at the destination successfully.

Life does not give a second chance to repeat experiences. Yes - another very different door of opportunity might open, but is it you that is shown that door?

You might want opportunities. When they come, do you have the capacity to grasp them?

An inner BaZi compass guiding you along the difficult pathways of life will not deprive you of the joy of living. Traveling the path of least resistance gives you more time to enjoy and laugh. The eventual good outcome gives you that peace of mind.

When challenges appear, the real "journeying" replaces the carefree time of feeling joy. Personal preparation is a result of forward thinking, a consequence of BaZi foretelling of the journey ahead.

Life will not be joyful when you constantly lose your way.

In planning a journey, you plan timelines and destinations. In planning well, you can live a life well-designed. Positioning is what gets you ahead.

THE IMPORTANCE OF DESIGNING DESTINY

At certain times, you need to fundamentally change the reality you created. You intuitively know your message does not resonate with who you really are, nor resonate with the change in your circumstance.

You begin to find answers.

You agonize about whether you have a better option of staying where you are or to leave an unhappy stagnancy to begin anew.

To create change from within or to align yourself with a mission bigger than yourself, you realize it is time for change.

But which option do you choose?

In life, in order to make the right decision, you need to study the situation, acquire the skills necessary to fulfill that mission. Then follow it with action.

Here are five calls for your action:
1. Design your <u>partnership, network and support team</u>
2. Design your <u>plan of execution and modes of implementation</u>
3. Design your <u>cash flow and financial health</u>
4. Design your <u>lifestyle, health and well-being</u>.
5. Design your <u>knowledge base</u>

STAYING AHEAD OF BUSINESS COMPETITION

There is constant change in the business environment. As economies and industries fluctuate, it is imperative to stay ahead of the game.

1. As a CEO or a key player, having the right advice for your corporation or business can help you forecast how and when the upcoming changes will happen for your corporation, business or industry.

2. This head start can help everyone, including you. If you are in corporate affairs, avoid future difficulties and maximize your company's positive position in order to have the best possible outcome.

3. The game of competition needs skills in maximizing corporate or business strengths and diminishing weaknesses.

4. Understand your own strengths and weaknesses to gauge the strength of your competitors and business associates.

5. Get to know yourself to understand their impact on your competitiveness

6. Decoding destiny is analysing your birth details. Improving your destiny and taking calculated steps is to stay ahead of competitors.

7. As a tool, BaZi gives you that chance to examine your key decisions and tactical approaches to secure eventual success.

It helps to define the art of positioning to win.

Businesses need to see immediate results. That is why Asians use Fengshui to design winning strategies. The result-driven solutions are aimed at achieving a return of investments within a time frame. They view Chinese metaphysics as an alternative AND ultimate guide to success.

Businesses can maintain employing staff only when they are seeing returns. It is the same with personal success.

Obstacles can impede your progress. Weaknesses can be self-sabotaging. In your quest for success, design your own winning ways.

As an entrepreneur making money, share your message. Achieve cascading financial abundance by sharing your passion more effectively with likeminded others. It is designing a living, creating wealth out of an asset when the timing is right. Making a difference in other people is one thing; finding life fulfilment doing it, is another.

THE IMPORTANCE OF KNOWING POTENTIALS

Bazi gives you the tools to position yourself to resonate with your natural strengths. Your capacities can help you to manage your purpose in life.

You have the option of either seeking wealth, finding support or giving support, leading and influencing others with charisma. You can be fully satisfied and rewarded when others find you likable enough to cooperate with you.

Finally, you realize that teamwork and networking works wonders for you rather than you competing on the same grounds and getting frustrated at being beaten in the game. Designing your dream team is not far-fetched.

To succeed in any area of life, it is essential to understand that there is a flow as well as a path of least resistance. Understanding this flow and this path leads to fantastic outcomes in positioning. You reap the benefits for the rest of your life if you follow the correct path.

You will be amazed at how life turns out when you stay inspired and fulfilled by taking the right path that eventually leads to ultimate success.

In seeking personal career success, approach your superiors for career advancements at favorable promotional periods for added advantages and boosts in self-confidence. Transform yourself into a charismatic, confident and attractive personality that every boss or network of people is genuinely looking for. Your power of influence and the way you communicate can be used to your advantage. Your likeability can be an asset.

BaZi can detect particular possibilities in your area of influence, performance and likability. They will help you to climb the ladder of success.

THE IMPORTANCE OF FORETELLING

It is possible to receive information about what lies ahead. If you care enough about excellent positioning, get a headstart in knowing the forecasts about the status of your company's financial security — it is the foretelling of events.

1. Personal forecasts can safeguard wealth accumulation and job security. Careful personal spending in view of difficulties can be in your control.

2. Crucial forward thinking is required when imminent upcoming luck cycle changes are analyzed and decoded early.

3. Times of loss are real. Making informed decisions is within human control. Minimize loss by not taking uninformed corporate risks.

4. Position yourself well when planning financial affairs. It is your life. Take control of your money and your life.

5. Preparedness is the key. Preparations should be in place before the arrival of good fortunes.

6. Good luck cannot be fully enjoyed if there is no preparedness to receive it full steam.

Positioning improves dramatically with the foretelling of the arrival of an effective game changer. That turning point you were waiting for could be the break through in:

- financial destiny of wealth creation
- business success
- career advancement
- good health announcement after a health scare

Then all you have to do is to tap into your personal mission, and turn it into your personal fortune.

It is at times of uncertainty that an inner intuitive compass or a crystal ball would be so valued when designing your lifestyle.

But how many get to see what lies ahead?

FORETELLING & FORWARD PLANNING

Knowing what lie ahead gives you more grounds to implement forward thinking and goal setting.

BaZi is beyond motivation and positive thinking. It is tailor-made advice to manage business, financial and personal success.

It helps you to manage:

- career advancement
- fulfilling relationships
- family harmony
- deep friendships
- filial children
- satisfying marriages

However, not everyone can see the writing on the wall to propel them to engage in forward planning. Valuable opportunities are lost as a result of indecision due to poor judgment even after receiving good information.

Another stumbling block to good progress can also be the constant shift in the goal post. Reposition the goal post. Keep your eye on the ball. Aim well.

Have you ever thought about forward planning as a guide to ultimate success?

If you have been having a spate of bad outcomes, acknowledge that turning point in your life by ending the self-pity and removing the stagnancy. If you can see light at the end of a tunnel then it is time to walk towards it. It is time for change. Light at the end of the tunnel is a sign that the bad period is coming to an end. The light reveals your change of luck.

What preparations did you make for the upturn while you were experiencing the downturn?

Bad luck will not last forever nor will good luck go on forever. Bad luck is only doom and gloom if you did not prepare for the downturn by laying low and managing your expectations.

Success comes down to action or inaction – well-timed or ill-timed. Good, well-timed decisions that lead to good outcomes; valuable and reliable skills, prompt and immediate action activates good human efforts.

- Forward planning has to take prominence.
- No more delays, ill-timed decisions that lead to bad outcomes.
- Inaction, procrastination are all effects of poor destiny designing.

If human effort is excellent, motivation can move a mountain if that mountain wants change.

Not many have the foresight to design their future destiny. BaZi foretelling brings you into the future to read your past. Is your future going to be an exact picture of the past?

TAKING CONTROL OF YOUR LIFE

During good luck cycles you have to prepare for lean times ahead. Good luck periods do not last forever and neither do bad luck periods go on forever.

This is the philosophy of yin and yang.

BaZi also has the capacity to inform you to hold back from taking impulsive decisions when you realize particular opportunities will lead to poor outcomes.

Here are seven tips to design your life.

1. Learn to understand yourself to understand others better.
2. Decode, design and master your destiny.
3. Gain insights into your destiny to choose better decisions and make better choices.
4. Select the path of least resistance if it leads to great outcomes.

5. Work smart, not work hard just to survive, if you are on a path of great resistance.

6. Manage your financial affairs well in good as well as bad times.

7. Know what lies ahead and learn to plan. Make strategic moves to avert danger and loss.

Don't make whatever limitations you admit to become a self-prophesying reality.

Live a well-designed life. But first know your destiny.

Thomas Carlyle said: *"Nothing is more terrible than activity without insight."*

About Siou Foon Lee

Siou-Foon was at a crossroads in her life after devoting herself to a satisfying high school teaching career and motherhood, and she decided it was time for self-development. Appreciative of the knowledge and heritage that came with her ancestors' discoveries; she was drawn to Chinese metaphysics study and went back to her roots to find out more. She studied Qi healing and went on to lecture in this field. Chinese healing ensures that Qi flowing freely and evenly will energise us. She learnt that a poor environment can adversely affect us. From there, she moved on to understand that this same energy governs the landscape and all aspects of life. This realisation sparked her interest in digging deeper into ancient methodology. She learnt that Qi balancing benefits one person, but Feng Shui benefits one whole household.

She left full time employment to follow her passion. Her choice of a Feng Shui career paid off when she was subsequently named the Australian representative, facilitator and professional trainer by an international Feng Shui organisation. She hosted numerous seminars for the principals, contributing further to the spread of traditional Feng Shui. She was chosen to speak in Germany at The First Classical Feng Shui World Conference after attaining mastery level. Besides being named the best student, Siou-Foon also won another prestigious honour that launched her respected international reputation when her peers selected her as the most helpful student.

A firm believer that "learning is a life long journey" she continued her passion for Chinese metaphysics, studying Yin and Yang House Feng Shui and also Zi Ping Astrology. The first step taken in 1994 on this journey never stopped. Wanting to taste natural spring water, she continued to find its source. She found drinking pure and crystal clear water so rewarding. The desire to acquire more knowledge drove her on to learn with masters who taught her to uncover the true depth and authenticity of these ancient practices. In her second wave of learning, she has had the ultimate privilege and good fortune to advance and seek more truths in such a complex environment. This is where Siou-Foon shares her values, integrity and dedication to the art of Feng Shui as practiced by these highly qualified but low profile masters from a long impressive lineage. Their extensive case studies and research speaks of their dedication and passion to preserve an ancient science.

Siou-Foon has appeared on SBS (Special Broadcasting Service, Australia) as a Chinese Massage Therapist. She is recognised for pioneering traditional Feng Shui in Australia. Over the years, Siou Foon introduced Feng Shui to TV viewers and radio listeners and actively participated in Mind, Body and Spirit Festivals and Shows popularizing Feng Shui; other mediums of media have also given extensive exposure to Siou-Foon. As a consultant, speaker and trainer, Siou-Foon has travelled widely throughout Australia, USA, India, UK, Singapore and Malaysia.

She believes that the external world desperately requires us to tap into our own positive and authentic potentials. When we tap into the power of these potentials we can create value. It is her passion, her vision to encourage as many people as possible to see this powerful reality. Her passion was to ignite, not only her own unique potentials to go far beyond simple symbolic Feng Shui, but to master an authentic ancient practice to keep this earth science alive.

Siou-Foon of Feng Shui Innovations is a speaker and bestseller co-author of two publications called *Cracking The Success Code* and *The Secret of Winning Big.*

To learn more about Master Siou-Foon Lee and Feng Shui please visit: www.fengshui-innovations.com.au or www.fengshuiinnovations.com – you can reach Siou-Foon via email: siou-foon@fengshui-innovations.com.au and contact her on +612 98260002.

CHAPTER 38

THE WILL TO SUCCEED:
ACTIVATING THE NINE QUALITIES TO ACHIEVE YOUR POTENTIAL

BY SUE HINES

Are you reaching or achieving your highest potential? If not, you are probably uncomfortable thinking that how well we fulfill our potential and the destiny we each reach, is in our own hands. Circumstances set boundaries, defining routes to achievement and influencing how we go about achieving, but free will determines *what* we do with our potential.

We inherit characteristics from the genes of our parents, their parents, and their parents' parents. Psychologist, Carl Jung, recognized the archetypal symbolism ancient astrologers used as psychological knowledge as they describe different qualities of human potential. Still relevant today, they are possibly equivalent to psychological DNA. What you inherit, and the astrology of your birth, set potential for what you can achieve.

Oscar Pistorius was born with a genetic defect that led to amputation of both his legs below the knees. His astrology shows Oscar had the potential of becoming a superb athlete. The 2012 Olympics saw Oscar defy the fate of his circumstances to choose his highest potential and effectively and brilliantly compete against the world's greatest able-bodied runners.

The difference between Oscar, who reaches such extraordinary peaks, and the other children born around the same time under the same stars, is how they use archetypal qualities of the psyche. There are nine core qualities in the psychological DNA and it is highly unlikely that you will get near achieving your highest potential without embracing and mastering them.

The laws of the universe allow us to predict, with more or less certainty, what might happen under specific conditions. Your free will defies that predictability. You get to choose if, how, and to what extent you will use your psychological qualities to fulfill your potential.

Professor Zimbardo cut short his 1971 Stanford Prison Experiment because volunteers arbitrarily assigned as guards or prisoners became sadistic and showed severe signs of stress. Zimbardo told the BBC in 2011, "It does tell us that human nature is not totally under the control of what we like to think of as free will, but that the majority of us can be seduced into behaving in ways totally atypical of what we believe we are."

We all face this danger. Not exercising choice as to *how* we live our lives, means we risk being seduced by circumstances that encourage us to live on autopilot, or risk living up to our full potential because we are under the seduction of conditions that do not make it easy or convenient to do so.

The nine core qualities are the keys to your success. They are highly interrelated, but are individually recognizable. Like your DNA, how they work in your life, their patterns of operation and degree of interaction is specific to you and your free will.

Grouped under the three headings of Mind, Heart, and Spirit, the nine Core Qualities of the human psyche are:

Mind	**Heart**	Spirit
Intuition	Honor	Optimism
Consciousness	Endurance	Enchantment
Courage	Faith	Ingenuity

1. QUALITIES OF THE MIND

Intuition

*This is the insight of the **Moon**, whose messages from spirit nourish your subconscious*

By your intuition, you know something directly without reasoning or thinking. It is the bridge between your conscious and unconscious and the intersection where instinct, senses, experience, feelings, reason and understanding meet. It treats all information equally, so it is important to take the time to work out priorities from what it gives you.

Intuition, your inner voice

- Is a pattern wizard, linking and connecting experiences, ideas, sensations, and thoughts from different times and places.

- Includes instinct; messages about your safety and wellbeing.

- Includes information below and on the periphery of awareness, like forgotten memories, glimpses, and visceral sensations.

- Involves more bits of information than reason and can take longer to sift, sort, and process.

Take time to get in touch with your intuition. It has valuable information for you.

CEOs rely more on intuition than quantitative data analyses and information, using gut feelings to guide business strategies. You cannot consciously hold and process immeasurable complexities of knowledge, understanding, foresight, market intelligence, and common sense needed in making strategic business decisions. Intuition is critical.

When you dismiss your intuition, hunch or gut feeling because you cannot "explain" it without checking or acknowledging it through your consciousness for veracity, your brain registers it as unnecessary and reduces the energy available for intuitive processing.

Consciousness

*This is the skill of **Mercury** that stimulates your mind and intellect and feeds communication*

Consciousness includes awareness, gathering and processing information, and directing your mind. It is about your intellect and communication with the world, being aware of and understanding yourself, others, the world, and the energy from each. Consciousness is recognizing your power to change and influence your world.

Your mental processes are designed to effect choice. Mastering and managing your mental processes means living your life by design rather than default. It is about making decisions. Every moment holds opportunity for choices and success depends on your ability to choose effectively.

You have to make choices knowing:

- What you perceive is contextual. Change the context, and your choices change.
- We all have blind spots. The information you have might be flawed.
- Your beliefs *about yourself* influence your choices.

As a social being, your life depends on communication.

In your interactions with others:

- Understanding means shared meaning. Communication means ensuring common meaning.
- Your words are actions. Your words "do" things to other people.
- Listening is active and creative. Other people's words "do" things to you.

Your job as CEO is to manage your identity and actions *and* those of the company. Allow that you are not infallible and make your choices anyway.

No matter how hard you prepare or try to avoid them, you will face doubt, fear and uncertainty. They are paralyzing and internally destructive. You cannot afford to let them stop your deciding.

Courage
*This is the energy of **Mars**, which feeds your drive and enthusiasm*

Everyone who ever accomplished something meaningful did so in the face of fear. If you have a passion, mission or gift to share with the world, you will meet challenges and you will have to muster courage.

1. Move forward in spite of fears. Courage is the mastery of fear – you do it anyway, even though you have fear.

2. Face challenges head on. Commit to pursuing your goal even if the fears become reality.

3. Be ready and prepared to respond to obstacles. Then protect and defend as best you can.

4. Change when you need to. Courage is not needless suffering. Make your goal big and meaningful enough that you find another way, a *how*, if the first fails.

5. Certainty of your Self and your convictions. The questioning voice is sure to start squawking sooner or later. Be steadfast.

6. Take initiative. It takes mental and emotional practice to step over your normal boundaries. Even small steps build that muscle.

Being in business means facing risks. This induces fears. Ask for advice, be realistic, do your homework, prepare, feel fear… and do it anyway.

Allowing fear to hold you back starts you down a slippery slope where doubt, worry and anxiety control you. Your progress slows or stops, you become less effective, and your self-confidence takes a dive.

2. QUALITIES OF THE HEART

Honor
*This is the grace of **Venus** that keeps you connected to others*

There is a fable about a shepherd boy who, to enjoy the spectacle of everyone rushing to help him, cried "Wolf!" when there was none. Frustrated, nobody came when one came for his sheep and he cried "Wolf!" This is about honor.

Honor is about personal responsibility and trusting yourself and others. It is something you feel pride in giving and as a privilege when receiving.

You have honor when you

- Know and focus on what serves you emotionally, physically, and spiritually.

- Treat yourself and others well, kindly, and with forgiveness, readily accepting and giving support.

- Are loved and love that you are loved.
- Have self-esteem and take pride in your personal and professional reputation.
- Keep good company.
- Negotiate effectively in your personal and business life.
- Are grateful and are readily able to express your gratitude.

Integrity is an essential leadership quality correlated with effective and optimal performance. Respect, honesty, fairness, and integrity attract success and abundance to your business through attracting quality staff and clients.

Disappointments in your own achievements, feeling stuck or powerless in a relationship or a job, result from broken promises you made to yourself. You have cried "Wolf!" and no longer trust yourself to show up and are in a self-sabotage loop. However, it is never too late to re-learn to honor yourself.

Endurance
*This is the power of **Saturn** and is where you meet your challenges and limitations*

Tap into your gift to the world, and the true value of the service you offer, to feel its energy propel you forward. A powerful reason or aspiration breeds commitment and a vision to pull you forward, set you on a consistent course, sustain you through tough times, give you resilience when facing adversity, and clarify what you need to do.

Strengthen your endurance with

- A **mindset** that accomplishment is a long-term process requiring patience and sustained action.
- **Planning and tracking** so you are well prepared and stay focused and productive.
- **Persistence** to do things when not motivated to and tenacity to hang on in spite of obstacles, challenges, and setbacks.
- **Momentum**, because if you stop for long enough, getting going is a monumental task.
- **Pacing** and energy management to regulate your stamina.

• **Developing resilience**, your ability to recover or bounce back.

Endurance is not suffering or passiveness. It is mental and inner strength to deal effectively with challenges. Doing **what is meaningful to you is crucial for the entrepreneur's inner strength and staying steady and focused.**

There is a fine balance between endurance and obstinacy. Obstinate is stubborn, inflexible, and intransigent while endurance is tenacious, resolute, persistent, and determined.

Faith
*This is the judgment of **Pluto**, which changes your destiny, again and again*

Everyone wants to make a difference in this world; to matter. Something inside you just *knows* you can change things for the better or that you can be of service. The signature of faith is that there is no proof. You run on confidence and trust.

Because life will challenge you, success is only possible if you have faith. For great success, faith needs to be the with-all-your-heart kind. Success will have a hard time finding you if you dance around the edges. This is your life, your future, your destiny, and your legacy. The capital you have to invest is faith.

Do you have that all-consuming faith?

1. You know you matter. When you know you can make a difference, you are called and you become a seeker, looking for ways to make it happen.

2. You define the faith. It is not given to or pushed on you, you choose it, embrace it, and make it part of you.

3. Faith commands. You are not *asking* for something. There is no option of failure.

4. Faith receives. When you are on your path, it feels like the universe is cooperating. Seize opportunity and express gratitude for good things that come your way.

Allowing others to sense your faith in yourself, your company and your vision, fosters confidence from the people you work with – partners, vendors and clients. It gives them faith.

Holding center on this can be hard. When you waiver, the only way is to rebuild, reinforce, or reaffirm your faith to regain your confidence in yourself and the future. Eliminate negative self-talk and put your faith in the future, not your circumstances.

3. QUALITIES OF THE SPIRIT

Optimism

*This is the benefit of **Jupiter**, that expands your horizons and fulfills your dreams*

If you believe your happiness comes from inside you and there is some more-or-less stable and predictable order to life, you are probably an optimist. If you believe you have relatively little or no control over events, you probably lean more pessimistic. Optimism is better. It is connected to better health, success, stress management, recovery from illness and longevity.

A serious disappointment or loss can wear you down over time and make you more pessimistic. You can increase optimism by recognizing your state and realigning your thoughts to more positive considerations.

1. Feel good without reason, and your mind will find supportive reasons.

2. Know the difference between disappointment and fear of disappointment so you can handle the fear.

3. Do not expect people to be consistently good and rational – they are not.

4. Identify and regulate your response to emotional setbacks.

5. Actively seek the positive, it rubs off on you and you find silver linings.

It is smart business to be optimistic so your optimism rubs off onto others. Your staff, vendors and customers will be happier and more likely to want to engage with you. You are also more likely to spot opportunities. Remember, nothing new is accomplished without hope.

Enchantment

*This is the spirit of **Neptune**, that heals and fills you with the universal lightness of being*

The multi-billion dollar entertainment industry is proof we love enchantment. Dictionaries define *"enchant"* as magic, bewitching, delighting, and joyful. Enchantment is about meaning. You are enchanted when something entertains you, holds your curiosity, or stimulates your imagination. Enchantment occurs when you become aware of simultaneous overt and covert meanings, or conscious, preconscious and unconscious messages.

1. The experience of enchantment is enriching and satisfying.

2. It may stimulate an intellectual reaction, but it is always about realizing meaning.

3. The emergence of meaning evokes delight. Enchantment occurs when your existence or something becomes clear.

4. The potent, euphoric sensation of meaning realization can counteract feelings of fragmentation and isolation.

5. It is a primary source of motivation or an end in itself.

6. It is recognition of, or identification with, the ideal that allows the unconscious to come to the fore.

The art of influence and persuasion involves forming, demonstrating or challenging beliefs. Enchantment forms the basis of any business negotiation and attempts to influence or persuade your customers, staff, or suppliers.

Unfocused enchantment wastes time. Because it is enriching and satisfying, enchantment easily tricks us, so keep checking whether it is serving the right goals.

Ingenuity

*This is the psyche of **Uranus** whose messages from spirit nourish your subconscious*

Creativity involves seeing something in a new way. Innovation is turning ideas and imagination into something real and new. Ingenuity is creativity *plus* innovation *plus* insight. Ingenuity solves a problem. We all have problems so we all need ingenuity.

Thomas Homer-Dixon called the space between a challenge and a solution "ingenuity gap." You are called to show up here daily. Smooth routine is the enemy of ingenuity because whenever you meet problems, ingenuity gets you solutions.

How do you exercise ingenuity?

1. Resourcefulness. Turn off your conscious, rational, logical mind and get out of the way.

2. Challenge the status quo. When facing apparently insurmountable problems, smooth routine stops you challenging your beliefs and assumptions.

3. Be willing to experiment. Even a failed experiment will teach you something useful.

4. Abandon or reject the traditional and conventional. Change your thinking paradigm to get the creative juices into that gap.

5. Be unique and stand out or apart. Doing things like everyone else limits your advantage.

Setting your business or brand apart from the competition means finding a new approach. Being entrepreneurial implies testing new waters, risking innovative ideas and finding better ways to do things.

If you are stuck, you need ingenuity. Do something different, unusual, or illogical in spite your rational mind's arguments against stepping out of routine.

About Sue

Sue Hines is "The Entrepreneur's Astrologer" and CEO of Aspects Galore. A life-long seeker and student of the art of finding meaning and purpose in life, Sue applies three decades of experience in marketing and consulting to help entrepreneurs find the center and bring out the best in their brands.

Sue uses astrology as a tool to guide entrepreneurs in gaining fresh perspective, insight and motivation to enhance their magical powers of choice. In the context of greater understanding, their confidence grows and decisions become easier as priorities become clearer. She employs astrology's wisdom to help them understand their potentialities and characteristics so their actions become more purposeful and meaningful. She guides them in the framing of their brand's positioning as unique, differentiated and of verifiable value – so they attract the business they want and lifestyle they desire.

Fascinated by the unique qualities of each person, Sue works with the one-of-a-kind spirit in business owners to bring out their highest potential. She helps them find and express their own particular form of vibrant, authentic living and seeks to serve entrepreneurs through her own brand of inspiring, teaching, healing and entertaining.

Sue hosts Bright Star Café, a weekly radio program on astrology and positive living on the CBS station, NewSky Radio. She is a published poet, has been a Reiki Master since 1998, and feels graced with the divine whisper of discontent – constantly challenging, always growing and becoming more. This is the gift she loves to share with others.

To download the free Special Report, "Entrepreneur's Archetypes of Success: Leveraging The 9 Qualities" or to learn more about The Entrepreneur's Astrologer and how you can gain a whole new perspective for yourself and your business, visit: www.AspectsGalore.com
Or call Sue Hines at +805-277-3581.

CHAPTER 39

FIVE PREMIUM STEPS FOR GOING ABOVE AND BEYOND IN ACHIEVING YOUR GOALS

BY VICENTE NJOKU MS

INTRODUCTION

The purpose of this chapter is to reveal five premium steps that you may consider as a resourceful tool, compelling gifts and pertinent skills that you could potentially explore to help you identify possibilities that could bring the best out of you as you pursue your goals during your lifetime. The reality of life has imposed on you the concept of challenge and responsibility, and this you have to deal with everyday and in every phase of your journey through life – and the only condition that could make a difference here is how you go about meeting your daily responsibilities. This reminds me of Newton's third law of motion in physics which stipulates that "for every action there is an equal and opposite reaction" (the physics classroom.com, 2012). The law emphasizes the notion that forces always comes in twos and they are always equal and opposite, and is based on this concept that birds learn to fly effectively and cars are built to withstand opposing forces.

Similarly, your challenges are opposing forces and cannot be greater than you as a person – as long as you learn to use and act on the necessary strategies that will help you excel, and just like the birds in the air and the cars on the road, you can handle any obstacle that may get in your way. You have an inborn strength that will assist you to counter the forces that exist between you and your challenges, and whether you balance it out well depends on what strategic approach you decide to implement under the circumstances. At this point in your life, you could bear with me that life is quite a challenge, and decisions you make most of the time could either make or mar your task ahead – thereby posing as a serious challenge or possible hindrance to bringing your dreams to reality. The sooner you realize this, the better the chances you have to develop your own strategy to accomplish your dreams. But again, dreams are meant to be dreamt and not all dreams are realized; but if you develop good strategic thinking as well as have a good strategic plan, these, when implemented at the right time and the right place may boost your chances of realizing your dream. As you forge ahead in this chapter, I have proposed five premium steps that could place you on the pedestal to success – as well as take you to the next level in your career, or help you overcome any challenges that may come ahead of you. These include:

1. the act of realization
2. the concept of having a definite goal
3. the implementation of success strategy
4. the act of actualizing your goals
5. going above and beyond

These concepts would be discussed to help you prepare and develop the right state of mind when it comes to problem solving, conflict resolution, and going above and beyond in your area of specialty or in any challenge you have planned to embark on in the future – both as an individual and as a group. These five premium steps when integrated and implemented as part of your conflict resolution strategy may serve as a cutting-edge concept and roadmap to enhancing your chances of accomplishing your dreams. But again, nothing is guaranteed in life, you just have to tough it up and get going as well as embrace your challenges.

Do not forget time waits for no man, and you have to be both physically and psychologically prepared for what is to come ahead of you or else you will be taken by surprise as you move along on this path, because most times surprises tip you off-balance and by the time you realize what has happened to you and try to regain your balance, years have gone past you and you cannot regain anytime you have lost in the course of your adventure in life. This reminds me of a Latin adage which states *tempus neminem manet* meaning 'time waits for no one' (yuni.com, 2012). Take advantage of time; do not let time creep up on you.

THE ACT OF REALIZATION

This may be referred to as the moment of truth and is characterized by self-awakening and the willingness to change or improve on certain things or areas in your life. Though you may not acknowledge this when it first dawns on you, but accepting the unraveling of reality as it is, provides you with the liberty to determine what your next move will be. At this point in your life, you should be able to differentiate your mere perception of things happening around you from the reality of life that you are part of, the things that you witness on a daily basis that motivate you to do something about improving your life. These are things that make you want to become a new and improved you as well as excel in all your endeavors and accomplish all your dreams.

I asked myself one question at some point in my life that changed my entire life today; and I would like for you to ask yourself this same question today as you read through this chapter. The question in context here is, "Are you happy with your current condition?" Because if you are not happy with your present status, you can make things happen by changing certain things in your life to become a better version of yourself. You have the capability of turning your life around for good. The scope of this concept could be approached from both an individual and group perspective, and the condition in this regard may include but is not limited to your current job, improving your school grades, going to college, improving on areas in your life such as losing or gaining weight, trying new nutrition/dieting regimen or even improving your business, working on your relationship or becoming a pro athlete, a movie star, a musician or anything humanly possible that you could set your mind on.

The premium lesson to be learned here is accepting that you need to make a change in your life and believe that you can do it despite any challenge that may come your way – taking necessary actions and using strategic steps to make this happen.

THE CONCEPT OF HAVING A DEFINITE GOAL

It is good to have multiple goals, but accomplishing them could be far-fetched due to divided attention. Having too many goals at a time may decrease the amount of time and energy that you put into one project because of split concentration. However, there are some select few that can handle multiple projects very well and have them accomplished in a timely manner. If you are one of them, "kudos" to you, but if you are not, it would be beneficial if you identify what you need to do with your time, and which goals you need to accomplish first. You will become more focused and productive when you prioritize your goals and set a timeline on when you want to have them achieved.

Following this strategy will simply decrease your stress level, decrease the chances of having a stress-related headache, decrease the risk of having increased blood pressure, and give you the opportunity to maximize your input as well as enhance the possibility of getting the most effective and competitive outcome. Having a definite goal in life is the premium concept to be learned here, since setting your goal would give you a sense of direction as well as the ability to decipher possible strategies that you could use to accomplish your dreams. But remember, you have to accept the responsibility that comes with setting your goals and you have to hold yourself accountable to accomplishing all your goals. I believe using this approach will help you go a long way to fulfilling your dreams both as a person and as a group.

THE USE OF STRATEGY TO SUCCEED

One thing I have learned thus far in life is that becoming successful always requires a strategy, and as you develop that strategy make sure you also have a contingency plan. Cutting-edge strategies in my opinion almost always incorporate the use of strategic thinking, strategic planning, and implementation strategy, and since you are endowed with the privilege to think and plan, using these concepts as resourceful tools will definitely increase your chances of becoming successful. Though you may not view them as strategies, if you think about it for a minute, these three steps that I pointed out here are essential in every aspect of your life, from household planning, improving on your school grades, improving on your business, including improving on your relationships, landing on your dream job or in fact, taking your career to the next level; the concepts could be applied to every aspect of your life or business that needs change or improvement. Critics say that strategic thinking is a combination of individual intellectual process – a mindset or method of intellectual analysis that encourages individuals like you and I to position ourselves as leaders and see things from a broader perspective – while strategic planning helps you as a person or as a group in developing steps necessary to reaching your desired goals (Swayne et al, 2008).

In my experience, the success strategy allows me to brainstorm ideas and come up with potential steps that could help me reach my set goals. Another thing that helped me a lot is prioritizing and writing out steps and setting up action plan or implementation strategy that will allow me to accomplish my goals in a timely manner. The premium lesson here is that you have to have a strategy to succeed in all your endeavors in life, and writing your goals and plan of action down on paper will constantly remind you of things you need to do to get your goals accomplished. Once that is imprinted in your conscious mind, your chances of bringing your goals to fruition would be magnified, thereby encouraging you to take precautionary measures as well as keep you motivated until your goals are achieved.

THE ACT OF ACTUALIZING YOUR GOALS

Now, it is time for you to bring your goals and dreams to reality; but what happens after that? Everyone would like to have their goals accomplished in their life time. You may ask why most people do not usually get to reach their goals in life? Could it be because they have not really tried or maybe they did not try hard enough? It could be any of the above or other factors that may impede a person from reaching a desired goal. It is not enough to identify your goal and develop steps to accomplish your mission in life. You should also have action plans that will take you in the direction of your goals and build upon those actions to keep you competitive as you move along, because getting to your desired goal is one thing and maintaining your goal and taking it to the next level is another.

Now that you have headed in the direction of achieving your goals; what next? This is where the concept of competition comes in because with the rate of technological evolution and a major shift from an industrial to a knowledge-based economic approach to society, you need to constantly upgrade your knowledge with what you do before it becomes obsolete to the system. Take for example, physicians engage in lifelong learning to constantly upgrade themselves with technology, current medical discoveries and break-through scientific journals, seminars, conferences, online tools and other resources that could help them prepare for license revaluation and medical practice. The premium lesson here is you need to be constantly upgraded/updated like the physicians and every other professional out there. First, it will help you to remain competitive in the market; and second, it will help you to keep your dreams alive.

GOING ABOVE AND BEYOND

Conversely, upgrading yourself on a regular basis is not the end of the project. It is true by now you must realize the project is a lifelong project and you just do not want to be competitive in the market, you also need to take your project to the next level. Taking my projects to the next level has always been part of my dream and I believe you would like to do the same either independently or as a group. The question here is, what are you doing to take your project above and beyond? For me, I developed an acronym which has helped me overtime to accomplish most of my goals and I called it CHIMP, which basically stands for consistency, honesty, innovation, motivation, and perseverance.

For example, if you are a CEO of a firm or even an ordinary employee, you are expected to be consistent with your overall performance and in doing so, your actions have to reflect honesty. In addition, with the use of innovative ideas you could come up with better and more compelling strategies that could help your organization accomplish their mission and purpose, and you have to convince and motivate your co-workers to share your dreams. By persevering, your goals could be accomplished. This concept could help you become exceptional in life as well as help you excel in areas of your life that you need improvement – including school, business, relationships and so on. The premium lesson here is, you need to be consistent with your performance to receive exceptional outcome, and when you establish your performance, more doors will open for you and it is up to you to decide on which direction you would like to go.

CONCLUSION

The five premium steps for going above and beyond in achieving your goals in life make up a compelling strategy that has to be revised constantly, written down and implemented as part of your strategic approach to advancing to the next level of life, and as emphasized in the chapter, the direction of concept implementation here is limitless.

However, it is up to you to identify which areas of your life that you need to incorporate the strategy the most, and based on your findings, apply key necessary concepts to help set you in the right direction to fulfill your dreams. I hope you find this one-of-a-kind strategy useful in your journey to becoming a success in what you do. Remember, you always have to put in your best effort in everything you are doing and hope for the best.

References

Strategic Management of Health Care Organizations (6th ed.)
by Swayne, L., Duncan, W., & Ginter, P. (2008). San Francisco: Wiley.

The Physics Classroom (2012). *Newton's third law of motion*:
http://www.physicsclassroom.com/class/newtlaws/u2l4a.cfm

Yuni.com (2012). *Latin quotes and Latin phrases*: http://www.yuni.com/library/latin_7.html

About Vicente

Author of *Entangled by Intrigue* and other works, Vicente Njoku is a Nutritionist who graduated at the top of his class from New York Institute of Technology (NYIT) in 2010 with a Master of Science (M.S.) in Nutrition. His goal is targeted towards helping individuals across the globe realize their goals in life, using strategic concepts as well as gaining insight in the use of food as a resourceful tool to optimize human health and prevent disease.

As a nutrition and health expert, Vicente advocates health, fitness, and overall well being of individuals and is particularly focused on disease prevention and alternative medicine, with a future research prospect in the beneficial effects of antioxidants.

With a work background in healthcare and research, Vicente has prepared and presented numerous health-related issues including selected topics on health education and promotion projects; the importance of diet and exercising; patient and staff communication enhancement skills, and issues on entrepreneurship/leadership skills.

Vicente is a member of the University of Nevada, Reno (UNR) Alumni association since 2008; New York Institute of Technology (NYIT) Alumni association since 2010, *Sigma Alpha Pi* and an Honors Society member: the National Society of Leadership and Success (NSLS) since 2011 and with outstanding performance, and in 2012 Vicente received NSLS-national distinguished membership excellence award.

Contact Information:
Email: Vincent.Njoku@yoursuccessgps.com
Website: www.yoursuccessgps.com
Phone: 702 758 8678

CHAPTER 40

TURN THE CORNER

BY ERIC PENARANDA

In 2007, I was part of a three-person development team tasked with constructing the national headquarters for a major restaurant corporation. The project in its entirety was high profile and staffed with one of the most talented design professionals in modern time. In particular, the principal architect was well known in many circles as a prodigy in the field. His reputation spanned nearly a half-century with a cult-like following. In short, this guy was incredible. During a preliminary design meeting in Atlanta, he made a short appearance to articulate the fundamentals of the project. At the close of his presentation, an immediate barrage of side bar questions began from the other participants, questions designed to extract some genius from this man's mind.

This was a prime opportunity to gather 'intel' and utilize it towards improving my career – yet I sat back and listened carefully. To my surprise, I focused on the questions being asked and discovered the pointed nature of the questions were structured in a manner to receive direct answers. I then noticed the responses were choreographed and monotone, as if this question has been asked hundreds of times. As the questioning continued, I came to the conclusion that the line of questioning did not allow this man to speak; pointed questions were received with pointed answers. As I listened further, there was a subtle transition which allowed the architect to pivot out of the Q&A session and leave the room.

Before he closed, I gathered my things and made my way ahead, the goal being to walk to his next location. After a casual interception, I teed up a very short and general statement that allowed him to speak towards something that was of interest to him at that very moment.

He stopped, waved his hand across the open office and told me to observe every person working at their desk. We stood quietly for about 30 seconds and watched. The majority of the 50+ junior architects wore headphones and appeared laser-focused at their desktop frantically working designing components of the building. It was clear they were focused on one thing and one thing only.

After the brief moment of silence, he casually said "I wish I could get them to turn the corner." Most would immediately follow up this statement with a direct question; yet again I waited and listened. "They focus on accomplishing one task yet often forget about what that task changes," he said. After a quick pause he continued, "They need to learn to turn the corner and see what is on the other side."

In layman's terms he was describing the multi-faceted nature of architecture and the need to observe all the angles of any decision. For instance, if a building roof structure is modified, it may change the load design which will change the steel components, concrete design and all connections. It also may change the esthetic components such as glass, finish metal, finish concrete, etc.

This brief interaction forever changed my approach to making any decision. This experience taught me to take a three dimensional approach to addressing nearly everything. Turn the corner – expose untapped opportunities by finding creative angles that ensure you are not leaving opportunity on the table.

TIME, VALUE AND MONEY...

Time: Your greatest asset

Value: How is your time measured and how much is it worth?

Money: How much does your time produce over an hour, a day, a week or a month?

Sometimes I find myself sidetracked with non-income-producing activities such as browsing MSN.com or searching for a ski destination for my wife and I. Both serve their purpose, one builds my current events database and the other keeps my family active and sane. If you manage your time properly, you have established a 7-day allotment of time for working, living and playing. The problem is one week is a fixed cycle; we do not get extensions or bonus hours.

So, how have you divvied up your greatest asset to produce income? Let's start with a quick snapshot at my work week matrix based on a total of 50 hours:

• Business development - 15 Hours

• Lunch - 5 Hours

• Business planning - 5 Hours

• Busy work - 10 Hours

• Executing business - 15 Hours

First, business development must take close to the majority of any business owners work week. In my business, the most critical element of commercial real estate is keeping the pipeline active. On average, transactions can take 4 months or more to execute from initial showing to document execution, add another 2 months to receive actual payment. You can quickly see that a 6 month cycle can create a huge cash flow issue if business development is set aside. As a side note, I always track pursuits and active calls on a weekly basis as a mechanism to hold me accountable for shots on goal. If you don't take the shot, you can't score.

Lunch, yes I calculate lunch as income-producing time. As a former colleague would always remind me of the importance of lunch by the saying, "Never eat alone." The fact is everyone eats lunch at some point, so you might as well make it productive. I have taken lunch with warehouse managers, property owners, attorneys, bankers, contractors, office mates and even friends. It doesn't matter who it is, so long as you get to know that person and learn a thing or two.

I always set aside one day before the start of the New Year to establish my business plans and objectives for the coming year. However, during the week, I work more at a micro level to implement objectives and learn new areas of development.

Busy work is a necessary evil. Less than 10 hours per week is ideal, 0 is impossible. Delegation is key to reducing hours, hand off what you can and efficiently manage what you can't.

Executing business is the easy part but largely critical to any business. Whether I am showing property, negotiating terms or even reviewing contracts, time accumulates and it must be tracked.

At the end of a work week, calculate how much time was spent where. Track your progress over the course of one month, overlay this total with your overall production then compare to your anticipated value. This will not only net you the greatest return, but also enable you to efficiently manage this non-renewable resource. The goal is to refine your workweek to improve efficiency and focus more on income-producing activities.

GET OUT OF THE BOX, AND THEN LOOK IN...

I often find myself peering deep into any business that I encounter where the goal is to try and understand the business model. What are the operating costs? Where is the margin? How do they execute the upsell? Like I'm at a zoo, I stare and wonder what are they doing and why?

One day my wife told me that during trips to Disney World, she observes the park as a business and picks up on ways that Disney has refined the operation to maximize not only profit but also guest experience. This is the mindset of an entrepreneur; find diverse avenues to provide a best-in-class product and service.

Being immersed in the inner workings of your business, it is difficult to visualize how you are perceived by the customers walking through the door. Often you can miss some of the most obvious flaws or gaps in your operation, because you are not looking from the outside in. Remove yourself from the operational mindset of your business and observe it as a customer. Take yourself through the transactional process mentally and physically. Be a client so you can effectively serve your client.

SERVE YOUR CLIENTS AND IN TURN,
THEY WILL SERVE YOU...

Some time ago, during the beginning stages of a real estate transaction, a broker declined to bring his client to a building I represented because the offering fee was not above market and did not include a monetary bonus package. Keeping my ear to the group, I discovered who his client was and what they were hunting for. Interestingly, this business model was a functional perfect fit for my facility. I decided to reach out to the broker in hopes of convincing him to bring his client over for a space tour, not to my surprise, his tune changed dramatically as his client was leaving the country in a matter of hours.

It turns out; this very busy client from London provided his broker a month of advanced notice to schedule a property tour so that in one day he could view all available options to secure a location for occupancy within 2 months time. Instead of putting his client first, the broker decided to short list the properties offering the largest fee. During the tour, the client was extremely disappointed that no property met his requirements and was considering holding off on his building pursuit which would change his business strategy dramatically.

With an hour to spare, I quickly set up the building tour with the broker. Upon arrival, the client quickly ascertained that I had not only performed my homework on his functional needs, but also on the company and their business strategy. In short, the building was ideal, and he quickly executed a long-term lease on the facility. Within one year, the business was performing so well that he appointed me alone to expand his operation so that he could occupy the entire facility.

The moral of the story is your client's best interests are your priority, always. Building the perception of client-first business is generally not an overnight success story, so take time to ensure the service being performed is executed at the highest level. Build the brand of a company that looks on its clients business as if it were your own.

BE A SPECIALIST...

Take two doctors; one is a general practitioner providing a wide range of medical services to its patients. The other is a spinal cord surgeon providing a small range of very specific procedures. Take a wild guess to which doctor takes home the larger annual income.

From another angle, consider two business owners offering automotive services. You own a rare European car that is in need of a carburetor overhaul. Owner #1 offers general automotive service on any make and model. Owner #2 is a specialist in fuel delivery systems solely for European cars; this owner has performed thousands of overhauls and is well known as the expert. For the same money Owner #2 is a clear choice, the business model focuses on the service needed with the expertise to offer high-level solutions.

The point here is generalists rarely strike it big. Why? The business model is easy entry, minimal experience and largely diversified. Specialty services historically drive higher rates given the specific and rare nature of the service. Pair a rare business line with a high level of service and become the expert.

CHANGE IS GOOD...

Through the course of our lives we will experience every part of the economic cycle, on multiple occasions. Unless you are a doctor or lawyer, your business has a chance of becoming completely obsolete.

I say this because after years of hard work to become an expert in the field of real estate development, I found myself not only out of projects but also out of options, or so it seemed. Every path I took led me closer to the realization that my area of expertise has become nonexistent until I came to the conclusion that I needed to change and adapt to the situation happening around me.

With a mind full of commercial real estate experience I decided to pursue the path of brokerage. I joined an international real estate firm in 2009 which happened to be the worst year for commercial real estate brokers in modern history. Though a tough year financially and spiritually, I came to realize that the change I made was for the best. I entered into a field that many were fleeing, yet after 3 years of hard work and dedication, I finally arrived at the #1 real estate company in the world with a portfolio of almost 4 million square feet, poised for the return of tenants and buyers.

Change can be best when times are bad. For example, during the downturn, the commercial real estate industry spawned the new business line of assessment consulting, generating a new source of fee-based services for clients. The key is to evaluate the angles of your business, find and expand your menu of specialties, and execute with a level of service that is second to none.

SUPPORT THE SUPPORT...

Employees can make or break your company in a matter of moments. Take time from your schedule to ensure they are happy and incentivized. Pay attention to office chatter, gossip spreads like wildfire and is detrimental to company perception and office morale. Be careful to avoid micromanaging conversations, but be mindful of the underlying message.

Close employee interactions with, "Is there anything I can do for you?" Execute this in a sincere manner to show your attention to their needs.

Occasionally sit down with each employee in a comfortable location (preferably not your office) to discuss their satisfaction with the company and the efficiency of internal operations. Avoid structuring the conversation as an employee performance review; the goal is to offer a setting so their voice can be heard but not criticized.

No matter how hard you try, not one individual will view the company like you unless their name is listed next to yours under the Division of Corporations. Understand this, then discover what drives your support staff. Everyone has a motivation button, find it and push it.

GAUGE PERFORMANCE WITH A TARGET...

I have never met someone that has arrived at the top without hard work, these people do exist, however, it is more a function of luck or the inheritance of another. The key element is hard work, without it an arrival at success is likely a dream. Of course, there is no guarantee that is correlated with the amount of work invested, which is why your most important asset (time) must be measured.

A very successful businessman once told me that every December he sets a business and personal plan for the upcoming year. It just happened that this year he derived a plan to run 300 miles before the New Year. He separated the main objective into small monthly goals to accurately measure his performance and adjust based on personal schedule interruptions. Every month he targeted 25 miles, some months he completed less and some months more. The idea is to understand the level of progression against your main objective and adjust accordingly.

Approach every venture with a plan, a goal and a timeframe. Planning the strategy is extremely important to build the framework to arrive at the objective. Without a vetted plan, the execution stage will likely become a false start. Next, put a target on the board to measure your time invested. Be aggressive; conservative goals encourage complacency so set the bar high and push yourself to reach the top. Finally, set the stopwatch. Limit your performance levels and objectives to a specific timeframe. Above all, putting it to paper without a plan, a goal and a timeframe and you are shooting in the dark.

I was incredibly fortunate to have that conversation in 2007, a simple one-line statement forever changed the way I identify, execute and operate my business. It allowed me to turn the corner in my business by creating a multi-faceted approach to every situation, condition and decision.

Turn the corner in your business and see what is on the other side.

About Eric

Eric Penaranda is a native Floridian raised in Tampa while being surrounded by the Development and Construction Industry through the family business. He is blessed with his loving wife Lindsay and two amazing pups Marley and Cooper. Eric is a graduate of The University of North Florida, where he received a Bachelor of Science in Construction and Real Estate Development.

Currently, Eric is an associate within the Industrial Services Group of CBRE where he specializes in the sale and leasing of industrial properties in the Central Florida commercial real estate market. Prior to joining CBRE, Eric provided leasing services for over 1 million square feet of industrial real estate from 2009 to 2012. From 2001 to 2009 he developed and constructed over 3 million square feet of real estate and successfully negotiated over $500 million in project contracts. Eric was also recently featured in *Newsweek* magazine as one of America's PremierExperts®.

As an innovative entrepreneur, Eric also owns and operates a seasonal Christmas tree business in Winter Park, Florida, whereby he has successfully built and maintained a brand that is well known for delivering a quality product with a focus on superior service.

If you would like more information about Eric Penaranda, or would like to discuss commercial real estate in any market, visit: www.EricPenaranda.com or call him at: 407-222-2424.

CHAPTER 41

CREATING INVESTMENT INCOME WITH TRANSPARENCY

BY C. GRANT CONNESS & ANDREW M. COSTA

Perhaps the saddest things we see daily at Global Wealth Management are the shocked faces of new clients when they realize that their broker's investment strategy was really no strategy at all, or the look of despair on someone's face when they learn they cannot retire as planned because they lost 40% of their investments almost overnight. As a result, of these stories and others like them, our primary goal became creating investment income with transparency for our clients. In other words, we choose not to hide fees or the real rate of return on investments we make. In fact, we believe transparency should be a goal of our entire industry; therefore, it became our mission to help investors seek transparency.

To achieve transparency in a business that normally operates in the dark alleys of buried fees and selling and not advising requires a strategy not normally found in an investment firm. The primary difference between our philosphy and that of our competition equals the difference between advising and selling. We advise; others sell.

As a general rule, an Investment Advisor has an obligation when working with his clients to act as a fiduciary. A broker when working with his clients acts on a suitability basis. As fiduciary advisors to our clients with significant financial worth, we have a greater burden than do brokers at the average investment outfit. The fiduciary standard requires us to recommend not what might be an appropriate investment for a client, but we must recommend *only* those investments that are in the best interest of our clients. To that end, and with a desire for complete transparency in mind, we recommend and encourage investors to answer the following questions to ascertain whether they are receiving the best advice or not.

Do you have mutual funds? If yes, you might not be transparent.

Do you have a Broker or a Fiduciary Advisor?

Did you create an Initial Plan or receive a blueprint? If not, how will you measure the meeting of your investment needs? Your portfolio may not be transparent.

Is anyone following up with you to tell you what your investments have done? If yes, good for you, if no, it may be time to check in with your financial professional.

Ask anyone about how they feel presently and, say, how they differ from ten or twenty years prior, and that person can likely laundry list for you how different his life is from then until now. While most of our clients can tell how they have changed physically from 30 to 60, many of them have no idea that their investment needs have changed as well.

We share the story of our client, a physician, who likely would not have treated a 40-year-old patient exactly the way he would a 60-year-old patient. Yet when it came to his retirement investing, he had been doing exactly that. The doctor was 60 years old and approaching retirement, but his investments were risk/growth oriented for the aggressive portfolio of a 40-year-old in his earning prime. When we first met with him, his entire portfolio carried a risk of 40-50% and was loaded with mostly mutual funds. It is imperative that investors approaching retirement transition from growth-driven investing to income-driven investing. Our analysis of his portfolio determined that he had a high-risk, growth portfolio that included a mega insurance policy with a sizeable cash value that would have been lost if not removed before he died, several variable annuities with hidden fees galore and a large amount invested in 30-year bonds.

The repair of our client's portfolio began with lowering his risk by changing his investment strategy. We advised him to move his mutual funds to a transparent, wholesale portfolio that eliminated the fees to an intermediary, and by doing so, saved the client about 2/3 of his former investment costs. Next, we lowered his maximum downside significantly and shortened the duration on his bond portfolio from 30-year bonds to 10-year or less bond maturities. We advised him that he was paying considerable tax on gains inside his mutual funds, and we recommended ways to make his portfolio more tax efficient. Finally, we found our client a retirement income annuity with a similar income and death benefit as his variable annuities, but with less expense – a 1% fee down from a 4% fee – and less risk.

Why do we take so much time to educate and protect our clients? We do so because we have seen relatives and friend's parents suddenly lose half of their retirement in years like 2008, and we want to keep others from having to give up on their retirement plans.

We consider it our professional duty to share our vision of transparent investing and the ways transparency can benefit investors. Transparency begins with the right analysis, by asking the right questions. Through experience, we have noted four key elements of a secure and successful investment plan: (1) risk and appraisal analysis to determine hidden risks and costs, (2) establishing transparent investment goals, (3) developing a transparent income plan and (4) transparent communications. We encourage investors to use our guide and help to achieve better results and to safeguard their retirement.

KEY ONE: RISK AND APPRAISAL ANALYSIS

After asking yourself the above questions, it is time for a risk analysis to determine the potential risk of the current portfolio. Nine times out of ten, the actual risk is not what an investor thought it was. A fiduciary advisor must investigate the investments the client has and what risk the client THINKS they are taking. If they *think* they have invested conservatively, but their actual potential risk is 20-30% loss in a year, that is not a conservative investor. If a client's risk is too great, the first step is to minimize the risk with a redesign of the client's portfolio. The second step is a cost or appraisal analysis of their portfolio with emphasis on the mutual funds. The hidden costs of mutual funds can be 2-3 times higher than the advertised fees. The difficulty in computing the actual costs of mutual funds is challenging even for experts in the field.

While most investors would check the expense ratio of a mutual fund--which is essentially the costs to own the fund that pay the portfolio manager and operating expenses--that number is not the bottom line. Looming above each of these mutual funds is a cloud of additional transaction and trading costs comprised of bid-ask spreads, opportunity costs, market-impact costs and brokerage commissions. Confused yet? Many of these costs are not mandatory to report because the SEC deems them too difficult to calculate due to the variances from fund to fund. If the SEC thinks those fees are too hard to calculate, a client has little chance of adequately doing so. It is prudent for an investor to engage the assistance of a fiduciary advisor to navigate the hidden costs and risks of mutual funds and other investments.

KEY TWO: TRANSPARENT INVESTMENT GOALS

A transparent investment goal balances on three things: an advisor as the quarterback who calls the correct plays, a balanced portfolio that generates a steady income stream and the ability to advise on invest-ments with minimum costs and fees. The goal of an advisor should be to manage the client's investments and expectations with superior service and with a mind toward minimizing the client's risk.

As highly conservative and investment managers, we feel like we hit our homeruns when the market is down because we protect the client's down side or blind side. Our philosophy is not to shoot for 12%to 15% returns as other firms do, because that does not allow us to protect that down side. Our experiences working in both sides of the industry estab-lished our belief that no investor should put all the eggs in one basket. Our fiduciary obligation to the client prohibits us from recommending only certain investment options. For example, an insurance agent can assist a client with retirement investing; however, he can only sell one type of product. If the client has $1,000,000 to invest, that investment will likely be made into an annuity because that is what the agent sells. Conversely, a fiduciary advisor might recommend that some of that cli-ent's million-dollar investment, maybe 20 or 30 %, be invested in an annuity and the balance in other investment options that will work together to minimize the overall risk to the client's portfolio while providing other investment needs to the portfolio.

Instead of simply dumping a client's money into a mutual fund portfolio and collecting a commission as some brokers might, spreading out investments into multiple asset classes can better meet the needs of the clients. The best advisors don't just "do" insurance or just "do" stocks. In fact, the only singularly minded thing a great advisor will do is advise clients. Many traditional brokerage firms put together packages of products (funds) for resale to the public. They make money for their shareholders first, themselves second and the client third. If a client purchases a product that does not meet their needs or is not right for them, oh well, the broker still made money for the firm. The practice of repackaging and reselling products at a higher cost to the client equates to the client purchasing at retail pricing. Just as it is more advantageous for the client to have a diverse investment portfolio, it is also more advantageous for a client to purchase investments at wholesale pricing.

KEY THREE: TRANSPARENT INCOME PLAN

If you were purchasing a new car and you had the choice to pay the wholesale or dealer price for the car or the regular retail price for the car, which would you choose? You would certainly want to pay the wholesale price and eliminate markup to the middleman. An investor should avoid markups paid to a middleman as well. Wholesale investments require doing things differently than other firms. For example, our RIA, Global Financial Private Capital hired a chief investment officer Christian Bertelsen. Chris and his team act as our primary money manager. They manage eight investment portfolios for us with a very low cost structure, very transparent portfolios. What is normal in the industry is for the person with whom you meet and from whom you receive advice to be the person also managing your money. We found that system to be very inefficient, because if an advisor is meeting with the client and spending adequate time learning his needs and assessing his risks, that advisor cannot also effectively be managing investments. Therefore, we designed an approach, in which the advisors coordinate the client planning and relationship building while some of the best professionals available manage the investments. Called a separately managed account in investing, it is vastly different from a mutual fund. A mutual fund is a retail product packaged and sold by somebody else. A broker can choose to sell you that product, and you will likely have no idea who is managing the changes of the investments within that mutual fund. Alternatively, a separately-managed account adds to the transparency of the investment strategy because the client owns a wholesale portfolio and knows exactly who the people are who are managing their money.

Our portfolio managers came from the institutional side of investing and are very highly recognized and respected in the management industry. There are really only a handful of top portfolio managers in the United States; they are like the Major League of investing. It makes the most sense to have major league players, the best in the business, manage client funds. We know from experience that if we are on the phone with a client and there is a change that needs to be made, then our investment committee deals with it while we continue to manage the other aspects of our business. Without a chief investment officer and investment committee, either the client or the portfolio would suffer due to inattention.

Another aspect of a transparent income plan is the 50/30/20 rule for individuals that are close to retirement or in retirement. The 50% represents the money that is conservatively invested in the market and actively managed. That 50% represents stabilized income. The next 30% is invested in more stable, less risky investments such as fixed products like fixed annuities, treasury bonds, CD's, and money market with no ties to the stock market. These investments typically provide guaranteed income. The final 20% goes into alternative investments; public non-traded REITs (real estate investment trusts) or note programs that generate a nice income but are not tied in any way to the stock and bond markets. One can adjust these percentages based on a specific client requests, but as a rule, this formula is a proven, effective strategy for which investors nearing retirement should strive.

When a prospective client is going through this process, we show them their blueprint or roadmap for retirement to demonstrate for them the income they can expect. Experience says that too many people have difficulty transitioning from their growth years into the new position of *this* (managing retirement investments) is their job now because they are no longer earning money to invest. If a person is earning a conservative 5-7 ½% a year off his or her investments, that person cannot afford to pay buried fees of 2-3%. This is what makes our transparent investment strategies with a fixed, low cost fee for managing the portfolio so appealing to so many clients. We provide them with the blueprint up front as to how much they have invested in each category as well as provide the transparent management costs they will pay for the services they receive.

KEY FOUR: TRANSPARENT COMMUNICATIONS

The best fiduciary advisors offer their clients opportunities to learn more about their investment advisors and allow the clients to offer feedback. Client advisory boards that are comprised of the firms most influential clients--we have nine ranging in position from CEO's of major corporations to a retired police officer—are a great way to elicit client feedback. An advisory board offers feedback on how to better-serve clients which allows an advisor to adjust his business quickly to meet client needs.

Client feedback told us that our clients prefer our smaller, intimate way of doing business. Consequently, based on our own client recommendations, we limit our new client base of full-service clients per year. While we desire not only to be the right fit for the client, we also want the client to be the right fit for our firm. If the client has a substantial portfolio but they want to manage and call all the shots, then they are likely not the right fit for us. Usually when one sits down with a broker or advisor, one must trust that their word is law, however, this typically requires a significant level of trust and confidence. In the interest of transparency, we not only tell our prospective clients about our firm, we also allow them to contact our client advisory board if necessary. Therefore, they get not only our perspective, but also those of the clients who have been working with us through the years.

Weekly newsletters from our investment management team called "Thought of the Week" gives our clients a snapshot into the minds of the people investing their money. By doing so, the client stays current on both his investments and the firm's outlook on the markets. Additionally, trading notes about what traded and why, can assist a client in better understanding why his retirement portfolio contains certain investments. We also highly recommend finding a fiduciary advisor who communicates with clients, as we do, a Monthly Market Update that features the chief investment officer briefing them about trends in the markets over the last month. It is our position that these transparent communications foster a greater comfort level for our clients.

Ultimately, transparency is a tool that builds stronger client relationships and contributes to our mission of providing comprehensive wealth management for our clients. With every client, we begin by assessing their risks, advise them of ways to minimize their risks and maximize their income using a broad spectrum of investment opportunities, and create total solutions for them that satisfy our fiduciary obligations to our clients. All along the investment journey, our clients receive communication and continued service from our entire team including our investment committee whose sole obligation is to manage their assets, not to make money for shareholders of the firm. We offer these things to our clients to insure that their retirement is comfortable and that they can continue to enjoy their lifestyle. We hope that in the future, our entire industry will follow suit.

About Grant

C. Grant Conness' steadfast adherence to the highest level of integrity, trust, and service to the affluent individuals and families whom he assists with their retirement and estate planning aspirations has earned him the respect of the South Florida community of which he has been a part for over 30 years. An investment Advisor Representative, financial author and Co-founder of Global Wealth Management, Mr. Conness also shares his passion for wealth management by educating and enlightening the local investment community through his various lectures, seminars and speaking engagements.

Mr. Conness is a co-host of the financial radio show the "Road to Retirement Income" and is an accredited course instructor with the Florida Bar on 1031 Exchanges.

Mr. Conness attended The University of Findlay, OH where he was a member of the National Championship Football Team and he holds a Bachelors of Business Administration from Florida Atlantic University.

He has been featured and quoted in major publications such as *The Wall Street Journal, USA Today,* and *Newsweek* and has appeared on major television networks such as NBC, ABC, CBS and FOX as a recognized investment advisor in his field.

Mr. Conness has given back to his community through local service and charitable groups including Rotary Club, Jason Taylor Foundation, and Kids in Distress. He resides in Ft. Lauderdale with his wife Jessica and four children. He is a passionate sports fan and enjoys boating, surfing, paddleboarding, and spending quality time with his family.

To contact Mr. Conness:
Call the Fort Lauderdale, Florida office direct at: 866.405.1031
Email: gconness@globalwma.com
Or visit the firm's website at: www.globalwma.com

About Andrew

Andrew Costa is a Financial Author and Co-Founder of Global Wealth Management, who has worked extensively in the field of financial management.

Mr. Costa is the co-host of the financial radio show "The Road to Retirement Income" on 610 WIOD and iheartradio.com. He has been featured and quoted in major publications such as *The Wall Street Journal, USA Today,* and *Newsweek* and has appeared on major television networks such as CBS, NBC, ABC, and Fox as a recognized professional expert in the investment management business.

Mr. Costa's hard work and diligence earned him the honor of being a Million Dollar Round Table Qualifier, and as a member of the Lincoln Presidents Club as a Gold Eagle Member.

Acting on his strong beliefs of giving back to the community, Mr. Costa devotes time to the Salvation Army, Petset-Humane Society of Broward County, and Kids in Distress.

Mr. Costa and his wife Liz have been married since March 2008 and have been residents of Ft. Lauderdale for more than 25 years. They are proud parents of their two sons, Dylan and Austin. Mr. Costa's hobbies include spending time with the family, golf, boating, traveling, and a passion for sports.

To Contact Mr. Costa:
Call the Fort Lauderdale, Florida office direct at 866.405.1031
email: acosta@globalwma.com
or visit the firm's website: www.globalwma.com

CHAPTER 42

KEEPING IT SIMPLE ISN'T STUPID — HOW TO TURN YOUR IRA ROLLOVER INTO 5% TO 7% INCOME FOR LIFE

BY STEVE JURICH

ONCE UPON A TIME, …a million dollars in a 401k and a free and clear home meant your money worries were over…You could retire, turn on your pension, collect fifty thousand a year in interest, and still pass on a million to your loved ones…

That was then, this is now.

Today, after the dot com crash, 9-11 and the 2008 "Black Swan," Americans are not sure where they stand. Is Wall Street on their side? Or is it a rigged game? As 78 million baby boomers march into retirement at a pace of 10,000 per day, they aren't worrying about the same things anymore. A recent MetLife study found that the number one fear in retiring Americans is no longer dying, it is running out of money.

It wasn't too long ago that Frank, a prospective client, came into my office looking kind of miffed and depressed. At first, I couldn't understand why. He seemed to be a very bright man, in pretty good health. As it turned out, he was sitting on a portfolio of roughly a million dollars and change. "What could be bad?" I wondered to myself.

He had worked as an engineer for a major Fortune 500 company and owned both company stock and a 401k that he had rolled over into an IRA. He was a happily married guy, 68 with three grown up kids. We shook hands, exchanged pleasantries, and sat down around my desk. The sunlight shone in a little bright at that time of the day, so I skewed the mini-blinds and asked how I could be of help.

"I just can't seem to get a handle on it," he said, with a sudden look of mental fatigue. "When I had my 401k in the 80s and 90s, it seemed I could do no wrong. I picked different kinds of sector funds, and almost all of them seemed to go up. If they fell, I would switch and still see nice gains. I contributed the max every year. Before I knew it, I was sitting on a million and then went up to over $1.4 million before I finally retired. Then came the dotcom bubble."

I listened as he opened his neatly organized book of statements, going back twelve months.

"Since then, I've hired the best advisors money can buy—and have never recovered. That's twelve years. I was told I could withdraw five percent a year safely back then, which turned out to be poor advice. My funds took a hit in 01 and 02, and I took income at the same time. The statements kept going down by thousands every month and really started to dwindle, so I cut back and even postponed a trip my wife and I had planned. It wasn't supposed to be like this. Besides the stocks, I tried natural gas partnerships, some TICs, and had a REIT not pan out."

I asked him who was managing his money currently.

"Been doing it myself for four years, and I'm not doing much better, but at least I don't have to pay someone for poor results."

We continued to talk, as he encouraged me to look through his holdings. His statement was at least nine pages. He had page after page, double sided, of mutual funds and ETFs that I recognized as overlapping. I searched for a trend in his investment strategy, hoping to find a pattern. None was apparent. He had at least seventy different holdings on his statements, mixed between stock and bond funds and ETFs.

I began to ask him why he owned some of them. Each item had its own justification. He felt like he was not being haphazard at all. In fact, he told a compelling story on almost each one.

The recurring theme was an article he read, or a newsletter guru offering special reports with the "5 Can't Miss Stocks, etc." He was a fan of both CNBC and Fox and bought favorite picks he heard about on those shows. I noticed several buy and sell entries for the SPY ETF. Clearly, he was floundering. Was he investing, or merely gambling with his money?

His portfolio reminded me of a person I read about who bet on every horse at each horse race. True, she had a winner in every race, but soon learned the odds are not in favor of the amateur bettor. Eighty percent of investors share twenty percent of the profits, while twenty percent of investors share eighty.

The lesson that Frank was learning—with hard won dollars—is the lesson of Secular Bear and Bull Markets. All markets move in cycles. There are small cycles with short durations of a month to a year that are like a storm that can be handled with a raincoat and an umbrella. And then there are large cycles that are very powerful, based on dynamic forces of supply and demand, which can last from ten to twenty years. These are more like hurricanes. Staying out of the path and not fighting the trend are recommended.

"WHEN IT COMES TO YOUR INVESTMENTS, ARE YOU STILL FIGHTING THE LAST WAR?"

Recall the 1980s and 1990s when baby boomers in their 30's, 40's and 50's poured money into their 401ks driving the demand for stocks. They created a hurricane.

Those same 78 million baby boomers are now in their 50s, 60s, and 70s - and naturally scaling back on risk and consumption. Rather than pouring money into the markets with every paycheck – they're taking money out to replace their paychecks. The hurricane has reversed.

This isn't a minor blip on the screen. It is a major reversal of a mega-trend. Any investor expecting the same results with stocks when the hurricane has switched direction will be disappointed. Staying in safer positions, making steady gains, paying yourself a solid income, and living to fight another day are the signs of a winning strategy in retirement.

INFORMATION IS EVERYWHERE, BUT PRACTICAL KNOWLEDGE IS HARD TO COME BY

In the past, stock investing was for the rich and the upper middle class. In the 1980s and 1990s, it became everyone's hobby, almost a recreation. USA Today became a dumbed down version of *The Wall Street Journal*. CNBC became wildly popular. The trend was everyone's friend—the rising tide lifted all boats. Everyone was an expert. The wealth effect kept the economy buzzing.

When a person is working and bringing home a paycheck, market losses and fees are ignored. The real problem is when a retired person starts treating investing like a job. Results are expected daily, weekly, and monthly—just like at work. Wall Street may have different ideas.

It isn't that do-it-yourself investors aren't smart. The problem is that they are ruled by emotions, specifically the emotions of fear and greed.

Emotions lead to bias. Psychologists have identified three kinds of 'bias' that affect our decisions:

• **Cognitive:** decisions we make because of a lack of understanding.

• **Emotional:** decisions we make because of our emotional makeup.

• **Social:** decisions we make based on how we see ourselves in the world.

There are quite a few types of cognitive biases that have been identified by the science of psychology. These biases are survival instincts—they are shortcuts in thinking that can save your life, but can be the result of errors in statistical judgment, memory, and social attribution.

"Cognitive dissonance" is one of the most well known types of cognitive biases. Cognitive dissonance is very common, and just about everyone has experienced it at least once in their lives. It is the feeling of tension or anxiety caused by holding two opposing beliefs or thoughts at the same time. Investors are overrun by cognitive dissonance because there are so many credible sounding and opposing opinions coming from so many news sources, 24/7/365.

"Illusory correlation" is another one of the more commonly known types of cognitive biases. It is very common in investing. Illusory correlation describes a situation where someone perceives a correlation, or relationship between two variables, when in reality, there is little or no relationship between the variables. One example that cost many investors money was the correlation between technology stocks in the 1990s and guaranteed profits. These thoughts got anchored in the minds of many.

"Hot cognition" is a newer term for certain types of cognitive biases. This type of bias is based on the mood of the person making decisions. Someone in a heightened state of emotion, such as anger, fear, and even joy, can make errors in judgment based on his or her emotional state. In the case of hot cognition, a person may make a decision too quickly, without the proper amount of reflection.

"Cold cognition" is also a relatively new type of cognitive bias. It is the complementary cognitive bias of hot cognition. Just as hot cognition describes decision making affected by heightened emotional states, cold cognition occurs when a person makes a decision while experiencing very little emotion. This type of low-energy and attention decision-making is also problematic. Instead of making decisions too fast and while emotionally charged, a person experiencing cold cognition makes decisions based on little reflection because of lack of interest.

It turns out, Frank, my prospective client, was in a state of mental fatigue caused by twelve years of dealing with all of the above.

To use the fifty-dollar word, Frank was stuck in "illusory correlation" believing that money in the market was the same as money in the bank or in an annuity. Not so. In his mind, "stocks always make 10%" and "always come back" after a fall. He got used to the "old normal."

WELCOME TO THE NEW NORMAL

Will investors ever return to the 'hey' days of the 1990s and recoup the money they lost, of the past twelve years? They may recoup the dollars, but they will never recoup the time.

So far, the 21st Century has not been kind to stock market investors. Baby boomers who experienced the thrills of the 1980s and 1990s have been hit hard. Their retirement dreams were built on the expectations of "conservative" yields in the eight to ten percent range and bond yields of six and seven percent. Didn't happen.

Two of the money giants of our time, John Bogle and Bill Gross of Pimco tell us that we had better deal with it and adjust to it until the next major trend comes our way. Until then, they are both saying "Welcome to the New Normal."

John Bogle is the founder of mutual fund giant Vanguard and is generally regarded as one of the most sober and intelligent stock market analysts of all time. Bill Gross is the vaunted manager of the $2 trillion family of mutual funds, Pimco.

Both are already famous enough and neither needs more money to live their lifestyle. When they make controversial statements, it may pay to listen. If they are sounding a warning, it may pay to listen.

Back in 2002, Mr. Bogle first used the term "new normal" to describe a new prolonged period of very tame returns equal in length to the twenty year bull market of 1980 to 2000. Mr. Gross made the term "new normal" famous in an article in 2010.

His premise? Half size economic growth can only logically lead to half size stock market returns over the long run. After an exploding economic period where budgets in government were finally balanced, we've moved to an imploding economic infrastructure getting crowded out by government debt.

How logical is it to expect 10% returns in an environment like we're in—especially when politicians in Washington are treating it like business as usual.

For the new generation of retired and retiring men and women, the new normal couldn't come at a worse time. Ironically, today's retiring baby boomers created the "old normal" when they were younger.

Think about it. Seventy eight million aging investors getting more conservative means less money going into stocks and less money spent at the malls. Less money going into mutual funds and markets means less demand, and lower returns. Logically and mathematically, we won't see a new prolonged bull market until the economy becomes authentically sound again. This isn't a pessimistic view, it is realistic.

Let's not forget another aspect of this "New Normal": as the government spirals deeper into debt, taxes will also rise which could further take money out of circulation for investments. Instead, it will be going to taxes. Taxes eat the economy—they are simply transfer payments that do not expand capital.

This generational shift in supply/demand fundamentals has experts like John Bogle (Vanguard) and Bill Gross (Pimco) projecting 2.5% to 4% returns for the next decade. While some investors may call their assessments pessimistic, these guys own some very fancy calculators and they are aren't afraid to use them. What if they're right?

"PENSION ENVY," A SYMPTOM OF THE NEW NORMAL

A person spends the first half of their lives accumulating money and paying into savings. They spend the second half of their lives trying to preserve their money and paying out of savings. In the past, thirty years on the job was rewarded with a pension. Today, the 401k and 403b has taken over. If you are going to have a pension, you will have to buy one on your own.

Research by the Center for A Secure Retirement found that two-thirds of middle-income Boomers believe their retirement will be different from that of previous generations. What will cause the difference? Pensions for one, debt for the other. Pensions and guaranteed income are what sixty percent (60%) of middle-income Boomers say they **envy most about the retirement of previous generations.**

In retirement, achieving a sustainable, reliable, guaranteed income is the most important goal of the investor. Even if one runs out of money, as long as they have sufficient income, they have a successful financial plan and will not live poor.

HOW TO BUY A PENSION: THE SIMPLE STRESS FREE WAY TO REACH YOUR RETIREMENT GOALS

Here's the problem: Most traditional investments are based on the concept of capital appreciation. You buy assets, such as shares of stock, and hope they appreciate in value so you can sell them later for a profit. Cash-flow investing works differently. With cash flow, you buy an asset not for its future value but for its ability to generate income. This income gives you flexibility: You can spend it if you want to or you can reinvest it. Cash flow reinvested is compounding growth. It is stabilizer for your entire investment plan.

THE NEED FOR A GUARANTEED LIFETIME
INCOME HAS NEVER BEEN GREATER

Some retirees will go back to working a job during retirement and like the idea. Others may be forced to do so because finances are running thin, but it is unlikely they will find the kind of work and kind of money they are hoping for. (If twenty-five and thirty-five year olds are having trouble finding work, sixty-five and seventy year olds won't fare much better.)

Your money has to last and it has to work hard. But what investment can be counted on to be there, come what may, good markets and bad?

It is a financial vehicle that has been around since Roman times, financed the Crusades in Europe, and has financed retirements in the U.S. and England since 1696. It has one of the best safety records of any financial instrument. It is known as an annuity. Today, there are 917 insurance companies, many of whom offer annuities. There are four kinds of annuities: immediate, fixed, variable, and fixed index, also known as a "hybrid" annuity. If you are looking for guaranteed cash flow, happier days, and more sleep at night, explore the world of hybrid index annuities. For details, feel free to visit us at MyAnnuityGuy.com™.

About Steve

Steve Jurich is the Managing Member of IQ Wealth Management and Editor of MyAnnuityGuy.com™. Steve, known as "My Annuity Guy" is an in-demand Retirement Coach and Wealth Manager known for innovative retirement planning solutions for affluent retirees.

As a Consumer Advocate and editor of MyAnnuityGuy.com™, Steve has made appearances on ABC, NBC, CBS, and FOX, and spoke recently at a Southwestern financial conference with Ron Insana of CNBC. He is the host of *Journey To Wealth* on Money Radio in Phoenix. Clients turn to Steve for generating secure income, cutting taxes, protecting assets from frivolous lawsuits, and simplifying retirement decisions.

Using his unique system known as the IQ Wealth Endowment Model, Steve combines proprietary annuities with special forms of life insurance to create a private, legal and tax advantaged fortress. Clients include physicians, engineers, teachers, and business owners.

To learn more about Steve Jurich and the IQ Wealth Endowment Model:
Call 1(888) 310-1776 and visit his company websites:
www.IQWealthGroup.com
www.MyAnnuityGuy.com

CHAPTER 43

THE WORLD THROUGH THEIR EYES

BY JOHN GAJKOWSKI
& NANCY COUTU

Our clients are usually 55-70 years old. …Middle America. …worked for large organizations or owned a small business and are scared about retirement. When can they retire? How much will it cost? Have they saved enough? What if there is another 2008 economic crisis after they retire?

Nancy and I are very much like them. We came from large middle class families where we started working young and saved. We worked our way through college for both large and small companies before starting our own. Our parents had 30+ years working for the same companies with the promise of a worry-free retirement. With good pensions, social security and little savings they did O.K. However, like most of our clients, we don't have big pensions and we now have to worry about the future of social security. We meet people every day who tell us stories of people they know who retired and ran out of money within 10 or 15 years. They want to know what they have to do to make sure it won't happen to them.

Early in our financial planning careers we decided that we should specialize in retirement planning, but not retirement planning the way banks, brokerage firms and insurance companies were doing it. We realized that retirement planning wasn't chasing the highest returns. We knew that information about whatever stock or bond or other popular investments of the day was not the most important issue for people. The most important issues of retirement planning are protecting and freeing up their most valuable asset, time, and bringing a high degree of certainty to their financial lives in a very uncertain world.

Unlike others in our field, we realized retirement planning was about developing a lifetime strategy with income that you could not outlive. For many people, their greatest fears are uncertainty and the gnawing feeling that one day they will run out of money. We wanted to address those fears and eliminate them with reasonable certainty. We believe this can only be done by spending a great amount of time with our clients to help them identify exactly where they are right now and what their ultimate goals are. Once we have established this, our responsibility is to sit in their chairs, look at the world through their eyes and bring our specialized financial expertise to them. We know that there is no shortage of investment ideas. Like our clients, we are constantly bombarded with ads on the latest and greatest investments. They come and go. We firmly believe that most investments have a purpose in various portfolios, but we focus on the ones that are appropriate to our clients' situation.

John and I became Certified Financial Planners™ and focused on becoming specialists in retirement and estate planning because we like helping people prepare for what should be the happiest years of their lives. Most people approaching retirement age are afraid to retire for fear they will outlive their money. They might not have the pensions that their parents and grandparents had. They will live years longer, which means their money has to keep up with inflation and last much longer. Often people retire and run out of money within 10-15 years. They don't know how to figure out how much "is enough." They see the price of goods going up while the return on their retirement savings has been disappointing. They know that the investments within their retirement savings plan at work offer no guarantees, but they don't know where to find safer alternatives.

We begin the process by explaining to them that they should not be focusing on the job they are retiring "from," but rather to think about and plan for what they are retiring "to" because they might spend 1/3 of their life in retirement. Then we have them document what their "required" expenses are right now. We inflate those numbers annually and project them to ages 90-95. Once we have those numbers established, we then add their "desired" expenses and do the projections. The nicest part of this work is that it is only on paper. It is safe to make alterations and adjustments here -before they retire. This gives them a realistic look at what the rest of their financial life would/could look like. We might make several adjustments, but we can usually arrive at some very realistic numbers.

Most of the time we are able to show them how they can have financial peace of mind with an income they will not outlive. We help them prepare for the retirement of their dreams. We love turning dreams into reality!

Of course, the sooner this planning starts the better. You can't be too young to think about retirement, and a small amount of regular savings over time can make for a lot of money! If you start planning while you are young, your goals might change along the way and the amounts you save might go up and down, but the magic of compounding will motivate you to continue as you see the balances go up. Over the long term, if you do happen to hit a bump in the road whereby your retirement plans need to change, it is a lot easier to handle when you have already been preparing for it.

I remember a couple I had been working with for several years, preparing for their retirement at age 60. They were doing all the right things: working hard, budgeting and saving. We would go over their expenses every year and tweak our projections based on the real rates of return and expenses vs. our projections

All was going well for them when one day I got a call from the wife. She was sobbing. She told me that her husband had just lost his job-at age 50! She was devastated. His job was very unique and they feared it would be difficult to find another job as his skill set was limited to that job for so many years. She was very disturbed because he said that he really didn't want to find another job. He was ready to retire! "What about our retirement plans," she quivered. "What are we going to do?" she sobbed. She was very distraught.

I told them to get all their benefits statements together and we scheduled an emergency meeting. When we reviewed their current situation I asked her, "What do you intend to do if your husband doesn't go back to work? Do you want to continue working as planned?" She said, "No." She would like to retire with him but she feared it was impossible.

They decided that if they retired now they would sell their home in an affluent suburb of Illinois and buy a smaller home in Arizona. We reworked the plan numbers, and as it turned out, both of them were able to retire and they moved to Arizona. If they had not been saving and planning for this day, albeit a little premature (10 years), they would not have been able to do this.

That was 25 years ago! They travel the world. They spend summers in the mountains of Arizona and the rest of the year in their beautiful home in Mesa. They send me a beautiful poinsettia every Christmas to thank me for helping them make their dreams come true. What a great job I have!

We tell people what they *need* to hear, not what they *want* to hear. It is our job to tell them what the future might look like before they make what could be the most important financial decision of their lives – retirement.

About John

John Gajkowski, CFP™, CLU®, ChFC®, CMFC®, CRPC® is a principal of Money Managers, Ltd. He was born in Berwyn, IL. John earned Bachelor of Science degrees in Political Science and Legal Studies from Illinois State University, Normal, IL.

John entered the financial planning industry in 1983 as a Registered Representative with American Express Investment Advisors (now Ameriprise). He was also an insurance agent of IDS Life Insurance Company, a wholly-owned subsidiary of American Express. Each year he earned the distinction of top producing representative. In 1987, he left to co-found Money Managers, Ltd., an independent financial planning firm.

He has custom-designed and presented retirement and estate planning seminars for Fortune 500 companies. He has presented numerous educational seminars to employees of AT&T, Jewel/Osco (Supervalu), McDonalds and Motorola, to name a few.

John is a FINRA Registered Representative with GF Investment Services, LLC, a Broker-Dealer in Sarasota, FL. He is a fully licensed General Securities Broker and Registered Principal, and is a licensed agent for the sale of Life, Disability, Medical, and Long-Term Care Insurance, as well as Fixed, Variable and Fixed-Indexed Annuities.

John is actively engaged in continuing education in the financial planning industry and has taught adult education courses on various financial topics for over 15 years.

John and his wife, Cathy, have 3 children: Lauren, Michelle and Jarrett.

Professional Designations:

CFP™	Certified Financial Planner™, conferred by the College of Financial Planning, Denver, Colorado, 1989. The focus of this curriculum was Investment and Tax Planning.
CLU®	Certified Life Underwriter®, conferred by the American College, Bryn Mawr, Pennsylvania, 1993. The focus of this curriculum was Insurance and Estate Planning.
ChFC®	Chartered Financial Consultant®, conferred by the American College, Bryn Mawr, Pennsylvania, 1993. The focus of this curriculum was Comprehensive Financial and Estate Planning.
CMFC®	Chartered Mutual Fund Counselor®, conferred by the College of Financial Planning, Denver, Colorado, 1997. The focus of this curriculum was the Analysis and Selection of Mutual Funds.
CRPC®	Chartered Retirement Plans Counselor®, conferred by the College of Financial Planning, Denver, Colorado, 2001. The focus of this curriculum was Retirement Planning.

About Nancy

Nancy Coutu, CFP™, CLU®, ChFC® is a principal of Money Managers, Ltd. and Money Managers Advisory. She was born in Chicago, Illinois. Ms. Coutu earned a Bachelor of Arts degree in Business Management with a double major of Finance and Economics from Loyola/Mundelein College, Chicago, Illinois.

Nancy entered the Financial Planning Industry in 1981 as a Registered Representative with American Express Investment Advisors. She was also an agent for IDS Life Insurance Company, a wholly-owned subsidiary of American Express.

After hiring and training one of the top Districts, Nancy left American Express to start her own independent financial planning firm.

Nancy is a FINRA Registered Representative with GF Investment Services, LLC, a Broker-Dealer in Sarasota, FL. She is a fully licensed General Securities Broker and Registered Principal. She is also a licensed agent for the sales of Life, Disability, Medical, and Long-Term Care Insurance, as well as Fixed, Variable and Fixed-Indexed Annuities.

She has custom-designed and presented Retirement and Estate Planning Seminars for Fortune 500 companies. She has presented numerous Educational Programs to employees of AT&T, Jewel Foods (Supervalu), McDonalds and Motorola, to name a few.

Nancy appeared on WGN's "People to People", CNBC, FOX News and most of the local TV news programs. She has been quoted in *Kiplinger's Personal Finance Magazine, Woman's Day* ™ magazine, the *LA Times,* and is often quoted in the *Chicago Tribune,* the *Daily Herald* and various other publications. Nancy's other honors include a nomination for the prestigious "NAWBO (National Association of Women Business Owners) New Venture Award" and Small Business recognition awards.

Ms. Coutu has been actively engaged in continuing education in the financial planning industry and is a member of the DuPage Estate Planning Council. She is a member of the exclusive Ed Slott's Master Elite IRA Advisor Group™.

Professional Designations:

CFP™	Certified Financial Planner™, conferred by the College of Financial Planning Denver, Colorado, 1983. The focus of this curriculum was Investment and Tax Planning.
CLU®	Certified Life Underwriter®, conferred by the American College, Bryn Mawr, Pennsylvania, 1993. The focus of this curriculum was Insurance and Estate Planning.
ChFC®	Chartered Financial Consultant®, conferred by the American College, Bryn Mawr, Pennsylvania, 1993. The focus of this curriculum was Comprehensive Financial and Estate Planning.

CHAPTER 44

WARNING: MINIMIZING RISK CAN LEAD TO A GOOD NIGHT'S SLEEP AND PEACE OF MIND

BY MICHAEL LADIN

Six Steps for Boomers and Business Owners to Mitigate Risk, Be Better Diversified, and Save Thousands of Dollars:

1) Understanding the Way Financial Advisors Recommend What They Do

2) Market Risk versus Safety: Some Market Advisors Sell Risk and Optimism, Some Sell Safety

3) Tax Risk and Tax Advantage Strategies

4) Keep Your Profits, Have A Plan Including Estate Tax Planning

5) Mitigate Inflation and Longevity Risk

6) Wealth Accumulation and Premium Financing

Minimizing risk in your life cannot only lead to achieving your financial goals, but also a more peaceful, healthier life and a better night's sleep. Have you ever woken up in the middle of the night worrying about your investments, your retirement, the economy, the global debt crisis, or somewhere else in the world? Ever ask yourself, "What's going to happen in the future? Will I have enough money to live on? What if I have an emergency? Will I be able help out my kids if they need me; or leave them money one day?" Our company's philosophy is a simple one: If you can afford to live your lifestyle comfortably, whatever that means to you, and minimize or eliminate risk with your investments, you should do just that.

It's important that your advisor is not restricted in the investment or insurance products that they can offer you. Otherwise, how do you know you are getting truly unbiased advice and if the recommendations are in your best interests? We work for our clients, not a company. Once we understand our clients' needs, wants, and goals, we shop the entire market place and place them with the best company that helps them accomplish just that. Again, it's imperative that the advisor you choose is not restricted in the products or investment they can offer you.

1. UNDERSTANDING RISK AND WHY FINANCIAL ADVISORS RECOMMEND WHAT THEY DO

Would you go to Vegas and gamble with your life savings? How ridiculous does that sound? Yet people are doing the same thing every day in the stock market and with their IRA's, 401k's, 403b's, college plans, and other various retirement plans. If your current financial advisor is a stockbroker, wealth manager, or the investment person at a bank, the reality is that you probably have most or all of your monies at risk. Why is that? Because they sell stock market products. Let me ask you this: "If we stop at the Porsche dealership in your town and wait a few minutes, a salesman is going to come over to us and try to sell us what? A Porsche, of course." Wealth managers and most investment advisors sell stocks, bonds, and mutual funds. Put simply, they specialize in stock market products, risk, and they add a dose of optimism to make the risk in any market condition acceptable to the investor. This is what they specialize in, investment growth and risk in the stock market.

Now what if you needed or wanted an insurance product such as a fixed annuity or life insurance? They will pull out of their drawer the one or two insurance companies' products that they are allowed to offer you. The danger in this is that it may NOT be the best product for you, but this is all they have to offer their clients. It's similar to asking that Porsche salesman for a family station wagon. That's not their specialty, but they will still try to sell you something. Likewise stockbrokers, wealth advisors, and investment advisors specialize in market products, growth, and beating the S&P. You have to really be ok with the risk and possibly losses. After all, it is your money.

As you near retirement or if you're in retirement, we want to look at guarantees to have a larger part of our portfolio. Growth advisors usually do not specialize in fixed insurance products or guaranteed income planning, which oftentimes can have a higher payout over your lifetime versus the 4% distribution rule. These products are more often used by advisors with an insurance background to lay a foundation to your income planning or financial plan. This is done to guarantee an income stream no matter what, and it guards against worst-case scenarios that the best diversified plans can't. With that said, be sure your advisor is not just an insurance-only advisor, or you can run into an overly conservative plan. Some investors choose two advisors. A stock market advisor for risk, and a conservative or guaranteed income planning insurance advisor for safety.

Over the years, the financial planning landscape has changed, and we have made sure we have too. We offer our clients both market products and insurance investments to keep the focus on their plans and their goals, not on what we have to offer. Non-market fixed products or investments are the foundation to a holistic plan. Without it, the next time the market tumbles, will you be asking yourself was I really diversified? Was I really prepared in the best possible way? Why didn't my stock market advisor tell me about this?

2. MARKET RISK VS. SAFETY: SOME MARKET ADVISORS SELL RISK AND OPTIMISM, SOME SELL SAFETY

"But I'm diversified and the market always comes back!" Sound familiar? When folks come into the office and tell me this, I know instantly they're working with a stockbroker. That thought process made sense in the 80's or 90's, but not now. It certainly doesn't make sense if you are in your mid-50's or older looking to build or hold on to your retirement savings. In 2003 and 2007, most diversified plans and blended portfolios of stocks, bonds, and mutual funds lost money. When your investment advisor tells you that you're in a conservative portfolio in the stock market; that means you will lose less money than someone in an aggressive portfolio. It does not mean that you won't lose money. If you're risk averse or very conservative, you don't want to lose your principal. The bottom line is if you can't swim -- that is, if you can't afford to lose any money -- it doesn't matter which end of the pool you jump in, you will drown. If you're in the stock market you stand the potential to lose money regardless of how diversified your blended portfolio is. If you need to live on the money at the time, this is critical.

Remember when the market is up, your broker's a hero, and everyone's happy. When the market turns down, the last advice you get is cash out. Why? Because then your advisor stops making money with your money. When I speak with couples who attend my dinner seminars, I ask them, "Do you think your stockbroker, after working together with you for 20 + years, will ever say, 'Thanks for letting me help you all these years, but now I have to send you to the guaranteed income planning guy down the street.'?" They always chuckle and say, "No, that would never happen." When you retire, the advisor who specializes in growth and stock market investments will often keep you in the market and continue to have your monies at risk. We see folks in their 60's, 70's, and 80's all the time in this very situation. They have the same portfolios as their kids in their 40' and 50's. That's just wrong, but it's not their fault. They simply did not know there are other investment options available to them, something their advisor didn't tell them. It is important to consciously decide what you are really trying to achieve and customize your financial plan with the right blend of market risk and safety.

3. TAX RISK AND TAX ADVANTAGED STRATEGIES

After analyzing your situation, you realize that you fall short of your income needs. What then? What if you're risk averse and not willing to lose any more than you have? Is there anything else to consider? What about taxes? Could we reduce, eliminate, or put off taxes, and give your money more time to work for you, not the government?

As if worrying about losses and market timing wasn't enough, now it's important to incorporate tax planning into your financial planning decisions. Most people worry all the time about the rate of return they are getting with no regard to the bottom line. As the old adage goes, "It's not what you make, but what you keep that counts." The risk now also stretches beyond stock market investing to tax strategies. If you're in a 40% tax bracket and earn 8% in a mutual fund, you'll net 4.8% after taxes. Consider a less risky tax-favored investment. It only needs to yield 4.8%, and the profits will continue to compound tax deferred. Investing in a tax-deferred vehicle means your money can compound interest for years, deferring income taxes and providing the potential to earn interest at a faster rate. While very few financial vehicles avoid taxes completely, insurance products allow you to defer paying them until retirement, a time at which you may be in a lower tax bracket. The higher the tax bracket, the more advantageous and important are utilizing tax-favored products and structures to your portfolio.

If you're a business owner, you have the opportunity to use business dollars, not only to attract, retain and keep high quality employees, but also to fund your own retirement. Non-Qualified Executive Bonus Plans became popular in the 80's when tax rates were higher to take advantage of the tax-deferred compounding and tax-favored status when accessing the money.

4) KEEP YOUR PROFITS; HAVE A PLAN INCLUDING ESTATE TAX PLANNING

People don't plan to fail, they simply fail to plan. Baby Boomers and retirees should not be in the market unless they have a plan for when the market goes up as well as a plan for when the market goes down. I can only think of one reason to be in the market and that's to make money! Can you think of another reason? But if you are like most people, you have a stockbroker or advisor without a comprehensive plan. You watch your brokerage statement and the market go up and down, but without any control to keep your profits. So why don't you have control over your retirement monies that you worked so long and hard to make? Has your broker ever called you up and said, "Hi Mr. Smith, I see your investments were profitable in XYZ company. Why don't we sell that and stick those profits in the bank? Maybe take your spouse on that cruise they have been talking about." Never happens, right? If anything, they tell you to sell and then want you to buy another investment, and you're right back in the market. That's equivalent to going to your broker one day and saying, "Here's my life savings. I hope and pray that one day when I need it, it will be there." Well hoping and praying isn't a strategy! We invest in the market and choose to take on the risk to make money in our younger years, when there is time to make up for downturns. In your 50's, you should have a plan and goal with your advisor to ensure that you keep your profits and don't just ride out the markets up's and down's and end up with nothing but fees, headaches, and losses.

Do you have a plan when the market goes down? Ever heard of a stop-loss? Or simply pre-determining maximum losses you're willing to take? If you owned a stock at $50, you set a stop loss at $45, so that if the stock hits $45, it's sold automatically. You lost 10%, but you knew that, and you were okay with it since it was a pre-determined plan. Otherwise, you just watch the stock continue to fall to $40, $35, $25, etc. Now you have a conversation with your broker that sounds something like this, "Its ok. Hang in there, hold on. Your sector's down, the markets down, everyone's down." The next thing you know, you spend the next 4, 5, 6 years chasing losses versus making money. Anyone investing in the stock market needs to have a definitive plan to keep their profits when the market's up, and a plan to preserve their profits and principal when the market's down.

The closer to retirement you are, the more important it is to protect principal and profits. Remember, the one thing you can run out of is time, time to make up for any bad decisions or market reversals. A significant loss in the years just prior to, or in retirement, can have a damaging impact on your lifestyle and your income. If a loss occurs earlier in life, you have time to recover a significant loss, an opportunity you do not have in your 50's or in retirement. Don't jeopardize a worry-free retirement because you were greedy or just didn't take the time to make a plan. Remember, nobody plans to fail, they simply fail to plan.

The Estate Tax laws are always changing. Seek out a Financial Advisor who specializes in Estate Planning Life Insurance and works with an Estate Planning attorney to get a well-balanced plan that will ensure your family has the money in hand when the IRS comes knocking, because the plan doesn't stop with you and your spouse. Be sure to have your Estate Planning in order. This includes a will, a trust, and in some cases, an irrevocable life insurance trust. If you think you don't have an Estate Plan, reconsider. The State and Federal Governments have one for you if you don't make one for yourself. What's the benefit in risking, investing, and working hard your whole life and then when you try to pass it on to your family or a charity, the IRS takes 40 to 75 %! Without a properly-structured estate plan, your wishes may not be fulfilled, and your loved ones could be hurt both emotionally and financially.

5. MITIGATE INFLATION AND LONGEVITY RISK

Proper planning will help you design a guaranteed retirement income strategy, which incorporates insurance and annuity vehicles to create opportunities for long-term growth as well as guarantee income throughout your retirement. A base, a foundation, a guarantee that you can count on is not only the basis of true diversification, but it also takes inflation and longevity risk out of equation. Many Fixed Index Annuities offer an Income Rider which guarantees growth rate, followed by an income stream for life; and unlike having to 'annuitize' the annuity, if there is money left in the account when the policyholder passes, it will pass on to the named beneficiary. Be sure to understand all the terms and conditions, as every annuity works differently. When it comes to fixed insurance products, the right annuity or life insurance product when used the right way can be an amazing retirement or Estate Planning tool. The wrong annuity used any which way can be a disaster. Those are typically the horror stories you read about in the paper or magazines. Be sure your advisor is independent, not working for any one company, so they can shop the marketplace to find you the best investment or product for your retirement needs.

6. WEALTH ACCUMULATION AND PREMIUM FINANCING

Given lessons learned in stock market investing, it is important to remember that more conservative retirement strategies, which typically have assets invested in the stock market, yield a smaller percentage. Other allocations should be set aside in proper life insurance planning which can include wealth accumulation and tax advantages, both for today and for retirement.

Business owners especially have an opportunity to meet certain business obligations such as Buy-Sell Agreement funding, Key Man or Golden Handcuff policies, even Non-Qualified Deferred Compensation Plans, to help fund their retirement, simultaneously saving them thousands of dollars. For wealthier families with $7 million and up or people who have most of their assets tied up in Real Estate or are heavily invested in the stock market, there is Premium Financing. A bank or Private Lender pays the premiums on their policy to help them get the Estate Planning, Business Planning, or Wealth-Accumulation-type policy that is needed. In return, the lender charges an interest rate and has first claim on their policy. This type of planning is very sophisticated and every deal is structured differently. When structured properly, it can be a powerful asset to any portfolio for Estate Planning protection and/or income planning needs. Be sure to find a qualified, experienced specialist. If it's not designed properly, there could be tax and debt collateral consequences. Not everyone can qualify for these types of policies and investments.

In conclusion, twenty-first century asset protection calls for more than just strategic asset allocation. Product allocation and buying instruments that can protect your monies from market declines throughout retirement is an effective means of protecting assets. Because the market does not provide security, you're going to want your financial strategies to include some secured income products, such as annuities, which are insurance products with guarantees, to provide a source of supplemental income throughout your retirement. Diversifying your retirement assets among a variety of vehicles, both through insurance products and investments, depending on what is appropriate for your situation, may offer you the best chance of meeting your retirement income goals and getting that better night's sleep.

About Michael

Michael Ladin, founder and CEO of Ladin Tax and Financial Group, also known as "The Baby Boomer & Business Owners Income Planning Coach," is a best-selling author, a financial and insurance planning expert who is regularly sought out by Business Owners, Baby Boomers, and Retirees for his advice on guaranteed income planning, wealth transfer, and tax-favored investment strategies that really work.

Michael started in the business 20 years ago, helping people to better understand risk versus safety. Since then, he has developed his customized retirement and income planning process, which minimizes risk while guaranteeing one's desired lifestyle. Michael shares his expertise on his radio show on NewsRadio 610 WIOD. Michael has been seen on NBC, CBS, ABC, Fox and/or affiliates, as well as in *The Wall Street Journal, USA Today,* and *Newsweek.* Michael is also a member of the National Ethics Bureau and the Million Dollar Round Table, organizations whose members demonstrate exceptional professional knowledge, strict ethical conduct and outstanding client service. MDRT is recognized internationally as the standard of excellence in the financial-planning and insurance business.

To learn more about Michael Ladin, attend a seminar, or how you can receive the free Special Report: "The 10 Mistakes Retirees Make" visit our website at:
www.LadinTax.com
To E-Mail Michael directly: Michael@Ladinfinancialgroup.com.
For contact by telephone: 305 444-4898

CHAPTER 45

SUCCESS MEANS NEVER HAVING TO WATCH YOUR BACK

BY STEVEN M. NETZEL

American Businessman and founder of financial firm Kohlberg Kravis Roberts, Henry Kravis, said, "A real entrepreneur is somebody who has no safety net underneath them." Many of the world's most successful entrepreneurs have built their businesses without financial assistance or help from anyone, and in fact, little more to recommend them than faith and sheer will.

There once was a young man working for Lockheed on airplanes at the airport in Albuquerque, NM. He came home exhausted everyday and smelling of jet fuel. One afternoon, the young man's roommate was interviewing for a sales position with an insurance company. The young man got the name of the insurance company and called the interviewer to ask, "Can anyone do this business?" After hearing the reply that in fact, all one needed was a license, the young man promptly bought the appropriate books, studied all weekend, took the licensing tests, and passed. He showed up at work with that license and began his new career the following Monday.

I was that young man, and since that day, I have shared Henry Kravis' opinion that one can build a successful business with little more than hard work and some guiding principles. Please do not misinterpret this story and assume that everyone can launch an insurance career in a weekend. Obtaining licensing is the relatively easy part. Building a business with few resources and no assistance is a major undertaking. As with any business, there were plenty of lean years during which one questions the decision to keep trying. Through hard work came a new definition of success: Success means never having to watch your back, because your happy customers will watch it for you. I have heard that one can only connect the dots after one is past certain milestones in life. While reflecting on the business I have built, I learned that anyone might achieve such a level of success, without the help of others, by following ten simple axioms.

1. HAVE FAITH.

Ninety percent of entrepreneurs give up in the first three years in business. That means that to succeed, a person has to believe he is the one in ten who can and will make it. Unwavering faith in a higher power gets many people through those agonizing first years. Set backs and failures are a sure thing. Faith is a foundational point one can return to at any time. Success brings great responsibility. Faith offers a point of reference, the steadfastness to do what is right, and a reminder that there will always be a way through a difficult situation.

2. SUCCESS IS SOMETHING INSIDE EACH ONE OF US.

Success is not something one achieves; it is something one has to realize from within oneself. One has to be strong enough to dig deep inside to find it. There are tough decisions to make to get to that level, and there are risks and chances one has to take. Success equals setting personal goals and working to achieve them. Success is greater than any individual is. Do not measure success by monetary achievement alone. There is a powerful scene in the movie *Wall Street* in which Charlie Sheen's character, Bud Fox, accuses his father of being an old machinist who is jealous of his success and his father tells him, "What you see is a guy who never measured a man's success by the size of his WALLET!"

Money does not equal success. Success is measured best by the relationships one builds. Some financial advisors—and other businessmen as well—choose the predominance of their clients based solely on the amount of money the client has to invest, thus measuring the client's merit on the size of his wallet. A better criterion would be to seek clients whose beliefs align with one's own beliefs, who one likes and wants to do business with, and who will fit into one's business family. Turning away a client because he is not a millionaire seems shortsighted. While there are an estimated 24.2 million millionaires on the planet with whom to do business, pursuing only those "worthy" clients leaves 99.5% of the world population to the competition.

3. SURROUND YOURSELF WITH PEOPLE WHO ARE BETTER THAN YOU ARE.

Keep humility in play. Realize that no matter how excellent you become in your business, there will always be someone more successful from whom you might learn a thing or two. Keep an open mind and learn from other people mistakes and experiences. No one has to reinvent the wheel. This is not to say that one should not implement new ideas; on the contrary, new ideas can improve any business. You do not have to be the one to invent every new idea; borrowing an idea or two or learning what not to do from others' experiences can be both beneficial and time-saving.

4. GOLDEN RULE: TREAT OTHERS THE WAY YOU WISH TO BE TREATED.

Never move a client into a bad position because it pays more money. For example, an investment that might make your company more money is not a good investment if it puts your client in a bad position. No one desires to be taken advantage of and fewer still would refer business to a company that took advantage of them. While it might be tempting to rush to open an account when the potential client demands it done hurriedly and before a relationship is established, remind them that your company builds relationships first. In a relationship-driven business where trust is important, think about how you wish to be treated if you were the customer.

5. PRACTICE RANDOM ACTS OF KINDNESS.

The more one gives, the more one receives in return. Make anonymous donations when possible. Try every day to help someone and expect nothing in return. The person who regularly gives becomes a magnet to people because we gravitate toward people who care. People want to feel good. Be the giving spirit who energizes people, not the person who is a vacuum and sucks the energy out of the room. The simple gesture of acknowledging, "That shirt is a great color on you" might brighten someone's day. When you give like that, the success will come out from inside of you. You magnetize people to you.

Everyone knows at least one person who randomly makes his or her day better. Think of a restaurant, for example, at which you might pay more or drive slightly out of the way for, simply because the staff remembers your name and treats you right. Most of the time people do not realize what they are looking for, but they are seeking something to give them a boost, a vote of confidence. Be the person who everyone wants to be around because when you are around the whole room seems a little happier.

6. GET TO KNOW PEOPLE.

Recognize that the people with whom you do business are *people* before they are *clients*. If you look at people as clients, then you are walking through life looking for business. The harder a person seaches for something the further and further away it becomes.

7. DO THE THINGS THAT OTHER PEOPLE ARE UNWILLING TO DO.

Help people. Do not sell to people. The successful businessperson does not get objections if he is helping clients. When you help someone, you fulfill a person's need. Clients, in turn, will fulfill your needs as well long term.

Help the clients that others might turn away. Setting minimums for clients immediately closes doors for a business. For example, if a business turns away the client who has only $60,000 to invest, that business also turns away the millionaire friends that client might be related to or attend church with. The referrals from that seemingly smaller client that other firms do not want to deal with because he is "too small" could have meant double the annual revenue for the business.

8. ADOPT AN ATTITUDE OF SUCCESS.

Honesty, confidence, and success go together. Desperate people reek of fear, not confidence. Customers rarely wish to do business with someone who seems desperate for the business, and who would sacrifice building a solid, business relationship for a quick sale. If someone is beating down the door and begging for the business, is one more inclined to do business with that person or less? Refer back to the Golden Rule.

9. DRAW A LINE IN THE SAND.

Be confident enough to draw a line in the sand. Tell people up front what your business goal is; if you are building a relationship-based firm, let clients know that. Plant the seeds of a relationship-based business and that is what you will grow. Establish how you will run your business and stand firm. Clients need to have 100% confidence in you that you are working in their best interest, and that your business stands for something. Do not be afraid to say, "I know you want to come in today to do business, but it is a holiday, and we are sending our loyal employees home to spend time with their families." Of course, the businessperson wants his clients to have confidence in him, but it is equally important to have confidence in those clients that they will remain clients, even if one cannot meet their needs immediately.

10. SUCCESS MEANS NEVER HAVING
TO WATCH YOUR BACK.

Our firm holds an annual holiday party that 250 people attended this year. We hosted an outdoor event with wine, food, and mingling clients. After the party, the group walked across the street to see live theater in the round. The party was a huge hit; everyone loved it. Every year we do these events, and they get bigger and bigger which is testimony to the growth of our business. The most exceptional measure of the year's success, however, is feeling exhausted at the end of the evening because we have hugged so many cherished clients! This is a better barometer to a business's success than profit or loss.

You do not have a client until you get a hug, because that is when it is real. Success means being able to walk anywhere and never having to check your back. Success means not being afraid to run into someone with whom you have done business because the client's needs came first, therefore, there is never a need to explain or apologize. If you put 250 customers at one venue where they can freely talk to each other, you had better hope you have done all the right things for the right reasons. When people can stand around drinking liquid courage and chatting, the truth is going to come out. You cannot control the conversation, the environment, or the event. The trust shown to clients to be able to talk to each other openly also increases their confidence and trust, so that they share your name with other people.

Success comes from digging deep into oneself to find the determination and strength to weather any storm – while on a quest to connect with people and meet their needs. Applying these axioms for success will help build any business, but it is perhaps necessary to add an 11th axiom for business success – **referrals**. Although meeting and getting to know new people is important to any business, too many businesses invest too much of their budget on advertising to gain new clients rather than building stronger bonds with their existing clients. Happy, existing clients refer other, like-minded clients. If one has successfully forged relationships with the right-fit clients, then the referrals are likely to be right-fit clients as well.

About Steven

Steven M. Netzel attended the University of Northern Iowa.

He has been honored to be nominated for "Ethics in Business Award" in 2008 by the BBB of Central Arizona. He believes that Honesty, Morals, Ethics and Integrity are the driving catalysts. Treat others as you wish to be treated is the way he does business and lives his life. Steve enjoys Golf, Tennis, Basketball, Racquetball, travel and his business.

Steve is a member of the Sun Lakes Rotary Club, National Ethics Bureau, the Chandler Chamber of Commerce, as well as being an Accredited Business with the Better Business Bureau of Central and Northwestern Arizona.

He and his wife Diane, along with their two children, stay actively involved in their kid's schools, their neighborhood, their community and their church.

CHAPTER 46

RELATIONSHIPS AND SERVE STRATEGIES

BY AZHAR KHAN

Customer Service is a term that has become so ingrained in our culture that we often miss out on the essential elements that form this require-ment for success. The term is used as though it's a foregone conclusion, but it takes a strategy and framework to give good customer service.

As you read this chapter, use the questions asked to redefine the param-eters that mentally define who you aim to serve both personally and in business. Start to consider the framework of how you plan to create behaviors to position yourself as a person who is ready to serve at any opportunity. The more you get specific about who you plan to serve, the greater the level of clarity you will discover about your relationships and the connections you make with people.

Write down the questions that are asked throughout this chapter. Then, create three columns. The first column is to document how you apply the question to yourself or your surroundings. The second is to represent the perceptions you have of those you know and admire most. In the third and last column, apply each question to those you admire least.

This process will help you balance the emotional and the mental factors. It will allow you to imagine the possibilities and get specific. Start with the following:

1. What defines the scope of the relationship you have...

   a) with others?

   b) with your customers?

   c) with your product or service?

2. Why do you have people in your life?
   Get really specific about this. Look at your role models, friends and friends of friends. Use a chart to map out who these people are and what level they play in influencing the direction of your life?

3. Who decides on what connections you make?

Is it you, your friends or your manager? Define the people that lead and chart your life's direction. Look for patterns in how you make, break or repair relationships and connections.

The more you write on these three questions, the deeper your insight will be.

In today's world, how you grow your relationships is rooted in the connections you make and nurture. How much heart you emotionally invest in the connection will determine the level of influence in which you operate.

Anyone or any group wanting to build multi-faceted relationships to be a success must adopt a strategy of being agile – in order to grow all the time. This strategy should be designed to grow in cycles. Even if what you offer is a product or service, you should not be transactional and base your support entirely on deliverables. You should seek to en-hance your presence, maintain your status and build your personal or business brand by interacting and producing a series of transforming experiences.

This way of thinking can be compared to the transformational lifespan of a butterfly.

Imagine your relationships are starting out just as a larva hatches. They slowly grow into caterpillars.

When you choose the people you associate with, it's just as a larva chooses the leaf to consume, which allows growth. The connections you make are just like the silk spun by a caterpillar, taking care to nurture and wrap each interaction as an encapsulating cocoon, which form the essence of your product or service.

Finally, the emergence of a butterfly is just like your results. It's your feedback and the chance to see what your experience delivered. This amazing transformation is literally what growth looks like when you choose to serve others in relationships.

HOW CAN YOU NOW BEGIN TO CREATE AN ENVIRONMENT THAT FOSTERS CHANGE?

Building relationships and creating emotional connections create an environment and build a platform for your voice to be heard. Eventually, you may have a career or have built a business to show for all the relationships you have created.

Building relationships is like streaming a group of connections together in what may seem to you like a good strategy at the time. However, most people only build their relationships with others who they perceive to have value at the moment of their first interaction.

Since most people only tend to judge on the surface, they often miss what could be a key player in the goal they wish to reach. An investment into how your connections serve you or your business needs to align with your vision, mission, or purpose. Character and behavior will play an important role in defining your service strategy. To do this keep asking, "Who needs me?"

I'll never forget walking into my first tech company. I was excited to be part of an emerging and exciting industry. We were at the beginning of something special, and back then, not many people understood how large the industry would get.

It was the classic 1980s mainframe scene. In those times, people wore business grey suits and the computers were large enough to fill a whole building floor.

I sat down for an interview and handed them my not-so-impressive resume. I was young and hadn't worked yet. After a short aptitude test, they said I didn't have a chance.

"You just don't have the aptitude to be a programmer," they told me.

My dad had a different view of my prospects. He thought computer people hung out in arcades all day and it was a waste of my time.

Surprisingly, I didn't have trouble consolidating the two opinions. My father thought I was too good for it, while the people I wanted to work with didn't think I was good enough.

I decided the opportunity was far greater than most people could see. This would be the industry of the future, and I would be part of it. If my resume wasn't good enough, I would demonstrate that I was good enough. If the industry was thought of as worthless, I would be the one to help make it meaningful.

The relationships and connections I created along the way propelled me to accomplish these goals.

WHY LEARN, WHY TEACH AND WHEN TO SHARE?

Currently, most industries hire based on some form of academic qualification. Back when I got started, you didn't get an education in computer programming. You had to find a way to learn from others and had to create relationships.

Today, this industry has prospered more than any other. Now I take the lessons I discovered then and teach others how to innovate, demonstrate and find success.

I help people concentrate and focus more on what they can actually bring to the table.

Therefore, consider making a list and define what your key competencies are. This list is not of your academic achievements, but the skillsets and behavioral habits you have built.

Now, build a strategy on negotiating and delivering what you believe are your strengths. This exercise will demonstrate your abilities and assist you to really focus on what you do. Refine this until you have a summarized pitch that you can use on the fly when someone asks you what you do or who you are.

WHAT CAN YOU DO TO DIFFERENTIATE YOUR SERVE STRATEGY?

If you are in business, you should consider the relationships you have developed with people and the social side of business. Many business deals are conducted in social settings. Your strategy should make allowances for this.

Within this framework you should consider the following three ground rules:

1. Groups are changing all the time.

2. Good products will develop in life cycles. A good example is cell phones. They continue to get better with every development.

3. Customers are fickle, and will come and go to the next best thing.

So, in order to survive, you need to be able to manage projects and people in an environment that is changing constantly. You need to know if your message is positively received and that the expectation is understood. You need to be able to demonstrate how deliverables should be met and always set a timeframe for acceptance testing. Those you intend to influence should not follow you simply for fear of keeping their jobs. They should be given the opportunity to speak freely and openly. Social researchers call this opportunity 'free space.'

It's been my experience that no person can be assured of their success just by looking at results. The path to success is often littered with broken relationships and connections unless the "Serve Strategy" is congruent and authentic.

But many successful companies have started to embrace a new methodology of creating teams, especially around social interaction.

Take the following example:
A group assembles in a boardroom, where there's a boss at the end of the table looking down on the nervous employees giving a rigid presentation. The presenters were given instructions to complete a task.

The defined hierarchy and chain of command separate the management from the team. The decision makers, the managers or leaders, sit upright, conscious of their authority and impose their judgment whilst the team members must comply or face subtle adverse action. This environment is toxic. Here, these people do what the boss says needs to be done – even when the boss asks them to do something they aren't good at.

So when the projects and business suffers, the people feel undervalued and have to work twice as hard to repair the situation. They make choices they believe will get them recognition rather than grow the business.

Let's take another example. There are groups of people standing around the water cooler, who have 'free space.' They might interrupt each other, form half an idea and then take a break before going back to work. They feel supported in their roles and duties. These people are not risk takers or work dodgers. They know that a balanced person gets better results. They know the difference between socializing and working, and when both are needed.

Look carefully, there's spontaneity from that disorder. Good stories are shared and when people get along, they socialize and sometimes meet outside of work for a meal. When an environment is considered free and open, there is a sense of safety that encourages participation and fosters innovation.

Problems are solved easier when their co-workers, surprisingly, can help them and they don't have to make it formal. New relationships form. Connections are deepened. People feel they are valued and productivity increases.

Traditional business people see these as two kinds of groups – one institutional, the other largely social – as opposites. In their perception, one group gets things done and the other drinks wine together on weekends.

But consider this, it's the second group – the informal group – that can be used for so much more. If an institutional business environment adopted more of the spontaneity that exists around the water cooler, the right people are more likely to get assigned the work they can do best.

WHEN SHOULD I LISTEN?

In the majority of businesses, managers are the ones creating groups to accomplish tasks. Often the groups they create are filled with the wrong people. The team members aren't given the opportunity to decide on the group dynamics. They almost never get to share their strengths and are not assured that their unique talents have been hand-picked for the role or purpose.

Imagine if we reconfigured the company's backend, and rewired a manager's head so that there was no hierarchy and chain of command. Managers had to say YES first to any request and only say NO after they agreed to try to resolve any problem or issue presented to them. How different do you think the workplace around you would be?

Organizational Structure is no longer about the pyramid, where hierarchies of senior managers sit on the top. It is increasingly more efficient to live in a matrix, where the context of the situation dictates how to move forward.

For example - you have twenty people that are tasked with doing four things. The challenge is to decide which people go into which group.

The dilemma is a classic one: Do you ask them what they want? That may waste too much time. Do you buddy them up with those they're sitting next to? That's fast and clean, but is it the best choice? Or do you choose based on past performance. That's a good idea if the tasks are the same as they have been for years. But that's rarely the case.

You have to let them tell you what they can do. You have to let them tell each other. You have to let them form their groups in real time, in a comfortable setting that mimics a water cooler, not a stiff boardroom. Why do that?

IN TEAMS, PEOPLE WANT TO ORGANIZE THEMSELVES – LET THEM!

Your team will tell you. People want to make their own groups, and they want to work on those things at which they excel. You cannot read minds and know an employee is a great painter unless they tell you.

If you are leading or managing teams, you should take the time to explore your leadership style and attitude towards relationships. Figure out how you let people form habits and expectations, and document when you offer others the opportunity to explore what works best for the team.

Take the time to document what you do, create a journal. This will provide you with a resource and give you a playbook to ignite new ideas. Consider how powerful that would be.

WHAT DO YOU DO WHEN CREATING YOUR TEAM ENVIRONMENT?

Find a way to reach a consensus fast without demoralizing others. How can you provide every situation with the opportunity to innovate and build on collective participation? You do this by developing connections first, and then facilitate change by reigniting the passion that drove the people into their work in the first place.

If you try and impose change and restriction, you will rapidly lose your voice, especially when you have to yell at people to get the job done.

KNOW YOUR HEART, KNOW YOUR MIND

The heart is the emotional processor of peoples' thoughts and feelings.

It's where our laughter comes from, and also our tears. It's what always brightens our day, and sometimes makes us wonder why we're doing something we don't want to do.

Then, there's the mind. This is the great filter – it compares our options, it studies what's bothering us. It filters out elements based on not just what we want, but what we need. A well-balanced professional must let both the heart and mind be part of the actions they commit to.

We want to be respected. We want to be where we're wanted, and be valued for our contribution. In our work lives, if we are where we are needed most, we will love our work.

The objective of your continuous success should positively aim to assure you align your appreciated talents to where you are needed the most.

INFORMATION IS THE NEW PROFESSIONAL CURRENCY

Your CV may never be the best. With several hundred applicants for each job today, you really have to be pretty special to be recognized. So, differentiating yourself through your character and personality is a key asset and differentiator to your intellectual horsepower.

What is important today are the relationships being formed around the water cooler. The relationships you build mean everything as you move forward, both in your job now and in the future. If you can communicate what you're good at and be surrounded by those who know your talents, your relationships will be your qualification. The maintenance of your connections will be key to your success.

After all, the barriers to education used to be closed off. Now education is open to everyone. Anyone can obtain qualifications, or learn skills online. It's what you do with the information out there, and how you use it to form relationships, that sets you apart from the millions of others.

Constantly ask yourself:

- "What is my serve strategy?"

- "How can I serve those around me?"

- "How can I serve myself and be remunerated for doing what I choose?"

These questions will keep you inspired and on the right track.

About Azhar Khan

Azhar Khan is an accomplished international speaker, consultant, mentor, and technology architect. For more than 20 years, Azhar has applied his technology background to a diverse range of industry solutions, often focusing on how people can work together to better solve industry issues.

Azhar moved to Australia in 2001 and spent more than 10 years researching personal development and interpersonal communication.

Born in Zimbabwe, Africa in 1971, Azhar began his own publishing company at the ripe age of only 24. This company later developed into an advertising agency, which worked with corporate companies and developed communities in third world countries.

This early introduction into the high-stakes corporate world is one Azhar still carries with him today to create solutions for business professionals and NGOs.

His ability to connect with anyone and understand multiple cultures is what helps him focus on understanding businesses with a global focus, combined with an aptitude for production.

His work with teams and employees adds purpose to any project, and he can find deep meaning in any activity, no matter how small.

Azhar truly is a unique talent when it comes to explaining esoteric technical jargon one minute, then motivating employees of all levels in the next.

For more information or to book Azhar, please visit: www.azharkhan.me

CHAPTER 47

LIFE LESSONS IN SUCCESS

BY CORINE PETERSON

My career today in real estate sales is not where I anticipated I would be after earning an accounting degree from Penn State University and an MBA in Finance from Pepperdine University. It's very interesting how an individual's career path can lead them through such a variety of experiences and into unexpected places. For almost two decades I've had the great privilege to work with some of the top executives in the real estate industry across the country. In fact, as a former national Vice President of Prudential Real Estate, I was responsible for managing a $300 million real estate portfolio. As a result, I had the experience of serving on the boards of several of the largest real estate firms through-out the United States. This type of background has given me a unique perspective on the real estate industry that is not available to most local realtors. It was during this time that I formulated certain principles that I believe can be translated into any business or profession to help anyone achieve great success. I would like to share those principles with you.

A. KNOWLEDGE IS POWER

As an expert in finance, I have been able to combine my formal educa-tion with the realities I faced on a daily basis in the high dollar, high en-ergy, and high intensity world of one of the largest real estate and finan-cial institutions in the country. Believe me, it could be a pressure cooker at times. But they were years of gaining knowledge that most people in real estate will never hear about. Not only did I have the opportunity to watch many real estate brokerage firms experience tremendous growth, but unfortunately, I also had to be there to pick up the pieces of firms that did not survive the collapse of the housing market beginning in 2007. I have found that there is a tremendous value in the knowledge one can obtain while working very closely with those that found great success as well as with those who faced calamity.

Whatever your circumstances might be, there are always lessons to be learned and knowledge to be gained. Don't look at negative circumstances as wasted time. There are very valuable lessons to be learned during difficult times. Fortunately for me, I was never the one that was in the tumultuous waves of loss that hit my industry. However, as a turn-around specialist, I had to be with those individuals in the storm and get them into the lifeboats. There were some situations that could not be saved, but I would always do whatever I could to make sure the individuals involved had the best opportunities possible to make their businesses work.

Being through those good and bad times over a number of years has equipped me with an arsenal of knowledge that I still use today when selling real estate. My title today may not sound as fancy and glamorous, but the basic skills I used in very high level meetings to negotiate multi-million dollar corporate deals are the same skills I use when working with a home owner. I think the big distinction today between my peers and me is the sharpness of those skills and the knowledge I have obtained through experience. I have been able to compile a rare combination of experience in both real estate and finance that enables me to provide my clients with a sophisticated level of knowledge and service unique to the real estate industry. My intention here is not to be boastful. I just want to make a point. If you want to be a leader in your field, make sure you are the most knowledgeable person. Allow your experiences, both positive and negative, to be life-lessons that will mold you and shape you into a resourceful person. You will find that people will flock to you, even if you are the "new kid on the block." Not only will your peers see you as an expert, more importantly, your clients will see the great distinction between you and your peers. That results in more business and greater potential for success.

B. IT'S NOT ALWAYS ABOUT WHAT YOU KNOW, IT'S ALSO ABOUT WHO YOU KNOW

Let's face it, having the right connections can never be a bad thing. I have had the privilege of working with some of the most successful people in my industry from across the entire country. I have always been careful to nurture the relationships I have with people. You always want to avoid burning bridges. Knowing the right people, in the right place, at the right time, can be pivotal to your success. There may be times you need to call someone about a specific issue or so they can introduce you to certain people who also have influence to help you achieve your goals.

C. ALWAYS ACT ETHICALLY

In my industry, I was known to be someone that could be trusted and always told the truth no matter how painful it may have been. I never shirked from my responsibility to act ethically at all times. As in any business, I have seen my share of unethical behavior. One thing that stands out to me with regard to those that function unethically is that their actions always have consequences that are negative in nature. It may not bite them right away, but it will in the long run.

I've had to make some very difficult decisions in relationship to some of the firms we financed. Unfortunately, I had to deliver the news on more than one occasion that we had no choice but to foreclose on a firm that we were financing. However, even when delivering difficult news, I didn't hide any of the facts or beat around the bush. I gave it to them straight. In business, it's always best to get all the information related to a transaction on the table so everyone knows where they stand. Don't let any surprises make their way into the picture. Otherwise, you will have to deal with additional issues that will only delay the work you are trying to accomplish. That's not to say you have to be cold and calculating. You can deliver difficult news with warmth, compassion, and empathy.

In my business today, I never focus on what I'm going to earn on a particular transaction. If I'm representing a buyer and I think that the property is worth significantly less than what it is listed for, I'm going to try to negotiate the right price for the property on their behalf. This may seem odd to some, but commission is never on my mind because I always think about the long-term relationship, rather than the short-term gain. There is nothing more important to me than my reputation. I never let anything get in front of my ethics and that commitment has always served me well.

D. BE COURAGEOUS

There are a lot of powerful, wealthy, and influential people leading some of the top real estate firms throughout the country. Most of these individuals are men. I will even take it a step further and say that most of these individuals are the "alpha male" type. They have an internal drive to be in charge and to dominate in any activity in which they participate. I remember monitoring the activity of one of our affiliates that had been doing well. However, they encountered some issues that caused their growth to be inhibited, and I noticed that their earnings were consistently trending downward. I worked with them to improve productivity, bring in new agents, and a number of other efforts to reverse their negative spiral. After concluding there needed to be a change in leadership, I went to the President of my company with the recommendation that we find someone else to take over the firm I had been monitoring and advising. He agreed and a plan was set in motion to execute a take-over. I was charged with the responsibility of finding new leadership for the firm and a date for a meeting was set.

When we arrived at the city where our meeting was to take place, we decided to have lunch before the meeting. At lunch the President said to me, "What are you going to say to these guys?" After I picked my jaw up from the table, I questioned emphatically, "What am I going to say to these guys?" I went on, "You are usually the one that handles these conversations." Much to my chagrin, he insisted I be the one to deliver the news. I had done a lot of consulting and advising, but, at that point, I had never had to explain to anyone that I was going to take his keys and his business from him and give the reigns of leadership to someone else. To make matters worse, the "someone else" was also his direct competitor. The man I had to confront was very large in stature, older than me, and definitely an alpha male. I knew he wasn't going to take this lightly.

To say I was nervous is an extreme understatement. However, I stepped up to the plate and courageously laid the facts on the table and asked for the keys. He gave me the keys and the transition began. It was something that had to be done. It was an extremely difficult task. It wasn't something I wanted to do. I would have been very comfortable sitting in a supportive role as the President asked for the keys. But sometimes you have to put your feelings aside and become courageous. I learned a new dimension of courage that day and it has served me well. If I can confront a powerful alpha male twice my size and ten years my senior, I know I'm well equipped to ask for a listing or close a sale. Sometimes courage has to be learned. Don't let fear direct your path. Be courageous and step outside your comfort zone. You will find that you have more courage than you even realized.

E. ALWAYS EXCEED EXPECTATIONS

I've heard from some of my clients that they have a perception that real estate agents are very lazy. That's not a perception I care to validate through my own activity. In fact, I take great strides in going the opposite direction of lazy. I constantly seek to go far beyond the expectations of my clients. I am very high energy and I am very willing to walk ten extra miles if necessary to make my business successful. My motivation is not necessarily just to please my clients. I am also very highly motivated by the expectations I set for myself. I have never allowed myself to accept mediocrity as a work ethic. That's not how I live my life. I go above and beyond for my clients as well as for the satisfaction I derive for myself knowing I have done everything I can possibly do to make a business transaction as successful as possible.

My clients see me do a lot of extra work for them that other agents will not do. I'm constantly available to my clients and constantly networking with others. My clients know they are getting value for their dollar when they work with me. I promptly answer every email, text message or phone message. I've even answered phone calls at 10:30 in the evening. The only time I don't answer my phone is when I'm sleeping. I want my clients to communicate with me and my clients want me to communicate with them. I customize all of my marketing materials for each client and make sure no one is shortchanged when it comes to marketing. When you achieve a reputation as one who provides great, outstanding, over and above customer service, people will line up to do business with you.

F. BE A CARING PERSON

As you can imagine with the great downward spiral of the real estate market starting in 2007, I had conversations with numerous real estate business owners who were finding themselves in unfortunate circumstances. I functioned as a turnaround consultant in those situations.

Sometimes people think high dollar business owners have ice running through their veins and they are emotionally great mountains of stability. I have not found that to be the case. Even the alpha males in my industry have a breaking point. Sometimes they need to know there is someone there that understands their crisis and genuinely cares about helping them through the situation.

I have found the same principle translates into the consumer market. Although the consumer typically isn't dealing with such large stakes, nonetheless, they still can be overcome with the stress resulting from their own crisis. A homeowner who is having a financially difficult time can also be at an emotional breaking point, and it then becomes my responsibility to understand the reason for their stress so I can be a voice of reason, comfort and consolation. I can be the one that helps them think through their crisis objectively and be part of a strategy that will help them get back on their feet again. The reality is that it may not be enough just to be sympathetic with people; you may have to help them develop a vision of where they're going from this point on. People will remember you more for your emotional support and friendship than for the sales contract you negotiate for them.

CONCLUSION

To summarize, my life lessons that have led to my success include:

- Knowledge is power
- It's not always about what you know, it's also about who you know
- Always act ethically
- Be courageous
- Always exceed expectations
- Be a caring person.

I'm sure you have also realized some of your own life lessons that have formed your path toward success. There isn't any one path to success, but I strongly believe the principles I have shared with you in this chapter are a foundational part of any success story. If you put these principles into action, I'm convinced opportunities will arise from places you didn't expect.

To your success!

About Corine

As the former national Vice President of Prudential Real Estate, Corine Peterson has the rare combination of experience in both real estate and finance that enables her to provide her clients with a sophisticated level of knowledge and service unique to the real estate industry.

While at Prudential, Corine was responsible for managing a $300 million real estate portfolio. As a result, she has the experience of serving on the boards of several of Prudential's largest real estate firms throughout the United States. This broad background gives Corine the inside knowledge not available to most local realtors.

Corine's educational background consists of an MBA in Finance from Pepperdine University as well as an Accounting degree from Penn State University. Corine's financial experience gives her the depth of knowledge to navigate the entire process of marketing a property through the details of closing the sale.

In today's ultra-competitive marketplace, your choice of a realtor is the single most important decision you will face when trying to sell your property. Corine Peterson will give you the competitive edge needed to distinguish your home from all of the other properties competing in today's real estate market.

CHAPTER 48

TAKING CONTROL OF YOUR FINANCIAL DESTINY

BY PETER GARCIA

Success comes in many forms through a variety of avenues and can be realized at almost any age. In recent years I have seen many very young entrepreneurs have great successes in their early lives. I also have had the privilege of helping older adults plan for a successful retirement after decades of "nose-to-the-grindstone" work, as well as guiding hundreds of clients toward achieving a position of financial security, comfort, and in many cases, becoming financially affluent through a systematic approach to wealth management.

One thing I have realized over the course of my career is that, whether your success and the corresponding wealth comes at an early age or from a lifetime of accumulation, you must have a strategic financial plan in place to maximize and preserve your hard-earned dollars.

Many individuals set their sights on retiring in financial comfort and with the peace of mind that they will not outlive their money. And rightly so, longevity risk is the greatest risk of all because it is the multiplier of all the other types of risks associated during your retirement years.

People want to retire successfully. That is, they want their money to work for them so they can enjoy a certain lifestyle and amenities during their "golden years." These "amenities" vary greatly from person to person. However, there are certain components of a financial strategy that must be in place for individuals as they transition into retirement in order to live through their years in retirement without having to depend on others or the government.

Some of the greatest worries retired individuals have expressed to me is, "I'm very concerned that I will outlive my money," and "I don't want to be a burden to my family." In helping my clients quell these concerns, I guide them through the four basic foundational legs that must be in place in their retirement years to help them live financially worry-free.

FOUR BASIC FOUNDATIONAL LEGS TO A WORRY-FREE RETIREMENT

First, you must have a specific amount of cash immediately available to you as an emergency fund in case a specific need arises. The exact amount will vary greatly depending on your acquired lifestyle and your particular comfort level. These assets could be held in a savings account, money market, fixed income portfolio or whole life insurance cash value.

Second, you will need to determine what your minimum income requirements will be, so you can make the transition into the next phase of your life, retirement. You will need to carve out a portion of your retirement assets in order to secure a guaranteed, lifetime, passive income stream* that you could never outlive.

This is the transition that most investors entering retirement fail to make. We've been working and saving to build our financial assets in anticipation of this day primarily through government sponsored retirement accounts and investing in the stock market. However, making the transition from saver and investor to retirement income is vitally important in order to secure an income stream – so that no matter what happens in the stock or real estate markets, your lifestyle won't be affected by the changes in your portfolio values.

Securing your retirement income for life is best accomplished using insured products. These funds must be in a secure income vehicle such as a fixed annuity or in some cases, a fixed income managed account. To avoid market risk as well as longevity risk, the safety of this investment vehicle is extremely important because it will be one of your primary income sources once you're retired. If you choose to use traditional growth type investments, once you are retired and start taking withdrawals, when the market drops, you will still need to pull money out and this could have a devastating effect on your funds when not properly insured for lifetime income. Thus, this is why I suggest using insured products for this leg of your retirement income plan.

Third, whenever possible, you should have a separate growth account in place that will serve as a hedge against inflation. This account could fluctuate with the markets since it's invested for growth. If you've taken the steps to secure your basic income needs as described above, you could use these assets as a hedge against future inflation as well as your "slush fund."

The fourth and final leg is, in my opinion, the most valuable because it brings so much of what financial planning should bring together, and what I have been promoting since 2004 when I first learned about it. It is a concept propagated by individuals such as Nelson Nash, founder of the Infinite Banking Concept™ and Best Selling author of the book, *Becoming Your Own Banker* and Pamela Yellen, Best Selling author of the book, *Bank On Yourself.*

BECOMING YOUR OWN BANKER

This concept, when engineered and utilized the way it is advocated, brings together basic economic principles, U.S. tax laws and life insurance contractual guarantees to build wealth safely and predictably in any economic environment. This results in a cash and debt management system, risk management, wealth creation, tax planning and, in my opinion, the most efficient wealth transfer strategy rolled up into one ideal system, utilizing a whole life insurance policy individually engineered and designed for each client's specific needs as the vehicle to accomplish this strategy. Let me explain:

1. **Central to a sound financial plan is a cash and debt management system:** Your premiums and cash value are constantly compounding in your policy even when you take out a loan (as long as you are using a non-direct recognition company). These plans, when properly designed to maximize the paid up additions rider, earn a very competitive rate of return. When you need to finance any purchase, you can borrow the funds from

your life insurance policy and pay cash for your purchase, then set up an amortization table in order to pay yourself back, with interest, just as an outside lender would have required. That is smart debt management and the part of the "banking" process that allows you to recapture part of the interest and lost opportunity costs that would otherwise have been paid out to the banks and credit card companies to your detriment.

Your policy will continue to pay you dividends even when you take out a loan so you'll continue to earn the dividend as though you never borrowed a penny.

2. **Risk management:** There is no stock or real estate market risk. In some states you also have asset protection from creditors, predators and frivolous lawsuits.

3. **Tax planning:** Life insurance cash value grows tax deferred and your basis comes out tax-free when you're ready to turn it into a passive income stream when you retire. Once the basis has been withdrawn, you can then borrow your earnings by switching the withdrawals to policy loans – which are not a taxable event. Policy loans would get paid from the death benefit proceeds plus any accrued interest due once the insured dies.

4. **Wealth creation:** When utilized the way it is advocated, you can use your financing needs as a wealth-creating strategy by borrowing the money from your policy to pay cash for your purchases, and then paying yourself back with interest, just as an outside lender would require of you.

For example, in the table below I have outlined how a typical auto loan would be amortized over a period of five years. Payments are front loaded with interest as you can see illustrated in the table below. You will also notice that over the five-year repayment period, you would have borrowed $15,782 and would have paid $19,200 of which a total of $3,412 is interest. This results in over 17 cents of every dollar paid is interest to the bank.

By creating your own personal financing system, you could pay yourself back the same way you would have paid a bank or credit card company. Wouldn't you like to recapture a portion of that volume of interest you would have paid the bank in this example? Plus, by recovering a portion of these lost dollars back to an entity that you own and control, you can now also recover a portion of what used to be your "lost opportunity costs" – since you have the money in an entity that you own and control instead of an outside lender.

Once you learn how to become your own banker for your financing needs, you can then learn how you could also increase the "velocity" of your money just like the commercial banks and credit card companies do. Understanding these basic economic principles - compounded over time in your favor, inside a tax-favored entity, with the features of a dividend-paying whole life insurance policy properly engineered - can help you build wealth safely and predictably, even in this or any economic environment.

Standard Credit Union Car Loan:
$15,782 Loan, 8% Loan Rate, 60 Month Financing Plan
Monthly Payment = $320.00

Year	Paid in One Year	Interest Paid in One Year	Interest % of Payments
1	$3,840.00	$1,165.92	30.3%
2	$3,840.00	$943.97	24.5%
3	$3,840.00	$703.60	18.3%
4	$3,840.00	$443.28	11.5%
5	$3,840.00	$161.35	4.2%
Totals	$19,200.00	$3,418.12	17.8%

Table credited to Mike Burril - *Mining The Gold In Your Money Flow*

5. **Estate planning and wealth transfer strategy:** Permanent life insurance creates an instant, permanent estate. The death proceeds do not pass through probate and they are paid directly to the named beneficiaries, income tax free under current tax laws.

Please note that this concept will not help you get rich quick but it will help you build lasting wealth and enjoy the fruits of your labor. It is a process that combines and compounds basic economic principals, current U.S. tax laws and life insurance contractual guarantees to help you build wealth safely and predictably in any economic environment. Plus, it helps everyone, young or old, to wean away from the dependence and bondage of the banks and credit card companies.

One individual in her mid 50's learned of this concept when she read Pamela Yellen's book, *Bank On Yourself*. She came into my office to tell me that she had heard about this concept years ago through her father. She finally discovered what her father had been doing all along, but he was never able to clearly explain it to her before he passed away. She said her father was a physician and was always borrowing money from himself and paying himself back. He simply called it his own bank. When she married, her father lent the money to pay cash for the newly-wed couple's house and then had them set up a mortgage payment plan to pay him back, with interest, just like a mortgage bank would have done. She said that they agreed on the terms that were convenient for all three of them and prepared an amortization schedule over a specified number of years.

Not only did this allow her to purchase the home with a favorable interest rate, but she was also able to pay the loan back on manageable terms. Little did she know that every loan payment she was making back to her father was going back into his life insurance policy to replenish the cash value and the death benefit. You see, she was the sole beneficiary of her father's life insurance policy. In her case, she was a double recipient of this concept. First, when her father loaned her the money for the house and second, when she received the tax free death benefit from the life insurance policy when her father passed away

She never quite understood what he was doing but after reading and learning about this concept, she immediately came in to my office to set up a plan like this for her family's financing needs.

The system of becoming your own banker will enable you to enjoy true financial security that comes from knowing you have a stable foundation and an account balance that is only going to grow. You can plan with some accuracy the amount of money you will have at various milestones in life as well as your retirement years. Will this system make you rich overnight? Absolutely not. Does this system have the ability to give you a definitive and predictable plan for your future? Absolutely! The choice is yours. You can take control of your financial destiny and this proven system can be one of the tools to help you achieve economic success.

*Fixed Insurance and Annuity product guarantees are subject to the claims-paying ability of the issuing company and are not offered by Global Financial Private Capital. Investment Advisory Services offered through Global Financial Private Capital, LLC, an SEC Registered Investment Advisor.

About Peter

Pelayo (Peter) Garcia is the founder and CEO of GBS Financial and My Legacy Group. With over twenty-four years dedicated to the insurance and financial services industry, he began his career with Merrill Lynch International Private Client Group, one of the world's leading wealth management and advisory organizations. There he offered sophisticated investors insightful investment advice, customized solutions and responsive service. Working in Caracas, Venezuela as a Private Banker for over ten years, he dealt with high net worth individuals and provided customized advice and solutions from a wide range of global investments, cross-currency financing and multi-generational estate planning services.

Upon his return to the United States, he joined New England Financial to continue his career in insurance and financial services. While there, he developed a strong business relationship with GBS Group, a highly reputable accounting firm in South Florida, working primarily with the Venezuelan entrepreneur community. He eventually merged his practice to be in closer proximity to the accounting firm and founded GBS Financial, a privately owned insurance and financial planning firm, becoming an independent insurance and financial advisor.

Working primarily with business owners, and high net worth clients, he began a business relationship with Heritage Living Trust, a national estate planning and legal documents company. His business continued to grow and accelerate as he integrated tax savings strategies, estate and retirement income planning to his growing clientele.

In the process of continuously expanding educationally and professionally, Peter mastered the principles of the Infinite Banking Concept™, a process utilizing time-honored economic principles, US tax laws and the provisions of life insurance contractual guarantees to build wealth safely and predictably in any economic environment by "becoming your own banker." Integrating this concept into his practice has allowed him to teach many clients to learn how to manage their money like a Fortune 500 CFO.

In 2008, Peter also became an Authorized Bank On Yourself™ Advisor. Combining this concept with his experience as a retirement income planning strategist, he has been able to help hundreds of people learn and implement this cash flow and debt management system and combine it with guaranteed lifetime income strategies to help his retired and pre-retired clients build wealth safely and predictably without the need to take excessive risk in the stock or real estate markets. His financial services firm now operates under the name of My Legacy Group.

Peter has began implementing the Values-Based Financial Planning philosophy to his practice in order to provide his high net worth clients comprehensive financial planning through this unique business model. He's brought together his team of subject matter experts in the areas of financial planning, institutional money management, insurance, tax and estate planning.

Peter is featured as one of America's PremierExperts® on the Consumer Advocate television program that will air on ABC, NBC, CBS and Fox affiliates throughout the country this spring. He was also featured as one of America's PremierExperts® Financial Trendsetters in *Newsweek* magazine.